AMERICAN STUDIES

AN ANNOTATED BIBLIOGRAPHY

VOLUME III

INDEX

AMERICAN STUDIES

AN ANNOTATED BIBLIOGRAPHY

VOLUME III

INDEXES

Edited by

JACK SALZMAN

Director, Columbia Center for American Culture Studies

on behalf of

THE AMERICAN STUDIES ASSOCIATION

The right of the
University of Cambridge
to print and sell
all manner of books
was granted by
Henry VIII in 1534.
The University has printed
and published continuously
since 1584.

CAMBRIDGE UNIVERSITY PRESS

CAMBRIDGE

LONDON   NEW YORK   NEW ROCHELLE

MELBOURNE   SYDNEY

Published by the Press Syndicate of the University of Cambridge
The Pitt Building, Trumpington Street, Cambridge CB2 1RP
32 East 57th Street, New York, NY 10022, USA
10 Stamford Road, Oakleigh, Melbourne 3166, Australia

© Cambridge University Press 1986

First published 1986

Printed in the United States of America

ISBN 0-521-26688-2 Vol. III
ISBN 0-521-32555-2 Set of three volumes

INDEXES

AUTHOR INDEX

Aaron, Daniel H 414; L 88, 203
Abadinsky, Howard SOC 606
Abbott, Carl H 1274-1275
Abbott, Shirley H 1404
Abel, Elie PC 645
Abel, Robert PC 322
Abeles, Ronald P. PC 833
Abell, Aaron I. R 99, 158
Abell, Troy D. R 269
Abellera, James PS 568
Aberle, David F. A-F 200
Abernethy, Francis Edward
     A-F 369
Abernethy, Thomas Perkins H 257,
     1405
Abrahams, Harold J. STM 1
Abrahams, Roger D. A-F 370-371,
     374
Abrahamson, James L. H 415
Abrams, Robert PS 68
Abramson, Doris E. L 204
Abramson, Harold J. SOC 77
Abramson, Paul R. PS 406-407;
     PSY 1
Abshire, David PS 106, 569
Achenbaum, W. Andrew STM 2
Acheson, Dean PS 570
Achor, Shirley A-F 257
Ackerman, Bruce A. PS 1
Adair, Douglass H 189
Adair, Gilbert PC 407
Adair, John R 25
Adams, Adeline Valentine Pond
     A-A 235
Adams, Charles C. A-F 347
Adams, Clinton A-A 287
Adams, Donald R., Jr. H 1646
Adams, J. Donald L 205
Adams, James Truslow H 48
Adams, William C. PC 711
Adkins, Douglas L. SOC 248
Adler, Dorothy R. H 1647
Adler, Judith E. SOC 510
Adler, Richard PC 738
Adler, Richard P. PC 712-714
Adler, Selig H 841; PS 571
Adorno, Theodor W. PS 506
Affron, Charles PC 408
Agar, Michael H. A-F 305;
     SOC 607
Agassi, Judith Buber SOC 511-512
Agee, James PC 409
Agee, William C. A-A 198
Ageton, Suzanne S. SOC 608
Ahearn, Frederick L. PSY 51
Ahlstrom, Sydney E. R 1, 130
Ahnebrink, Lars L 89

Aichinger, Peter PC 289
Aisenberg, Nadya PC 138
Aitken, Hugh G. J. H 1820;
     STM 3-4
Akin, William E. STM 5
Akinsanya, Sherrie K. A-F 330-
     331
Alba, Richard D. SOC 295
Albanese, Catherine L. R 2, 131,
     291
Albert, Ethel M. A-F 73
Albert, Peter J. H 213
Albin, Mel PSY 2
Albion, Robert G. H 1648
Albrecht, Stan L. SOC 249
Alcantara, Ruben R. A-F 79
Aldcroft, Derek H. H 1821
Alden, John Richard H 190
Aldiss, Brian W. PC 199-200
Aldrich, John H. PS 407-408
Aldrich, Richard M 37
Aldrich, Robert A. A-F 325
Aldridge, Alfred Owen L 39
Aldridge, John W. L 206-209
Alexander, Charles C. H 416;
     STM 369
Alexander, John K. H 191
Alexander, William PC 410
Alix, Ernest Kahler SOC 609
Allen, Charles L 313
Allen, David Grayson H 49
Allen, Edward B. A-A 170
Allen, Frederick Lewis H 417,
     1649
Allen, Garland E. STM 6-7
Allen, Richard V. PS 569
Allen, Walter L 437
Allen, William Francis M 202
Allend, Gerald A-A 483
Alley, Robert S. PC 715
Allison, Graham T. PS 572-573
Alloway, Lawrence A-A 18, 199;
     PC 411
Allport, Gordon W. PC 735;
     PSY 3
Allsop, Kenneth M 245
Allswang, John M. H 842, 1276
Almquist, Alan F. A-F 103
Almquist, Elizabeth McTaggart
     SOC 78, 328
Alstein, Howard SOC 217-218
Alt, James E. PS 2
Altback, Edith Hoshino H 698
Altback, Philip G. H 418
Altman, Irwin PSY 4
Altman, Rick PC 412
Altschuter, Glenn C. H 1406

Alvarez, A. L 210
Amacher, Richard E. L 40
Ambrose, Stephen E. PS 574
American Folklife Center M 131
Ames, Kenneth L. A-F 372
Ames, Russell M 132
Ames, Van Meter H 549
Amis, Kingsley PC 201
Ammer, Christine M 1
Ammerman, David L. H 175
Ammon, Harry H 192
Andersen, Wayne V. A-A 253
Anderson, Alan D. H 1277
Anderson, Arlow W. H 843
Anderson, Barbara Gallatin
    A-F 89
Anderson, Charles H. SOC 79
Anderson, Clive M 222
Anderson, Dennis R. A-A 146
Anderson, Eric H 1012
Anderson, Henry H 1595
Anderson, Karen H 699
Anderson, Kent PC 716
Anderson, Michael H. PC 897
Anderson, Oscar E., Jr. STM 8-
    9, 165
Anderson, Quentin L 90
Anderson, Robert Mapes R 27;
    SOC 610
Anderson, Terry Lee H 1822
Andreano, Ralph L. H 1823-1824;
    STM 394
Andrew, Ed SOC 513
Andrew, Laurel B. A-A 561
Andrews, Charles M. H 50
Andrews, Clarence A. H 1407
Andrews, Edward Deming A-A 355
Andrews, Faith A-A 355
Andrews, K. R. H 51
Andrews, Matthew Page H 52
Andrews, Wayne A-A 433-434
Andrews, William L. L 438
Angell, Roger PC 917
Angrist, Shirley S. SOC 328
Anson, Bert H 1095
Anthony, Gene M 366
Apostle, Richard A. SOC 80
Appelbaum, Eileen SOC 514
Apple, Michael PS 507
Apter, T. E. PC 169
Aptheker, Bettina H 700
Aptheker, Herbert H 193, 1013
Arac, Jonathan L 91
Archdeacon, Thomas J. H 1278
Archer, Gleason L. STM 10
Arens, W. A-F 24
Arensberg, Conard M. A-F 1
Argyris, Chris PC 836
Arieli, Yehoshva H 550
Arlen, Michael J. PC 717
Armstrong, David A. STM 11

Armstrong, Janice Gray PC 1036
Armstrong, Louise PSY 5
Armstrong, Tom A-A 314
Armstrong, William H. H 1096
Armytage, W. H. G. PC 202
Arnason, H. H. A-A 200
Arnold, Joseph L. H 1279
Aron, Betty PS 506
Aronowitz, Stanley PS 508
Arrington, Leonard J. H 1408;
    R 188
Art, Robert J. PS 300
Arthur, Eric A-A 435
Artis, Bob M 133
Arvin, Newton L 92
Aschenbrenner, Joyce A-F 166
Ashcraft, Norman A-F 25
Ashley, L. F. PC 114
Ashton, Dore A-A 19-20, 201-202,
    254
Asimov, Isaac PC 203
Asinof, Eliot PC 918
Asp, C. Elliot SOC 276
Asselineau, Roger L 439
Astin, Alexander W. SOC 81
Astro, Richard L 596
Athearn, Robert G. H 1409
Atheling, William, Jr. (pseudonym)
    PC 207-208
Athens, Lonnie H. SOC 611
Atherton, Lewis H 258, 1410
Atkins, Thomas R. PC 413
Atkinson, Brooks PC 323
Attebery, Brian PC 170
Atwell, Robert H. PC 919
Auchincloss, Louis L 440
Auletta, Ken SOC 445
Austin, Gilbert R. PSY 6
Austin, James C. PC 68
Avedon, Elliott M. A-F 2
Averitt, Robert H 1825
Averson, Richard PC 635, 707
Axtell, James L. A-F 201; H 53;
    R 249
Axthelm, Peter PC 920
Ayabe, Tsuneo A-F 26
Ayars, Christine Merrick M 2
Aydelotte, William O. H 1-2
Ayers, Linda A-A 143
Ayers, William A-A 356

Babb, Laura Longley PC 837
Babcock, Glenn D. H 1650
Bachman, Van Cleaf H 1651
Bachrach, Peter PS 3
Back, Kurt W. SOC 593
Backus, Rob M 246
Badash, Lawrence STM 12
Bader, Barbara PC 108
Baer, Michael PS 504

Bagdikian, Ben H. PC 646, 838;
  SOC 515
Bahr, Howard M. A-F 202; SOC 249-
  250, 263, 418
Baier, Kurt U. STM 13
Baigell, Matthew A-A 147, 203
Bailey, James O. PC 204
Bailey, John W. H 1097
Bailey, Kenneth K. R 115
Bailyn, Bernard H 3, 54-55, 194-
  195, 551, 589
Bain, Richard PS 429
Baird, W. David H 1098
Baker, Elizabeth C. A-A 71
Baker, Elizabeth Faulkner H 701
Baker, George R 215
Baker, Holly Cutting A-F 469
Baker, Houston A., Jr. L 441
Baker, Jean H. H 259
Baker, M. Joyce PC 414
Baker, Ronald L. A-F 373
Baker, Ross K. PS 107
Baker, Tod A. H 1411, 1484
Balakian, Nona L 211
Baldassare, Mark SOC 21
Baldwin, Alice M. R 44
Baldwin, Charles C. L 212
Baldwin, Richard S. STM 14
Balio, Tino PC 415-416
Balk, Alfred PC 839
Ball, Desmond PS 575
Ball, Donald W. PC 921
Ball, George W. PS 576
Ball, Howard PS 301
Ball, John PC 139
Ballace, Janice R. H 1521
Balliett, Whitney M 247-251
Baltzell, D. Catherine SOC 107
Baltzell, E. Digby H 552;
  SOC 446
Bane, Mary Jo SOC 251
Banham, Reyner A-A 593
Banks, Ann PC 324
Banner, James M. H 260
Banner, Lois W. H 702-703, 759
Banning, Lance H 261
Bannister, Robert C. STM 15
Bannon, John Francis H 1412
Banta, Martha L 442
Baraka, Imamu Amiri M 252-253
Baral, Robert PC 325
Baran, Paul PS 509
Barber, Benjamin R. PS 4
Barber, Edwin Atlee A-A 357
Barber, James D. PC 647; PS 108-
  109, 409-410
Barber, Red PC 922
Barcus, F. Earle PSY 7
Bardwick, Judith M. PSY 8-9;
  SOC 329
Barger, Harold H 1652-1654, 1826

Baritz, Loren STM 16
Barker, Danny M 254
Barker, David T. SOC 402
Barker, Philip PSY 10
Barker, Ruth PSY 135
Barker, Virgil A-A 148, 204
Barker-Benfield, G. J. H 704
Barnard, John H 1522
Barnes, Gilbert Hobbs R 91
Barnes, Henry Elmer PSY 11
Barnet, Richard J. PS 577-578
Barnett, A. Doak PS 579
Barnett, Louise K. L 93
Barney, Ralph D. PC 886
Barnouw, Erik PC 417, 718-722
Baron, Augustine PSY 12
Barr, Alfred H., Jr. A-A 222
Barr, Marleen S. PC 205
Barratt, John PS 671
Barrera, Mario SOC 83
Barret, Donala N. H 553
Barrett, Paul H 1280
Barrett, Rosalyn C. PSY 13
Barrett, William H 554
Barron, Milton L. SOC 84
Barsam, Richard Meran PC 418-419
Barsh, Russel Lawrence H 1099
Barth, Gunther H 844, 1281
Barth, Peter S. SOC 516
Barthold, Bonnie J. L 443
Bartlett, Lee L 213
Bartlett, Richard A. H 1413
Bartlett, Robert PS 302
Bartlett, Susan H 1462
Barton, Amy E. H 1690
Barton, John H. PS 580
Barton, Josef J. H 845
Baruch, Grace K. PSY 13
Barzun, Jacques M 38
Basch, Norma H 1941
Basler, Roy P. L 444
Basso, Keith H. A-F 3, 203
Bastin, Bruce M 203
Basu, Asoke SOC 501
Bataile, Gretchen M. PC 420
Bateman, Fred H 1414, 1827
Bates, Elizabeth Bidwell A-A 382
Bates, Ralph S. STM 17
Bathe, Dorothy STM 18
Bathe, Greville STM 18
Battcock, Gregory A-A 21-24, 255;
  PC 421
Battis, Emory H 56
Baugh, John A-F 167
Baum, Andrew PSY 14
Baum, Charlotte H 705
Bauman, Richard A-F 374
Baumgarten, Murray L 214
Baumol, William J. PC 326
Bauer, Raymond A. PS 303
Baur, John I. H. A-A 64, 179,
  205

Baxter, Annette K. H 706
Baxter, James Phinney, III
    STM 19
Baxter, John PC 422-423
Baxter, William T. H 1655
Bay, Christian PS 5
Bayley, Stephen H 1656
Baym, Nina L 94
Bayor, Ronald H. H 846
Beach, Joseph Warren L 215-216
Beal, Lee L. SOC 488
Beale, Howard H 419
Beall, Otho T., Jr. STM 20
Beam, George PS 469
Beard, Charles A. H 4, 1828
Beard, Mary R. H 4
Beardsley, Edward H. STM 21-22
Beardsley, John A-A 315
Beasley, Maurine L 341
Beatty, William K. STM 236
Beaver, Donald de B. STM 23
Beaver, Robert Pierce R 240, 250
Becher, Franklin D. PC 1010
Becker, Carl L. H 555-557
Becker, Gaylene SOC 396
Becker, George J. L 445
Becker, Howard Saul A-A 25;
    A-F 80; SOC 252
Becker, Peter A-A 484
Becker, Stephen PC 305
Becker, Susan D. H 707
Becker, William H. H 1829
Beckhardt, Benjamin H. H 1830
Becnel, Thomas H 1523
Bedini, Silvio A. STM 24-25
Bee, Robert L. H 1100
Beebe, Jack H. PC 800
Beeghley, Leonard SOC 447
Beer, Gillian PC 183
Beer, Thomas PC 69
Beer, William R. SOC 330
Beidler, Philip L 217
Beisner, Robert L. H 262
•Beisser, Arnold R. PC 923
Belasco, James Warren PC 1011
Belknap, Waldron Phoenix, Jr.
    A-A 171
Bell, Daniel H 420; PS 510-512
Bell, Leland V. PSY 15
Bell, Michael A-F 168
Bell, Michael Davitt PC 184
Bell, Whitfield J., Jr. STM 26-
    27
Bellah, Robert N. R 292-293
Belle, Deborah PSY 16
Bellows, George Kent M 15
Bellush, Bernard H 421
Belous, Richard S. SOC 482
Belsito, Peter M 367
Belz, Carl M 368
Benagh, Jim PC 924

Bender, Thomas H 1282-1283
Benedict, Burton A-F 27
Benedict, Ruth A-F 4
Benello, C. George PS 513
Benes, Peter A-A 241, 436;
    PC 1012
Benet, James PC 704
Benjamin, Samuel G. W. A-A 26
Bennett, David H. H 422
Bennett, John W. A-F 28-29, 81
Bensman, Joseph SOC 448
Benson, Adolph B. H 847
Benson, Lee H 263-264
Benson, Leonard G. SOC 253
Bent, Silas PC 840
Bentley, Eric L 218
Bentley, George R. H 265
Bercerra, Rosina M. PSY 17
Berch, Bettina SOC 517
Bercovitch, Sacvan L 41-44
Berelson, Bernard PS 411
Berendt, Joachim Ernst M 255
Beres, Louis Rene PS 581
Berg, Barbara J. H 708
Berg, William M. SOC 206
Berger, Arthur Asa PC 290, 306,
    723
Berger, Brigitte SOC 254
Berger, David H 848
Berger, Edward M 316
Berger, Harold PC 206
Berger, Max H 849
Berger, Michael L. PC 1013
Berger, Peter PS 304
Berger, Peter L. SOC 254
Berger, Raymond M. SOC 331
Bergerson, Frederic A. PS 305
Berghorn, Forrest J. SOC 397
Bergman, Andrew PC 424
Bergman, Elihu PS 324
Bergsten, C. Fred PS 582
Berk, Richard A. SOC 22, 255,
    650
Berk, Sarah Fenstermaker SOC 255
Berkhofer, Robert F., Jr. H 1101;
    R 251
Berkin, Carol Ruth H 709
Berkowitz, Alan D. H 1521
Berkowitz, Edward SOC 519
Berle, Beatrice Bishop A-F 258
Berlin, Edward A. M 256
Berlin, Ira H 1014
Berlin, Pearl PC 944
Berman, Edward H. PS 583
Berman, Larry PS 584
Berman, Myron H 850
Berman, Neil David PC 290
Berman, Ronald H 558; SOC 520
Bermingham, Peter A-A 180
Bernard, H. Russell A-F 264
Bernard, Jessie SOC 256-257, 332,
    521

Bernard, Richard M. H 851, 1284
Bernstein, Barton J. H 5
Bernstein, Irving H 1524-1525
Bernstein, Marver H. H 1657
Bernstein, Michael Andre L 219
Bernstein, Samuel J. L 220
Berry, Gordon L. PSY 18
Berry, Jeffrey M. PS 475
Berry, Mary Frances H 1015
Berryman, Charles L 446
Berthoff, Rowland T. H 6, 852
Berthoff, Warner L 95, 221
Berthron, Donald J. H 1102-1103
Bertolotti, David S., Jr. PC 1
Bertram, Christoph PS 585
Berwanger, Eugene H. H 266, 1415
Berzon, Judith R. L 440
Beschner, George M. A-F 305
Bessie, Simon Michael PC 841
Bestor, Arthur Eugene, Jr. R 189
Bethal, Elizabeth R. A-F 169
Bettelheim, Bruno PC 109;
  PSY 19
Betten, Neil H 1526
Betts, John Rickards PC 925
Betts, Richard K. PS 586-587,
  650
Bewley, Marius L 96-97
Bezilla, Michael STM 28
Bianco, Carla A-F 375
Bickel, Alexander M. PS 412
Bickman, Martin L 98
Bidwell, Percy W. H 1416
Bier, Jesse L 448
Bigelow, Gordon E. L 45
Bigsby, C. W. E. L 222-223, 449-
  450; PC 2-3
Bilbao, Jon A-F 93
Bilik, Dorothy Seidman L 224
Billias, George A. H 57
Billingsley, Andrew SOC 87
Billington, David P. STM 29
Billington, Ray Allen H 58, 559,
  1417-1419; R 258
Bilstein, Roger E. STM 30
Binder, Arnold SOC 653
Binderman, Murray B. A-F 465
Bing, Samuel A-A 358
Bird, Caroline SOC 333
Bird, Michael PC 536
Birkhead, Edith PC 185
Birmingham, Stephen H 853-854
Birnbaum, Robert SOC 258
Birr, Kendall STM 31
Birrell, Susan PC 951
Bishop, Robert Charles A-A 27,
  295-296, 359-360, 418
Biskind, Peter PC 425
Bissell, Richard E. PS 588
Bitton, Davis R 188
Bivins, John, Jr. A-A 361

Bjerkoe, Ethel Hall A-A 362
Bjork, Daniel W. PSY 20
Black, Lloyd D. PS 589
Black, Mary A-A 297
Blackburn, R. M. SOC 578
Blackford, Mansel G. H 1658
Blackmur, R. P. L 225-227
Blackwell, James E. SOC 88
Blaine, Martha Royce H 1104
Blair, Karen J. H 710
Blair, Walter L 1, 451
Blake, John B. STM 32
Blake, Nelson Manfred H 1285;
  L 228
Blakenship, Russell L 2
Blanchard, Kendall A-F 204
Blankenburg, William B. PC 900
Blanton, Wyndham Bolling STM 33
Blasing, Mutler Konuk L 452
Blassingame, John W. H 1015-1017
Blau, Joseph L. R 159, 300;
  SOC 127
Blau, Peter M. SOC 522
Blau, Zena Smith SOC 90
Blaugrund, Annette A-A 161
Blauner, Robert SOC 91
Blaxall, Martha H 711
Blechman, Barry M. PS 590
Bledstein, Burton H 560
Blegen, Theodore C. H 855
Blesh, Rudi M 257-259
Bletter, Rosemarie Haag A-A 623
Bleyer, Willard G. PC 842
Blish, James (William Atheling,
  Jr. pseudonym) PC 207-208
Block, Jean F. A-A 594
Bloesch, Donald G. R 271
Bloom, Harold L 453-454
Bloomfield, Maxwell H 1942
Blos, Peter PSY 21
Blotner, Joseph L 229
Blovin, Francis X. H 1286
Blu, Karen I. A-F 205
Bluem, A. William PC 724
Bluestein, Gene L 455
Bluestone, Barry PS 514
Blum, Albert A. H 1527
Blum, Harold P. PSY 22
Blum, John Morton H 423-424
Blumberg, Paul SOC 449
Blumstein, Philip PSY 23
Boas, Franz A-F 30
Boatright, Mody C. A-F 376-377
Bode, Carl L 99, 456-457
Bodley, John H. A-F 31
Bodnar, John H 856, 1528-1529
Bogan, Louise L 230
Bogardus, Emory S. SOC 92
Bogardus, Ralph F. L 231
Bogart, Leo PC 725, 843
Boggs, John Whitehorn A-F 95

Bogle, Donald PC 426
Bogue, Allan G. H 2, 268, 1420-1421; PS 468
Bohan, Peter A-A 363
Bohannan, Paul A-F 82
Bohi, Charles W. A-A 456
Boles, John B. H 1018; R 68
Bollens, John C. SOC 23
Boller, Paul F., Jr. H 561-562; L 458
Bolton, Roger H 1462
Bolton, S. Charles R 45
Bolton-Smith, Robin A-A 139
Bonacich, Edna SOC 93
Bone, Robert L 459
Bonner, Thomas N. STM 34-35
Bonnifield, Paul H 425
Bonomi, Patricia H 59; PS 413
Bonwick, Colin H 169
Bookchin, Murray PS 6
Boorsch, Suzanne A-A 426
Boorstin, Daniel J. H 7-8, 60, 564-565; PC 4; PS 7; STM 36
Borchert, James H 1287
Borden, Morton H 197
Bordin, Ruth H 712
Bordman, Gerald PC 327-328
Borenstein, Israel H 1674
Boretz, Benjamin M 39
Boring, Edwin G. PSY 24
Boryczka, Raymond H 1530
Bosk, Charles L. STM 37
Bost, James S. L 46
Boswell, Thomas D. SOC 147
Botsch, Robert Emil H 1531
Boulding, Elise A-F 324
Bourguignon, Henry J. H 1943
Bourne, Dorothy Dulles SOC 94
Bourne, James R. SOC 94
Boutilier, Mary A. PC 926
Bouton, Jim PC 927
Bowden, Charles SOC 24
Bowden, Edwin T. L 460
Bowden, Henry Warner R 132, 252
Bowen, William G. PC 326
Bower, Robert T. PC 726
Bowers, William L. H 426
Bowes, Frederick P. H 61
Bowles, David Gordon PS 516
Bowman, William W. PC 875
Boyd, Lois A. R 241
Boyd, Thomas Alvin STM 38
Boyer, L. Bryce PSY 25
Boyer, Paul S. H 1288; R 26
Boyer, Walter E. M 134
Boykin, A. Wade PSY 26
Boyle, Richard J. A-A 181
Boyle, Robert H. PC 928
Boynton, Percy H. L 100, 232
Boyte, Harry C. PS 414
Bozeman, Theodore Dwight R 133

Brackenridge, R. Douglas R 241
Bradbury, John M. L 233
Bradbury, Katharine L. SOC 25
Bradbury, Malcolm L 234
Braden, Charles S. R 190-191
Braden, Waldo W. H 1422
Braestrup, Peter PC 648
Braiker, Harriet B. PSY 147
Brain, James Lewton SOC 398
Braithwaite, John SOC 623
Brams, Steven J. PS 415
Branca, Patricia STM 40
Brand, Oscar M 135
Brandes, Joseph H 857
Brandes, Stuart H 1831
Brandfon, Robert L. H 1423
Brandon, Ruth STM 41
Brannon, Robert PSY 56
Braroe, Niels Winther A-F 206
Bratton, J. S. PC 110
Braudy, Leo PC 427
Brauer, Ralph PC 727
Braun, D. Duane M 369
Braun, Sidney L 461
Braver, Carl M. PS 110
Braverman, Harry PS 517
Brawley, Benjamin L 462
Braxton, Bernard SOC 335
Bray, Robert C. · H 1424
Breckenridge, Adam C. PS 111, 416
Breen, Timothy H. H 62-63, 1019
Breines, Wini H 427
Breitenbach, Edgar A-A 320
Bremer, Francis J. H 64, 179
Bremner, Robert H. H 9-10
Brenton, Myron SOC 259
Bretall, Robert W. R 148
Bretnor, Reginald PC 209-211
Bretton, Henry L. PS 518
Brewington, Marion Vernon A-A 242
Breyer, Stephen PS 306
Bridenbaugh, Carl A-A 364; H 65-70; R 6
Bridge, R. Gary SOC 260
Bridges, Hal R 192
Bridgman, Richard L 463
Brieger, Gert H. STM 42-43
Briggs, Charles L. A-F 259, 378
Briggs, John W. H 858
Briggs, Martin S. A-A 535
Briggs, Vernon M., Jr. SOC 95
Brigham, Clarence S. PC 844-845
Bright, Arthur Aaron, Jr. STM 44
Bright, Charles D. STM 45
Brindze, Ruth PC 728
Bringhurst, Bruce H 1659
Brinkley, Alan H 428
Brislin, Richard PSY 27

Broad, William SOC 612
Broadhead, Robert S. SOC 261
Brock, Leslie V. H 1832
Broder, Patricia Janis A-A 2, 236
Broderick, Dorothy M. PC 111
Brodhead, Richard H. L 101
Brodie, Bernard PS 591
Brodtkorb, Paul, Jr. L 501
Brody, David H 1533-1535
Brody, Eugene B. PSY 28
Brody, J. J. A-A 3
Broehl, Wayne G., Jr. H 859
Brogan, Denis W. SOC 1
Bromberg, Walter PSY 29
Bromley, David G. R 193
Broner, E. M. L 483
Bronfenbrenner, Urie SOC 262
Bronson, Bertrand Harris M 136
Brooks, Courtney G. STM 46
Brooks, H. Allen A-A 595
Brooks, Henry M 40
Brooks, John PC 5
Brooks, Nancy A. SOC 582
Brooks, Paul L 464
Brooks, Van Wyck L 102-107
Brosnan, John PC 428
Brotz, Howard SOC 96
Broussard, James H. H 269
Broven, John M 204-205
Brown, Andreas A-A 348
Brown, B. Katharine H 71
Brown, Bernard E. PS 519
Brown, Charles T. M 370
Brown, Dee H 1105
Brown, Denise Scott A-A 630
Brown, E. Richard STM 47
Brown, Harold PS 592-593
Brown, Herbert Ross PC 70
Brown, Howard PSY 30
Brown, Janet L 465
Brown, John A. H 1232-1233
Brown, Lee PC 846
Brown, Les L 730; PC 729
Brown, Letitia Woods H 1020
Brown, Lorin W. A-F 259
Brown, Milton Wolf A-A 28-29, 206
Brown, Muriel A-F 15
Brown, Peter G. PS 307
Brown, Ralph H. H 1425
Brown, Ray PC 731
Brown, Robert Eldon H 71
Brown, Roger H 270
Brown, Rollo Walter M 41
Brown, Sanborn C. STM 278
Brown, Seyom PS 594
Brown, Sterling A. L 466
Brown, T. Allston PC 329
Brown, Theodore A. H 1318
Brown, Thomas N. H 860

Browne, C. A. M 42
Browne, Gary Lawson H 1289
Browne, Henry J. H 1536
Browne, Pat PC 154
Browne, Ray B. PC 6-10, 154, 1014
Brownell, Blaine A. H 1290, 1322
Browning, Don S. PSY 31
Brownlow, Kevin PC 429-430
Brownmiller, Susan PSY 32
Bruce, Alfred W. STM 48
Bruce, Dickson D., Jr. H 1426-1427
Bruce, Philip Alexander H 72-74
Bruce, Robert V. STM 49-50
Bruce-Novoa, Juan D. L 467
Bruchey, Stuart W. H 1660-1661, 1833
Brucker, Herbert PC 847
Brugger, Robert J. PSY 33
Brunhouse, Robert L. H 198
Brunn, Harry O. M 260
Brunvand, Jan Harold A-F 379-380
Bruss, Paul L 235
Bryan, William Alfred L 468
Bryant, Clifton D. SOC 613
Bryson, Lyman PC 732
Brzezinski, Zbigniew PS 8, 595
Buchanan, A. Russell H 429
Buchanan, James M. PS 69-71
Buck, Peter STM 51
Budd, Louis J. L 469
Budds, Michael J. M 261
Buder, Stanley H 1537
Buel, Richard H 199
Buell, Emmett SOC 97
Buell, Lawrence L 108
Buerkle, Jack V. M 254
Buettner, Stewart A-A 30
Buffington, Albert F. M 134
Bugbee, Bruce W. H 1944
Buhle, Mari Jo H 713
Buitrago Ortiz, Carlos A-F 260
Buley, R. Carlyle H 1428, 1662
Bull, Hedley PS 596
Bullock, Penelope L. PC 848
Bullough, Bonnie PSY 34
Bullough, Vern PSY 34
Bunce, Richard PC 733
Bundy, William P. PS 597
Bunting, Bainbridge A-A 437, 562
Bunzel, Ruth L. A-F 16
Burawoy, Michael SOC 523
Burch, William R., Jr. SOC 3
Burchard, John Ely A-A 438; H 1328
Burchell, R. A. H 861
Buren, James E. PSY 186
Burg, David F. H 1291
Burge, Rabel J. PC 12
Burger, Edward J., Jr. STM 52
Burgess, Ann W. SOC 633

Burham, Jon C. PSY 35
Burk, John N. M 71
Burke, Doreen Bolger A-A 182
Burke, Russel A-A 154
Burkhart, Lynne C. A-F 296
Burling, Robbins A-F 348
Burlingame, Roger STM 53-56
Burner, David H 430
Burnham, David PS 520
Burnham, Jack A-A 256
Burnham, Walter Dean PS 417-418, 423
Burns, Arthur R. H 1834
Burns, James MacGregor PS 9-10, 413, 419
Burns, Rex PC 71
Burr, Wesley PSY 36-37
Burris, Beverly H. SOC 524
Burrison, John A. A-F 381
Burroughs, Alan A-A 149
Burrow, James G. STM 57-58
Burrows, Edwin G. A-F 83
Burt, Richard PS 598
Burt, Ronald S. H 1835
Burton, E. Milby A-A 365
Busch, Lawrence SOC 525
Bush, Donald J. PC 1016
Bush-Brown, Albert A-A 438
Bushman, Richard L. R 47
Busnar, Gene M 371
Buss, Allan R. PSY 38
Buss, Terry F. SOC 526
Butcher, Margaret Just L 470
Butler, Joseph T. A-A 59, 366
Butler, Robert N. SOC 399
Butler, Stuart M. SOC 527
Butterfield, Herbert PS 521
Buttitta, Tony L 236
Button, James W. SOC 528
Byrkit, James W. H 1538
Byrneside, Ronald M 10

Cada, Joseph H 862
Cadogan, Mary PC 143
Cady, Edwin H. L 109-110; PC 929
Cafferty, Pastora San Juan SOC 98
Caffin, Charles Henry A-A 150, 248, 326
Cahn, Edgar S. A-F 207
Cahn, Robert A-A 321
Cain, Louis P. H 1836
Calas, Elana A-A 32
Calas, Nicholas A-A 31-32
Calder, Jenni PC 431
Caldwell, John A-A 275
Caldwell, Patricia L 47
Calhoun, Daniel Hovey H 566; SOC 529; STM 59
Calhoun, Richard B. SOC 400

Califano, Joseph A. PS 112
Calleo, David P. PS 599-600
Callow, Alexander B., Jr. H 1292
Callow, James T. L 111
Calvert, Monte A. STM 60
Calverton, V. F. L 471
Camarillo, Albert A-F 261
Cambell, Angus PSY 39; SOC 2
Cambell, Barbara Kuhn H 714
Cambell, Bruce F. R 195
Cambell, Charles S. H 271
Cambell, Edward D. C., Jr. PC 433
Cambell, Lyle A-F 208
Cambell, Russell PC 434
Cambon, Glauco L 237
Cameron, Evan William PC 432
Cameron, Rondo H 1837
Campa, Arthur Leon M 137
Campbell, Angus PS 420-421
Campbell, Ballard PS 308
Campbell, Rex R. SOC 150
Camus, Raoul F. M 43
Canby, Henry Seidel L 112
Canny, N. P. H 51
Cantor, Milton H 715, 1539
Cantor, Muriel G. PC 734
Cantor, Norman PC 11
Cantril, Hadley PC 735
Caplovitz, David SOC 450
Caplow, Theodore SOC 263
Caras, Tracy M 64
Card, Josefina J. PSY 40
Carden, Joy M 44
Carden, Maren Lockwood R 196; SOC 336
Carey, Daniel J. L 239
Cargen, Leonard SOC 264
Cargill, Oscar L 238
Carlson, Eric T. PSY 149
Carlson, Leonard A. H 1106
Carlson, Peter H 1540
Carmean, E. A. A-A 33-34
Carmichael, Stokeley SOC 99
Carnegie Commission on the Future of Public Broadcasting PC 736
Carney, George O. M 3
Carnoy, Martin PS 309
Caro, Robert A. H 1293
Carossa, Vincent P. H 1663
Carpenter, Charles H., Jr. A-A 167
Carpenter, Edmund PC 649
Carpenter, Frederic I. L 472
Carr, Lois Green H 126
Carr, Patrick M 138
Carroll, Berenice H 716
Carroll, Charles F. H 1664
Carrott, Richard G. A-A 563
Carson, Clayborne PS 522
Carson, Rachel STM 61

Carson, William G. B. L 113
Carstensen, Vernon H 11
Carter, Anne P. H 1838
Carter, Douglass PC 713, 738-739, 850
Carter, Elizabeth PSY 41
Carter, Everett L 114-115
Carter, Lin PC 171
Carter, Paul PC 212
Carter, Paul A. H 431-432; R 100, 116
Carter, Samuel, III H 1107
Cartwright, William H. H 12
Carwardine, Richard R 69
Cary, Diana Serra PC 435
Cary, Lorin Lee H 1530
Case, Robert O. M 45
Case, Victoria M 45
Casey, Ralph D. PC 849
Cash, Wilbur J. H 567
Cashman, Sean Dennis H 433
Casper, Barry M. SOC 530
Cass, Ronald A. PC 737
Cassedy, James H. H 75
Cassell, Joan A-F 84
Castells, Manuel PS 523; SOC 26
Castleman, Craig SOC 27
Castile, George Pierre A-F 85
Cath, Stanley H. PSY 42
Cathers, David M. A-A 368
Caton, Christopher SOC 435
Catton, Bruce H 272
Catudal, Honore PS 601
Caudill, Harry M. H 1429; SOC 28
Caudill, William A-F 86
Caughie, John PC 436
Cauhape, Elizabeth SOC 265
Cavaioli, Frank J. H 952
Cavallo, Dominick H 1294; PSY 2
Cavan, Sherri A-F 87-88
Cavell, Stanley PC 437
Cayton, Horace T. SOC 111
Cawelti, John G. PC 72-73, 270
Ceaser, James W. PS 422, 428
Cecil, Mirabel PC 186
Centers, Richard PSY 43
Ceplair, Larry PC 438
Cerulli, Dom M 262
Chadwick, Bruce A. A-F 202; SOC 263
Chafe, William H. H 717-718, 1022
Chaffee, Steven PSY 52
Challinor, Joan R. A-F 55
Chalmers, David M. R 259
Chamber, William N. PS 423
Chamberlain, J. E. H 1108
Chamberlain, John H 434
Chambers, William N. H 200
Chambliss, William J. SOC 614

Champigny, Robert PC 140
Chandler, Alfred D., Jr. H 1665-1667, 1839
Chandler, Joseph Everett A-A 536
Channing, Steven H 273
Chapman, Arthur H. PSY 44
Chapple, Steve M 372
Charmaz, Kathy SOC 401
Charney, Hanna PC 141
Charney, Maurice L 240
Charren, Peggy PC 740
Charters, Samuel Barclay M 206-209, 263
Charvatt, William L 116-117
Chase, Gilbert M 4, 46
Chase, Judith Wragg A-A 35
Chase, Richard Volney L 3, 473
Chase, William C. H 1945
Cheape, Charles W. H 1295
Cheek, Neil H. PC 12; SOC 3
Chemers, Martin M. PSY 4
Chenault, Lawrence R. SOC 100
Cheney, Martha Candler A-A 36
Chenoweth, Lawrence PC 13
Cherlin, Andrew J. SOC 266
Chernin, Kim SOC 338
Cherry, Conrad R 134, 283
Chesler, Phyllis PSY 45-46
Chester, Edward W. PC 741
Chester, Ronald H 568
Child, Herbert STM 63
Child, Irvin L. PSY 47
Childs, Alan W. PSY 48
Chilman, Catherine PSY 49
Chindahl, George L. PC 330
Chiswick, Barry R. SOC 98
Chinoy, Ely SOC 531
Chiu, Ping H 863
Choate, J. Ernest, Jr. H 1430
Choate, Julian, Jr. PC 275
Chomsky, Noam PS 602
Christ, Jacob PSY 92
Christensen, Edwin O. A-A 298, 369
Christgau, Robert M 373
Christian, Barbara L 241
Christians, Clifford G. PC 683
Christie, Robert A. H 1541
Christman, Margaret C. PC 1027
Christopher, Milbourne PC 331
Chrystal, K. Alec PS 2
Chudacoff, Howard P. H 1296
Chung, Norman H. SOC 310
Church, Robert L. H 569
Churchill, Allen PC 332-333
Churchill, Charles W. SOC 101
Cioffi, Frank PC 213
Cirino, Robert PC 14
Ciucci, Giorgio A-A 439
Clapp, Priscilla PS 665
Clard, Kenneth B. SOC 195

Clarens, Carlos PC 439
Clareson, Thomas D. PC 214-217
Clark, Charles E. H 76
Clark, Dennis H 864-865
Clark, Edward W. R 257
Clark, Garth A-A 370
Clark, Harry Hayden L 474
Clark, Jerry E. H 1109
Clark, Kenneth B. SOC 102
Clark, Margaret A-F 89, 262
Clark, Norman H. H 435
Clark, Paul F. H 1542
Clark, Reginald PSY 50
Clark, Robert Judson A-A 371, 596
Clark, Robert L. SOC 402
Clark, Thomas A-F 170
Clark, Victor S. H 1668
Clark, William J. A-A 249
Clarke, Duncan L. PS 603
Clarke, Erskine R 80
Clarke, James W. PS 113
Clarke, Peter PC 851
Clay, Grady PC 1017
Clebsch, William A. R3, 135
Clecak, Peter H 436
Clemens, Paul G. E. H 1840
Clerk, John P. SOC 631
Cletus, Daniel E. H 1543
Clifton, James A. A-F 209, 297
Clinard, Marshall B. SOC 615
Cline, Ray PS 604
Clinton, Catherine H 719
Cloward, Richard A. PS 378; SOC 493
Clowse, Converse D. H 1841
Clurman, Harold L 242
Cobb, Jonathan SOC 502
Coblentz, Patricia A-A 27, 360
Cochran, Clarke E. PS 11
Cochran, Thomas C. H 1669-1673
Cochrane, Glynn A-F 298
Cochrane, Rexmond C. STM 65-66
Cochrane, Willard W. H 1842
Cockburn, Alexander PS 524
Coddington, Alan H 1843
Coe, Ralph T. A-A 4
Coffey, Jon W. PS 12
Coffey, Kenneth J. PS 605
Coffin, Margaret M. A-F 382
Coffin, Tristram Potter A-F 383-387; PC 930
Coffman, Stanley K., Jr. L 243
Cogley, John PC 440, 742
Cohen, Anne B. A-F 388
Cohen, Bernard H 866; SOC 616
Cohen, Bernard C. PC 852; PS 606
Cohen, Cheryl M 218
Cohen, David Steven A-F 90, 389
Cohen, David K. PS 98
Cohen, George M. A-A 38

Cohen, Hennig A-F 386; L 475-476
Cohen, I. Bernard STM 67
Cohen, L. M. PSY 180
Cohen, Lester H. H 201
Cohen, Naomi W. H 867; SOC 103
Cohen, Steven M. SOC 104
Cohen, Norm M 139
Cohen, Patricia Cline STM 68
Cohen, Raquel E. PSY 51
Cohen, Ronald D. A-F 19; H 1297
Cohen, Sarah Blecher L 244
Cohen, Stanley PC 650, 931
Cohen, Warren I. PS 607
Cohn, Jan A-A 440
Cohn, Nik M 374
Cohn, Ruby L 245
Cole, Barry G. PC 743
Cole, Bernard A-A 325
Cole, Donald B. H 868
Cole, Jonathan R. STM 69
Cole, Lewis PC 932
Cole, Wayne S. H 437
Coleman, A. D. A-A 322
Coleman, James S. PS 486; SOC 4, 267
Coleman, Richard P. SOC 451
Coleman, William STM 70
Coles, Harry L. H 274
Coles, Robert SOC 452
Colgan, Susan A-A 403
Collier, James Lincoln M 264-265
Collier, John H 1110
Collins, John M. PS 608
Collins, Robert M. PS 310
Collins, Thomas W. A-F 32
Colson, Elizabeth H 1111
Colton, Ray C. H 1431
Combs, James E. PS 551
Commager, Henry Steele H 202, 570, 869
Commons, John R. H 1544
Comstock, George A. PC 744; PSY 52
Comstock, Helen A-A 372
Conant, Michael PC 441
Condie, Spence J. SOC 250
Condit, Carl W. A-A 441, 564; H 1298; STM 71-74
Condon, Eddie M 266
Condon, Thomas J. H 77
Cone, Edward T. M 39
Cone, James H. M 210; R 156
Cone, Thomas E. STM 75
Conferences on Research in Income and Wealth H 1844
Conforti, Joseph A. R 81
Conkin, Paul K. H 438-439, 571, 606
Conklin, Nancy Faires A-F 349
Conlin, Joseph R. H 1545
Conn, Peter L 246

Conn, Richard A-A 5
Connell, R. W. PS 525
Connolly, Cyril L 247
Connolly, Thomas E. H 841
Connolly, William PS 13-14
Conot, Robert STM 76
Conover, Pamela Johnson SOC 340
Conrad, John P. PSY 53
Conrad, Peter L 248
Conrad, Peter SOC 617
Conrad, Susan Phinney H 720
Conroy, Hilary H 870
Constant, Edward W., II STM 77
Contreras, Belisario R. A-A 39
Converse, Philip E. PS 420-421,
    424; PSY 39
Conzen, Kathleen Neils H 871
Cook, Adrian H 872
Cook, Bruce L 249; M 211
Cook, Charles M. H 1946
Cook, Edward M., Jr. H 78
Cook, Elizabeth C. L 48
Cook, Harold E. M 140
Cook, Jim PC 442
Cook, Sherburne F. H 1112
Cook, Sylvia Jenkins L 250
Cook, Warren H 79
Cooke, Edward S., Jr. A-A 373
Cooke, Hereward Lester A-A 40
Cooley, John R. L 477
Cooley, Thomas L 118
Coolidge, John A-A 565
Coombs, Steven Lane PC 671
Cooney, Margaret SOC 664
Cooper, Grace Rogers STM 78
Cooper, Jerry M. H 1546
Cooper, Joseph PS 114
Cooper, Mark N. SOC 453
Cooper, Wendy A. A-A 374
Cooper-Clark, Diana PC 142
Cooperman, Stanley L 251
Cope, Jackson I. L 478
Copland, Aaron M 48-50
Coppa, Frank J. PC 745
Corbin, David A. H 1547
Cord, Robert L. R 301
Cordasco, Francesco H 873
Corio, Ann PC 334
Corn, Joseph J. STM 79
Corn, Wanda A-A 41
Corner, George W. STM 80
Cornfield, Robert M 141
Cornillon, Susan Koppelman L 479
Corsini, Raymond J. PSY 131
Cortes, Fernando PS 72
Corwin, Norman PC 15
Coser, Lewis H 477
Coser, Lewis A. SOC 532
Cott, Nancy F. H 721-722
Cotterill, R. S. H 1113
Cotter, Cornelius PS 425

Cotton, James Harry H 572
Coughtry, Jay H 1023
Countryman, Edward H 203
Couperie, Pierre PC 307
Courlander, Harold M 142
Courtwright, David T. STM 81
Couser, G. Thomas L 480
Covey, Cyclone H 80
Cowan, Helen I. H 874
Cowan, Louise L 252
Cowan, Ruth Schwartz STM 82
Cowdrey, Albert E. H 1432
Cowell, Henry H 51
Cowie, Alexander L 4
Cowley, Malcolm L 253-258
Cox, Allan SOC 533
Cox, Annette A-A 207
Cox, John H. H 275
Cox, LaWanda H 275
Crabb, Cecil V., Jr. PS 465, 609
Crafton, Donald PC 443
Craig, E. Quinta L 259
Craig, Lois A. A-A 442
Craig, Patricia PC 143
Crampton, C. Gregory H 1114
Crane, Verner W. H 81, 1115
Cranz, Galen A-A 443
Craven, Avery O. H 276-277
Craven, Thomas A-A 42
Craven, Wayne A-A 237
Craven, Wesley Frank H 82-83,
    1116
Cravens, Hamilton STM 83
Crawford, Richard M 52
Creamer, Daniel H 1674
Creedon, Carol F. PSY 81
Crenson, Matthew A. PS 311
Crepeau, Richard C. PC 933
Crester, G. A. PSY 54
Cremin, Lawrence A. H 573-574
Crick, Bernard PS 73
Cripps, Thomas PC 444-445
Croan, Melvin PS 736
Crockett, Norman A-F 171
Cronin, Thomas E. PS 115-116
Cronon, William H 84
Crosby, Alfred W. H 1117
Crosby, Donald F. H 440
Crosby, Faye J. SOC 341
Cross, Donna Woolfolk PC 746
Cross, John R. SOC 624
Cross, Robert D. R 160
Cross, Whitney R. R 70
Crotty, William J. PS 426-427
Crouch, Tom D. STM 84
Crouse, Timothy PC 853
Crowley, J. E. H 85
Crunden, Robert M. H 441, 575
Crystal, Stephen SOC 403
Csida, Joseph PC 335
Csida, June Bundy PC 335

Cudacoff, Howard P. H 1298
Cuddihy, John Murray R 294
Cuff, Robert D. H 442
Culbert, David H. PC 747
Culhane, Paul PS 476
Cullen, Ruth M. SOC 147
Cumbler, John H 1548
Cumings, Bruce PS 610-611
Cummings, Abbott Lowell A-A 537
Cummings, Paul A-A 288
Cummings, Richard H 13
Cummings, Tony M 222
Cummings, W. P. H 86
Cunliffe, Marcus H 278; L 5
Cunningham, Noble E., Jr.
  A-A 43; H 279-280
Cunz, Dieter H 875
Curran, Robert Emmett R 161
Curran, Thomas J. H 876
Current, Richard N. H 1433
Curry, Larry A-A 183
Curry, Leonard P. H 1024
Curti, Merle H 14, 576-578, 1434
Curtin, Philip D. H 1025
Curtis, David PC 446
Curvin, Robert SOC 618
Cutten, George Barton A-A 375
Czitrom, Daniel J. PC 651

Daems, Herman H 1839
Dahl, Barbara B. PSY 136
Dahl, Robert A. PS 15-17, 74-75
Dain, Norman STM 85-86
Dal Co, Francesco A-A 439
Dale, Edward Everett H 1118, 1435
Daley, Charles V. PC 652
Dallas, Karl M 375
Dallek, Robert PS 612-613
Daly, John Charles PS 614
Daly, Kathleen SOC 667
Daly, Robert L 49
Dana, Richard H. PSY 55
Danbom, David B. H 1299
Dance, Daryl Cumber A-F 390
Dance, Stanley M 267
Daner, Francine Jeanne A-F 91
Dangerfield, George H 281-282
Danhof, Clarence H. H 283
Daniel, Robert L. H 15
Danielian, N. STM 87
Daniels, Arlene Kaplan PC 704
Daniels, Bruce C. H 87, 1436
Daniels, George H. STM 88-91
Daniels, Les PC 308
Daniels, Roger H 877
Danto, Arthur C. A-A 44
Danziger, Edmund Jefferson, Jr.
  H 1119
Darby, Michael R. H 1845
Dardis, Tom L 260

Darling, Richard L. PC 112
Datcher, Linda SOC 250
Dathorne, O. R. L 481
Daum, Arnold R. H 1815; STM 393-
  394
Davenport, Guy L 482
Davenport, Thomas G. A-A 58
David, Deborah S. PSY 56
David, Hans T. M 53
David, Paul A. STM 92
David, Paul T. PS 312, 428-429
Davidson, Abraham A. A-A 151,
  208
Davidson, Cathy N. L 483
Davidson, Donald L 261
Davidson, James West R 284
Davidson, Marshall B. A-A 376,
  444
Davidson, Stephen M. SOC 534
Davidson, R. Theodore A-F 263
Davies, John D. STM 93
Davies, Margery W. H 723
Davies, Philip PC 447
Davis, Allen F. H 878, 1300
Davis, Angela Y. H 724
Davis, Bob M 367
Davis, David Brion H 1026; L 119
Davis, Douglas A-A 45
Davis, George A-F 174
Davis, James W. PS 430
Davis, Karen SOC 454
Davis, Lance E. H 1846-1847
Davis, Lawrence B. H 879
Davis, Lynn E. PS 593
Davis, Moshe H 880
Davis, Nathan M 268
Davis, Nuell Pharr STM 94
Davis, Patricia A. SOC 404
Davis, Pearce H 1675
Davis, Richard Beale L 50-51
Davis, Robert E. PC 653
Davis, Ronald L. M 5
Davis, Ronald L. F. H 1437
Davis, Vincent PS 117
Davis, W. Allison A-F 172-173,
  299
Davis-Sacks, Mary Lou SOC 410
Davison, Archibald T. M 54
Dawidowicz, Lucy S. R 162
Dawley, Alan H 1549
Day, Clarence A. H 1438
Day, Dawn SOC 106
Day, Robert C. PC 941
Deal, Terrence E. A-F 300
Dean, John P. SOC 242
Dearing, Mary R. H 284
Deaux, Kay SOC 535
DeBenedetti, Charles H 443;
  PS 526
Debo, Angie H 1120-1123
DeBrizzi, John A. SOC 536

de Camp, L. Sprague PC 172
DeCanio, Stephan J. H 1439
Deckard, Barbara Sinclair
  PSY 57
Decker, Scott H. SOC 619
Deedy, John G., Jr. PC 854
Deegan, Dorothy Yost L 484
Deer, Harriet PC 16
Deer, Irving PC 16
Deetz, James PC 1018-1019
Degler, Carl N. H 16, 285, 725,
  1027, 1440
DeGrazia, Sebastian PC 17
DeJong, Gerald F. H 881
DeLaguna, Frederica A-F 5
Delamater, John SOC 342
Delany, Janice H 726
Delany, Samuel R. PC 218
De Laurentis, Teresa PC 448
De Lerma, Dominique Rene M 6
Del Castillo, Adelaida R.
  A-F 283
Del Rey, Lester PC 219
DeLuca, Stuart M. PC 748
DeMartino, Nick PC 785
Dembo, L. S. L 262
D'Emilio, John SOC 343
Deming, Barbara PC 449
Demos, John Putnam H 88; R 27
DeMott, Robert J. L 485
Dempsey, John J. PSY 58
Denisoff, R. Serge M 143-144,
  376-377
Denison, Edward F. H 1848-1849
Denker, Joel SOC 537
Denmark, Florence L. PSY 174
Dennis, Everette E. PC 654-655,
  855
Dennis, Jack PS 527
Dennison, Sam M 378
Denny, Margaret L 486
Densmore, Frances M 145
Dentler, Robert A. SOC 107-108
DeRochemont, Richard H 35
De Rosier, Arthur H. H 1124
Derr, Jill M. R 242
Dervin, Brenda PC 661
De Santis, Hugh PS 615
Desmarais, Charles A-A 337
Desroche, Henri R 197
Destler, I. M. PS 616-617
Dethloff, Henry C. H 1850
De Toledano, Ralph M 269
Dettelbach, Cynthia Golomb
  PC 74
De Turk, David A. M 146
Detweiler, Frederick G. PC 856
Detweiler, Robert L 487
De Usabel, Gaizka S. PC 450
Deutsch, Francine PSY 59
Deutsch, Helene PSY 60

Deutsch, Karl W. PS 76
Devine, Donald J. PS 18
DeVolpi, A. STM 95
DeVoto, Bernard Augustus H 89,
  1441
Dew, Charles H 286
DeWeerd, Harvey A. H 444
Dewhurst, C. Kurt A-A 299-300
Dexter, Dave M 270-271
Dexter, Elisabeth Anthony H 727-
  728
Dexter, Lewis A. PS 303
D'Harnoncourt, Rene A-A 7
Dial, Adolf L. H 1125
Diamond, Ailyn L 488
Diamond, Edwin PC 656, 749-750
Diamond, Sigmund STM 96
Diaz-Guerrero, Rogelio A-F 313
Dick, Everett H 1442
Dickason, David Howard A-A 46
Dickerson, Oliver M. H 204
Dickey, James L 263
Dickinson, Joan Younger H 729
Dickinson, John N. H 1301
Dickinson, Robert E. H 1443
Dickson, Harold E. A-A 47
Diehl, Carl H 580
Dieter, Melvin Esterday R 272
Dietz, Mary Lorenz SOC 620
Diggins, John P. H 581, 882;
  PS 19
Dillard, J. L. A-F 350
Dillenberger, Jane A-A 48-49
Dillenberger, John A-A 48
Dillman, Don A. SOC 66
Dillon, Katherine V. PS 753-754
Dillon, Merton H 287
DiMeglio, John PC 336
DiMona, Joe PC 334
Dimont, Max I. H 883
Diner, Hasia R. H 884
Diner, Stephen J. H 1302
Dinerstein, Herbert S. PS 618,
  742-743
Dinitz, Simon PSY 53
Dinkin, Robert J. H 90
Dinnerstein, Leonard H 885-888;
  SOC 109-110
Dippie, Brian W. H 1126
Diskin, Martin PS 619
Distefanis, Proto PC 307
Divine, Robert A. H 889; PS 620-
  623
Dixler, Elsa H 825
Dixon, Bernard STM 97
Dizer, John T. PC 292
Dizikes, John PC 934
Dje Dje, Jacqueline Cogdell
  M 147
Dobelstein, Andrew W. SOC 538
Dobie, J. Frank L 489

Dobkowski, Michael N. R 260
Dobrovolsky, Sergei P. H 1674
Dobson, John M. H 445
Dobyns, Henry F. A-F 92
Dockstader, Frederick J. A-A 6
Dodd, Lawrence C. PS 118
Dodder, Laura SOC 644
Dodds, John W. H 446
Doehrman, Steven R. SOC 410
Doenecke, Justus D. H 288
Doering, Susan G. SOC 270
Doerner, William SOC 665
Doezema, Marianne A-A 50
Doherty, Robert J. A-A 323
Dolan, Jay P. H 890; R 71
Dollard, John A-F 172; SOC 455
Dolson, Frank PC 935
Domhoff, G. William PS 77;
  SOC 456-458
Donald, David H 289-290
Dondoe, Dorothy Anne L 490
Donegan, Jane B. STM 98
Donhauser, Paul S. A-A 378
Donnelly, Marian Card A-A 538
Donovan, Robert J. PS 624-625
Doody, Terrance L 491
Dooley, Roger PC 451
Dorfman, Ariel PC 18, 309
Dorfman, Joseph H 1851
Dormon, James H., Jr. L 120
Dornbusch, Sanford M. PC 95
Dorr, Aimee PC 801
Dorson, Richard M. A-F 391-401
Doty, Robert A-A 324
Doucet, Michael J. H 1881
Douglas, Ann L 121
Douglas, Frederic A-A 7
Douglas, Mary R 117
Douglass, William A. A-F 93
Douvan, Elizabeth PSY 176
Dove, George N. PC 144
Dover, Cedric A-A 51
Dow, George Francis H 91
Dowd, James J. SOC 405
Dowdy, Andrew PC 452
Dowie, James Iverne H 891-892
Dowling, Harry F. STM 99-100
Downer, Alan S. L 264
Downes, Randolph C. H 1127
Downie, Leonard, Jr. PC 857
Downing, Antoinette F. A-A 445
Downs, Anthony PS 78, 313;
  SOC 25, 29
Downs, James F. A-F 301
Drake, James A. PC 38
Drake, St. Clair SOC 111
Drake, Thomas E. R 92
Dranov, Paula M 379
Draper, Theodore H 442, 448;
  PS 626
Drepperd, Carl William A-A 278

Drexler, Arthur A-A 465
Drinan, Robert F. R 302
Drinnon, Richard L 492
Driskell, David C. A-A 52
Driver, Harold E. A-F 210
Drucker, Peter F. PS 528-529
Drummond, Robert R. M 55
Drury, Clifford M. H 1128
Druxman, Michael B. PC 337
Duberman, Lucile SOC 344
Dublin, Thomas H 730-731
DuBoff, Richard B. H 1676
Dubofsky, Melvyn H 1550
DuBois, Ellen Carol H 732
Ducheneaux, Karen H 1180
Ducker, James H. H 1551
Duff, John B. SOC 112
Duffey, Bernard L 265, 493
Duffy, Martin SOC 435
Duffy, John STM 101-103
Dugger, Ronnie H 582; PS 119
Duis, Perry R. H 1304
Dulles, Foster Rhea PC 19;
  PS 627
Dumont, Richard G. PSY 61
Duncan, Francis STM 166-167
Duncan, Hugh Dalziel A-A 566
Duncan, Otis Dudley SOC 522, 579
Dundes, Alan A-F 402-404
Dunlap, George Arthur L 494
Dunlap, Thomas R. STM 104
Dunn, Richard S. H 92
Dunn, Thomas P. PC 220-221
Dunn, William M. PS 314
Dunson, Josh M 148
Dunwell, Steve STM 105
Dupre, J. Stefan STM 106
Dupree, A. Hunter STM 107-108
Duran, Livie Isauro A-F 264
Duran, Richard P. A-F 265
Durgnat, Raymond PC 453
Durham, Philip PC 271
Durso, Joseph PC 936-937
Dusenbury, Winifred L. L 495
Dworkin, James B. PC 938
Dworkin, Ronald PS 20
Dye, Nancy Schrom H 733
Dye, Thomas R. PS 315-316
Dyer, Richard PC 454
Dykstra, Robert H 1305
Dyson, Lowell K. H 449

Eakin, Paul John L 122
Ealy, Steven D. PS 79
Eames, Edwin A-F 302
Eames, S. Morris H 583
Earl, Polly Anne STM 298
Earle, Alice Morse H 93-94
Earle, Carville V. H 1677
Earle, Edward W. A-A 327

Early, James A-A 567
Earnest, Ernest L 266, 496
East, Robert A. H 1678
Easterlin, Richard A. H 1847, 1852
Eastman, Elaine Goodale H 1129
Easton, David PS 80-82
Easton, Loyd D. H 584
Eaton, Allen H. A-F 405-406
Eaton, Anne Thaxter PC 128
Eaton, Clement H 291, 585, 1444
Eaton, Leonard K. A-A 597-598
Eauclaire, Sally A-A 338
Eberhart, Richard L 267
Eberlein, Harold Donaldson A-A 539-540
Eberly, Philip K. PC 751
Ebert, John A-A 301
Ebert, Katherine A-A 301
Eccles, William J. H 95
Eckert, J. Kevin SOC 406
Eco, Umberto PC 145
Eddy, Elizabeth M. A-F 303-304
Edel, Leon L 497
Edelman, Murray PS 83
Edgell, G. H. A-A 599
Edgerton, Gary R. PC 455
Edmonson, Munro S. A-F 191
Edmunds, R. David H 1130-1131
Edward, Joyce PSY 62
Edwards, Arthur C. M 7
Edwards, George C. PS 120-121, 317
Edwards, George Thornton M 56
Edwards, Harry PC 939-940
Edwards, Herbert W. L 535
Edwards, Lee R. L 488
Edwards, P. K. H 1552
Edwards, Rem B. R 136
Edwards, Richard H 1553, 1568
Edwards, Richard C. H 1554
Egbert, Donald Drew A-A 53
Egerton, John SOC 268
Eggan, Fred A-F 211
Eggert, Gerald H 1555
Egoff, Sheila A. PC 113-114
Ehrenreich, Barbara H 734-735; SOC 345-346
Ehrlich, Richard D. PC 220
Ehrlich, Richard L. H 893
Eichner, Alfred S. H 1679
Eiseman, Alberta SOC 113
Eisen, Arnold M. R 163
Eisen, Jonathan M 380-382
Eisenberg, Bernard PS 497
Eisenstein, Sarah SOC 539
Eisenstein, Zillah R. PS 21
Eisinger, Chester E. L 268
Eisinger, Peter K. SOC 114
Eitzen, D. Stanley PC 941
Ekirch, A. Roger H 96

Ekrich, Arthur A., Jr. H 450, 586
Elazar, Daniel J. H 1306
Elder, Glen H., Jr. SOC 269
Elder, William Voss, III A-A 379-380
Eldredge, Charles C. A-A 152
Eldersveld, Samuel PS 431
Eliades, David K. H 1125
Elias, Robert SOC 621
Eliot, Marc PC 752
Elkins, Stanley H 1028
Eller, Ronald D. H 1445
Ellinger, Esther Parker L 123
Elliott, Emory L 52-54
Elliott, Mark PS 628
Ellis, David M. H 1446-1447
Ellis, John STM 109
Ellis, John Tracy R 28, 164
Ellis, Joseph J. L 55
Ellis, Lewis Ethan PS 629
Ellis, Richard E. H 292
Ellison, Harlan PC 753
Ellman, Mary L 498
Ellsworth, Lucius F. H 1925
Ellwood, Robert S., Jr. R 198-199
Elovitz, Mark H. H 894
Elsner, Henry STM 110
Elson, Louis C. M 57-58
Ely, Catherine Beach A-A 184
Emerson, Everett L 56
Emery, Edwin PC 858-859
Emme, Eugene M. STM 111-112
Emmet, Boris H 1680
Engel, J. Ronald SOC 31
Engel, Lehman PC 338
Egelbourg, Saul H 1681
Engle, Paul H 736
Engler, Robert PS 318
Engerman, Stanley L. H 1031, 1855
English, Deirdre H 734-735; SOC 346
English, Peter C. STM 113
Englund, Steven PC 438
Engs, Robert Francis H 1029
Enloe, Cynthia H. PS 477
Enos, John Lawrence STM 114
Enthoven, Alain C. PS 630
Entwise, Doris R. SOC 270
Epps, Edgar SOC 139
Epstein, Barbara Leslie H 737
Epstein, Cynthia Fuchs SOC 347-348
Epstein, Dena J. M 59, 149
Epstein, Edward J. PC 754, 860
Epstein, Edward Z. PC 549
Epstein, Laurily Keir PC 861
Epstein, Melech H 895
Erenberg, Lewis A. H 1307
Erens, Patricia PC 456

Erickson, Charlotte H 896, 1556
Erickson, Jack T. A-A 302
Erikson, Erik PSY 63-65
Erikson, Kai T. R 29
Erlich, Lillian M 272
Erlich, Richard D. PC 221
Ernst, Robert H 897
Eschbach, Lloyd Arthur PC 222
Escobar, Javier I. PSY 17
Escott, Colin M 383
Escott, Paul D. H 293
Espelie, Ernest M. H 892
Espinosa, Jose E. A-A 303
Essien-Udom, E. U. H 1030
Essig, James D. R 93
Esslin, Martin PC 755
Esslinger, Dean R. H 899
Estes, Carroll L. SOC 407
Estes, J. Worth STM 115
Estren, Mark James PC 310
Etheridge, Elizabeth W. STM 116
Etheridge, Lloyd PS 631
Ettling, John STM 117
Etulain, Richard W. H 1507;
    PC 272
Etzioni, Minerva PS 632
Eulau, Henry PS 84-85
Evangelina, Enriquez A-F 282
Evans, Christopher R 200
Evans, Daryl Paul SOC 662
Evans, David M 212
Evans, Dorinda A-A 172
Evans, Elizabeth H 738
Evans, Richard J. H 739
Evans, Sara SOC 349
Evans, Susan H. PC 851
Evans, W. McKee H 294, 1132
Everhart, Robert B. SOC 271
Everette, Michael W. A-F 248
Everson, David H. PS 432
Everson, William K. PC 457, 462
Ewen, David M 60, 384-386;
    PC 339-341
Ewen, Elizabeth PC 20
Ewen, Lynda Ann H 1557
Ewen, Stuart PC 20
Ewers, John C. H 1133
Ewing, George W. M 387
Ewing, John A. PSY 66
Ezell, Edward Clinton STM 118
Ezell, Linda Newman STM 118

Fabre, Genevieve L 269
Fabricant, Solomon H 1682
Faderman, Lillian H 740
Fagen, M. D. STM 119-120
Failey, Dean F. A-A 381
Fairbanks, Jonathan L. A-A 54,
    382
Falco, Maria J. PS 86

Falconer, John I. H 1416
Faler, Paul G. H 1558
Fales, Dean A. A-A 383
Falk, Richard PS 719
Falk, Robert L 124, 499
Fallows, James PS 633
Fallows, Marjorie R. SOC 115
Fallwell, Marshall, Jr. M 141
Farber, Manny PC 458
Farber, Stephen PC 459
Farbero, Norman L. A-F 133
Farish, Hunter Dickinson R 94
Farran, Dale Clark PSY 67
Farrar, Ronald T. PC 657
Farrell, Jack T. M 288
Farrell, James J. STM 121
Farrell, Michael P. SOC 403
Farrell, Warren T. SOC 344
Farrer, Clair A-F 60
Fasold, Ralph W. A-F 368
Faulkner, Harold U. H 1853
Faulkner, Robert Kenneth H 1947
Faulkner, Robert R. M 388-389
Fauset, Arthur Huff R 222
Faust, Drew H 587
Fawcett, Anthony M 390
Fawcett, Stephen B. PS 373
Fay, Bernard H 205
Feagans, Lynne PSY 67
Feagin, Joe R. SOC 31
Feather, Leonard M 273
Feder, Judith PS 319-320
Feder, Norman A-A 8-9
Feeney, William F. PS 798
Feest, Christian A-A 10
Fehrenbacher, Don Edward H 295,
    1448, 1948
Feidelson, Charles, Jr. L 500-
    501
Feigelman, William SOC 272
Fein, Albert H 1308
Fein, Isaac M. H 900
Feinberg, Joel PS 22
Feinberg, Richard E. PS 634
Feingold, Henry L. H 901; R 165-
    166
Feinstein, Karen Wolk H 741
Feinstein, Marnin H 902
Feis, Herbert H 451; PS 635-638
Feiveson, Harold A. PS 659
Feld, Sheila PSY 177
Feldberg, Michael H 296, 903
Feldman, Harvey W. A-F 305
Feldman, Saul D. A-F 34
Feldstein, Martin H 1854
Feldstein, Stanley H 904
Felix, David H 452
Fell, James E., Jr. H 1683
Fell, John L. PC 460-461
Fell, Marie Leonore H 905
Fellman, Anita Clair STM 122

Fellman, Michael STM 122
Felshin, Jan PC 944
Fenichel, Carol STM 257
Fenin, George N. PC 462
Fenno, Richard F. PS 122-124
Fenstermaker, J. Van H 1684
Ferguson, Charles A. A-F 351
Ferguson, Otis PC 463
Ferguson, Thomas PS 433
Ferm, Deane William R 137
Fermi, Laura H 588, 906
Fernandez, John P. SOC 116
Fernett, Gene M 274-275
Ferrell, Robert H. PS 639
Ferris, William A-F 407-408;
    M 150, 213
Ferriss, Abbott L. PSY 68
Feshbach, Seymour PC 756
Fetterly, Judith L 502
Feuer, Jane PC 464
Feuerlicht, Roberta Strauss
    H 907
Fey, Harold E. H 1134
Ffrench, Florence M 61
Fiedler, Leslie A. L 503-505;
    PC 75-76, 342
Field, Donald R. PC 12
Field, G. Lowell PS 87
Field, Tiffany M. PSY 69
Fielding, Raymond PC 465-466
Fiering, Norman R 138-139
Fife, Alta A-F 409-410
Fife, Austin A-F 409-410
Figley, Charles R. PSY 70
Filler, Louis PC 77
Findlay, James F., Jr. R 72
Fine, David M. L 125
Fine, Elsa Honig A-A 55
Fine, Sidney H 1559
Fineberg, Harvey PS 367
Finholt, Richard L 126
Fink, Gary M. H 1560, 1623
Fink, Leon H 1561
Fink, Lois Marie A-A 56
Finkelman, Paul H 1949
Finkelstein, Sidney M 276
Finkle, Lee PC 862
Fiorina, Morris P. PS 125
Fisch, Harold L 270
Fischer, Claude S. SOC 32
Fischer, David Hackett H 17, 297
Fischer, Frank PS 321
Fish, Carl Russell H 298
Fish, John Hall SOC 33
Fisher, Dexter L 506
Fisher, Harold A. PC 887
Fisher, Louis PS 126-127
Fisher, Marvin STM 123
Fisher, Miles Mark M 151
Fisher, Sethard SOC 117
Fisher, William Arms M 62

Fishkin, James PS 23-24, 41
Fishlow, Albert H 1685
Fishman, Joshua A. A-F 352
Fishman, Mark PC 863
Fishman, Priscilla SOC 118
Fishwick, Marshall W. A-A 446;
    PC 10, 21-22
Fisk, Elizabeth C. SOC 308
Fisse, Brent SOC 623
Fitch, James Marston A-A 447-448,
    568
Fitchen, Janet M. A-F 306
Fitchen, John PC 1020
Fite, Gilbert C. SOC 540
Fitzgerald, Francis PS 640
Fitzgerald, Oscar P. A-A 384
Flack, J. Kirkpatrick STM 124
Flaherty, David H. H 97-98
Flanigan, William H. PS 468
Flatham, Richard E. PS 25-26
Fleenor, Juliann E. PC 187
Fleming, Donald H 589; STM 125
Fleming, Sandford H 99
Flexner, Eleanor H 742
Flexner, James Thomas A-A 173-
    175, 185-186; STM 126
Fliegelman, Jay H 590
Flink, James J. STM 127-128
Flower, Elizabeth H 591
Fluck, Winifred L 507
Flynn, Charles PC 540
Foerster, Norman L 508-509
Fogarty, Robert S. H 453
Fogel, Robert William H 2, 1031,
    1686, 1855
Fogelson, Robert M. H 1309-1310
Folb, Edith A. A-F 175
Foley, Daniel J. A-A 316
Foley, Mary Mix A-A 449
Foley, Suzanne A-A 261
Folsom, Burton W., Jr. H 1311
Folsom, James K. PC 273-274
Foner, Anne SOC 409
Foner, Eric H 206, 299-300, 1032
Foner, Philip S. H 743, 1033,
    1562-1563; M 152
Foote, Henry Wilder M 63
Foote, Shelby H 301
Forbes, Harriette M. A-A 243
Forbes, Jack D. H 1135-1136
Ford, Alice A-A 304
Ford, Daniel STM 129
Ford, Edwin H. PC 859
Foreman, Grant H 1137
Forgie, George B. H 302
Forman, Henry Chandlee A-A 450,
    541
Forman, John Henry PC 467
Formisano, Ronald P. H 303
Fornatale, Peter PC 757
Forrest, Gary G. PSY 71

Forster, Colin H 18
Forsyth, David P. PC 864
Foss, Dennis C. PSY 61
Foster, Brenda SOC 650
Foster, Charles I. R 73
Foster, George PS 815
Foster, Hal A-A 57
Foster, Lawrence R 201
Foster, Mark S. H 1312
Foster, Stephen H 100
Fought, John A-F 358
Foulks, Edward F. SOC 557
Fowler, Loretta H 1138
Fowlkes, Martha R. SOC 273
Fox, David J. PSY 165
Fox, Elaine SOC 274
Fox, Kenneth H 1313
Fox, Richard W. STM 131
Fox, Sanford J. H 101
Framo, James L. PSY 89
Francaviglia, Richard V. A-A 569
Francis, Andre M 277
Franck, Thomas M. PS 641
Francois, Edouard PC 307
Frank, Lawrence PC 942
Frank, Robert J. H 1497
Frank, Robert Shelby PC 758
Frankenstein, Alfred A-A 187
Frankfort, Roberta H 744
Franklin, Anderson J. PSY 26
Franklin, H. Bruce L 127, 510;
    PC 223-224
Franklin, John Hope H 304, 1034
Franklin, Kay SOC 34
Frantz, Joe B. PC 275
Fraser, James H. PC 115
Fraser, Walter J., Jr. H 1449-
    1450
Frazer, Robert W. H 1451
Frazier, E. Franklin R 223;
    SOC 119-121
Frederick, John T. L 128
Fredericks, Casey PC 225
Frederickson, George H 1035
Frederickson, George M. H 592
Fredman, Stephen L 511
Freedman, Anne PS 530
Freedman, Estelle B. H 745
Freedman, Lawrence PS 642-643
Freedman, P. E. PS 530
Freehling, William M. H 305
Freeland, Richard M. PS 644
Freeman, Donald B. H 1228
Freeman, Jo H 746-747
Freeman, Lucy PC 146
Freeman, Richard B. SOC 541
Freidel, Frank H 454
French, Brandon PC 468
French, John R. P., Jr. SOC 410
French, Philip PC 469
French, Warren L 271-274; PC 470

Frese, Joseph R. H 1687-1688
Freyer, Tony Allan H 1689
Friar, Natasha A. PC 471
Friar, Ralph E. PC 471
Frickey, Edwin H 1856
Fried, Edward R. PS 736
Fried, Frederick A-A 305
Fried, Marc SOC 459
Friedan, Betty SOC 350-351
Friedenberg, Edgar SOC 275
Friedheim, Robert L. PS 332
Friedland, Roger SOC 35
Friedland, William H. A-F 176;
    H 1690
Friedlander, Lee A-A 238
Friedman, Alan Warren L 275
Friedman, Jean E. H 748
Friedman, Kathi V. PS 27
Friedman, Lawrence J. R 95
Friedman, Lawrence M. H 1950
Friedman, Lester D. PC 472
Friedman, Martin A-A 209
Friedman, Milton H 1857-1858;
    PS 28
Friedman, Nathalie S. SOC 584
Friedman, Samuel R. SOC 542
Friedman, Saul S. H 908
Frienze, I. PSY 72
Fries, Sylvia Doughty H 102
Frisbie, Charlotte J. A-F 212
Frisch, Michael H. H 1314
Frith, Simon M 222, 391
Fritz, Henry E. H 1139
Frohlich, Norma PS 88
Frohock, W. M. L 276-277
Frosch, John PSY 73
Frost, Frederick PC 834
Frothingham, Octavius Brooks
    R 140
Fry, Gladys-Marie A-F 411
Frye, Hardy T. SOC 122
Fryer, Judith L 129
Fryer, Russell G. PS 29
Fuchs, Estelle A-F 213, 307
Fuchs, Lawrence H. H 909; PS 478
Fuchs, Victor SOC 411
Fuchs, Wolfgang PC 317
Fulenwider, Claire Knoche
    SOC 352
Fuller, Edmund H 306; L 278
Fuller, Robert C. PSY 74
Fundaburk, Emma Lila A-A 58
Funnell, Chalres E. H 1315
Furman, Nelly PSY 135
Furner, Mary O. STM 132
Furniss, Norman F. H 307; R 101
Furst, Jill L. A-A 11
Furst, Peter T. A-A 11
Fusfeld, Daniel R. H 1564
Fuss, Peter H 593
Fussell, Edwin L 130, 512

1858

Gablik, Suzi A-A 121
Gabriel, Ralph Henry H 594-595
Gaddis, John L. PS 645-646
Gage, John T. L 279
Gagey, Edmond M. PC 343
Gagne, Cole M 64
Gaillard, Frye M 153
Galambos, Louis P. H 1691-1693
Galbraith, John Kenneth H 1859-1861
Galenson, Walter H 1565
Galishoff, Stuart STM 133
Gallaher, Art, Jr. A-F 94
Gallick, Rosemary H 799
Galliher, John F. SOC 624
Gallimore, Ronald A-F 95
Gallman, Robert E. H 1694, 1862
Gallner, Sheldon M. PC 943
Gallo, Patrick J. SOC 123
Galloway, David D. L 280
Gambill, Edward L. H 308
Gambino, Richard H 910-911
Gammond, Peter M 278
Gannon, Michael V. R 30
Gans, Herbert J. PC 23, 658; SOC 36, 124, 543
Gansler, Jacques PS 647
Garbarino, James PSY 75; SOC 276
Garber, Herbert PSY 6
Garcia, Antonio M 167
Garcia, Juan Ramon H 912
Gardiner, Dorothy PC 147
Gardiner, Harold C. L 281
Gardner, Albert Ten Eyck A-A 250, 269
Gardner, Burleigh B. A-F 173, 308
Gardner, Emelyn Elizabeth A-F 412
Gardner, Hugh SOC 37
Gardner, John L 282
Gardner, Mary B. A-F 173
Garland, Phyl M 214
Garnel, Donald H 1566
Garofalo, Reebee M 372
Garon, Paul M 215
Garraty, John A. H 309
Garretson, Lucy R. A-F 35
Garrett, Wendell D. A-A 59, 542
Garrison, Dee SOC 544
Garrow, David J. SOC 125
Gartner, Lloyd P. H 913; H 1005
Garvan, Anthony N. B. A-A 543
Garvan, Beatrice B. A-A 385
Gassiot-Talabot, Gerald PC 307
Gassner, John L 283-284
Gastil, Raymond D. A-F 36
Gates, Paul Wallace H 310-311, 1452, 1951
Gatewood, Willard B., Jr. R 102

Gati, Charles PS 648
Gatzke, Hans W. PS 649
Gaustad, Edwin Scott R 4-5, 48
Gaventa, John SOC 38
Gayle, Addison, Jr. L 513
Gearing, Frederick O. A-F 214
Gebhard, David A-A 451, 600
Geddes, Gordon E. H 103
Gedo, John E. PSY 76
Geduld, Harry M. PC 473
Gee, Helen A-A 339
Geer, Blanche A-F 80; SOC 252
Geerken, Michael SOC 277
Geherin, David PC 148
Gehman, Richard M 266
Geiles, Richard J. SOC 318
Geilhuffe, Nancy L. A-F 266
Geis, Michael L. A-F 353
Geismar, Maxwell L 285-288
Geist, Christopher D. PC 24
Gelatt, Roland M 8
Gelb, Leslie H. PS 650
Geldzahler, Henry A-A 60, 210
Gelfand, Mark I. H 1316
Gelfant, Blanche Housman L 514
Gellman, Irwin F. PS 651
Gelpi, Albert L 515
Genovese, Eugene D. H 1036-1037
George, Alexander L. PS 652-653
George, Carol H 749
George, Linda K. SOC 412
George, Peter J. H 1863
Georges, Robert A. A-F 413
Gerald, J. Edward PC 865
Gerber, Ellen W. PC 944
Gerdts, William H. A-A 61-62, 137, 153-154, 188-189, 251
Gerlach, Luther P. A-F 37
Gerlach, Russel L. H 914
Gerow, Maurice M 346
Gerson, Louis L. PS 479
Gerson, Robert A. M 65
Gersoni-Stavn, Diane PSY 77
Gewalt, Gerard W. H 1952
Gewehr, Wesley M. R 49
Gibb, George S. H 1695
Gibbons, Don C. SOC 625
Gibbs, Lois Marie SOC 545
Gibson, Arrell Morgan H 1140, 1453
Gibson, Charles H 104
Gibson, Donald B. L 516
Gibson, Florence E. H 915
Giddens, Paul H. H 1696
Giddins, Gary M 279
Giebelhaus, August W. H 1697
Giedion, Sigfried A-A 601; PC 1021
Giele, Janet Zollinger SOC 353
Gies, Francis STM 135
Gies, Joseph STM 135

Gieske, Millard L. H 455
Gifford, George E. PSY 78
Gilbert, Charles H 1736
Gilbert, Dennis SOC 460
Gilbert, Douglas M 392; PC 344
Gilbert, Felix H 207
Gilbert, Glenn G. A-F 309
Gilbert, Gorman H 1698
Gilbert, James B. H 597
Gilbert, Michael Francis PC 149
Gilbert, Neil PS 322
Gilbert, Robert E. PC 759
Gilbert, Sandra M. PC 188
Gilder, George F. SOC 354
Gildrie, Richard P. H 105
Gilgen, Albert R. PSY 79
Gillett, Charlie M 393-394
Gillette, William H 312
Gilligan, Carol PSY 80
Gilman, William N. L 486
Gilmartin, Gregory A-A 629
Gilmore, Al-Tony H 1038
Gilmore, Grant H 1953
Gilmore, Michael T. L 57, 131
Gilpin, Robert STM 136
Gilpin, W. Clark R 285
Gimbel, John PS 645
Ginger, Ray H 313
Gipson, Lawrence H. H 106
Girgus, Sam B. L 289; PC 25
Gitler, Ira M 280
Gitlin, Todd PC 659
Gizelis, Gregory A-F 414
Glaab, Charles N. H 1317-1318
Glaberman, Martin H 1567
Glad, Paul W. H 314
Gladwin, Thomas A-F 310
Glanz, Dawn A-A 281
Glanz, Rudolf H 916-919
Glasgow, Douglas G. A-F 177
Glasser, Morton A-F 311
Glassie, Henry A-A 452; A-F 410,
  415
Glazer, Nathan H 456; R 167;
  SOC 125-129
Glazer, Nona Y. PSY 81
Gleason, Philip R 168
Gleason, Ralph M 281
Glenn, Jules PSY 82
Glessing, Robert J. PC 866
Glick, Clarence E. SOC 130
Gliedman, John SOC 626
Glittenberg, Jo Ann E. A-F 325
Glock, Charles Y. SOC 80
Gloster, Hugh M. L 517
Gluck, Sherna H 750
Glut, Donald F. PC 480
Goddard, Chris M 282
Goddard, Harold Clarke L 132
Godfrey, Audrey M. R 242
Godfrey, Kenneth W. R 242

Goen, C. C. R 50
Goethals, Gregor T. PC 760
Goetze, Rolf SOC 39
Goetzmann, William H. A-A 190;
  H 314, 598, 1454-1455
Goffman, Erving A-F 38-43, 96;
  SOC 355
Goffin, Robert M 283
Gohdes, Clarence L. F. L 133
Goist, Park Dixon H 1319
Golab, Caroline H 920
Gold, Diane E. SOC 40
Goldberg, Arnold PSY 83
Goldberg, Herb SOC 356
Goldberg, Isaac M 395
Goldberg, Joe M 284
Goldberg, Roberta SOC 546
Goldberg, Steven SOC 357
Goldberger, Paul A-A 602-603
Goldblatt, Burt PC 373
Golden, Joseph L 290
Goldfield, David R. H 1320-1322
Goldin, Claudia Dale H 1039
Goldin, Milton M 66
Goldman, Albert M 396
Goldman, Eric F. H 457-459
Goldman, Judith A-A 270
Goldman, Mark H 1456
Goldman, Ralph PS 429
Goldman, Ralph M. H 19
Goldschmidt, Walter A-F 97
Goldschneider, Calvin SOC 131,
  158
Goldsen, Rose K. PC 761
Goldsmith, Arnold L. L 291
Goldsmith, Raymond W. H 1864-1865
Goldson, Rose Kohn SOC 181
Goldstein, Donald M. PS 753-754
Goldstein, Jeffrey H. PC 945
Goldstein, Jonathan H 1699
Goldstein, Malcolm L 292
Goldstein, Richard PC 946
Golsteine, Herman H. STM 137
Goldstine, Sidney SOC 131
Gonsiorek, John C. PSY 84
Gonzalez, Nancie L. A-F 267
Goode, James M. A-A 453
Goode, Judith Granich A-F 302
Goodenough, D. PSY 185
Goodin, Robert E. PS 89-91
Goodman, Abram V. H 921
Goodman, Cary SOC 41
Goodman, Emily Jane PSY 46
Goodman, Kristen L. SOC 249-250
Goodman, Mary Ellen A-F 44
Goodman, Paul SOC 413
Goodrich, Carter H 1866-1867
Goodrich, Lloyd A-A 63-64
Goodwin, Carole SOC 132
Goodwin, Craufurd D. PS 323
Goodwin, Leonard PSY 85

Goodwyn, Lawrence H 316
Goodyear, Frank H., Jr. A-A 65
Goodykoontz, Colin Brummitt
   R 74
Gordon, Albert I. SOC 133
Gordon, Andrew J. A-F 65
Gordon, Beverly A-A 386
Gordon, David M. H 1554, 1568
Gordon, Laura Kramer SOC 596
Gordon, Linda H 751
Gordon, Michael PSY 86
Gordon, Milton M. SOC 134-135,
   461
Goren, Arthur A. H 922
Goro, Herb SOC 42
Gospel, Howard F. H 1700
Gossett, Louis Y. L 293
Gossett, Thomas F. H 599
Gottfried, Martin L 294; PC 345
Gottlieb, David SOC 414
Gottman, Jean SOC 43
Gottschalk, Stephen R 203
Goulart, Ron PC 78, 311
Gould, Jean L 295
Gould, Mary Earle A-A 544
Gould, Roger PSY 87
Gould, Stephen Jay STM 138
Gove, Walter R. SOC 277
Govenar, Alan B. SOC 595
Gover, Geoffrey A-F 45
Gow, Gordon PC 474
Gowans, Alan A-A 59, 454-455;
   PC 26
Graber, Doris A. PC 660; PS 655
Graebner, Norman A. PS 656
Graff, Harvey PSY 88
Graglia, Lino A. H 1954
Graham, Otis L., Jr. H 460-461
Graham, Philip PC 346
Grambasch, Paul V. SOC 279
Grame, Theodore C. M 154
Granger, Bruce L 58-59
Grant, Barry K. PC 475
Grant, H. Roger A-A 456; H 1701,
   1868
Grantham, Dewey W. H 1457-1458
Gray, Colin S. PS 657-658
Gray, Dorothy H 752
Gray, Richard L 296
Gray, Virginia PS 316, 324;
   SOC 340
Graymount, Barbara H 1141
Grebler, Leo SOC 136
Greeley, Andrew M. H 923; SOC
   98, 137-138, 278
Green, Abel PC 347
Green, Archie M 155
Green, Benny M 285
Green, Constance McLaughlin
   H 1040, 1323-1325; STM 139
Green, Douglas B. M 156

Green, Geoffrey L 478
Green, George D. H 1702
Green, Harvey H 753
Green, James R. H 462, 1569-1570
Green, Jonathan A-A 340
Green, Martin L 518
Green, Michael D. H 1142
Green, Norma Kidd H 1143
Green, Robert J. PSY 89
Green, Samuel M. A-A 66
Green, Stanley PC 348-349
Greenberg, Bradley S. PC 661,
   762
Greenberg, Clement A-A 67
Greenberg, Daniel STM 140
Greenberg, Edward S. PS 325
Greenberg, Harvey R. PC 476
Greenberg, Jay R. PSY 90
Greenberg, Joel PC 484
Greenberg, Martin H. PC 249-250,
   264
Greenberg, Sanford PS 116
Greenberg, Stanley SOC 44
Greenblum, Joseph SOC 222
Greene, Jack P. H 107
Greene, Lorenzo Johnston H 1041
Greene, Mott T. STM 141
Greene, Suzanne Ellery PC 79
Greene, Victor R. H 924, 1571
Greenstein, Fred I. H 463;
   PS 92, 434, 531-532
Greenstone, J. David PS 481
Greenwald, Maureen Weiner H 754
Greenway, John A-F 416; M 157;
   SOC 5
Greenwood, Ted PS 659
Greer, Edward H 1572
Greer, Germaine SOC 358
Gregory, Frances W. H 1703
Gregory, Horace L 297
Gregory, Ross H 464
Gressley, Gene M. H 1869
Greven, Philip J. H 108; R 51
Gribbin, William R 52
Gridley, Mark C. M 286
Griffen, Clyde H 1326
Griffen, Nard M 287
Griffen, Sally H 1326
Griffin, Clifford S. R 82
Griffin, Rachel A-A 68
Griffiths, John PC 226
Grimes, Alan P. H 755
Grimes, Bruce PC 919
Grimes, Ronald L. A-F 268
Grimsted, David L 6
Grimwood, James M. STM 46, 369
Grinnell, George Bird H 1144
Grinstein, Hyman B. H 925
Griswold, A. Whitney PS 660
Griswold del Castillo, Richard
   H 926

Grob, Gerald N. H 1573; STM 142-145

Grodinsky, Julius H 1704

Grogg, Sam L., Jr. PC 530

Groia, Philip M 216

Gronberg, Kirsten SOC 462

Gropper, Rena C. A-F 98

Groom, Bob M 217

Grose, Peter PS 661

Gross, Bertram PS 533

Gross, Edward SOC 279

Gross, Robert H 208

Grossman, Loyd M 397

Grossman, Michael B. PC 662

Grossman, William L. M 288

Grossner, Alfred PS 662

Groueff, Stephane STM 146

Grow, Lawrence A-A 457

Grubb, W. Norton PSY 91

Gruber, Carol S. H 465

Grunebaum, Henry PSY 92

Guback, Thomas H. PC 477

Gubar, Susan PC 188

Gubrium, Jaber F. A-F 99

Guckin, John P. M 300

Guffey, George R. PC 258

Guida, Louis M 218

Guilbaut, Serge A-A 211

Guillemin, Jeanne A-F 215

Gumina, Deanna Paoli H 927

Gummere, Richard Mott L 60

Gumperz, John J. A-F 354

Gunn, Giles L 519; R 6

Gunn, James PC 227

Gunn, Janet Varner L 520

Gunnerson, Dolores A. H 1145

Gunther, Erna H 1146

Gura, Philip F. L 134-135

Guralnick, Peter M 398-399

Guralnick, Stanley M. STM 147

Gurian, Jay P. SOC 6

Gurin, Patricia SOC 139

Gurman, Richard J. S. A-A 458

Gurock, Jeffrey S. H 928

Gurwitt, Alan R. PSY 42

Gutierrez, Aronando SOC 145

Gutman, Amy PS 30

Gutman, Herbert G. H 1042-1043, 1574

Guttentag, Marcia SOC 359

Guttmann, Allen H 466; L 521-522; PC 447

Guzman, Ralph C. SOC 136

Gwaltney, John Langston A-F 178

Habakkuk, H. J. STM 148

Habegger, Alfred L 136

Haber, Carole PSY 93

Haber, Samuel STM 149

Haberland, Wolfgang A-A 12

Hacker, Andrew PS 435; SOC 7

Hacker, Helen Mayer SOC 344

Hadden, Jeffrey K. PC 663

Hadley, Charles D. PS 447

Hadley, Jack PS 319

Hadlock, Richard M 289

Hadwiger, Don F. PS 326; SOC 547

Haefele, Edwin T. PS 327

Haeger, John Denis H 1705

Hagan, William T. H 1147-1149

Hahn, Steven H 1459

Haines, Francis H 1150

Hair, P. E. H. H 51

Haites, Erik F. H 1706

Halamandaris, Val J. SOC 433

Halbertstam, David PC 664, 948

Hale, Janice E. SOC 140

Hale, Nathan G. PSY 94

Halem, Lynne Carol SOC 280

Hall, Ben M. A-A 604; PC 1022

Hall, David H 109

Hall, David D. R 31-32

Hall, Edward T. A-F 6-7

Hall, Jacquelyn Dowd H 756

Hall, James B. PC 27

Hall, Kermit L. H 1955

Hall, Michael Garibaldi H 110; STM 378

Hall, Peter Dobkin H 601

Hall, R. Cargill STM 150

Hall, Raymond L. SOC 141

Hall, Robert L. A-F 100

Hall, Stuart PC 28

Halle, Louis J. PS 663

Haller, John S., Jr. STM 151-153

Haller, Mark H. H 878; STM 154

Haller, Robin M. STM 153

Halliburton, R., Jr. H 1151

Hallmark Cards, the editors of PC 49

Halperin, Morton H. PS 328, 664-665, 775

Halperin, Samuel H 929

Halpern, Ben R 169; SOC 142

Halsell, Grace SOC 143

Halsey, William M. R 170

Halttunen, Karen H 317

Hambrick-Stowe, Charles E. R 33

Hamermesh, Daniel S. SOC 415

Hamilton, Charles V. SOC 99

Hamilton, Holman H 318

Hamilton, Richard F. SOC 463

Hamilton, Roberta SOC 360

Hamlin, Talbot Faulkner A-A 459, 570, 605

Hamm, Charles M 9-10, 400

Hammack, David C. H 1327

Hammel, William PC 29

Hammerslough, Philip A-A 363

Hammett, Ralph W. A-A 460

Hammond, Bray H 1707

Hammond, Charles Montgomery, Jr. PC 763
Hammond, John Winthrop STM 155-156
Hampsten, Elizabeth L 137
Hampton, Benjamin B. PC 478
Hand, Wayland D. A-F 417-419
Handel, Leo A. PC 479
Handler, Edward PS 482
Handlin, David P. A-A 571
Handlin, Lilian H 209
Handlin, Mary Flug H 1870
Handlin, Oscar H 209; 930-933, 1328, 1870; R 62
Handy, Robert T. R 7-8, 21, 141
Handy, W. C. M 219
Hanlan, J. P. H 1575
Hanle, Paul A. STM 157
Hanna, Mary T. PS 483
Hannerz, Ulf A-F 179
Hanrahan, John PS 329
Hansen, Asael T. A-F 334
Hansen, Chadwick R 34
Hansen, Klaus J. R 204
Hansen, Marcus Lee H 934
Hansen, Niles A-F 269
Hansen, Roger D. PS 666-667
Hanson, Dirk STM 158
Haralambos, Michael M 220
Harap, Louis L 523
Harder, Marvin A. PS 374
Harding, Brian L 138
Harding, Vincent H 1044
Hardy, Stephen PC 949
Hare, Maude Cuney M 11
Hareven, Tamara H 1576
Harlan, David R 53
Harland, Gordon R 142
Harley, Sharon H 757
Harman, David SOC 284
Harmon, Jim PC 480
Haroutunian, Joseph R 143
Harper, Alan H 467
Harper, Douglas A. SOC 627
Harper, Howard M., Jr. L 298
Harper, Michael S. L 524
Harper, Ralph PC 150
Harrell, David Edwin, Jr. R 261, 273
Harrington, Michael H 1871; PS 31-32
Harris, Barbara J. H 758
Harris, Carl V. H 1329
Harris, Charles S. SOC 416
Harris, Charles W. PC 276
Harris, Howell John H 1577
Harris, Janet C. PC 950
Harris, Louis SOC 417
Harris, Marvin A-F 8
Harris, Neil A-A 69; PC 350

Harris, Seymour E. H 1791
Harris, Trudier L 525
Harris, William C. H 319
Harris, William H. H 1045
Harrison, Bennett PS 514
Harrison, Harry PC 200
Harrison, John M. PC 867
Harrison, Max M 290
Harrison, Selig S. PS 668
Harry, Joseph SOC 361
Hart, James D. PC 80
Hart, John Fraser PC 1023
Hart, M. Marie PC 951
Hart, Mary L. M 150
Hart, Philip M 67
Hart, Phillip SOC 88
Hart, Robert A. PS 669
Hartley, Edward Neal STM 159
Hartman, Mary S. H 759
Hartmann, Sadakichi A-A 70, 258, 341
Hartmann, Susan M. H 760
Hartsock, Nancy PS 33
Hartwick, Harry L 299
Hartz, Louis H 602; PS 34
Harvey, A. McGehee STM 160-161
Harvey, Carol D. H. SOC 418
Harwell, Richard B. M 68
Harwood, Alan A-F 270
Haskell, Elizabeth PS 330
Haskell, Molly PC 481
Haskell, Thomas L. STM 162
Haskins, George Lee H 1956
Haskins, Jim M 291
Hassan, Ihab L 300-301
Hassler, Donald PC 228
Hassler, Warren W. H 20
Hassrick, Peter H. A-A 138
Hassrick, Royal B. H 1152
Hastie, Reid SOC 628
Hatch, Elvin SOC 45
Hatch, Nathan D. R 286
Hatcher, Harlan L 302
Hatt, Paul K. SOC 579
Hattaway, Herman H 320
Hauck, Richard Boyd L 526
Haugen, Einar A-F 355
Haupton, Lawrence M. H 1153
Haveman, Robert H. PS 331
Havens, Daniel F. L 139
Haviland, Virginia PC 116
Havinghurst, Robert J. A-F 213, 216, 299
Hawes, Joseph M. H 1330
Hawkins, Gordon SOC 654
Hawkins, Martin M 383
Hawley, Ellis W. H 468, 1872
Hayano, David M. SOC 548
Haycraft, Howard PC 151-152
Hayden, Delores A-A 461-462
Hayes, Michael T. PS 484

Hays, Samuel P. H 469-470
Hazard, Lucy Lockwood PC 277
Hazard, Patrick D. PC 764
Hazen, Helen PC 189
Heaps, Willard A. M 158
Heath, Jim F. H 471
Heath, Milton S. H 1873
Heath, Shirley Brice A-F 351
Heath, Stephen PC 448
Hechinger, Fred SOC 419
Hechinger, Grace SOC 419
Heckelman, A. Joseph PS 670
Hedges, James Blaine H 1419, 1708-
    1709
Hedin, Naboth H 847
Heelas, Paul L. F. PSY 95
Hefner, Robert J. A-A 381
Heilbut, Tony M 221
Heilman, Samuel C. A-F 102
Heimert, Alan R 54-55
Heinz, John P. SOC 549
Heizer, Robert F. A-F 103
Heller, Nancy A-A 212
Hellman, John PC 293
Helm, June A-F 271
Helmer, John PSY 96
Hemphill, Herbert Walde, Jr.
    A-A 306-307
Hemphill, Paul M 159
Hench, John B. H 195
Henderson, Edwin B. PC 952
Henderson, Harry B., III L 527
Henderson, James Youngblood
    H 1099; SOC 85
Henderson, John P. H 1578
Hendler, Herb M 401
Hendricks, Glenn A-F 272
Hendricks, Gordon PC 482
Hendrickson, David C. H 247
Hennesey, James R 171
Hennessey, Timothy M. PS 332
Hennessy, Bernard C. PS 425
Hennessy, Brendan PC 190
Henretta, James A. H 111
Henry, Anne W. D. A-A 572
Henry, Joseph STM 163-164
Henry, Jules A-F 47, 312
Hentoff, Nat M 292-294, 336-337;
    SOC 144
Henzke, Lucile A-A 387
Herberg, Will R 118
Herman, Judith Lewis SOC 281
Hermann, Janet Sharp H 1046
Herndon, Marcia M 160
Hero, Alfred O., Jr. PS 671
Herrera-Sobek, Maria M 161
Herreshoff, David H 604
Herring, George C. PS 672
Herron, Ima Honaker L 528
Herschensohn, Bruce PC 765
Herscher, Uri D. H 605

Hersh, Blanche Glassman H 761
Hersh, Seymour M. PS 673
Hershberg, Theodore H 1331
Hershkowitz, Leo H 1332
Herskovits, Melville J. A-F 180
Hertz, Susan Handley SOC 464
Hertzberg, Hazel W. H 1154
Hertzberg, Steven H 935
Herzog, Kristin L 140
Heskett, John H 1710
Hess, Robert PSY 163
Hess, Stephen PC 868-869
Hess, Thomas B. A-A 34, 71, 213
Hettinger, Herman S. PC 766
Hevener, John W. H 1579
Hewlett, Richard G. STM 165-167
Heyl, Barbara Sherman SOC 629
Heyman, Therese Thau A-A 328
Hibbard, Benjamin H. H 1957
Hickey, Tom SOC 420
Hickman, Bert G. H 1874
Hicks, George L. A-F 48, 104
Hicks, Granville L 529
Hicks, Jack L 304
Hicks, John H 472
Hicks, John D. H 321, 1501
Hickson, Mark L., III SOC 61
Hidy, Muriel E. H 1712
Hidy, Ralph W. H 1711-1712
Higashi, Sumiko PC 483
Higbee, Edward C. H 473
Higginbotham, Don H 210
Higgins, W. Robert H 211
Higgs, Robert H 1047
Higgs, Robert J. L 530; PC 953
Higham, Charles PC 484
Higham, John H 606, 936; R 262
Highwater, Jamake A-A 13; H 1155
Higley, John PS 87
Hildebrand, Grant H 1713
Hilfer, Anthony Channell L 305,
    531
Hilgard, Ernest R. PSY 97
Hill, David B. PS 436
Hill, Forest G. H 1714
Hill, Frank Ernest STM 267-268
Hill, Hamlin L 1
Hill, Robert F. A-F 71
Hill, Ruben PSY 36-37
Hill, Samuel S., Jr. R 9-10, 119-
    120
Hill, Stephen SOC 550
Hillegas, Mark PC 229
Hillier, Bevis A-A 388
Hillier, S. H 86
Hills, Patricia A-A 72-73, 191
Hilsman, Roger PS 674
Hime, Virginia H. A-F 37
Himelstein, Morgan Y. L 306
Himmelberg, Robert F. H 474
Himmelstein, Hal PC 767

Himmelstein, Jerome L. SOC 630
Hindle, Brooke PC 1024; STM 168-173
Hindus, Michael Stephen H 1958
Hines, Thomas S. A-A 596
Hinckley, Barbara PS 437
Hinsley, Curtis M., Jr. STM 174
Hintz, Howard W. L 532
Hipple, John L. PSY 98
Hipple, Lu B. PSY 98
Hippler, Arthur E. A-F 181
Hipshern, Edward Ellsworth M 69
Hirsch, David H. L 141
Hirsch, Herbert SOC 145
Hirsch, Paul Morris M 402
Hirsch, Susan E. H 1580
Hirschman, Albert O. PS 534
Hirschman, Lisa SOC 281
Hirshfeld, Daniel S. STM 175
Hirshson, Stanley P. H 322
Hirshorn, Paul A-A 606
Hitchcock, H. Wiley M 12-13
Hitchcock, Henry-Russell A-A 464-465
Hite, Shere PSY 99
Hoare, Ian M 222
Hobbs, Robert Carleton A-A 214
Hoberman, J. PC 485
Hobson, Fred H 1460; L 231
Hobson, Wilder M 295
Hoch, Paul PC 954
Hochschild, Arlie Russell SOC 421
Hochschild, Jennifer L. SOC 465
Hodeir, Andre M 296
Hodge, Francis L 142
Hodge, William H. A-F 49, 217
Hodgson, Godfrey H 475
Hoebel, E. Adamson H 1190, 1264
Hoerder, Dirk H 212, 1581
Hoeveler, J. David, Jr. L 307
Hoffer, Peter C. H 112
Hoffman, Abraham H 937
Hoffman, Charles H 1875
Hoffman, Daniel L 143, 308
Hoffman, Frederick J. L 309-313
Hoffman, Lois Wladis SOC 374
Hoffman, Ronald H 213
Hoffman, Stanley PS 675
Hoffman, William STM 176
Hofling, Charles K. PSY 100
Hofstadter, Richard H 21, 476, 607-609; STM 177
Hofstetter, C. Richard PC 768
Hohenberg, John PC 870
Holahan, John PS 319-320
Holden, Jonathan L 314
Holder, Alan L 315
Holder, Preston H 1156
Holifield, E. Brooks R 35, 144
Hollander, Paul H 610

Hollander, Samuel H 1715
Holli, Melvin G. H 938, 1333
Hollick, Ann PS 676
Hollinger, David STM 178
Hollinger, Richard C. SOC 631
Hollingshead, August B. SOC 466-468
Hollingsworth, Ellen Jane H 1334
Hollingsworth, J. Rogers H 1334
Hollon, W. Eugene H 1461
Holloway, Mark R 205
Hollowell, John PC 295
Holman, C. Hugh L 533
Holmes, Ronald M. SOC 632
Holmstrom, Lynda Lytle SOC 382, 633
Holroyd, Stuart L 534
Holstein, Jonathan A-A 389
Holt, Michael F. H 323
Holt, Pat M. PS 609
Holt, Thomas H 1048
Holtsmark, Erling B. PC 173
Holtzman, Abraham PS 485
Holtzman, Wayne H. A-F 313
Holway, John PC 955
Homer, William Innes A-A 74, 342
Honigmann, John J. A-F 10
Hood, Fred J. R 83
Hood, Graham A-A 390
Hood, Jane C. SOC 283
Hooker, Richard J. H 22
Hoole, Francis W. PS 332
Hoopes, Donelson F. A-A 282
Hoover, Dwight W. H 1157
Hopkins, Anne H. SOC 511
Hopkins, Charles Howard R 103, 114
Hopkins, Jerry M 403-404
Hopkins, Raymond F. PS 677
Horn, Marilyn PC 1025
Horn, Maurice C. PC 307, 313-314
Horning, Clarence PC 1026
Hornung, Clarence P. A-A 271
Horowitz, David H 1158
Horowitz, Irving L. PS 333, 535-536
Horowitz, Ruth A-F 274
Horricks, Raymond M 312
Horsman, Reginald P. H 611, 1159
Horton, James Oliver H 1049
Horton, Lois E. H 1049
Horton, Rod W. L 535
Horwitch, Mel STM 179
Horwitz, Morton J. H 1959
Horwitz, Richard P. A-F 105
Hostetler, John A. A-F 106-108
Hough, Leslie S. H 1623
House, John W. SOC 469
House, Peter PS 334-335
Houseman, Gerald L. SOC 470
Hovenkamp, Herbert STM 180

Howard, Alan A-F 109
Howard, Helen Addison L 536
Howard, John Tasker M 14-15, 70
Howard, Leon L 7, 61
Howard, Richard L 316
Howat, John K. A-A 75
Howe, Daniel Walker H 324; R 145
Howe, Irving H 477, 939
Howe, Louise Kapp SOC 362
Howe, Mark Antony DeWolfe M 71
Howe, Mark DeWolfe R 303
Howell, Joseph T. A-F 110
Howells, Coral Ann PC 191
Howsden, Jackie SOC 552
Hoyt, Harlowe R. PC 352
Hraba, Joseph A-F 111
Hsu, Francis L. K. A-F 11, 50;
  SOC 146
Hubbard, Cortlandt Van Dyke
  A-A 540
Hubbard, W. L. M 16
Hubbell, Allan Forbes A-F 356
Hubbell, Jay B. L 537-539
Huber, Joan SOC 363
Huber, Richard M. H 23
Huddleston, Lee Eldridge H 1160
Hudson, Arthur Palmer M 162
Hudson, Charles H 1161
Hudson, Frederick PC 871
Hudson, John A. H 547
Hudson, Winthrop S. R 11, 295,
  340
Huebel, Harry Russell PC 30
Huettig, Mae D. PC 486
Huf, Linda L 540
Hufford, David J. A-F 420
Huggins, Nathan I. H 1050
Hughes, Carl Milton L 541
Hughes, Everett C. A-F 80; SOC
  252
Hughes, Glenn L 8
Hughes, Jonathan R. T. H 1876-
  1877
Hughes, Rupert M 72
Hughes, Thomas Parke STM 181-183
Hughto, Margie A-A 370
Hull, N. E. H. H 112
Hulteng, John L. PC 872
Hultkrantz, Ake A-F 218
Hummel, Charles F. A-A 385
Hummel, Ralph P. PS 336
Hummer, Patricia M. H 762
Humphrey, David C. H 214
Humphrey, Seth K. H 1162
Hundley, Norris, Jr. H 940
Hunt, David C. A-A 190
Hunt, H. Allan SOC 516
Hunt, Michael H. PS 678
Hunter, Carman St. John SOC 284
Hunter, Edna J. PSY 101, 136
Hunter, James Davison R 274

Hunter, Louis C. STM 184-185
Hunter, Sam A-A 29, 76, 215
Huntington, Gertrude Enders
  A-F 108
Huntington, Samuel P. PS 35, 595,
  679
Hurley, F. Jack A-A 343-344
Hurst, James Willard H 1960-1962
Hurston, Zora Neale A-F 421
Hurt, R. Douglas H 478
Huss, Roy PC 487
Hussey, Jeannette M. STM 252
Hutchinson, John H 1583
Hutchinson, William H. H 1716
Hutchison, William R. R 84, 104,
  146
Huth, Hans H 612
Hutson, James H. H 219
Huxtable, Ada Louise A-A 607-608
Hvidt, Kristian H 941
Hyde, George E. H 1163-1165
Hyman, Harold M. H 1963
Hyman, Paula H 705
Hyman, Ray A-F 149
Hyman, Stanley Edgar L 317
Hymes, Dell A-F 12, 219, 354,
  357-358
Hymowitz, Carole H 763
Hynds, Ernest C. PC 873

Ianni, Francis A. J. A-F 112,
  182, 314
Ichihashi, Yamato H 942
Iglehart, Alfreda P. SOC 364
Imai, Ryukichi PS 580
Imershein, Allen W. STM 186
Immerman, Richard H. PS 680
Inge, M. Thomas PC 31
Ingham, John N. H 1717
Ingles, Thelma SOC 593
Innes, Stephen H 113, 1019
Innis, Harold A. PC 665
Iorizzo, Luciano J. H 943
Irish, Jerry A. R 147
Iriye, Akira PS 681-682
Irons, Peter H 1964
Irwin, John T. L 144
Irwin, W. R. PC 174
Isaac, Rhys R 56
Isaacs, Edith J. R. L 542
Isaacs, Neil D. PC 953, 956-957
Isenberg, Michael PC 488
Isham, Norman Morrison A-A 545
Isham, Samuel A-A 155
Israel, Jerry H 479; PS 683
Issari, M. Ali PC 489
Isserman, Maurice H 480
Itzkoff, Seymour W. SOC 285
Iverson, Peter H 1166-1167
Ives, Edward D. A-F 422

Izenberg, Jerry PC 958
Izenour, Steven A-A 606, 630

Jackman, Mary R. SOC 471
Jackman, Robert W. SOC 471
Jackson, Anthony H 1335
Jackson, Arthur M 297; PC 398
Jackson, Blyden L 543
Jackson, Bruce A-F 423-425; M 163
Jackson, Carl T. R 206
Jackson, George Pullen M 164, 223
Jackson, Gregory H 1462
Jackson, John Brinckerhoff A-A 466, 573
Jackson, Joseph A-A 546, 574
Jackson, Kenneth T. H 1336
Jackson, Martin A. PC 562
Jackson, Patrick B. SOC 634
Jackson, Rosemary PC 175
Jacobs, Constance H 706
Jacobs, Diane PC 490
Jacobs, James B. SOC 635
Jacobs, Jane H 1337
Jacobs, Jerry SOC 636
Jacobs, Lewis PC 491-492
Jacobs, Norman PC 666
Jacobs, Robert D. L 388
Jacobs, Ruth Harriet SOC 422
Jacobs, Stephen W. A-A 467
Jacobs, Wilbur R. A-F 220
Jacobson, Gary C. PS 438-440
Jacobus, John A-A 29
Jacoby, Russell PSY 102
Jaenen, Cornelius J. H 1168
Jaffa, Harry V. H 325
Jaffee, A. J. SOC 147
Jaffee, Bernard STM 187
Jaher, Frederic Cople H 888, 1338
Jakle, John A. H 1463
James, Janet Wilson H 764; R 243
James, Jennifer SOC 665
James, John A. H 1878
James, Joseph Bliss H 1965
James, Sidney V. R 57
Jamieson, Perry D. H 344
Jamison, A. Leland R 22-23
Janis, Harriet M 259
Janis, Irving PS 684
Janis, Sidney A-A 216
Janowitz, Morris SOC 9
Janowsky, Oscar I. SOC 148-149
Jantz, Harold S. L 62
Jarrell, Randall L 544-547
Jarvie, Ian C. PC 493
Jasen, David A. M 298
Jaye, Michael C. L 548
Jedry, Christopher M. H 114
Jeffrey, Julie Roy H 765

Jencks, Charles A-A 610
Jencks, Christopher SOC 286, 472-473
Jenkins, Adelbert H. PSY 103
Jenkins, Brian H 944
Jenkins, Reese V. STM 188
Jenkins, William A-A 345
Jenkinson, Philip PC 494
Jenks, Leland H. H 1879
Jennings, Francis H 1169
Jennings, Jesse D. A-F 241
Jennings, M. Kent PS 537
Jensen, Arthur R. PSY 104
Jensen, Jay W. PC 682
Jensen, Joan M. H 810
Jensen, Merrill H 215, 1464
Jensen, Richard H 326
Jeremy, David J. H 1719
Jernegan, Marcus W. H 1584
Jerome, V. J. PC 495
Jervis, Robert PS 685
Jeuck, John E. H 1680
Jewett, Robert PC 33
Jewkes, John STM 190
Jick, Leon A. R 172
Jilek, Wolfgang G. A-F 221
Johannsen, Albert PC 81
John, Elizabeth A. H. H 1170
Johnson, Abby L 319
Johnson, Arthur Menzies H 1720-1723; STM 191
Johnson, Charles A. R 75
Johnson, Clifton H. R 224
Johnson, Conrad PS 307
Johnson, Daniel M. SOC 150
Johnson, E. W. PC 303
Johnson, Fridolf A-A 271
Johnson, Guy B. M 176-177
Johnson, H. Earle M 73-74
Johnson, Herbert A. H 1956
Johnson, James P. H 1724
Johnson, James Turner H 115
Johnson, James Weldon M 224
Johnson, John W. H 1966
Johnson, Marilynn A-A 426
Johnson, Michael L. PC 295
Johnson, Nicholas PC 769
Johnson, P. PSY 72
Johnson, Paul E. R 76
Johnson, Richard H. H 116
Johnson, Robert Alan SOC 287
Johnson, Ronald L 319
Johnson, Thomas C. STM 192
Johnson, Una E. A-A 289
Johnson, William PC 496
Johnson, William O., Jr. PC 959
Johnston, Norman A-A 468
Johnstone, John W. C. PC 875
Jonaitis, Aldona A-A 14
Jonas, Manfred PS 686
Jonas, Steven STM 193-194

Jones, Alice Hanson H 1880
Jones, Anne Goodwyn L 549
Jones, Archer H 320
Jones, Charles O. PS 337
Jones, Daryl PC 278
Jones, Donald G. R 96
Jones, Douglas L. H 117
Jones, Enrico E. PSY 105
Jones, Everett PC 271
Jones, Faustine Childress
  SOC 288
Jones, Howard Mumford H 613-617;
  L 9, 63
Jones, James H. STM 195
Jones, James W. H 118
Jones, Landon Y. SOC 423
Jones, LeRoi: see Baraka, Amiri
Jones, Louis C. A-F 426-427
Jones, Maldwyn Allen H 945
Jones, Peter D'A. H 938
Jones, R. P. M 299
Jones, Reginald L. PSY 106
Jones, Rufus M. H 119
Jones, Russell T. PSY 173
Jordan, Alice M. PC 117
Jordan, Cathie A-F 95
Jordan, Philip D. R 105
Jordan, Terry G. A-A 469;
  A-F 428; H 946, 1465
Jordy, William H. A-A 611-612
Jorgensen, James SOC 424
Jorgensen, Joseph G. A-F 51, 222;
  SOC 151
Jorstad, Erling R 121-122
Joselit, Jenna Weissman H 947
Josephson, Hannah H 766
Josephson, Matthew H 1725; STM
  196
Josephy, Alvin M. H 1171-1172
Jowett, Garth PC 497-498
Judd, Charles M. SOC 260
Judd, Jacob H 120
Judds, Jacob H 1687-1688
Jungk, Robert STM 197

Kacklin, Carol Nagy PSY 129
Kadarkay, Arpad PS 36
Kadushin, Charles SOC 532
Kael, Pauline PC 499
Kaestle, Carl F. H 618
Kagan, Norman PC 500
Kagle, Steven K. L 67
Kahan, Jerome H. PS 687
Kahl, Joseph A. SOC 460, 474
Kahn, Alfred J. SOC 289
Kahn, Frank J. PC 770
Kahn, Herman PS 688
Kahn, Roger PC 960
Kaiser, Harvey H. A-A 470
Kaiser, Karl PS 689

Kakar, Sudhir STM 198
Kalb, Madeleine G. PS 690
Kalinch, David B. SOC 631
Kalish, Richard SOC 425
Kallen, Horace M. H 619
Kalnein, Wend von A-A 282
Kalstone, David L 320
Kalzman, Natan PSY 52
Kamerman, Sheila B. SOC 289
Kamieniecki, Sheldon PS 338
Kamin, Leon J. PSY 107
Kaminsky, Stuart M. PC 501
Kammen, Michael G. H 216, 620
Kanahele, George S. M 165
Kando, Thomas M. PC 34
Kane, Kathryn PC 502
Kane, Patricia E. A-A 409
Kann, Mark E. PS 19, 538-539
Kanter, Arnold PS 665
Kanter, Kenneth Aaron M 405
Kanter, Rosabeth Moss SOC 290,
  553
Kantowicz, Edward R. H 948
Kantrowitz, Nathan SOC 152
Kaplan, Bert PSY 108
Kaplan, E. Ann PC 503-504
Kaplan, Harold L 145-146
Kaplan, Milton PC 869
Kaplan, Milton Allen PC 771
Kaplan, Morton PS 37
Kaplan, Stephen S. PS 590
Kaprow, Allan A-A 259
Karamanski, Theodore J. H 1726
Karanikas, Alexander L 550
Kardiner, Abram A-F 13
Kargon, Robert H. STM 199-200
Karimi, Amir Massoud PC 505
Karl, Barry D. H 621
Karl, Frederick L 321
Karnig, Albert K. SOC 153
Karno, Marvin PSY 17
Karolevitz, Robert PC 876
Karpf, Stephen Louis PC 506
Karsten, Peter SOC 554
Kashima, Tetsuden R 207
Kasinsky, Renee Goldsmith
  SOC 638
Kasson, John F. H 1339; STM 201
Kater, John L., Jr. R 123
Kattenburg, Paul M. PS 691
Katz, Jack SOC 475
Katz, James E. PS 333
Katz, Jonathan H 24
Katz, Leslie A-A 238
Katz, Michael B. H 1881
Katz, Sedelle PSY 109
Katz, Stanley N. H 121
Katzman, David M. H 767, 1051
Kauffman, Henry J. A-A 308, 391-
  392, 471
Kauffmann, Stanley PC 507

Kaufman, Allen H 622
Kaufman, Charles H. M 75
Kaufman, Debra R. PSY 110
Kaufman, Elliott A-A 458
Kaufman, Fredrick M 300
Kaufman, H. G. SOC 555
Kaufman, Herbert PS 339
Kaufman, I. PSY 189
Kaufman, Martin STM 202
Kaufmann, Edgar, Jr. A-A 575
Kaufmann, Helen L. M 17
Kaufmann, William W. PS 692-693
Kaul, A. N. L 147
Kay, Karyn PC 508
Kaye, Marvin PC 354
Kaysen, Carl H 1791
Kazdin, Alan E. PSY 111
Kazin, Alfred L 322-324
Kebede, Ashenafi M 18
Keech, William R. PS 441
Keefer, Lubov M 76
Keeler, Theodore E. H 1882
Keeley, Joseph PC 772
Keeran, Roger H 1585
Kegley, Charles W. R 148
Keil, Charles M 225
Keiser, R. Lincoln A-F 183
Keith, Jennie SOC 426
Kellaway, William H 122
Keller, Kate Van Winkle M 126
Keller, Morton H 327, 1727
Keller, Robert H., Jr. R 253
Keller, Rosemary Skinner R 245-
    246
Kellman, Steven G. L 551
Kelly, Fred C. STM 203
Kelly, Gail P. H 949
Kelly, J. Frederick A-A 547
Kelly, Lawrence C. H 1173-1175
Kelly, Patrick STM 204
Kelly, R. Gordon PC 118
Kelso, William A. PS 38
Kemble, Howard R. STM 386
Kendrick, John W. H 1883
Kennan, George F. PS 694-698
Kennard, Sara Sue A-F 185
Kenneally, James J. H 1586
Kennedy, Allan A. A-F 300
Kennedy, David M. H 481; STM 205
Kennedy, Gail STM 206
Kennedy, J. H. H 1176
Kennedy, Robert F. PS 699
Kennedy, Roger G. A-A 472
Kennedy, Susan Estabrook H 768
Kennedy, Theodore A-F 184
Kenner, Charles L. H 1177
Kenner, Hugh L 325-326
Kent, Laura SOC 594
Kenyon, Gerald S. PC 968
Kerber, Linda K. H 623, 769-770
Kerckhoff, Alan C. PSY 112; SOC
    476

Kern, Montague PC 877
Kern, Robert H 1587
Kernell, Samuel PS 440
Kerr, Howard L 148
Kerr, K. Austin H 1728
Keshet, Harry F. SOC 311
Kessel, John PS 442
Kessell, John L. H 1178-1179
Kessler, Suzanne J. PSY 113
Kessler-Harris, Alice H 771-772
Kessner, Thomas H 950
Kester, Marian M 367
Ketcham, Ralph H 217
Ketchum, Alton PC 35
Ketchum, Robert Glenn A-A 321
Ketchum, William C., Jr. A-A 393
Kett, Joseph F. PSY 114; STM 207
Ketterer, David PC 230
Kettner, James H. H 1967
Keveles, Daniel J. STM 208
Key, V. O., Jr. PS 443-444
Key, Wilson Bryan PC 667
Keyser, Les PC 509
Keyssar, Helene L 552
Kichingbird, Kirke H 1180
Kidney, Walter C. A-A 473
Kidwell, Claudia PC 1027
Kiefer, Christie W. A-F 113
Kiefer, Monica PC 119
Kieniewicz, Teresa L 149
Kiev, Ari A-F 275
Killian, James R., Jr. STM 209
Killian, Lewis M. SOC 46, 154
Kim, Choong Soon A-F 52
Kim, Illsoo SOC 155
Kim, Sung Bok H 1729
Kimball, Fiske A-A 474, 548
Kimball, Solon T. A-F 1, 114,
    315
Kindillien, Carlin T. L 150
Kindleberger, Charles P. H 1884
King, Anthony PS 700
King, John Owen L 553
King, Richard H. H 624; L 327
King, Stephen PC 176
Kingman, Daniel M 19
Kingsbury, Martha A-A 68
Kingston, Carolyn T. PC 120
Kinnard, Douglas PS 340
Kinney, Charles B., Jr. H 123
Kinzer, Donald L. R 263
Kirby, Jack Temple PC 668
Kirby, John B. H 1052
Kirby, Michael A-A 77
Kirk, John T. A-A 394-395
Kirker, Harold A-A 576
Kirkland, Edward C. H 625, 1730-
    1732
Kirkpatrick, Martha PSY 115-116
Kirkpatrick, Price A-F 143
Kirman, William J. PSY 117

Kirschner, Don S. H 1340
Kirst, Michael W. PS 402
Kirwan, Albert D. H 1466
Kislan, Richard PC 355
Kissinger, Henry A. PS 701-703
Kistiakowsky, George B. STM 210
Kitano, Harry H. L. SOC 156
Kitchen, Helen PS 704
Kitses, Jim PC 510
Klaffky, Susan E. A-A 381
Klamkin, Charles A-A 309
Klamkin, Marian A-A 309, 396
Klapp, Orrin E. PC 36
Klapper, Joseph PC 37
Klausner, Samuel Z. SOC 557
Klehr, Harvey PS 540
Klein, Barbro Sklute A-F 429
Klein, Herbert S. H 1053-1054
Klein, Malcolm W. SOC 639
Klein, Marcus L 328-329
Klein, Maury H 1733
Kleiner, Robert J. A-F 189
Klepper, Paul PS 445
Kleppner, Paul H 328
Klingaman, David C. H 1467
Klinkowitz, Jerome L 330-332
Kloman, Erasmus H. PS 341
Klose, Gilbert C. STM 394
Kluckhohn, Clyde A-F 53, 223,
   227; PSY 118; STM 215
Kluckholm, Florence Rockwood
   A-F 14
Kmen, Henry A. M 20
Knapp, Herbert A-F 430
Knapp, Mary A-F 430
Knight, Arthur PC 511
Knight, Damon PC 231-233
Knight, Grant C. L 151, 333
Knight, Stephen PC 153
Knights, Peter R. H 1341
Knoke, David SOC 558
Knoll, Tricia SOC 157
Knowlton, Evelyn H. H 1739
Knuston, Jeanne PS 541
Kobin, Solomon SOC 639
Kobre, Sidney PC 878
Kobrin, Francese SOC 158
Koch, Adrienne H 218
Koch, Donald A. PC 68
Kochman, Thomas A-F 359
Koehler, Lyle H 773
Koeper, Frederick A-A 526
Kofsy, Frank M 301
Kohlberg, Lawrence PS 542
Kohlstedt, Sally Gregory STM 211
Kohn, Melvin L. SOC 477, 559
Koke, Richard J. A-A 156
Kolb, Harold H. L 152
Kolchin, Peter H 1055
Kolker, Robert Phillip PC 512
Kolko, Gabriel H 482, 1734; PS
   342, 705

Kolko, Joyce PS 705
Kolodin, Irving M 77
Kolodny, Annette L 554
Komarovsky, Mirra SOC 478
Kongas-Maranda, Elli K. A-F 432
Konig, David Thomas H 1968
Kootz, Samuel A-A 217
Koppes, Clayton R. STM 212
Koppett, Leonard PC 961
Korall, Burt M 262
Korchin, Sheldon J. PSY 105
Korn, Bertram W. H 951
Kornblum, William SOC 479
Korson, George A-F 433-435
Koskoff, David E. H 1735
Kostelanetz, Richard A-A 78
Koster, Donald N. H 626
Kotkin, Amy J. A-F 459
Kouser, J. Morgan H 1468
Kouwenhoven, John A. A-A 475;
   H 1342
Kovel, Ralph M. A-A 397
Kovel, Terry H. A-A 397
Kowet, Don PC 962
Kozloff, Max A-A 79
Kraditor, Aileen S. H 329, 627,
   774
Kramer, Aaron L 153
Kramer, Dale L 334
Kramer, Hilton A-A 80
Kramer, Judith SOC 159
Krane, Dale PS 301
Kranzberg, Melvin STM 204, 213-
   214
Krapp, George Phillip L 555
Krasner, Stephen D. PS 706
Kraus, Clyde Norman R 287
Krause, Sydney J. L 556
Krauss, Rosalind A-A 215
Krech, Shepard, III H 1181
Krehbiel, Henry Edward M 78-79,
   166
Kreinberg, Lew SOC 24
Kreuziger, Frederick A. PC 234
Krieger, Susan SOC 365, 560
Krieghbaum, Hillier PC 879
Kriesberg, Louis SOC 291
Krinsky, Carol Herselle A-A 613
Krislov, Samuel PS 343-344
Kristol, Irving PS 39-40
Kroeber, A. L. A-F 224; STM 215
Kroos, Herman E. H 1736, 1923
Krueger, Karl M 80
Krutch, Joseph Wood L 335
Kubler, George A-A 476; PC 1028
Kuehn, Thomas J. STM 216
Kuhn, Annette PC 513
Kuhns, William PC 669
Kuklick, Bruce H 628
Kulka, Richard A. PSY 176
Kumar, Martha J. PC 662

Kuniholm, Bruce R.   PS 707
Kunitz, Stephen J.   A-F 230
Kunkel, Peter   A-F 185
Kunstadt, Leonard   M 263
Kupferberg, Herbert   M 81
Kupperman, Karen Ordahl   H 1182
Kurath, Gertrude Prokosch   M 167
Kurath, Hans   A-F 360
Kurtz, Donald V.   A-F 316
Kurtz, Stephen A.   A-A 614
Kurtz, Stephen G.   H 219
Kushner, Gilbert   A-F 85
Kusmer, Kenneth L.   H 1056
Kutler, Stanley I.   H 483, 1969–
    1970
Kutsche, Paul   A-F 115
Kuykendall, John W.   R 85
Kuznets, Simon S.   H 1885–1888
Kyriazi, Gary   PC 356

LaBarre, Weston   A-F 116, 225
Labov, William   A-F 361-363
Labunski, Richard   PC 773
LaCivita, C. J.   SOC 22
Lacour-Gayet, Robert   H 330
Lacy, William B.   SOC 525
Ladd, Everett C.   PS 446-447;
    SOC 292
Lader, Lawrence   H 484
Ladner, Joyce A.   SOC 160, 366
LaFarge, Oliver   A-A 15; H 1183
LaFeber, Walter   H 331; PS 708-
    709
LaForse, Martin W.   PC 38
Lagemann, Ellen Condliffe   H 775-
    776
La Gory, Mark   SOC 47
LaGrie, Roger P.   PS 568
Lagumina, Salvatore J.   H 952
Lahee, Henry Charles   M 82
Lahue, Kalton C.   PC 514
Laing, Dave   M 406
Lainoff, Seymour   L 461
Lake, Robert W.   SOC 48
Lakoff, Sanford A.   STM 106, 217
Lamar, Howard R.   H 1469
Lamb, Michael E.   PSY 119
Lampard, Eric E.   H 1470
Lancaster, Clay   A-A 477-478
Land, Audrey C.   H 126
Landau, Jon   M 407
Landes, Ruth   A-F 317
Landrum, Larry N.   PC 154
Landsberg, Hans H.   H 1653
Lane, Ann J.   H 1057
Lane, John R.   A-A 81
Lane, Robert E.   PS 543
Lane, Roger   H 1343-1344
Lanes, Selma G.   PC 121
Lang, Gladys Engel   PC 774

Lang, Iain   M 302
Lang, Kurt   PC 774
Lang, Paul Henry   M 83
Langdon, George D.   H 127
Langford, Richard E.   L 336
Langley, Lester D.   PS 710
Langner, Thomas S.   A-F 143
LaPrade, Ernest   PC 357
Laqueur, Walter   PS 711
Larabee, Benjamin W.   H 124
Larabee, Leonard Woods   H 125
Lardner, John   PC 963
Larkin, Oliver W.   A-A 82
Larkin, Ralph W.   SOC 427
LaRose, Robert   PC 834
Larrabee, Eric   PC 39
Larsen, Lawrence   H 1345
Larsen, Susan C.   A-A 81
Larson, Gary D.   PS 345
Larson, Henrietta M.   H 1737-1739
LaRuffa, Anthony L.   A-F 276
Lasansky, Jeanette   A-A 398
Lasch, Christopher   H 629-631;
    SOC 293
Lash, Joseph P.   PS 712
Laslett, John H. M.   H 1588
Laslett, Peter   PS 41
Lasswell, Harold D.   PS 93-96,
    544-545, 713
Latner, Richard B.   H 332
Latourette, Kenneth Scott   H 632
Lauer, Jeanette C.   SOC 11, 294
Lauer, Robert H.   SOC 11, 294
Laufe, Abe   PC 358
Laugenbach, Randolph   H 1576
Laughlin, Ledlie Irwin   A-A 399
Laumann, Edward O.   SOC 480, 549
Laurie, Bruce   H 715, 1589
Laurie, Joe, Jr.   PC 347, 359
Laurie, Margaret A.   SOC 105
Lauth, Thomas P.   PS 301
Lavender, David   H 1471
Lavin, David D.   SOC 295
Lawrence, David Herbert   L 557
Lawrence, Elizabeth Atwood
    A-F 117
Lawrence, John Shelton   PC 33
Laws, G. Malcolm, Jr.   A-F 436-
    437
Lawson, Michael L.   H 1184
Lawson, Steven F.   H 485
Layman, Emma McCloy   R 208
Layton, Edwin T., Jr.   STM 218-
    219
Lazarsfeld, Paul F.   PC 775;
    PS 411
Lazerson, Marvin   H 1346; PSY 91
Lea, Zilla Rider   A-A 400
Leab, Daniel J.   PC 515
Leach, Douglas Edward   H 128-129
Leach, William   H 777

Leacock, Eleanor Burke A-F 226, 318
Lears, T. J. Jackson H 633
Lease, Benjamin L 154
Leavitt, Judith Walzer STM 220, 275-276, 309
Legergott, Stanley H 1889-1890
Lechevalier, Hubert A. STM 221
Leckie, Robert H 25
Ledeen, Michael PS 714
Leder, Lawrence H. H 130-131
Lee, A. Robert L 558
Lee, Alfred McClung PC 880
Lee, Charles PC 82
Lee, David R. H 787
Lee, Dorothy A-F 54
Lee, Edward M 303
Lee, Hector A-F 438
Lee, James Melvin PC 881
Lee, L. E. L 559
Lee, Robert Edson PC 279
Lee, Ronald Demos H 26
Lee, Susan Previant H 1891
Leemon, Thomas A. A-F 319
LeGales, Richard T. SOC 58
Leggett, John C. SOC 49
Leghorn, Lisa SOC 367
Legman, Gershom A-F 439
LeGuin, Ursula K. PC 235
Lehman, Milton STM 222
Lehmann-Haupt, Hellmut L 10
Leiderman, P. Herbert PSY 69
Leighton, Alexander H. A-F 320
Leighton, Dorothea A-F 223, 227
Leinwoll, Stanley PC 776
Leis, Philip E. A-F 48
Leisy, Ernest E. PC 296
Leites, Nathan PC 637; PS 96
Lekachman, Robert PC 854
Leland, Joy A-F 228
Lemay, J. A. Leo L 65-66
Lemon, James T. H 1472
Lemons, J. Stanley H 778
Lender, Mark Edward PSY 120
Lenihan, John H. PC 516
Lens, Sidney PS 715
Leon, J. J. PSY 54
Leonard, Eugenie Andruss H 779
Leonard, Neil M 304
Leone, Mark P. H 221
Lerman, Paul SOC 561
Lerner, Gerda H 780-781
Lerner, Michael PS 532
Leserman, Jane SOC 368
Lesher, Stephan PC 777
Lesser, Gerald S. PC 714, 778
Lessing, Lawrence STM 223
Lester, Richard A. SOC 562
Lettieri, Daniel J. PSY 121-122
Leuchtenberg, William E. H 486-488

Leupp, Francis E. H 1185
Levenstein, Harvey A. H 1590
Leventhal, Herbert STM 224
Leventman, Paula Goldman SOC 563
Leventman, Seymour SOC 159
Leverenz, David L 67
Levering, Patricia W. PC 877
Levering, Ralph B. PC 877; PS 716
Levey, Joseph M 305
Levi, Ken R 209
Levi, Margaret PS 346
Levin, Beatrice S. STM 225
Levin, G. Roy PC 517
Levin, Gail A-A 214, 218
Levin, Harry L 155, 337
Levin, Harvey J. PC 779-780
Levin, N. Gordon PS 717
Levin, Robert M 329, 340
Levine, Andrew PS 42
Levine, Charles H. PS 347
Levine, Edward M. H 953
Levine, Gene M. SOC 161
Levine, Lawrence W. R 225
Levine, Robert A. PSY 123
Levine, Stuart A-F 229
Levinson, Daniel J. PSY 124
Levinson, Henry Samuel R 149
Levinson, Maria Hertz PS 506
Levison, Andrew SOC 481
Levitan, Sar A. SOC 296, 482
Levitan, Teresa A. PS 452
Levitas, Gloria A-F 63
Levy, Alan Howard M 84
Levy, Babette May H 132
Levy, Jerrold E. A-F 230
Levy, Leonard H 333, 1971
Levy, Lester S. M 408-410
Lewels, Francisco J., Jr. PC 670
Lewington, Mike PC 442
Lewis, Eugene H 1892
Lewis, George PC 40
Lewis, Harold G. H 1591
Lewis, Hylan A-F 118
Lewis, Jerry M. PSY 100
Lewis, Merrill L 559
Lewis, Michael SOC 483
Lewis, Oscar SOC 162
Lewis, Philip C. PC 360
Lewis, R. W. B. L 156
Lewis, Ronald L. H 1058
Lewis, W. David H 1740
Lewis, William PS 714
Lewisohn, Ludwig L 11
Lewy, Guenter PS 718
Ley, Sandra PC 1029
Ley, Willy STM 226
Leyburn, James G. H 954
Liberty, Margot A-F 256, H 1186
Licht, Jennifer A-A 260
Licht, Walter H 1592

Lichten, Frances A-A 310
Lichtenstein, Nelson H 1593
Lieb, Sandra R. M 266
Lieber, Robert PS 744
Lieber, Todd M. L 561
Lieberson, Stanley SOC 163
Liebling, A. J. PC 882
Liebmann, Charles S. R 173
Liebow, Elliot A-F 186
Lifton, Robert Jay H 27; PS 719;
    PSY 125-126
Light, Ivan H. SOC 164
Lightfoot, Sara Lawrence SOC 297
Lightman, Allan J. A-F 55
Lillydahl, Jane A-F 324
Lincoln, C. Eric R 223, 226-227
Lindberg, Gary L 562
Lindblom, Charles E. PS 75, 97-
    98
Linders, Peter H. H 1940
Lindey, Christine A-A 83
Lindquist, G. E. E. H 1187
Lindsay, Vachel PC 518
Lindstrom, Diane H 1347
Lindzey, Gardner PSY 127
Lineberry, William P. PC 964
Lingeman, Richard H 489, 1473
Lingenfelter, Richard E. H 1594
Link, Arthur S. H 490-491
Linsky, Martin PC 781
Linton, James PC 498
Linton, Ralph A-F 231
Lipke, William C. A-A 265
Lipman, Jean A-A 297, 311-314
Lippard, Lucy A-A 84-86
Lippman, Walter PS 720
Lippy, Charles H. R 58
Lipset, Seymour Martin PS 99,
    348, 448, 486, 536, 546-547;
    SOC 12, 292
Lipsky, Richard PC 965
Lipsyte, Robert PC 966
Lipton, Lawrence L 338
Liska, George PS 721
Liston, Robert A. SOC 484
Litman, Barry Russell PC 782
Litoff, Judy Barrett STM 227
Little, Nina Fletcher A-A 157,
    401
Littlefield, Daniel C. H 1059
Littlefield, Daniel F., Jr.
    H 1188-1189
Littler, Craig P. H 1700
Litton, Glenn PC 394
Litwack, Leon F. H 1060; R 228
Lively, Robert A. L 157
Livermore, Shawn H 334
Livesay, Harold C. H 1741, 1773,
    1893
Livingston, Jane A-A 315
Livingston, John C. SOC 166

Llanes, Jose A-F 277
Llewellyn, K. N. H 1190
Lloyd, James B. L 12
Lock, Andrew J. PSY 95
Locke, Alain M 21
Lockridge, Kenneth A. H 133-135
Lockwood, Charles A-A 479; H 1348
Lodge, David L 339
Loehlin, John C. PSY 127
Loetscher, Lefferts A. R 21;
    R 59
Loewen, James W. H 955
Lofland, Lyn H. SOC 428
Lofton, John PC 883
Loggins, Vernon L 563
Lohr, N. Gordon A-A 407
Lokke, Virgil L. L 196
Lomask, Milton STM 228
Lomax, John A. M 169
London, Joan H 1595
Long, Clarence D. H 1596
Longstreet, Stephen M 306
Longstreth, Richard A-A 577
Lonn, Ella H 335
Lonner, Walter J. PSY 27
Looney, Robert F. A-A 283
Loosley, Elizabeth W. A-F 139
Lopata, Helena Znaniecki SOC 167,
    429-430
Lopiano, Donna PC 919
Lopreato, Joseph SOC 168
Lord, Priscilla Sawyer A-A 316
Loshe, Lillie D. L 158
Loth, Calder A-A 480
Lott, Bernice SOC 369
Louder, Dean R. PC 1041
Lounsbury, Myron O. PC 519
Lourie, Margaret A. A-F 349
Louv, Richard SOC 13
Love, Glen A. L 340
Lovecraft, Howard Phillips
    PC 177
Lovejoy, David S. R 60
Loveland, Anne C. R 86
Lovell, John, Jr. M 227
Low, J. O. A-F 155
Lowance, Mason I. L 68
Lowe, Carl PS 487
Lowenfish, Lee PC 967
Lowens, Irving M 85-86
Lowenthal, Leo PC 41
Lowi, Theodore J. PS 349, 488
Lowie, Robert H. A-F 232
Lowitt, Richardson L 341
Loy, John W. PC 921, 968
Lubove, Roy H 492, 1349-1350,
    1742
Lucas, Henry S. H 956
Lucas, John A. PC 969-970
Lucas, Paul R. R 36
Luccock, Halford E. L 342

Lucie-Smith, Edward A-A 87
Ludmerer, Kenneth M. STM 229
Ludwig, Allan I. A-A 244
Ludwig, Jack PC 971
Ludwig, Richard M. L 564
Luebke, Frederick C. A-F 119; H 957
Lundberg, Donald E. H 1743
Lundsgaarde, Henry P. A-F 120
Lunt, Paul S. A-F 156-157
Lunt, Richard D. H 1597
Luomala, Katherine A-F 334
Lupien, Tony PC 967
Lupoff, Dick PC 315, 319
Lupton, Mary Jane H 726
Luraghi, Raimondo H 336
Lurie, Edward STM 230
Lurie, Jonathan H 1894
Lurie, Nancy Oestreich A-F 226, 229
Luttberg, Norman R. PS 436
Lutwack, Leonard L 343
Lutz, Alma H 782
Lyndon, Michael M 228
Lyle, Jack PSY 158
Lyman, Stanford M. H 958; SOC 169-170
Lynd, Helen Merrell SOC 50-51
Lynd, Robert S. SOC 50-51
Lynd, Staughton H 634
Lyndon, Donlyn A-A 483
Lynen, John F. L 565
Lynes, Russell A-A 88, 481
Lynn, Catherine A-A 402
Lynn, Kenneth S. L 159, 344, 566
Lynn, Laurence E. PS 350
Lynn, Robert W. R 87
Lyon, James K. L 345
Lyon, Phyllis PSY 134
Lyons, Eugene H 493
Lyons, John O. L 567
Lyons, Nathan A-A 347
Lystad, Mary PC 122
Lyttle, David L 568
Lyttleton, Humphrey M 307-308

Maass, John A-A 578-579
Mabee, Carleton STM 231
Mabey, Richard M 411
MacAndrew, Elizabeth PC 192
MacAvoy, Paul W. H 1744
MacAvoy, Thomas T. R 174-175
MacCann, Donna Rae PC 123-125
MacCann, Richard Dyer PC 520-521
Maccoby, Eleanor Emmons PSY 128-129
MacConnell, Dean A-F 121
Macdonald, Dwight PC 522
MacDonald, J. Fred PC 783
MacDowell, Betty A-A 299-300

MacDowell, Marsha A-A 299-300
Mackenzie, Calvin G. PS 114
MacKenzie, Kenneth M. R 106
MacKethan, Lucinda Hardwick L 569
MacKinnon, Catharine A. SOC 370
Mackling, June A-F 294
MacKuen, Michael Bruce PC 671
MacLean, Robert M. L 570
MacLeod, Anne Scott PC 126
MacMinn, George R. PC 361
Macorquodale, Patricia SOC 342
Macy, John W., Jr. L 13; PC 784
Madden, David L 346
Maddox, Brenda PC 672
Maddox, Robert James PS 722
Madigan, Mary Jean A-A 403
Madsen, Axel PC 523
Madsen, William A-F 278
Madson, John H 1474
Magdol, Edward H 1475
Magnuson, Norris R 107
Magny, Claude-Edmonde L 347
Maher, James T. A-A 615
Mahoney, Richard D. PS 723
Mahony, Sheila PC 785
Maier, Pauline H 220
Mails, Thomas E. H 1191
Main, Jackson T. H 221-223
Maisel, Louis S. PS 449
Maizlish, Stephen E. H 1476
Majka, Linda C. SOC 564
Majka, Theo J. SOC 564
Mak, James H 1706
Malbin, Martin PS 489
Malcolm, Janet PSY 130
Maldonado-Denis, Manuel A-F 279
Male, Roy R. L 571-572
Malin, Irving L 348
Malinchak, Alan A. SOC 431
Malone, Bill C. M 170-172
Malone, Michael P. H 1477
Maltby, Richard PC 524
Maltin, Leonard PC 525
Malveaux, Julianne SOC 250
Malzberg, Barry N. PC 236
Mamber, Stephen PC 526
Manaster, Guy J. PSY 131
Manchester, Herbert PC 972
Mancini, Janet K. SOC 52
Mandelbaum, David G. A-F 187
Mandelbaum, Seymour J. H 1351
Mander, Jerry PC 786
Mandle, Jay R. H 1061
Mandle, Joan D. SOC 371
Mangels, William F. H 1745
Mangione, Jerre H 494-495, 959
Mangum, Garth L. SOC 172
Mani, Lakshmi L 160
Manieri-Ella, Mario A-A 439
Mankiewicz, Frank PC 787

Manlove, C. N.   PC 178
Manly, John Matthews   L 349
Mann, Arthur   H 28
Mann, Brenda J.   A-F 142
Mann, Philip A.   PSY 132
Manners, Robert A.   A-F 290
Manning, Frank E.   PC 43
Manning, Kenneth   STM 233
Manning, Thomas G.   STM 234
Manning, Willard G., Jr.   PC 800
Mansbridge, Jane J.   PS 43
Mansfield, Harvey C., Jr.   PS 44
Manvell, Roger   PC 527
Mapp, Edward   PC 528
Marable, Manning   PS 548
Marbut, F. B.   PC 884
Marcell, David W.   H 635
Marchant, Donald A.   PS 368
Marcorelles, Louis   PC 529
Marcus, Alfred   PS 351
Marcus, Griel   M 412-414
Marcus, Jacob Rader   H 960-961
Marcuse, Herbert   PS 45-46
Mardock, Robert W.   H 1192
Maret, Elizabeth   SOC 372
Margolies, Edward   L 350; PC 156
Margolis, Michael   PS 47
Maril, Robert Lee   SOC 565
Marini, Stephen A.   R 61
Mark, Joan   STM 235
Marker, Lise-Lone   PC 363
Markides, Kyriakos S.   SOC 173
Markle, Gerald E.   SOC 666
Marks, Geoffrey   STM 236
Marling, Karal Ann   A-A 219
Marmor, Theodore R.   PS 320, 352;
   SOC 534
Marovitz, Sanford E.   L 485
Marrocco, W. Thomas   M 7
Marsden, George M.   R 275-276
Marsden, Michael T.   PC 10, 272,
   530
Marsella, Anthony J.   PSY 133
Marsh, G. E.   STM 95
Marsh, Margaret S.   H 783
Marshall, F. Ray   H 1598
Marshall, Howard Wright   A-A 482
Marshall, Richard   A-A 261
Marshall, Victor W.   SOC 432
Martin, Albro   H 1746
Martin, Calvin   H 1193
Martin, Del   PSY 134
Martin, Edgar W.   H 1895
Martin, George T., Jr.   SOC 596
Martin, Harry W.   SOC 173
Martin, James Kirby   H 224;
   PSY 120
Martin, Jay   L 161
Martin, John Bartlow   PC 791
Martin, Robert K.   L 573
Martin, Ronald E.   L 162

Martinez, Tomas M.   SOC 640
Marty, Martin E.   PC 854; R 12,
   124-125
Marx, Gary T.   SOC 174
Marx, Leo   L 574
Marzik, Thomas D.   H 969
Marzio, Peter C.   A-A 285
Masnick, George   H 1462
Mason, Bobbie Ann   PC 127
Mason, Daniel Gregory   M 87-88
Mason, Edward S.   H 1747
Mason, John L.   PC 531
Massa, Ann   L 351
Massengale, John Montague
   A-A 513, 629
Massey, Mary Elizabeth   H 784
Mast, George   PC 532-534
Materer, Timothy   L 352
Mates, Julian   PC 364
Mathews, Donald G.   R 88, 97
Mathews, W. S. B.   M 89
Mathews, Zena   A-A 14
Matlaw, Myron   PC 44, 365
Mattelart, Armand   PC 309
Matthaei, Julie A.   H 785
Matthews, Brandor   PC 366
Matthews, Donald R.   PS 441
Matthews, Elmora Messer   A-F 122
Matthews, J. H.   PC 535
Matthews, Jane de Hart   H 770;
   L 353
Matthews, Sarah H.   SOC 373
Matthiessen, Francis Otto   L 163
Maurer, David W.   A-F 364
Maxfield, Michael G.   SOC 658
Maxwell, D. E. S.   L 575
May, Earl Chapin   PC 367
May, Elaine Tyler   H 786
May, Ernest R.   H 337; PS 724-725
May, Henry F.   H 636-637; R 108
May, John R.   PC 536
May, Robert E.   H 338
Mayer, Egon   SOC 175
Mayer, Harold M.   H 1352
Mayfield, John   H 339
Mayhew, Edgar de N.   A-A 404
Maynard Aubre de L.   STM 237
Maynard, Richard A.   PC 537-538
Mays, Benjamin Elijah   R 229
Mazey, Mary Ellen   H 787
Mazlish, Bruce   STM 238
Mazmanian, Daniel A.   PS 450
Mazur, Mary Ann   PSY 109
Mazzaro, Jerome   L 354
McAdam, Douglas   PS 559; SOC 176
McArthur, Colin   PC 539
McAuliffe, Mary   H 496
McAvoy, Thomas T.   R 174-175
McCabe, Cynthia Jaffee   A-A 89
McCaffrey, Lawrence J.   H 962
McCaghy, Charles H.   SOC 641

McCallum, Frances T. STM 239
McCallum, Henry D. STM 239
McCallum, Ian A-A 616
McCardell, John H 1478
McCarthy, Albert PC 368
McCarthy, Albert J. M 294, 309
McCarthy, Kathleen D. H 1353
McCarthy, Mary L 576
McCarthy, Todd PC 54
McClave, Heather L 577
McClellan, James E., Jr. A-F 315
McClelland, Doug PC 541
McClelland, Kent A. SOC 451
McClelland, Peter D. H 29, 1896
McClennan, Robert PS 726
McClure, Robert D. PC 802
McCole, C. John L 355
McCombs, Maxwell I. PC 906;
    PSY 52
McConnel-Genet, Sally PSY 135
McConnell, Frank D. PC 542
McConnell, Grant H 1748; PS 490
McCorkle, Donald M. M 90
McCormick, John L 356
McCormick, Richard H 340; PS 451
McCormick, Thomas J. PS 727
McCoubrey, John A-A 145, 158
McCoy, Donald R. H 497
McCoy, Drew R. H 225
McCraw, Thomas K. H 1897
McCubbin, Hamilton I. PSY 136
McCue, George M 22
McCulloh, Judith M 172
McCullough, David STM 240-241
McCurdy, David A-F 70
McCutcheon, Lynn Ellis M 415
McDaniel, George W. A-F 440
McDermott, John F. H 638;
    PSY 172
McDonagh, Edward C. SOC 177
McDonald, Forrest H 341; STM 242-
    243
McDonald, Michael J. H 1479
McDonald, William F. H 498
McDowell, John Holmes A-F 441
McDowell, John Patrick H 1480
McElvaine, Robert S. H 499
McFadden, George L 357
McGee, Mark Thomas PC 543
McGeehan, Robert PS 728
McGiffert, Michael H 136
McGinnis, Tom SOC 298
McGoldrick, Monica PSY 41
McGouldrick, Paul F. H 1749
McGovern, James R. H 1062
McGowan, John J. PC 798
McGraw, Thomas K. STM 244
McGregor, Alexander Campbell
    H 1750
McIntyre, Ruth A. H 137
McKearin, George S. A-A 405-406

McKearin, Helen A-A 405-406
McKee, Jesse O. H 1194
McKelvey, Blake H 1354-1355
McKelvey, Jean Trepp H 1599
McKem, Lucy M 202
McKenna, Wendy PSY 113
McKennon, Joe PC 369
McKinzie, Richard D. A-A 90
McKitrick, Eric L. H 342
McLanathan, Richard B. K.
    A-A 91-92
McLaughlin, John B. SOC 178
McLaughlin, Loretta STM 245
McLaurin, Melton Alouza H 1600
McLaurin, W. Rupert STM 232
McLean, Albert F., Jr. PC 370
McLemore, S. Dale SOC 179
McLoughlin, William G., Jr.
    R 13, 62, 109, 277-278, 305
McLuhan, Marshall PC 45, 649,
    673
McMallum, Frances T. STM 239
McNall, Sally Allen L 578;
    SOC 53
McNall, Scott G. SOC 53
McNally, Fiona SOC 566
McNamara, Brooks A-A 549; PC 371
McNickle, D'Arcy H 1134, 1195
McNitt, Frank H 1196
McPhee, William N. PS 411
McPherson, Barry D. PC 968
McPherson, James M. H 343, 1468
McQuaid, Kim PS 491; SOC 519
McRae, Barry M 311
McRoberts, Jerry William A-A 220
McShine, Kynaston A-A 159
McWhiney, Grady H 344
McWilliams, Carey H 963-964, 1601-
    1602
McWilliams, Wilson C. H 639
Mead, Margaret A-F 15-17, 56,
    233, 321-322; SOC 14
Mead, Sidney E. R 14, 150, 296-
    297
Meadow, Robert G. PS 100
Medcalf, Linda SOC 567
Mednick, Martha Tahara Shuch
    SOC 374
Meehan, Diana M. PC 788
Meeks, Carroll L. V. A-A 580
Mehan, Hugh A-F 323
Mehling, Harold PC 789
Meier, August B. H 1063, 1603;
    SOC 180
Meier, Matt S. H 965-966
Meigs, Cornelia PC 128
Meikle, Jeffrey L. H 1751
Meinig, D. W. H 1481; PC 1031
Meisel, Louis K. A-A 221
Meiselas, Susan PC 372
Meister, David SOC 568

Melchor, James R. A-A 407
Melchor, Marilyn S. A-A 407
Melder, Keith E. H 788
Melendy, H. Brett H 967-968
Melko, Matthew SOC 264, 337
Mellard, James M. L 358
Mellen, Joan PC 544-545
Mellers, Wilfred H. M 24
Mellquist, Jerome A-A 93
Melman, Seymour PS 353-356
Melody, William PC 790
Melosh, Barbara STM 247
Melosi, Martin V. H 1356
Melton, Gary B. PSY 48
Melton, J. Gordon R 15, 120
Meltzer, Milton A-A 325
Melville, Margarita B. A-F 280
Mendel, Douglas PS 729
Mendelowitz, Daniel Marcus
  A-A 94
Mendelsohn, Harold PC 674
Menez, Herminia Q. A-F 442
Mercer, Lloyd H 1898
Merchant, Larry PC 973-974
Meringoff, Laurene Krasney
  PC 714
Merino, Barbara Dubis H 1775
Merk, Frederick H 30, 345, 1482
Merk, L. B. H 345
Merrens, Harry Roy H 138
Merrill, Dana K. L 579
Merrill, George P. STM 248
Merrill, John C. PC 655, 885-887
Merrill, Kenneth R. H 640
Merritt, Raymond H. STM 249
Merritt, Richard L. H 139
Merry, Bruce PC 157
Mertens, Wim M 91
Mertz, Paul E. H 500
Messenger, Christian K. L 580
Messent, Peter B. PC 179
Messer, Robert L. PS 357, 729
Messerschmidt, Donald A. A-F 18
Messick, Hank PC 373
Metraux, Rhoda A-F 17
Metz, Donald L. SOC 569
Meyer, Donald PC 83
Meyer, Donald B. R 126, 211
Meyer, Marshall W. PS 358
Meyer, Robert, Jr. PC 374
Meyer, Roy W. H 1197; L 14
Meyer, Stephen, III H 1604
Meyer, Susan E. A-A 272
Meyer, Ursula A-A 262
Meyers, Margaret G. H 1899
Meyers, Marvin H 346
Meyers, Mary Ann R 212
Meyers, Walter Earl PC 237
Meyersohn, Rolf PC 39
Michael, Jack L. PSY 140
Michael, Sonya H 705

Michael, Stanley T. A-F 143
Michener, James A. PC 975
Mickel, Jere C. PC 375
Mickelson, Anne Z. L 359
Middlekauf, Robert H 140-141,
  226
Middleton, Richard M 229
Milbrath, Lester W. PS 492
Miller, David L. H 641
Miller, Dorothy C. A-A 222
Miller, Douglas T. H 347
Miller, Gale SOC 570
Miller, Glenn T. R 306
Miller, Howard S. STM 251
Miller, James E., Jr. L 581
Miller, Jim M 416
Miller, Joanne SOC 559
Miller, John Chester H 227-228,
  348
Miller, Lillian A-A 95; STM 252
Miller, Nathan H 1752
Miller, Perry H 142, 642-647;
  L 164; R 55, 151
Miller, R. Baxter L 582
Miller, Randall M. H 969; PC 546;
  R 89
Miller, Robert Moats R 127
Miller, Roberta Balstad H 1357
Miller, S. M. SOC 571
Miller, Stuart Creighton H 970;
  PS 730
Miller, Tice L. L 165
Miller, Warren PS 452
Miller, Warren E. PS 420-421
Miller, Wayne Charles PC 297
Miller, Wilbur R. H 1358
Miller, Zane L. H 1359-1360
Millgale, Michael L 360
Millman, Marcia SOC 642
Mills, C. Wright SOC 181, 485-
  486
Mills, Frederick V. R 63
Mills, Joshua E. PC 757
Mills, Ralph J., Jr. L 361
Milne, Gordon L 584-585
Milner, Murray, Jr. SOC 487
Milton, David H 1605
Milton, John R. PC 280
Milvasky, J. Ronald PSY 137
Mims, Edwin H 1483
Miner, H. Craig H 1198-1199
Miner, Horace A-F 123
Minge, Ward Allen H 1200
Minow, Newton N. PC 791
Minter, David L. L 586
Mintz, Alan L. SOC 224
Mintz, Jerome R. A-F 443
Mintz, Sidney W. A-F 281, 290
Mirande, Alfredo A-F 282
Mishler, Elliot G. STM 253
Mitchell, Broadus H 1900

Mitchell, Lee Clark L 166
Mitchell, Lee M. PC 791
Mitchell, Sally PC 84
Mitchell, Stephen A. PSY 90
Mitchell, William E. A-F 124
Mitchell-Kernan, Claudia PSY 18
Mitford, Jessica PC 888
Mithun, Marianne A-F 208
Mitroff, Ian I. STM 254
Mixer, Knowlton A-A 550
Mixon, Wayne L 167
Miyakawa, T. Scott H 870
Mizener, Arthur L 587-588
Mock, Elizabeth A-A 617
Modell, John SOC 83
Moe, Terry M. PS 493
Moen, Elizabeth A-F 324
Moers, Ellen PC 193
Mohl, Raymond A. H 1297, 1361
Mohr, J. C. STM 255
Mohr, Walter H. H 1201
Moline, Norman T. H 1362
Moliterni, Claud PC 307
Mollinger, Robert N. L 589
Monaco, James PC 47-48, 547
Monaco, Paul PSY 88
Mondello, Salvatore H 943
Monkkonen, Eric H. H 1363
Montague, Susan P. A-F 24
Montell, William Lynwood A-F 444-445
Montero, Darrel SOC 182-183
Montgomery, Charles F. A-A 408-409; PC 1032
Montgomery, David H 1606-1607
Moock, Peter R. SOC 260
Moody, Kate PC 792
Moody, Richard PC 376
Mooney, James H 1202
Moore, Arthur H 648
Moore, Charles W. A-A 483-484
Moore, David G. A-F 308
Moore, Deborah Dash R 176
Moore, Harry H. STM 256
Moore, James R. R 110
Moore, Joan W. SOC 136, 184, 643
Moore, Lorna G. A-F 325
Moore, R. Laurence R 213
Moore, Robert L. R 210
Moore, Winfred B., Jr. H 1449-1450
Moorhead, James H. R 288
Mora, Magdalena A-F 283
Morantz, Regina STM 257
Mordden, Ethan PC 377-378, 548
Moreland, Laurence W. H 1411, 1484
Morella, Joe PC 549
Morey-Gaines, Ann-Janine R 298
Morgan, Alan M 312
Morgan, David H 790

Morgan, Edmund M. H 229
Morgan, Edmund S. H 143-145; R 37, 307
Morgan, Hal A-A 348
Morgan, Helen M. H 229
Morgan, Howard Wayne A-A 192; H 349-350; L 168; STM 258
Morgan, John S. STM 259
Morgan, Kathryn A-F 188
Morgan, Lewis Henry A-F 234
Morgan, Richard E. PS 360
Morgan, William H. A-A 485
Morgenstern, Dan M 313
Morin, Edgar PC 550
Morishima, James K. A-F 338
Morison, Elting E. H 649; STM 260-261
Morison, Samuel Eliot H 31, 146-148; L 69
Moritz, Albert F. A-A 286
Morland, John Kenneth A-F 59, 76, 125
Morley, David A-A 632
Morris, Charles H 650
Morris, Milton D. H 1064
Morris, Norman S. PC 793
Morris, Richard B. H 149, 230, 1608
Morris, Robert C. H 351
Morris, Ronald L. M 314
Morris, Wesley L 590
Morris, Wright L 591
Morrison, Chaplain W. H 352
Morrison, Hugh A-A 486
Morrison, Theodore PC 379
Morrow, William PS 506
Morse, Arthur D. H 501
Morse, David M 417
Morse, John D. A-A 273
Mosco, Vincent PC 794
Moseley, James G. R 16
Moses, Montrose J. L 592
Moses, Wilson Jeremiah L 593
Mosher, Frederick C. PS 361
Moskos, Charles C., Jr. SOC 185
Moskowitz, Samuel PC 238-240
Mosley, Leonard H 1753
Moss, Frank E. SOC 433
Mossberg, Christer Lennart L 594
Most, Glenn W. PC 158
Mott, Frank Luther PC 85-86, 889
Mowrer, O. Hobart PSY 138
Mowry, George E. H 502-505
Moyer, Albert E. STM 262
Moynihan, Daniel Patrick PS 362, 480; SOC 128-129
Mrozek, Donald PC 976
Muehlbauer, Gene SOC 644
Mueller, Charles W. SOC 575
Mueller, John H. M 92

Mueller, Robert Kirk SOC 572
Mulder, John M. R 17
Mulder, Ronald A. H 506
Mulholland, James A. STM 263
Mulkern, John R. PS 482
Mullen, Patrick B. A-F 446
Mullen, R. D. PC 241
Muller, Edward N. PS 550
Muller, Peter O. SOC 54
Mullin, Gerald W. H 1065
Mullroy, Elizabeth D. A-A 489
Mumford, Lewis A-A 488, 581, 618-
  619; H 1364; L 169
Munro, Eleanor A-A 96
Munroe, John A. H 150
Murch, Alma Elizabeth PC 159
Murdock, Kenneth L 70
Murgia, Edward A-F 284
Murphey, Murray G. H 591
Murphy, Paul L. H 1972
Murphy, Robert F. A-F 5
Murphy, Sharon M. H 811
Murphy, Thomas PS 363
Murray, Andrew A. R 264
Murray, Edward PC 551-552
Murray, H. A. PSY 118
Murray, James P. PC 553
Murray, Richard N. A-A 144
Murray, Robert K. H 507-508
Murrell, William PC 316
Murtagh, William J. A-A 551
Mushkat, Jerome H 1365
Mussulman, Joseph A. M 94
Musto, Daniel F. PSY 139
Myers, Jerome K. SOC 488-489
Myers, Margaret C. H 1754
Myers, Minor, Jr. A-A 404
Myers, Ramon H. PS 731
Myers, Robert E. PC 242
Myers, Robert J. PC 49
Myerson, Joel L 135, 170
Myles, Lynda PC 570
Myrdal, Alva PS 732
Myrdal, Gunnar SOC 186

Nabokov, Peter A-F 235
Nachbar, Jack PC 24, 554
Nachbar, John G. PC 530
Nadeau, Robert L. L 362
Nadworny, Milton J. H 1609
Naef, Weston J. A-A 328
Nagel, James L 595-596
Nagel, Paul C. H 651
Nagel, Stuart S. PS 364
Naisbitt, John SOC 15
Naison, Mark H 509
Nanry, Charles M 315-316
Naroll, Raoul A 19
Nasatir, Mort M 262
Nasaw, David H 652

Nash, Dennison A-F 126
Nash, Gary G. H 151-152, 231
Nash, George H. H 653
Nash, Gerald D. H 1755, 1902
Nash, Michael H 1610
Nash, Roderick H 654; STM 264
Nathan, George Jean PC 380-381
Nathan, Hans PC 382
Nathan, James A. PS 733
Navasky, Victor S. PC 555
Naylor, David A-A 620
Nee, Brett De Bary SOC 187
Nee, Victor G. SOC 187
Needham, Gwendolyn Bridges
  PC 197
Needleman, Jacob R 214-215
Neff, Donald PS 734
Neidle, Cecyle S. H 791
Neil, J. Meredith A-A 446
Neithammer, Carolyn H 1203
Nelkin, Dorothy A-F 176
Nelli, Humbert S. H 791-793
Nelsen, Anne Kusener R 230
Nelsen, Hart M. R 230
Nelson, Cary L 363
Nelson, Daniel H 1611, 1756
Nelson, Joel I. SOC 490
Nelson, Martha J. H 825
Nelson, Ralph H 1757
Nelson, Richard R. PS 365
Nelson, William E. H 353, 1973-
  1974
Nelson, William R. STM 265
Nesbitt, Elizabeth PC 128
Nesteby, James P. PC 556
Netschert, Bruce C. H 1784
Nettels, Curtis P. H 1903-1904
Nettl, Bruno M 10, 173-175
Netzer, Dick PS 366
Neu, Irene D. H 1758, 1795
Neugarten, Bernice L. A-F 216
Neuhau, Richard PS 304
Neuringer, Charles PSY 140
Neusner, Jacob R 177-178
Neustadt, Richard PS 367
Neve, Brian PC 447
Nevins, Allan H 354-356, 1759;
  STM 266-268
Nevins, Deborah A-A 451
Nevins, Francis M., Jr. PC 160
Newcomb, Horace PC 795-796
Newcomb, Rexford A-A 490-491
Newhall, Beaumont A-A 329
Newhouse, John PS 735-736
Newman, Ronald B. A-F 465
Newman, William M. SOC 188
Newmeyer, Frederick J. A-F 365
Newton, Esther A-F 127
Newton, Jan M. SOC 603
Newton, Norman T. A-A 492
Newton, Wesley Phillips H 1740

Nicholls, Peter PC 243
Nichols, Bill PC 557-558
Nichols, David A. H 1204
Nichols, James Hastings R 152
Nichols, Roger L. H 887
Nichols, Roy F. H 357
Nicholson, Joseph William R 229
Nicolson, Marjorie Hope PC 244
Nie, Norman H. PS 453, 472
Niebuhr, H. Richard R 18
Niehaus, Earl F. H 974
Nielsen, George R. SOC 189
Nielsen, Georgia Panter H 792
Nielson, David Gordon H 1066
Nieman, Donald G. H 1975
Niemi, Richard G. PS 454, 537
Nies, Judith H 793
Nimmo, Dan PS 551
Nisbet, Robert PS 552
Nishimoto, Richard S. A-F 340
Nissenbaum, Stephen R 26
Niven, John H 358
Noble, David F. STM 269
Noble, David W. H 655; L 597
Noble, Grant PC 797
Noble, Jeanne H 794
Noble, Peter PC 559
Noebel, David A. M 418
Noel, Mary PC 87
Noel-Hume, Ivor A-F 57-58
Noffsinger, James Philip A-A 493
Noggle, Burl H 510
Nolan, Charles J. L 171
Noll, Roger G. PC 798, 977
Norbeck, Edward A-F 60
Nordlinger, Eric A. PS 48
Norelli, Martina R. A-A 160
Norris, James D. H 1760
North, Douglass C. H 1846, 1905
North, Joseph H. PC 560
Norton, Mary Beth H 709, 795
Norton, Paul F. A-A 59, 552
Norton, R. D. SOC 55
Novak, Barbara A-A 161, 193-195
Novak, Michael H 656; PC 978;
   PS 494, 553-554; SOC 190
Noverr, Douglas A. PC 979
Novotny, Ann H 975; STM 270
Nozick, Robert PS 49
Nuechterlien, Donald E. PS 363
Numbers, Ronald L. STM 271-276,
   309
Nurnberger, Ralph D. PS 106
Nye, F. Ivan PSY 36-37
Nye, Russel Blaine H 232, 360,
   511, 657; L 71; PC 50

Oberdorf, C. P. PSY 141
Oberholzer, Emil, Jr. H 153
O'Brien, David J. R 179

O'Brien, David M. PS 368
O'Brien, Mary PS 50
O'Brien, Michael H 658
O'Broin, Leon H 976
Ochsner, Nancy L. SOC 594
O'Connell, Brian J. SOC 191
O'Connor, Carol A. H 1485
O'Connor, Edward D. R 279
O'Connor, Francis V. A-A 98-100
O'Connor, James PS 369
O'Connor, John E. PC 561-562,
   799
O'Connor, Thomas H. H 361
O'Connor, William V. L 364-365
O'Dea, Thomas R 216
Odell, John S. PS 737
O'Doherty, Brian A-A 101
O'Donnell, James H., III H 1205
Odum, Howard W. M 176-177
Oehser, Paul H. STM 277
Ogbu, John U. A-F 326-327
Oglesby, Carole A. PC 980
O'Grady, Joseph P. H 977
O'Hara, Frank A-A 102
Ohashi, Kenzaburo L 366
Okun, Morris A. SOC 308
Olander, Joseph D. PC 249-250,
   264
Olderman, Raymond M. L 367
Oleson, Alexandra STM 278-279
Oliver, James K. PS 733
Oliver, Paul M 230-234
Oliver, Richard A-A 494
Olmstead, Allan L. H 1761
Olsen, Otto H. H 362
Olson, Alison G. H 154
Olson, Eric H 27
Olson, James C. H 1206
Olson, Kenneth E. M 95
Olson, Laura Katz SOC 434
Olson, Lawrence SOC 435
Olton, Charles S. STM 280
O'Neill, Charles Edward R 308
O'Neill, George SOC 299
O'Neill, Nena SOC 299
O'Neill, William L. H 512-513,
   659, 796-797
Opler, Marvin K. A-F 143, 334;
   PSY 142
Oppenheimer, Bruce I. PS 118
Oppenheimer, Joe A. PS 88
Oppenheimer, Valerie Kincade
   H 798
Orbach, Michael K. A-F 128
Ordeshook, Peter C. PS 105
Oriard, Michael PC 298
Orloff, Katherine M 419
Ormsbee, Thomas H. A-A 410
Ornstein, Jacob A-F 309
Ornstein, Michael D. SOC 573
O'Rourke, Timothy G. PS 455

Ortiz, Flora Ida SOC 300
Ortiz, Roxanne Dunbar H 1207-1208
Osborne, William A. R 265
Osgood, Henry O. M 317
Osgood, Herbert Levi H 155-156
Osgood, Robert E. PS 738-743
Osofsky, Gilbert H 1067
Ostendorf, Berndt L 598
Oster, Harry M 235
Osterweis, Rollin G. H 1486-1487
Ostrander, Gilman H 660
Ostransky, Leroy M 318-320
Ostroff, Eugene A-A 330
Ostrom, Vincent PS 371
O'Sullivan, Judith H 799
Oswald, John Clyde L 599
Otten, Terry L 368
Otto, Celia Jackson A-A 411
Oubre, Claude F. H 1068
Ourada, Patricia K. H 1209
Overton, Richard C. H 1762
Owen, Barbara M 96
Owen, Bruce M. PC 800
Owen, Dennis E. R 120
Owen, Marguerite STM 281
Owens, Gwendolyn A-A 196
Owens, Leslie Howard H 1069
Owsley, Frank L. H 363
Oye, Kenneth PS 744
Ozanne, Robert H 1613-1614
Ozawa, Martha N. SOC 574

Pace, C. Robert SOC 301
Pachon, Harry SOC 184
Packarce, Francis R. STM 282
Packard, Vance SOC 16, 491
Packenham, Robert A. PS 745
Padilla, Elena A-F 285
Page, Benjamin I. PS 456
Pagter, Carl R. A-F 404
Paige, Harry W. M 178
Paine, Jeffrey Morton PC 563
Painter, Nell Irvin H 1070
Palen, J. John SOC 56
Paletz, David L. PC 676
Palm, Risa A-F 324
Palmer, Bruce H 1906
Palmer, Edward L. PC 801
Palmer, Jerry PC 161
Palmer, John L. PS 372
Palmer, Robert M 236, 420
Palmer, Robert R. H 233
Palmer, Tony M 421
Palmore, Edmare SOC 436
Palsson, Mary Dale H 886
Palumbo, Dennis J. PS 373-374
Pampel, Fred C. SOC 437
Panassie, Hugues M 321-322
Pap, Leo SOC 192
Papashvily, Helen Waite L 172

Papenfuse, Edward C. H 126, 1763
Parcel, Toby L. SOC 575
Pare, Richard A-A 495
Paredes, Americo A-F 447-448;
  M 179
Paredes, J. Anthony A-F 236
Paredes, Raymond A-F 286
Parenti, Michael J. SOC 193
Park, Robert E. PC 890
Park, Roberta J. A-F 46
Parkay, Forrest W. SOC 194
Parker, Gail Thain STM 283
Parker, Katherine SOC 367
Parker, Richard SOC 492
Parker, Seymour A-F 189
Parker, Stanley SOC 438
Parker, William M. H 1764
Parker, William N. H 1847
Parkinson, Thomas L 369
Parks, Edd Winfield L 173
Parks, Rita PC 564
Parks, Roberta J. PC 950
Parman, Donald L. H 1210
Parmet, Herbert S. H 514
Parmet, Robert D. H 1615
Parrinder, Patrick PC 245
Parrington, Vernon Louis L 15
Parry, Ellwood A-A 103
Parry, J. H. H 157
Parsons, Elsie Clews H 1211
Parsons, J. PSY 72
Parsons, Talcott SOC 195, 302
Partridge, William L. A-F 129,
  304
Paskoff, Paul E. H 1765
Passell, Peter H 1891
Passer, Harold C. H 1766
Pasteur, Alfred B. PSY 143
Patchen, Martin SOC 196
Paterson, Thomas PS 746
Patridge, Bellamy STM 284
Pattee, Fred Lewis L 16-19;
  PC 89
Patterson, Daniel W. M 180
Patterson, James T. H 515;
  PS 375
Patterson, Thomas E. PC 675, 802
Patton, James Welch H 816
Paul, Doris A. PC 489
Paul, Rodman Wilson H 1488
Paul, Sherman L 370
Pavlos, Andrew J. R 217
Payne, George Henry PC 891
Payne, Ladell L 600
Peak, G. Wayne PS 505
Pearce, Roy Harvey H 1212; L 601-
  602
Pearsall, Marion A-F 114, 130
Pearson, Edmund Lester PC 90
Pearson, Helen Wallenstein
  PSY 122

Peary, Danny PC 565
Peary, Gerald PC 508, 565-567
Peattie, Lisa SOC 585
Peck, Merton J. PC 798
Peden, William L 371
Pederson, Paul B. PSY 133
Pegels, C. Carl SOC 439
Peirce, Neal R. H 1489
Peirce, William Spangar PS 376
Peisch, Mark L. A-A 621
Pel, Mario PC 677
Pells, Richard H. H 516
Pelto, Gretel A-F 311
Pencak, William H 158
Pendleton, John PC 66
Penick, James L., Jr. STM 285
Pennings, Johannes SOC 576
Pennington, Nancy SOC 628
Penrod, Steven D. SOC 628
Penzoldt, Peter PC 180
Peplau, Letitia Anne PSY 144
Pepper, Adeline A-A 412
Perdue, Theda H 1213
Perin, Constance A-F 61
Perkins, Bradford H 364-365;
  PS 747
Perkins, Dexter PS 748
Perkins, Edwin J. H 159, 1767
Perlman, Bennard B. A-A 224
Perlman, Daniel PSY 144
Perlman, Selig H 1616
Perloff, Marjorie L 372
Perman, Michael H 366
Peroff, Nicholas C. H 1214
Perrin, Richard W. E. A-A 582
Perrucci, Robert PSY 145;
  SOC 610, 645
Perry, John Curtis PS 792
Perry, Louis B. H 1617
Perry, Mary-Ellen H 753
Perry, Richard S. H 1617
Persons, Stow H 662-663,; L 603
Pertschuk, Michael PS 377
Pessen, Edward H 367, 1618
Peshkin, Alan SOC 303-304
Peters, Thomas J. SOC 577
Peters-Campbell, John A-A 196
Petersen, William SOC 197
Peterson, Charles E. A-A 496
Peterson, Donald R. PSY 146
Peterson, Julia J. STM 286
Peterson, Mark A. PSY 147
Peterson, Merrill D. H 664
Peterson, Rebecca A-A 632
Peterson, Richard A. M 377;
  PC 51
Peterson, Robert PC 981
Peterson, Theodore PC 682
Peterson, Trudy Huskamp H 1768-
  1769
Petrie, Dennis W. L 373

Petrocik, John R. PS 453
Petter, Henri L 72
Pettigrew, Thomas F. SOC 198
Pettit, Arthur G. PC 281
Pettit, Norman R 38
Pettitt, George A. A-F 62
Peyer, Bernd L 374
Pfaltzgraff, Robert L., Jr.
  PS 749
Pfeffer, Leo R 309-311
Phelan, James L 604
Phelen, John M. PC 678
Philliber, William W. SOC 57
Phillips, E. Barbara SOC 58
Phillips, E. Larkin PSY 148
Phillips, George Harwood, Jr.
  H 1215-1216
Phillips, Paul C. H 1770
Phillips, Robert L 375
Phillips, Ulrich Bonnel H 1490
Philp, Kenneth R. H 1217
Piazza, Thomas SOC 80
Pichaske, David M 422
Pichierri, Louis M 97
Pickering, Ernest A-A 497
Piehl, Mel R 180
Piepkorn, Carl Arthur R 19
Pierce, Albert C. PS 568
Pierce, Hazel Beasley PC 246
Pierce, John C. PS 457
Piercy, Josephine K. L 73
Pierpont Morgan Library PC 129
Pierre, Andrew J. PS 750
Pierson, William H., Jr. A-A 498,
  583
Pietroforte, Alfred M 181
Pike, Burton L 376
Pike, Martha V. PC 1036
Pilcher, William W. A-F 131
Pilgrim, Dianne H. A-A 144
Pilisuk, Marc PSY 145
Pilkington, William T. PC 282
Pinckney, Pauline A-A 245
Pincus-Witten, Robert A-A 105
Pinsker, Sanford L 377
Piotrkowski, Chaya S. SOC 305
Pipkin, John SOC 47
Pitcher, Evelyn Goodenough
  SOC 375
Pitkin, Hanna F. PS 51
Pitt, Leonard H 978
Pitz, Henry C. A-A 106; PC 1045
Pivar, David J. H 800
Piven, Frances F. PS 378;
  SOC 493
Pizer, Donald L 174
Placksin, Sally M 323
Plagens, Peter A-A 107
Platt, Alan PS 751
Platt, Charles PC 247-248
Platt, Gerald M. SOC 302

Platt, Harold L. H 1366
Pleasants, Henry M 324-325, 423
Pleck, Elizabeth Hafkin H 722,
  1071
Pleck, Joseph H. SOC 317, 376
Plesur, Milton R 181
Plimpton, George PC 982
Plinkington, William T. L 605
Plischke, Elmer PS 752
Pochman, H. A. H 665
Pocock, J. G. A. H 160
Podhoretz, Norman L 378
Poen, Monte N. STM 287
Poesch, Jessie A-A 108
Poirier, Richard L 606-607
Pole, J. R. H 161, 666-667
Polenberg, Richard H 517-518
Polich, M. Suzanne PSY 147
Polishook, Irwin H. H 120
Poll, Solomon SOC 199
Pollard, James E. PC 892-893
Pollock, Bruce M 424
Pollock, Ross PS 312
Polsby, Nelson W. PS 92, 101,
  458-459
Polyzoides, Stephanos A-A 622
Pomer, Marshall I. SOC 494
Pomerleau, Cynthia STM 257
Pomeroy, Earl S. H 1491-1493
Pool, Ithiel de Sola PC 679-680;
  PS 303
Pope, Daniel H 1771
Pope, Robert G. R 39
Popple, Charles S. H 1739
Porte, Joel L 175
Porter, Alan L. STM 216
Porter, Bruce SOC 618
Porter, Carolyn L 608
Porter, Dennis PC 162
Porter, Edwin PSY 158
Porter, Glenn H 1772-1773, 1907
Porter, H. C. H 1218
Porter, James A. A-A 109
Porter, Joseph C. A-A 190
Porter, Kenneth W. H 1738
Porter, Roger B. PS 379
Porter, W. M 158
Porter, William E. PC 984
Porterfield, Amanda R 244
Post, Robert C. STM 289
Postal, T. A. STM 95
Poston, Dudley, Jr. H 1494
Potamkin, Harry Alan PC 568
Potter, David M. H 32-33, 368-
  370
Poulsen, Richard C. PC 1037
Poulin, A., Jr. M 146
Pound, Louise A-F 449
Powdermaker, Hortense A-F 21,
  190; PC 569
Powell, Arthur G. H 668

Powell, Earl A. A-A 143
Powell, Lawrence H 371
Powell, Peter J. H 1219-1220
Powell, Sumner Chilton H 162
Powell, Walter W. SOC 532
Powers, Edwin H 163
Powers, Richard Gid PC 52
Powers, Ron PC 803
Powers, Thomas PS 555
Powers, William K. H 1221
Powledge, Fred PC 383
Prager, Arthur PC 130
Prandy, K. SOC 578
Prange, Gordon W. PS 753-754
Prassel, Frank R. H 1495
Pratt, Annis L 609
Pratt, Joseph A. H 1774
Pratt, Waldo Selden M 98
Prebish, Charles S. R 218
Pred, Allan H 1367
Prendergast, Roy M. M 425
Pressly, Nancy L. A-A 176
Presthus, Robert PS 556
Preston, Howard L. H 1368
Previts, Gary John H 1775
Price, Don K. STM 290
Price, Jacob M. H 1776, 1908
Price, Steven D. M 182-183
Priest, Loring Benson H 1222
Primm, James N. H 1909
Pritchard, John Paul L 176
Proffer, Carl R. L 379
Propper, Alice M. SOC 646
Prosper, Peter Anthony, Jr.
  H 1619
Prout, Henry G. STM 291
Prown, Jules David A-A 162-163
Prpic, George H 979
Prucha, Francis Paul H 1223-1225
Pruitt, Dean G. PS 755
Prus, Robert SOC 647
Pryse, Marjorie L 610
Przeworski, Adam PS 72
Puchala, Donald J. PS 677
Puckett, Newbell Niles A-F 450
Pulos, Arthur J. PC 1038
Punnett, Susan SOC 453
Punter, David PC 194
Pupin, Michael STM 292
Purcell, Edward A., Jr. STM 293
Purdy, Jim PC 576
Pursell, Carroll W., Jr. STM 214,
  285, 294-296
Putz, Manfred L 380
Pye, Michael PC 570
Pyne, Stephen J. STM 297

Quan, Robert Seto SOC 200
Quandt, Jean B. H 1369
Quandt, William B. PS 756

Quarles, Benjamin H 1072
Quebedeaux, Richard R 128, 280-281
Quen, Jacques M. PSY 149
Quick, Michael A-A 164
Quilligan, Maureen L 611
Quimby, Ian M. G. A-A 177, 413; A-F 451; PC 1039-1040
Quinn, Arthur Hobson, L 20-21
Quinn, David B. H 86, 164
Quirante, Jacinto A-A 110

Rabinowitz, Clare PSY 187
Rabinowitz, Howard N. H 1073
Rabkin, Eric S. PC 181, 249-250, 256, 259
Raboteau, Albert J. R 231
Rader, Benjamin G. PC 983-984
Radosh, Ronald H 1620
Rae, Douglas PS 102
Rae, John B. STM 299-301
Raffaele, Joseph A. SOC 648
Raffel, Marshall W. STM 302
Rahill, Frank PC 384
Rahill, Peter J. H 1226
Rahv, Philip L 381, 612, 615
Rainbolt, John C. H 1910
Raine, Alden PS 460
Rainey, Buck PC 276
Rainwater, Clarence E. PC 91
Rainwater, Lee SOC 451
Rakove, Jack N. H 234
Ramazani, Ruhollah K. PS 758
Ramirez, Bruno H 1621
Ramsey, Frederic M 326-327
Randall, Richard S. PC 571
Randel, William Pierce A-A 111
Randolph, J. Ralph H 1227
Rankin, Hugh F. L 74
Ranney, Austin PC 804; PS 380, 413, 461-462
Ransom, Roger L. H 1074
Raphael, Marc Lee H 980
Rathbone, Eliza E. A-A 34
Rathbone, Perry T. A-A 112
Rathbun, John W. L 22
Ratner, Sidney H 1912
Ravenal, Earl C. PS 759
Ravitch, Diane H 1371; SOC 306
Rawick, George P. H 1075
Rawls, John PS 52
Ray, Arthur J. H 1228
Rayback, Joseph G. H 1622
Read, Kenneth E. SOC 377
Read, William H. PC 681
Reagan, Barbara H 711
Reagan, Michael D. PS 381
Real, Michael R. PC 53
Record, Jeffrey PS 760
Redburn, F. Stevens SOC 526

Redd, Lawrence N. M 238
Redden, Sister Mary Maurita PC 195
Redding, J. Saunders L 616
Redfield, Robert A-F 22
Redlich, Frederick C. SOC 468
Redlich, Fritz H 1777
Reed, Henry Hope, Jr. A-A 499, 520
Reed, James STM 303
Reed, John Shelton SOC 59-60
Reed, Marl E. H 1623, 1778
Reel, A. Frank PC 805
Reep, Diana C. PC 92
Rees, Albert H 1624
Reese, Gustave M 99
Reese, Kenneth M. STM 345
Reeve, Kay Aiken H 1496
Reeves, Clement PSY 150
Reeves, Earl PC 900
Regier, C. C. PC 895
Reich, Michael H 1554, 1568
Reid, John Phillip H 1229
Reidenbaugh, Lowell PC 985
Reiman, Jeffrey H. SOC 495
Reimers, David M. H 887; R 266; SOC 110
Reingold, Nathan STM 304-306
Reis, Claire Raphael M 100
Reisler, Marc H 981
Reisner, Robert G. M 328
Reiss, Albert J., Jr. SOC 579
Reiss, David SOC 307
Reiss, Ira L. PSY 151
Reissman, Leonard SOC 496
Reitberger, Reinhold PC 317
Renan, Sheldon PC 572
Rennie, Thomas A. C. A-F 143
Renshon, Stanley PS 557
Renwick, Roger deV. A-F 387
Reps, John H 165, 1372-1374
Rescher, Nicholas STM 13
Reston, James PC 896
Rettig, Richard A. STM 307
Reuss-Ianni, Elizabeth A-F 112; SOC 580
Reuter, Peter SOC 649
Reveley, W. Taylor, III PS 761
Revell, Peter L 382
Reverby, Susan STM 308
Revett, Marion S. PC 385
Revi, Albert Christian A-A 414-416
Reynolds, David K. A-F 133
Reynolds, Quentin James PC 93
Rezneck, Samuel H 235
Rhinelander, John B. PS 811
Rhoads, William B. A-A 500
Rhode, David W. PS 407
Rhodes, Colbert SOC 440
Rhodes, Lynette I. A-A 317

Rhodes, Robert C. SOC 161
Rhodes, Robert E. L 239
Ribalow, Harold U. PC 986
Rice, Bradley R. H 1284, 1375
Rice, Edward LeRoy PC 386
Richard, Olga PC 123
Richards, Eugene S. SOC 177
Richards, Jeffrey PC 573
Richards, Pamela SOC 650
Richardson, Barbara L. PSY 110
Richardson, Edgar Preston
  A-A 165-166
Richardson, F. L. W., Jr.
  A-F 328
Richardson, James F. H 1376
Richardson, Richard C., Jr.
  SOC 308
Richardson, Robert D., Jr. L 177
Richey, Elinor H 801
Richey, Russell E. R 20
Richstad, Jim PC 897
Rickert, Edith L 349
Ricks, George Robinson M 184
Riddle, Ronald M 185
Rideout, Walter B. L 383
Ridgely, J. V. L 178
Ridgeway, James PS 524
Riedel, Johannes M 334
Riemer, Jeffrey W. SOC 581-582
Riesman, David SOC 17, 286
Riess, Steven A. PC 987
Rifkind, Carole A-A 501-502
Riker, William H. PS 103-105
Riley, Dick PC 251
Rimlinger, Gaston V. H 519
Ringe, Donald A. L 179; PC 196
Ringer, Benjamin B. SOC 201-202
Rinhart, Floyd A-A 331-332
Rinhart, Marion A-A 331-332
Rippley, La Vern J. H 982
Rischin, Moses R 182
Risjord, Norman K. H 236, 372
Risse, Guenter B. STM 309
Rist, Ray A-F 329
Ritchie, Andrew C. A-A 113
Ritter, Frederic Louis M 101
Ritter, Lawrence S. PC 988
Rivelli, Pauline M 329
Rivera, Feliciano H 965-966
Rivers, William L. PC 682-683,
  855, 898-900
Roach, Hildred M 25
Roark, James L. H 373
Robb, John Donald M 186
Robbins, Carla Anna PS 762
Robbins, Roy M. H 34
Robbins, William G. H 1497
Roberts, Bertram H. SOC 489
Roberts, Donald F. PC 691;
  PSY 52
Roberts, Joan I. A-F 330-331

Roberts, John Storm M 26, 426
Roberts, Randy PC 989
Robertson, R. J. PC 543
Robertson, Thomas S. PC 714
Robinson, Cecil L 617
Robinson, Cervin A-A 623
Robinson, David PC 574
Robinson, Donald L. H 237
Robinson, Evelyn Rose PC 131
Robinson, Glen O. PC 684
Robinson, Jerry PC 318
Robinson, Michael J. PC 685
Robinson, Sidney K. A-A 624
Robinson, Willard B. A-A 503-505
Rockwell, John M 27
Roddick, Nick PC 575
Rodgers, Daniel T. H 1625
Rodgers, Harrell R., Jr. SOC 583
Rodgers, Willard L. PSY 39
Rodnitzky, Jerome L. M 187
Roe, Frank Gilbert H 1230
Roeber, A. G. H 1976
Roebuck, Julian B. SOC 61, 200,
  651
Roelofs, H. Mark PS 558
Roemer, Kenneth M. L 618
Roffman, Peter PC 576
Rogers, Dave M 427
Rogers, David SOC 309-310
Rogers, Joel PS 433
Rogers, Meyric R. A-A 417
Rogers, Theresa F. SOC 584
Rogin, Michael Paul H 1231
Rogg, Eleanor Meyer SOC 203
Rohrbough, Malcolm J. H 1498,
  1977
Rohrer, John H. A-F 191
Rohrer, Gertrude Martin M 188
Rolle, Andrew F. H 983
Rollins, Peter C. PC 577
Romasco, Albert U. H 520-521
Romo, Ricardo A-F 286
Ronco, William SOC 585
Rooney, John F., Jr. PC 990, 1041
Root, Deane L. PC 387
Root, Waverly H 35
Ropes, Hannah Anderson STM 310
Rorabaugh, W. J. H 374
Rosa, Joseph G. PC 283
Roschco, Bernard PC 901
Rose, Al M 330
Rose, Anne C. L 180
Rose, Arnold SOC 186, 586
Rose, Barbara A-A 114, 163, 225-
  226
Rose, Bernice A-A 290
Rose, Dan A-F 332
Rose, Harold Wickliffe A-A 553
Rose, Lislie PS 763
Rose, Mark H. PC 252-253, 258;
  STM 311

Rose, Peter I. SOC 204-205
Rose, Willie Lee H 375, 1076
Rose-Ackerman, Susan PS 496
Rosen, David M. M 189
Rosen, George STM 312-313
Rosen, Marjorie PC 578
Rosen, Philip T. PC 806
Rosen, Ruth H 802
Rosenau, James N. PS 764
Rosenbaum, Jonathan PC 485
Rosenbaum, Max PSY 152
Rosenbaum, Patricia L. SOC 62
Rosenberg, Bernard PC 55
Rosenberg, Bruce A. A-F 452-453;
  H 1499
Rosenberg, Carroll Smith R 90
Rosenberg, Charles E. H 1978;
  STM 314-315, 380
Rosenberg, Emily S. H 522
Rosenberg, Harold A-A 115-118
Rosenberg, Jan SOC 378
Rosenberg, Nathan STM 316-318
Rosenberg, Rosalind H 803
Rosenberg, Stanley D. SOC 408
Rosenblatt, Roger L 619
Rosenbloom, David H. PS 344
Rosenblum, Naomi A-A 29
Rosenblum, Robert A-A 227
Rosenfeld, Paul M 28
Rosenkrantz, Barbara Gutman
  STM 319
Rosenstone, Steven J. PS 474
Rosenthal, Alan PC 579-580
Rosenthal, Kristine M. SOC 311
Rosenthal, M. L. L 384-385
Rosenwaike, Ira H 1377
Rosner, David STM 308, 320
Rosow, Eugene PC 581
Rosowski, Susan J. PC 286
Ross, A. Michael SOC 206
Ross, Ishbel L 620
Ross, John Munder PSY 42
Ross, Lillian PC 582
Ross, Murray PC 583
Ross, Richard E. H 1497
Ross, T. J. PC 487, 584
Rossi, Peter H. SOC 602, 667
Rossiter, Clinton H 238
Rossiter, John R. PC 714
Rossiter, Margaret W. STM 321-
  322
Rosten, Leo C. PC 585, 902
Rostow, Walt W. H 1913; PS 765-
  766
Roszak, Theodore PC 56
Rotella, Elyce J. H 804
Roth, John K. R 153
Roth, Leland M. A-A 506
Roth, William SOC 626
Rothchild, Donald PS 744
Rothman, Barbara Kate SOC 379

Rothman, David J. H 376-377;
  STM 323
Rothman, Robert A. SOC 497
Rothman, Sheila H 805
Rothstein, Robert PS 767
Rothstein, William G. STM 324
Roucek, Joseph S. PS 497
Rourke, Constance L 181, 621-622;
  PC 388
Rourke, Frances PS 768
Rourke, Francis E. PS 742-743
Rouse, Beatrice A. PSY 66
Roussopoulos, Dimitrios PS 513
Rowe, Ann E. L 182
Rowe, John H 984
Rowe, John Carlos L 183
Rowland, Benjamin M. PS 600
Rowland, Willard D., Jr. PC 807
Rowse, Alfred L. H 166, 985
Roy, Ralph Lord R 267
Royster, Charles H 239
Rubel, Arthur J. A-F 287
Rubel, Paula G. A-F 134
Rubin, Barry PS 769
Rubin, Irene PS 347
Rubin, Israel A-F 135
Rubin, Joan L 623
Rubin, Lillian B. SOC 312, 441,
  498
Rubin, Louis D. L 386-388, 534,
  624-625
Rubin, Morton A-F 136
Rubin, Richard L. PC 686; PS 463
Rubin, Steven Jay PC 586
Rubinstein, Charlotte Streifer
  A-A 119
Ruble, D. PSY 72
Rublowsky, John A-A 120; M 29
Ruby, Robert H. H 1232-1233
Rucker, Bruce W. PC 687
Rucker, Egbert Darnell H 669
Rudich, Norman L 626
Rudisill, Richard STM 325
Rudolph, B. G. H 986
Rudolph, Frederick H 670
Rudwick, Elliott H 1063, 1077,
  1603; SOC 180
Ruehlmann, William PC 163
Ruether, Rosemary Radford R 245-
  246
Ruland, Richard L 389
Rule, James PS 559
Rumberger, Russell PS 309
Rumlet, Richard P. H 1779
Rusk, Ralph Leslie L 184
Russell, Don PC 389
Russell, Francis H 1979
Russell, Howard S. H 1234, 1500
Russell, John A-A 121
Russell, Ross M 331
Russell, Tony M 239

Russett, Bruce M. PS 770-771
Russett, Cynthia Eagle STM 326-327
Russianoff, Penelope PSY 153
Russo, Vito PC 587
Rust, Art, Jr. PC 991
Rutland, Robert A. H 36; PC 903
Rutman, Darrett B. H 167-168; R 40
Ruzek, Sheryl Burt SOC 380
Ryan, Mary P. H 806-808
Ryan, William PSY 154
Ryerson, Richard H 240

Sabato, Larry J. PS 464
Sabini, John PSY 155
Sablosky, Irving L. M 102
Sachs, Carolyn E. SOC 587
Sadler, Julius Trousdale, Jr. A-A 480
Safa, Helen Ichen A-F 63, 288
Safford, Carleton L. A-A 418
Safran, Nadav PS 772
Sager, Clifford J. PSY 156
Sagi, Abraham PSY 119
Saint-Gaudens, Homer A-A 122
Saldich, Anne Rawley PC 808
Sale, Kirkpatrick H 523
Sale, Roger PC 132
Salisbury, Neal H 1235
Salisbury, Richard R. A-F 137
Saloutos, Theodore H 524, 1501
Salsbury, Stephen H 1667, 1780
Salt, Barry PC 588
Saltzgaber, Jan M. H 1406
Samora, Julien H 987; SOC 207
Sampson, Henry T. PC 390, 589
Samuels, Charles PC 391
Samuels, Louise PC 391
Samuels, Robert E. H 1698
Sanday, Peggy Reeves A-F 333
Sandeen, Ernest R. R 282
Sandel, Michael PS 53
Sander, Ellen M 428
Sanders, Ronald H 988
Sanderson, Richard Arlo PC 590
Sandler, Irving A-A 123, 228
Sandler, Martin W. PC 740
Sandmaier, Marian SOC 652
Sandowsky, Alvin PSY 152
Sandoz, Ellis PS 465
Sandoz, Mari H 1236
Sands, Pierre N. PC 591
Sanford, Trent Elwood A-A 507
Sanger, Mary Bryna SOC 499
San Giovanni, Lucinda PC 926; SOC 334
Sann, Paul PC 57
Santayana, George L 627
Sargeant, Winthrop M 332

Sargent, Pamela PC 254
Sarna, Jonathan D. R 183
Sarotte, Georges-Michel L 628
Sarris, Andrew PC 592
Sarson, Evelyn PC 809
Sasaki, Tom T. A-F 237
Satz, Ronald N. H 1237
Sauer, Carl Ortwin H 1238
Saum, Lewis O. H 1239; L 185
Saunders, Harold H. PS 773
Saunders, Richard H 1781
Savage, William W., Jr. H 1240-1241; M 429; PC 284
Savary, Louis M. M 430
Savelle, Max H 672-673
Saveth, Edward N. H 989
Savin, Marion B. STM 1
Savitt, Todd L. STM 328
Sawers, David STM 190
Sawhill, Isabel V. PS 372
Sayre, Nora PC 593
Sayre, Robert F. H 1242; L 629
Says, Mollie PSY 122
Scammon, Richard M. PS 466
Scanzoni, John H. SOC 208, 313
Scarborough, Dorothy M 190
Schach, Paul A-F 366
Schaeffer, Norma SOC 34
Schafer, Donna E. SOC 397
Schafer, Roy PSY 157
Schafer, William J. M 333-334, 431
Schaffer, Daniel A-A 625
Schapiro, Meyer A-A 229
Scharf, Lois H 809-810
Scharf, Peter SOC 653
Scharfman, Melvin A. PSY 82
Schattschneider, E. E. PS 498
Schatz, Ronald W. H 1626
Schatz, Thomas PC 594
Schauffler, Robert Haven M 30
Schaver, Frederick PS 54
Schechtman, Joseph PS 774
Scheele, Raymond L. A-F 290
Scheflen, Albert E. A-F 25
Scheiber, Harry N. H 1782
Scheick, William J. L 186
Scheiner, Seth M. H 1078
Schelling, Thomas C. PS 775
Schendel, Dan E. SOC 610
Schevitz, Jeffrey M. SOC 588
Schick, Frank PC 94
Schickel, Richard M 103; PC 595-596
Schiesl, Martin J. H 1379
Schiffer, Margaret Berwind A-A 419
Schiller, Dan PC 904
Schiller, Herbert I. PC 688
Schilpp, Madelon Golden H 811
Schlenker, Jon H 1194

Schlereth, Thomas J. PC 1042-1043
Schlesinger, Arthur M., Jr.
  H 378, 525-528, 674-675
Schlesinger, Arthur M., Sr.
  H 241
Schlissel, Lillian H 812
Schmandt, Henry J. SOC 23
Schmookler, Jacob STM 329
Schnaiberg, Allan SOC 500
Schneer, Cecil J. STM 330
Schneider, David M. A-F 64
Schneider, Herbert Wallace H 676;
  R 129
Schneider, John C. H 1380
Schneider, Joseph W. SOC 617
Schneider, Louis PC 95
Schneider, William PS 348
Schnier, Jacques Preston A-A 263
Schoen, Cathy SOC 454
Schoenberg, Sandra Perlman
  SOC 62
Schoener, Allon H 990
Schofield, Janet Ward SOC 209
Scholes, Percy A. M 104
Scholes, Robert L 390; PC 255-
  256, 259
Schon, Donald A. STM 331
Schooler, Carmi SOC 559
Schorer, Mark L 391
Schrag, Peter SOC 210
Schram, Glenn N. PS 55
Schramm, Sarah Slavin H 813
Schramm, Wilbur PC 683, 689-691,
  810; PSY 158
Schreiber, Carol Tropp SOC 381
Schroeder, Gertrude G. H 1783
Schudson, Michael PC 905
Schuller, Gunter M 335
Schultz, Duane P. PSY 159
Schultz, George A. H 1243
Schultz, Lynn Hickey SOC 375
Schulz, David A. SOC 72
Schulz, Max F. L 630-631
Schumach, Murray PC 597
Schumpeter, Joseph A. H 1914
Schurr, Sam H. H 1654, 1784
Schusky, Ernest Lester A-F 238-
  239
Schuyler, Hamilton STM 332
Schwab, Karen SOC 409
Schwabe, Calvin W. STM 333
Schwantes, Carlos A. H 1627
Schwartz, Anna J. H 1857-1858
Schwartz, David PS 561
Schwartz, Gary A-F 138
Schwartz, H. W. M 432
Schwartz, Marvin D. A-A 420, 426
Schwartz, Nancy Lynn PC 598
Schwartz, Pepper PSY 23
Schwartz, Sandra PS 561
Schwartz, Sanford A-A 124

Schwartz, Tony PC 692, 811
Schwarz, Hans-Peter PS 689
Schwarz, Jordan A. H 1785
Schwarz, Meg PC 812
Schwieder, Dorothy H 1628
Scollon, Ronald A-F 240
Scollon, Suzanne B. K. A-F 240
Scott, Andrew MacKay H 815
Scott, Anne Firor H 814-815
Scott, Jack PC 992
Scott, John SOC 589
Scott, Marvin B. SOC 108
Scott, Mel H 1381
Scully, Diana SOC 382
Scully, Vincent J., Jr. A-A 445,
  508-509, 584, 626
Seal, John R. STM 377
Seale, William A-A 421, 464
Searing, Helen A-A 510
Sears, David O. PS 543
Sears, Robert R. STM 334
Seaton, Douglas P. H 1629
Sebeok, Thomas A. PC 145
Secord, Paul F. SOC 359
Seda, Elena Padilla A-F 290
Sedlak, Michael W. H 569, 1786
Seeger, Pete M 191
Seely, John R. A-F 139
Seelye, John L 77
Seeman, Helene Zucker A-A 221
Segal, Charles M. R 255
Segal, Geraldine R. SOC 211
Segalman, Ralph SOC 501
Seilhamer, George O. L 23
Seip, Terry L. H 379
Seitz, William Chapin A-A 230,
  264
Selby, Henry A. A-F 3
Seldes, Gilbert PC 59, 693
Sellers, Charles Coleman STM 335
Selzer, Michael PS 776
Selznick, Gertrude J. SOC 212
Selznick, Philip PS 382
Semmingsen, Ingrid H 991
Sen, Amartya PS 56
Seninge, Stephen F. SOC 172
Senior, Clarence SOC 181
Sennett, Richard H 1382, 1389;
  SOC 502
Seranton, Philip H 1915
Serban, George PSY 160
Sernett, Milton C. R 232
Servan-Schreiber, Jean-Louis
  PC 694
Sessions, Gene A. R 219
Sessions, Roger M 105-107
Severens, Kenneth A-A 511
Sewell, Richard H. H 380
Sexton, Patricia Cayo SOC 213,
  590
Seymour, Flora Warren H 1244

Seymour, Harold PC 993
Shade, William G. H 748
Shadoian, Jack PC 599
Shadwell, Wendy J. A-A 274
Shafer, Henry Burnell STM 336
Shaffer, William R. PS 467
Shahan, Robert W. H 640
Shale, Richard PC 600
Shanabruch, Charles R 184
Shanet, Howard M 108-109
Shannon, Fred A. H 381
Shannon, Lyle SOC 214
Shannon, Magdaline SOC 214
Shannon, William V. H 992
Shapiro, David A-A 231
Shapiro, Henry D. H 677
Shapiro, Judah H 993
Shapiro, Nat M 336-337
Shapiro, Yonathan H 994
Share, Allen J. H 1502
Sharfman, I. Harold H 995
Sharkansky, Ira PS 317, 383
Sharkey, Robert P. H 1916
Sharlin, Harold Issadore H 1917
Sharp, Willoughby A-A 265
Shatzkin, Roger PC 566-567
Shaw, Arnold M 240-241, 338, 433
Shaw, Donald L. PC 906
Shaw, Lois Banfill SOC 442
Shaw, Peter L 78
Shayon, Robert Lewis PC 813-814
Shea, Daniel B. L 79
Shea, John G. A-A 423
Shead, Richard M 110
Shearer, Derek PS 309
Shecter, Leonard PC 994
Sheehan, Bernard W. H 1245;
  R 256
Sheehan, Margaret A. PC 685
Sheehan, Neil PS 777
Sheehy, Gail PSY 161
Shelly, Donald A. A-A 318
Shepherd, James F. H 1787, 1932-
  1933
Shepherd, John M 434
Shergold, Peter R. H 1630
Sherman, Frederic Fairchild
  A-A 178
Sherman, Michael SOC 654
Sherwin, Martin J. STM 337
Sherwood, Morgan B. STM 285
Sherwood, Roger A-A 622
Shibutani, Tamotsu SOC 655
Shields, Jerry STM 176
Shifflett, Crandall A. H 1503
Shindler, Colin PC 601
Shine, Ian STM 338
Shockley, John Staples H 996
Short, K. R. M. PC 602
Shover, John L. H 37
Shryock, Richard Harrison
  STM 20, 339-342

Shulman, Julius A-A 622
Shupe, Anson D. R 193; SOC 315
Shurr, William H. L 80
Shurtleff, Harold R. A-A 554
Sidorsky, David SOC 215
Sidran, Ben M 31
Sieber, R. Timothy A-F 65
Siegal, Harvey Alan SOC 63
Siegel, Adrienne PC 96
Siegel, Irving H. SOC 591
Sienicka, Marta L 392
Siepmann, Charles Arthur PC 815
Sigal, Leon V. PC 907; PS 788
Silberman, Charles E. SOC 216
Silberstein, Richard A. SOC 295
Silbey, Joel PS 468
Silbey, Joel H. H 382
Silet, Charles L. P. PC 420
Silk, Leonard SOC 503
Silk, Mark PS 779; SOC 503
Silver, Maury PSY 155
Silverberg, Robert H 997
Silverman, Arnold R. SOC 272
Silverman, David Wolf PC 854
Silverman, Kenneth L 81
Sim, R. Alexander A-F 139
Simkins, Francis Butler H 816
Simmons, A. John PS 57
Simmons, Charles L 211
Simmons, Marc A-F 289
Simmons, Steven J. PC 816
Simon, George T. M 339, 435
Simon, Herbert A. PS 384
Simon, John PC 603
Simon, Rita James SOC 217-218,
  656-657
Simoni, Arnold PS 58
Simpson, Charles R. SOC 592
Simpson, Dick PS 469
Simpson, George Eaton R 233
Simpson, Ida Harper SOC 593
Simpson, Lewis L 632-633
Sinclair, Andrew H 817
Sinclair, Bruce STM 343-344
Sinclair, John M 340
Singal, Daniel Joseph L 393
Singer, Jerome PSY 14
Singer, Robert D. PC 756
Singh, Amritjit L 394
Singletary, O. H 383
Siracusa, Carl H 1631
Sitkoff, Harvard H 1079
Sitney, P. Adams PC 604-605
Sitterson, Joseph Carlyle H 1504
Sizer, Sandra S. R 77
Skaggs, Merrill Maguire L 634
Skardal, Dorothy Burton L 635
Sklar, Kathryn Kish R 247
Sklar, Robert PC 606, 817
Sklare, Marshall R 185; SOC 219-
  222

Skogan, Wesley G. SOC 658
Skolnick, Jerome H. SOC 659
Skolnik, Herman STM 345
Skornia, Harry J. PC 818
Skowronek, Stephen H 529
Sky, Alison A-A 512
Slater, Peter Gregg H 169
Slater, Philip E. PSY 162
Slawski, Edward J. PC 875
Slawson, John SOC 223
Sleeper, James A. SOC 224
Slide, Anthony PC 607
Sloan, Douglas H 678
Sloan, John A-A 15
Sloan Commission on Cable Communi-
    cations PC 819
Sloane, William PC 133
Slobin, Mark M 436
Slotkin, Richard L 636
Slout, William Lawrence PC 392
Slusser, George E. PC 258-259
Small, Kenneth A. SOC 25
Small, William PC 820
Smead, Elmer E. PC 821
Smelser, Marshall H 384
Smith, Abbot Emerson H 17
Smith, Alfred G. H 1505
Smith, Alice Kimball STM 346-347
Smith, Allan Gardner L 187
Smith, Anthony PC 695, 822, 908
Smith, Bernard L 24
Smith, Bill PC 393
Smith, C. Ray A-A 627
Smith, Carter STM 270
Smith, Cecil M 111; PC 394
Smith, Charles Edward M 327
Smith, Daniel H 530
Smith, Elwyn A. R 310
Smith, Frances Foster L 188
Smith, Gerard PS 780
Smith, H. Shelton R 21, 268
Smith, Henry Nash H 385; L 189-
    190
Smith, Herbert F. PC 97
Smith, James Morton H 171
Smith, James Ward R 22-23
Smith, John E. R 154
Smith, Julian PC 608
Smith, K. Wayne PS 630
Smith, Kathryn A-A 484
Smith, Leo M 341
Smith, Leverett T., Jr. PC 995
Smith, Merritt Roe STM 348
Smith, Page H 243, 818, 1506
Smith, Robert A-A 145
Smith, Robert A. STM 349
Smith, Roger PC 98
Smith, Ronald A. PC 970
Smith, Stan L 395
Smith, Timothy L. R 78
Smith, Valene L. A-F 140

Smith, Walter B. H 1918
Smoke, Richard PS 653
Smuts, Robert W. H 819
Snetsinger, John PS 781
Snodgrass, Jon SOC 660
Snow, Robert P. PC 696
Snyder, Richard C. PS 755
Snyder, Robert L. PC 609
Sobchack, Vivian PC 610
Sobel, Bernard PC 395
Sobel, Robert H 1788-1789;
    PC 697
Sochem, June H 820-821
Sofaer, Abraham D. PS 782
Sokol, David M. A-A 29
Sokol, Martin L. M 112
Sokoloff, Natalie J. SOC 383
Solberg, Wintor U. R 41
Solmon, Lewis C. SOC 594
Solomon, Stanley J. PC 611
Solotorovsky, Morris STM 221
Soltow, James H. H 1912
Soltow, Lee H 1919-1920
Somers, Dale A. PC 996
Sonheim, Alan A-A 126
Sonneck, Oscar George Theodore
    M 113-114
Sonnedecker, Glenn STM 350
Sonnichsen, C. L. PC 285
Sontag, Frederick R 153
Sorauf, Frank PS 470
Sorensen, Thomas C. PS 783
Sorin, Gerald H 386
Sorkin, Alan L. SOC 225
Sorlin, Pierre PC 612
Sosin, Jack M. H 172-173
Sostek, Anita M. PSY 69
Souchon, Edmond M 330
Soule, George H. H 1921
South, Stanley A-F 66
Southern, Eileen M 32
Sowell, Thomas H 998; PS 562
Spaeth, Sigmund M 30, 437-438
Spain, Rufus B. R 111
Spalding, Walter Raymond M 115
Spanier, John PS 784-786
Spann, Edward K. H 1383
Spatz, Jonas PC 613
Speaight, George PC 396-397
Spear, Allan H. H 1080
Spears, Jack PC 614
Spell, Lota M. M 33
Spellman, A. B. M 342
Spence, Barbara Barrow H 1693
Spence, Clark C. STM 351
Spencer, Benjamin T. L 191, 396
Spencer, Frank STM 352
Spencer, Robert F. A-F 241
Spender, Stephen L 637
Spengemann, William C. L 638
Sper, Felix L 639

Sperounis, Frederick P. SOC 314
Spicer, Edward H. A-F 67-68, 242-243, 334; H 1246
Spies, Werner A-A 127
Spiller, Robert E. L 25-26, 640-642
Spindler, George D. A-F 69, 244, 335-337
Spindler, Louise A-F 69, 244
Spitz, Robert Stephen M 439
Spitze, Glenna SOC 363
Spivey, Ted R. L 397
Spoto, Donald PC 615
Spradley, James P. A-F 70, 141-142
Sprafkin, Joyce N. PSY 163
Spragens, Thomas A. PS 59
Spragens, William C. PC 823
Sprague, John D. PS 72
Springer, Marlene L 643
Sproat, John G. H 387
Spruill, Julia Cherry H 822
Spuhler, J. N. PSY 127
Spykman, Nicholas PS 787
Sredl, Katherine SOC 22
Srole, Loe A-F 143, 158
St. Claire, Leonard SOC 595
Staats, Arthur W. PSY 164
Stacey, William A. SOC 315
Stack, Carol B. A-F 100, 192
Stack, John F., Jr. H 999
Stage, Sarah STM 353
Staicar, Tom PC 260
Staines, Graham L. SOC 317
Stampp, Kenneth M. H 388-390, 1081
Stands in Timber, John H 1186
Stanford, Charles L. L 644
Stanford, G. S. STM 95
Stanley, Liz SOC 384
Stanley, Robert H. PC 698
Stanley, Peter PS 792
Stanley, Timothy M. PS 736
Stannard, David H 38, 174
Stanton, Phoebe B. A-A 585
Stanton, William STM 354-355
Staples, Robert SOC 385-387
Starck, Kenneth PC 900
Starobin, Robert S. H 1082
Starr, Kevin L 192
Stastny, Charles SOC 661
Stasz, Clarice SOC 505
Staudenraus, P. J. H 1083
Stauffer, Donald Barlow L 27
Stauffer, Helen Winter PC 286
Stave, Bruce M. H 1384
Stavins, Ralph L. PC 824
Stearns, Jean M 344
Stearns, Marshall M 343-344
Stearns, Mary Lee A-F 245
Stearns, Raymond P. STM 356

Stebbins, Theodore E., Jr. A-A 275
Steckmesser, Kent Ladd PC 287
Stedman, Raymond William H 1247
Steed, Robert P. H 1411, 1484
Steere, Geoffrey H. SOC 397
Stegner, Wallace H 1507
Stein, Arthur SOC 238
Stein, Benjamin PC 60
Stein, Harry H. PC 867
Stein, Herbert H 531
Stein, Herman O. SOC 127
Stein, Howard F. A-F 71
Stein, Leon H 1632
Stein, Robert PC 699
Stein, Roger B. A-A 128; H 680
Steinberg, Charles S. PC 698, 700
Steinberg, Leo A-A 129
Steinberg, Ronnie H 1633
Steinberg, Stephen SOC 212, 226
Steinbruner, John D. PS 788
Steiner, Gary A. PC 825
Steinmann, Anne PSY 165
Steinmetz, Suzanne K. SOC 318
Steinson, Barbara J. H 823
Stekert, Ellen J. A-F 448
Stellman, Jeanne Mager H 824
Stengel, Robert PC 785
Stepto, Robert L 506, 524, 645
Sterba, James PS 60
Stern, Madeleine B. H 391; PC 99
Stern, Mark J. H 1881
Stern, Nancy STM 357
Stern, Robert A. M. A-A 513, 628-629
Stern, Stephen A-F 454
Sterner, Richard SOC 186
Stevens, John D. PC 657
Stevens, Rosemary STM 358
Stevenson, Robert M 34
Stevick, Phillip L 398
Steward, Julian H. A-F 290
Stewart, A. SOC 578
Stewart, Abigail J. PSY 166
Stewart, Debra W. SOC 388
Stewart, Grace L 646
Stewart, R. F. PC 164
Stewart, Randall L 647
Stewart, Rex M 345
Stewart-Baxter, Derrick M 242
Stilgoe, John R. A-A 514; STM 359
Stillerman, Richard STM 190
Stillinger, Elizabeth A-A 424
Stimpson, Catharine B. H 825
Stineback, David C. R 255
Stobaugh, Robert PS 789
Stocking, George W., Jr. A-F 5, STM 360
Stoddard, Karen M. PC 616

Stoever, William K. R 42
Stoff, Michael B. H 532
Stokes, Anson Phelps R 311
Stokes, Donald E. PS 420-421
Stokes, Geoffrey M 440
Stoll, Clarice Stasz SOC 389
Stone, Alan H 1922; PS 349
Stone, Gregory P. PC 100
Stone, Michelle A-A 512
Stone, Ralph H 533
Storey, Edward A-F 314
Storey, Walter Rendell A-A 425
Stott, William A-A 349
Stoudt, John Joseph A-A 130, 319
Stout, Janis P. L 648
Stoutamire, Albert M 116
Stovall, Floyd L 28
Stover, Donald W., Jr. PS 386
Stover, John F. H 1790; STM 361-363
Stowe, William W. PC 158
Straight, Michael PS 387
Strand, Mark A-A 232
Strange, Adeline Cook H 1667
Strasser, Susan H 826
Strassmann, Wolfgang Paul STM 364
Strauman, Heinrich L 399
Straus, Murray A. SOC 318
Street, David SOC 462, 596
Street, James H. H 1508
Strickland, Donald A. STM 365
Strickland, Rennard H 1248
Strickland, Stephen PC 739
Strickland, Stephen P. STM 366
Strodbeck, Fred L. A-F 14
Strouse, James C. PC 701
Strout, Cushing H 681-683; L 649; R 24
Struick, Dirk J. STM 367
Struyk, Raymond J. PS 388
Stryker, Roy A-A 350
Stuart, Paul H 1249
Stuart, Reginald C. H 684
Stub, Holger R. SOC 443
Stubbs, G. T. PC 114
Stuckey, W T. PC 101
Studensky, Paul H 1923
Stupak, Ronald J. PS 363
Suchman, Edward A. SOC 242
Sudnow, David A-F 144
Sue, Stanley A-F 338
Sugar, Maurice H 1634
Sugarman, Barry A-F 145
Suid, Lawrence H. PC 617
Sullivan, Daniel J. SOC 107
Sullivan, John L. PS 457
Sullivan, Teresa A. SOC 597
Sullivan, Theodore L. SOC 453
Sundquist, Eric J. L 193-194
Sundquist, James L. PS 471

Supple, Barry E. H 1723
Surrey, David S. SOC 662
Susser, Ida SOC 64
Sutch, Richard H 1074, 1911
Sutherland, Anne A-F 146
Sutherland, Daniel E. H 1635
Sutherland, Edwin H. SOC 663
Sutherland, John PC 102
Suttles, Gerald D. SOC 462
Sutton, Francis X. H 1791
Sutton, Walter L 400, 650
Sutton-Smith, Brian A-F 2
Suvin, Darko PC 241, 261
Swain, Donald C. STM 285, 368
Swain, Doug A-A 515
Swan, John C. M 117
Swan, L. Alex SOC 319
Swank, Scott T. A-A 131; A-F 451
Swann, Charles E. PC 663
Swann, Leonard A., Jr. H 1792
Swanson, Roger PS 790
Swartz, Jon D. A-F 313
Sweet, Leonard I. R 248
Sweet, William Warren R 43, 79
Sweezy, Paul PS 509
Swenson, Loyd S., Jr. STM 46, 369
Swenson, Robert W. H 1951
Swerdlow, Joel PC 787
Swierenga, Robert P. H 1793
Swift, Carolyn PSY 163
Swoboda, Henry M 118
Sylla, Richard E. H 1794, 1912
Symons, Julian PC 165
Syndor, Charles S. H 244
Szajkowski, Zosa H 1000
Szanton, Peter PS 573
Szarkowski, John A-A 351-352
Szasz, Ferenc Morton R 112
Szasz, Margaret C. H 1250
Szasz, Thomas S. PSY 168-170
Szatmary, David P. H 245
Szwed, John F. A-F 197

Taft, John SOC 320
Taft, Lorado A-A 239
Taft, Philip H 1636-1637
Taft, Robert A-A 132, 333
Tageson, C. William PSY 171
Talbot, Daniel PC 618
Talbot, David PC 644
Talbot, George A-A 334
Talbott, G. Douglas SOC 664
Tallmadge, Thomas E. A-A 516
Tangri, Sandra Schwartz SOC 374
Tanis, James R 64
Tanner, Paul O. W. M 346
Tanner, Tony L 401, 651
Targ, Dena B. SOC 645
Tashjian, Ann A-A 246

Tashjian, Dickran A-A 133, 246;
L 402
Tate, Allen L 403
Tate, Thad W. H 175
Tatum, George B. A-A 145, 517,
555
Tatum, Stephen PC 288
Taubman, Howard L 29
Tawa, Nicholas E. M 35, 441
Taylor, Arthur M 347
Taylor, Billy M 348
Taylor, George Rogers H 1795,
1924-1925
Taylor, Gordon O. L 195
Taylor, Graham D. H 1251
Taylor, John Russell PC 398
Taylor, Joshua Charles A-A 49,
134-135
Taylor, Paul S. SOC 227
Taylor, Philip H 1001
Taylor, Robert J. H 176
Taylor, Sherril W. PC 826
Taylor, Theodore B. PS 659
Taylor, Walter Fuller L 30-31
Taylor, William R. L 652
Tax, Meredith H 827
Teaford, Jon C. H 1385-1386
Tebbel, John PC 702, 909
Tedlow, Richard S. H 1796
Tefft, Stanton K. A-F 72
Telander, Rick PC 997
Temin, Peter H 1797, 1926-1928;
STM 370
Tentler, Leslie Woodcock H 828
Terborg-Penn, Rosalyn H 757
Terkel, Studs (Louis) H 534;
M 349; SOC 65, 598
Teske, Robert Thomas A-F 455
Thach, Charles C. H 246
Thayer, Frederick PS 389
Thayer, H. S. H 685
Thayer, Lee PC 703
Theodoratus, Robert James
A-F 147
Thernstrom, Stephan H 1387-1389
Thielbar, Gerald W. A-F 34
Thigpen, Kenneth A. A-F 456
Thistlethwaite, Frank H 392
Thom, Gary PS 61
Thomas, Dana L. PC 910
Thomas, Dorothy Swaine A-F 339-
340; H 1888
Thomas, Emory M. H 393
Thomas, Isaiah PC 911
Thomas, John L. PS 62
Thomas, Lorenzo M 218
Thomas, Robert J. H 1690
Thomas, Sari PC 619
Thomas, William I. SOC 228
Thomas-Lycklama a Nijeholt, G.
SOC 506

Thompson, Daniel C. SOC 229
Thompson, Don PC 315, 319
Thompson, Frank J. STM 371
Thompson, G. R. L 196
Thompson, Gerald H 1252
Thompson, Harold W. A-F 457
Thompson, James C. PS 791-792
Thompson, James J. R 113
Thompson, Kenneth W. PS 663, 793-
795
Thompson, Oscar M 119
Thompson, Robert Luther STM 372
Thompson, Roger H 829
Thompson, Stith A-F 458
Thomson, David PC 620
Thomson, Henry Douglas PC 166
Thomson, Raymond H. A-F 68
Thomson, Virgil M 120
Thorelli, Hans B. H 1798
Thorman, George SOC 321
Thorndike, Robert M. PSY 27
Thornton, J. Mills H 394
Thornton, William E., Jr.
SOC 665
Thorp, Margaret Farrand A-A 252;
PC 621
Thorp, Willard L 404
Thrasher, Frederic M. SOC 230
Thurow, Lester C. PS 499
Tice, James A-A 622
Tichener, Trebor Jay M 298
Tichi, Cecelia L 653
Tien, Hung-Mao PS 796
Tillman, Seth P. PS 797
Timmerman, John H. PC 182
Tindall, George Brown H 1509
Tipton, Steven M. R 117, 220
Tirro, Frank M 350
Titon, Jeff Todd M 243
Tobey, Ronald C. STM 373-374
Tobin, James H 1791
Toeplitz, Jerzy PC 622
Tolchin, Martin PS 391
Tolchin, Susan PS 391
Toldson, Ivory L. PSY 143
Toll, Robert C. PC 399-401
Toll, William H 1002, 1084
Tolles, Frederick B. H 1799
Tomasi, Silvano M. H 1003
Tomaskovic-Devery, Donald PS 359;
SOC 571
Tomkins, Calvin A-A 136
Tomlinson, Charles L 405
Tomsich, John H 395
Torre, Susana A-A 518
Torrens, Paul R. SOC 599
Tosches, Nick M 192
Tostlebe, Alvin S. H 1800
Toth, Emily H 726
Tow, William T. PS 798
Townsend, John Rowe PC 134

Towsen, John H. PC 402
Trachtenberg, Alan H 396, 1390
Tracy, Berry B. A-A 137, 426
Tracy, Patricia J. R 65
Trask, David F. H 397
Trattner, Walter I. PS 392
Travis, David A-A 353
Travis, Dempsey M 351
Trefousse, Hans L. H 398
Trejo, Arnulfo D. A-F 291
Tremblay, Kenneth R., Jr.
    SOC 66
Trennert, Robert A., Jr. H 1254-
    1255
Trent, Robert F. A-F 459
Trent, William Peterfield L 32
Trenton, Patricia A-A 138
Trescott, Martha Moore STM 375
Trescott, Paul B. H 1801
Trigger, Bruce G. A-F 246
Trilling, Lionel L 654
Trini, Styllianoss SOC 647
Trinterud, Leonard J. R 66
Trow, Martin A. PS 486
Troyen, Carol A-A 275
Troyer, Ronald J. SOC 666
Truettner, William H. A-A 139
Truman, David B. PS 500
Truzzi, Marcello A-F 51; PC 61
Tseng, Wen-Sheng PSY 172
Tucci, Douglass Shand A-A 519
Tuchman, Barbara PS 799
Tuchman, Gaye PC 704, 827, 912
Tuchman, Maurice A-A 233, 266
Tucker, Frank H. PC 705
Tucker, G. S. L. H 18
Tucker, Marcia A-A 215
Tucker, Nicholas PC 135
Tucker, Robert W. H 247; PS 742-
    743, 800
Tucker, William SOC 507
Tudor, Andrew PC 623
Tullock, Gordon PS 71
Tullos, Allen A-F 460
Tully, Alan H 177
Tunis, Edwin STM 376
Tunis, John PC 998
Tunnard, Christopher A-A 520
Tunstall, Jeremy PC 706
Turner, Frederick M 352
Turner, Frederick Jackson H 1510
Turner, Geoffrey H 1256
Turner, Lorenzo Dow L 655
Turner, Paul R. A-F 367
Turner, Paul V. A-A 586
Turner, Samuel M. PSY 173
Turow, Joseph PC 828
Tushnet, Mark V. H 1980
Tuska, Jon PC 624
Tuttleton, James W. L 656
Tuveson, Ernest Lee R 289

Twin, Stephanie L. PC 999
Twombly, Wells PC 1000
Tygiel, Jules PC 1001
Tyler, Alice Felt H 399
Tyler, Moses Coit L 82-83
Tyler, Parker PC 625-626
Tyrnauer, Gabrielle SOC 661
Tyson, James PS 801

U.S. Congress, Committee on Foreign
    Affairs, Subcommittee on Africa
    PS 802
U.S. Congress, Senate Committee
    on Foreign Relations PS 803
Udell, Jon G. PC 913
Udelson, Joseph H. PC 829
Uhlman, Thomas M. SOC 231
Ulanov, Barry M 353-354; PC 27,
    62
Ullman, Joseph C. SOC 535
Ulman, Lloyd H 1638
Ulmer, Melville J. H 1802
Ulrich, Carolyn F. L 313
Ulrich, Laurel H 830
Umphlett, Wiley Lee L 657
Underhill, Ruth M. A-F 247;
    H 1257-1258; M 193
Underwood, Kenneth Wilson SOC 67
Unger, Irwin H 535; H 1929
Unger, Rhoda Kessler PSY 174
Unrau, William H 1199
Unruh, David R. SOC 444
Unterbrink, Mary M 355
Upton, L. F. S. H 1259
Upton, William Treat M 121
Urban, Wayne J. H 1639
Urofsky, Melvin I. H 1004
Uselding, Paul J. H 1836
Usher, Dan PS 563
Uslander, Eric M. PS 786
Utley, Robert M. H 1511, 1260,
    1267
Utter, Robert Palfrey PC 197

Vaillant, George C. A-A 16
Valentine, Bettylou A-F 194
Valentine, Charles A. A-F 195,
    341
Valines, Stuart PSY 14
Valliant, George E. PSY 175
Van Alstyne, Richard W. H 248,
    400
Van Arsdale, Peter W. A-F 325
Van Deusen, Glyndon H 401
Van Doren, Carl L 33
Van Heyningen, W. E. STM 377
Van Horn, Carl E. PS 393
Van Ness, John R. A-F 115
Van Ravenswaay, Charles A-A 587;
    PC 1044

Van Tassel, David D. STM 378
Van Til, Jon SOC 68
Van Tine, Warren R. H 1640
Van Vechten, Carl M 122
Varady, David P. SOC 232
Varian, Elayne H. A-A 268
Varma, Devendra PC 198
Vassal, Jacques M 194
Vatter, Harold G. H 1930-1931
Vaughan, Alden T. H 178-179, 1261;
  R 257
Vaughan, Thomas A-A 521
Vaughn, Jack A. L 34
Vedder, Clyde B. SOC 440
Vedder, Richard K. H 1467
Vendler, Helen L 406
Venturi, Robert A-A 630
Verba, Sidney PS 453, 472
Verhoff, Joseph PSY 176-177
Vermeule, Cornelius A-A 427
Vernier, Paul PS 307
Vernon, Raymond PS 804
Vetrocq, Marcia E. A-A 586
Veysey, Laurence R. H 686;
  SOC 69
Victor, Richard H. K. PS 394
Vidich, Arthur J. SOC 448
Vietze, Peter PSY 69
Vieyra, Daniel I. A-A 631
Vigil, James D. A-F 292
Vigtel, Gudmund A-A 282
Viguera, Ruth Hill PC 128
Vincent, Ted PC 1002
Vinovskis, Maris A. H 39
Viola, Herman J. H 1262
Viorst, Milton H 536
Viteritti, Joseph P. PS 395
Vlach, John Michael A-A 428;
  A-F 461
Vlahos, Michael PS 805
Vogel, Amos PC 627
Vogel, Morris J. STM 379-380
Vogel, Virgil J. STM 381
Vogeler, Ingolf H 1803
Voget, Fred W. A-F 23
Vogt, Evon Z. A-F 73, 148-149
Voight, David Q. PC 1003-1004
Von Breton, Harriette A-A 600
Vorspan, Max H 1005
Vos, Nelvin L 407
Voss, Arthur L 35
Voss, Frederick STM 252
Voss, John STM 279
Vulliamy, Graham M 356

Wachorst, Wyn STM 382
Wacker, Peter O. A-A 588
Wacker, R. Fred SOC 233
Waddell, Jack O. A-F 248-249
Wade, Nicholas SOC 612

Wade, Richard C. H 1085, 1352,
  1391
Wadlington, Warwick L 658
Wagar, W. Warren PC 262
Wagenknecht, Edward L 36; PC 628
Wagensteen, Sarah D. STM 385
Waggoner, Hyatt H. L 37, 408,
  659
Wagner, Geoffrey PC 63
Wagner, Jon SOC 390
Wagner, Linda N. L 409
Wagoner, Harless D. H 1804
Wakelyn, Jon L. H 1475; R 89
Walcutt, Charles Child L 660
Waldmeir, Joseph J. PC 299
Waldo, Dwight PS 396
Waldo, Terry M 357
Walker, Alexander PC 629-631
Walker, Charles R. A-F 328
Walker, Cheryl L 661
Walker, Clarence E. R 234
Walker, David A. H 1805
Walker, Deward E., Jr. A-F 250-
  251
Walker, Don D. H 1806
Walker, Katherine Sorley PC 147
Walker, Lester A-A 522
Walker, Mort PC 320
Walker, Robert H. H 402; PC 103
Walker, Samuel H 1392
Walker, Savannah Waring PC 730
Walker, Wyatt Lee M 195
Walkowitz, Daniel J. H 1641
Wallace, Anthony F. C. A-F 252;
  H 1263; STM 383
Wallace, Ernest H 1264
Wallace, Phyllis A. SOC 250
Wallace, Ronald L 410
Walsh, Jeffrey L 411
Walsh, Margaret H 1807
Walsh, Mary Roth SOC 600
Walsh, Richard H 249
Walshok, Mary Lindenstein H 1642
Walters, Ronald G. H 403;
  STM 384
Walton, Gary M. H 1706, 1787,
  1911, 1932-1933
Walton, Ortiz M 36
Walzer, Michael PS 63-64
Wandersee, Winifred H 831
Wangensteen, Owen H. STM 385
Warch, Richard H 180
Ward, David H 1394
Ward, Scott PC 714
Ware, Caroline F. H 1395, 1808
Ware, Charles Richard M 202
Ware, Norman J. H 1643
Ware, Susan H 832-833
Waring, Janet A-A 429
Warken, Philip W. H 1934
Warner, Alan PC 494

Warner, John Anson A-A 17
Warner, Sam Bass, Jr. H 1396-1398
Warner, W. Lloyd A-F 74, 151-158
Warren, Donald I. SOC 508
Warren, James Belasco H 1809
Warren, Roland L. SOC 70
Warrick, Patricia S. PC 263-264
Warshow, Robert PC 632
Warwick, Edward PC 1045
Washburn, Wilcomb E. H 1265-1267
Washington, Joseph R., Jr. R 235-236
Wasko, Janet PC 633
Waskow, Arthur I. SOC 235
Wasserstrom, Richard A. PS 65
Wasserstrom, William PC 104
Waterman, Robert H., Jr. SOC 577
Waterman, Thomas Tileston A-A 556
Waters, Donald J. A-F 462
Watkins, Lura Woodside A-A 430
Watson, Gregg A-F 174
Watson, O. Michael A-F 249
Watson, Richard L. H 12
Wattenberg, Ben J. PS 466
Watters, David H. A-A 247
Watts, Ann Chalmers L 548
Watts, Emily Stipes L 662
Watts, Thomas D. PSY 178
Waugh, Coulton PC 321
Wax, Murray PSY 179
Waxman, Chaim I. SOC 236
Wayne, Michael H 404
Wayne, Stephen PS 121, 473
Weales, Gerald L 412
Weaver, Paul PS 40
Weaver, Robert B. PC 1005
Weaver, Thomas A-F 75
Weaver, W. Timothy SOC 322
Webb, Stephen Saunders H 181
Webb, Walter P. H 1512-1513
Webber, Thomas L. H 1086
Weber, G. H. PSY 180
Weber, Ronald PC 301, 914
Weber, Timothy P. R 290
Webster, Grant L 414
Wechsler, Jeffrey A-A 234
Weeber, Stanley C. SOC 651
Weed, Perry L. SOC 237
Weglyn, Michi H 537
Weigle, Martha A-F 259, 293
Weigley, Russell H 40
Weil, Martin PS 806
Weiler, Lawrence PS 751
Weimer, David L 663
Weimer, David L. PS 397
Weinberg, Edgar SOC 591
Weinberg, Helen L 415
Weinberg, Martin S. SOC 391
Weinberg, Thomas S. SOC 392
Weiner, Charles STM 347

Weinstein, Allen H 538, 1935
Weinstein, James H 539-541
Weisband, Edward PS 641
Weisberg, Herbert F. PS 454
Weisberger, Bernard PC 915
Weisbord, Robert G. SOC 238
Weiss, Harry G. STM 386
Weiss, Melford S. A-F 159
Weiss, Nancy J. H 1087-1088
Weiss, Richard PC 105
Weiss, Robert S. SOC 323
Weiss, Thomas H 1827
Weisskopf, Tom PS 516
Weissman, Dick M 442
Weissman, Julia A-A 307
Weissman, Michaele H 763
Weitenkampf, Frank A-A 276
Weitze, Karen A-A 586
Wekerle, Gerda A-A 632
Welch, Richard E. H 542
Welch, Susan SOC 153
Weller, Robert H. H 1494
Welling, William B. A-A 335
Wells, Camille A-A 523
Wells, Katherine Gladney M 123
Wells, L. Jeanette M 124
Wells, Murray C. H 1810
Wells, Robert V. H 41, 182
Wellstone, Paul David SOC 530
Welsch, Janice R. PC 634
Welsch, Roger L. A-A 589; A-F 463-464
Welter, Barbara H 834-835
Welter, Rush H 687-688
Wepman, Dennis A-F 465
Weppner, Robert S. A-F 160
Werner, Craig Hansen L 416
Wertenbaker, Thomas Jefferson A-A 557-558
Wertham, Frederic PC 106
Wertheim, Arthur F. PC 830
Wertheim, Michael S. PC 11
Wertheimer, Barbara Mayer H 836
Wertz, Dorothy G. H 837
Wertz, Richard W. H 837
Weslager, C. A. A-A 524
West, James A-F 161
West, Ray B., Jr. L 417
West, Stanley A. A-F 294
West, Thomas L 418
Westbrook, Perry D. L 664
Westbrook, Wayne W. L 665
Westby, David L. SOC 324
Westfried, Alex Huxley SOC 239
Wetzel, Richard D. M 125
Wexler, Imanuel PS 807
Wexler, Philip PSY 181
Weyl, Nathaniel PS 501
Whalen, Charles W., Jr. PS 808
Whalley, Joyce Irene PC 136
Whannel, Paddy PC 28

Wheeler, William Bruce H 1479
Whetmore, Edward J. PC 64
Whiffen, Marcus A-A 525-526, 559-560
Whipple, Thomas King L 419
Whisnant, David E. H 1514-1515
Whitaker, Jennifer Seymour PS 809
Whitcomb, Ian M 443
White, David Manning PC 55, 65-66, 322, 635, 707
White, Edward M. PC 67
White, Eugene Nelson H 1936
White, G. Edward H 1981-1982
White, Gerald T. H 1811
White, John H., Jr. STM 387-388
White, John I. M 196
White, Leonard D. H 250, 405
White, Llewellyn PC 831
White, Lucia H 691
White, Margaret B. SOC 325
White, Morton H 251, 675, 689-691; R 155
White, Newman Ivey M 197
White, Philip L. H 1812
White, Richard A-F 253
White, Ronald C. R 114
White, Theodore H 543
Whitehill, Walter Muir A-A 431
Whiteman, Paul M 358
Whiting, Beatrice B. A-F 342
Whitt, J. Allen SOC 71
Whitten, Norman E. A-F 197
Wholstetter, Roberta PS 810
Whorton, James C. STM 389-390
Whyte, William Foote A-F 343-344; SOC 240
Whyte, William H., Jr. SOC 601
Wick, Wendy C. A-A 279
Wicker, Elmus R. H 1937
Wickes, George L 420
Wiebe, Robert H. H 42, 544-545
Wiecek, William M. H 1963
Wiener, Jonathan M. H 406
Wiener, Phillip P. H 692
Wik, Reynold M. STM 391-392
Wilcox, R. Turner PC 1046
Wilcox, Roger PSY 182
Wild, James H 693
Wildavsky, Aaron PS 398-399
Wilder, Alec M 444
Wilder, Amos N. L 421
Wilder, Mitchell A. A-A 320
Wiley, Bell I. H 407
Wilgus, D. K. A-F 466
Wilhelm, Hubert G. H. A-A 590
Wilkins, Mira H 1813-1814
Wilkins, Thurman H 1268
Willerman, Lee PSY 183
Williams, Benjamin Buford L 198
Williams, Bernard PS 56

Williams, Carol Traynor PC 636
Williams, Colin J. SOC 391
Williams, Frederick PC 834
Williams, Henry Lionel A-A 527
Williams, Hermann Warner, Jr. A-A 167
Williams, John E. A-F 76
Williams, Julia A-A 212
Williams, Kenny J. L 199
Williams, Lee E. H 1089
Williams, Lee E., II H 1089
Williams, Loretta J. SOC 241
Williams, Martin T. M 359-363
Williams, Melvin D. R 237
Williams, Ottalie K. A-A 527
Williams, Paul M 445
Williams, Peter W. A-F 77
Williams, Phyllis H. A-F 467
Williams, Richard H. PSY 184
Williams, Robin M., Jr. SOC 18, 242
Williams, T. Harry H 43, 408-410
Williams, Walter L. H 1269
Williams, William Appleman H 44-46
Williamson, Chilton H 694
Williamson, Edward C. PS 564
Williamson, Harold F. H 1786; STM 393-394
Williamson, Jack PC 265
Williamson, Jeffrey G. H 1938-1940
Williamson, Joel H 1090-1091
Willie, Charles Vert A-F 199; SOC 243, 326
Willrich, Mason PS 811
Wills, Garry H 252-253; PS 565
Wilmer, Valerie M 364
Wilmerding, John A-A 75, 141-143, 168-169
Wilmeth, Don B. PC 403-404
Wilmore, Gayraud S. R 156, 238-239
Wilson, Charles Reagan R 98
Wilson, Edmund L 38, 200, 422-429, 666
Wilson, Graham K. PS 502
Wilson, James Q. PS 400-401, 503
Wilson, Joan Hoff H 546
Wilson, John F. R 17, 299
Wilson, John Stewart M 365
Wilson, Kenneth M. A-A 432
Wilson, Margaret Gibbons H 838
Wilson, Richard Guy A-A 144, 591
Wilson, Robert A. SOC 72
Wilson, Robin Scott PC 266
Wilson, Ruth Mack M 126
Wilson, William J. SOC 244-245
Wiltse, Charles M. H 411
Winchester, Alice A-A 313
Winick, Charles PC 708

Winks, Robin W. PC 167-168
Winn, Marie PC 832
Winslow, Ola E. H 183
Winter, Robert A-A 633
Winters, Yvor L 430, 667-668
Wirths, Claudine G. PSY 184
Wirt, Frederick M. PS 402
Wischnitzer, Rachel A-A 528
Wise, Arthur PS 403
Wise, David PS 404
Wise, Jennings C. H 1270
Wise, Sue SOC 384
Wisely, William H. STM 395
Wishart, David J. H 1516
Wissler, Clark A-F 254-255
Wister, Francis Anne M 127
Witham, Barry L 236
Withers, Carl: see West, James
Witherspoon, Gary H 1271
Withey, Stephen B. PC 833
Witkin, H. PSY 185
Witney, Dudley A-A 435
Wittke, Carl H 1007-1008; PC 405
Wolcott, Harry F. A-F 345-346
Wolf, Bryan Jay A-A 197
Wolf, Daniel A-A 336
Wolf, David PC 1007
Wolf, Deborah Goleman A-F 163
Wolf, Eleanor P. SOC 246
Wolf, Eric R. A-F 290
Wolf, Frank PC 835
Wolf, Stephanie H 1399
Wolfe, Alan PS 66, 567, 812
Wolfe, Charles K. M 198-199
Wolfe, Don M. H 695
Wolfe, Gary K. PC 267-268
Wolfe, Richard A-A 420
Wolfe, Richard J. M 128
Wolfe, Thomas PS 813
Wolfe, Tom A-A 634; PC 303
Wolfenstein, Martha A-F 322;
    PC 637
Wolfinger, Raymond E. PS 474
Wolfram, Walt A-F 368
Wolfskill, George H 547
Wolgast, Elizabeth H. SOC 393
Woll, Allen L. PC 638-639
Wollen, Peter PC 640
Wollheim, Donald A. PC 269
Wolseley, Roland E. PC 916
Wolters, Raymond H 1092
Wong, Bernard P. A-F 164
Wood, Charles L. H 1816
Wood, Forrest G. H 412
Wood, Gordon S. H 254
Wood, James N. A-A 328
Wood, James Playsted PC 709
Wood, James R. SOC 558
Wood, Michael PC 641
Wood, Nancy A-A 350
Wood, Peter H. H 1093

Wood, W. Raymond A-F 256
Woodman, Harold D. H 1817
Woodruff, Diana S. PSY 186
Woods, Patricia Dillion H 1273
Woodward, C. Vann H 413, 1094,
    1517-1518
Woodward, Gloria PC 124-125
Woodward, Kathleen L 431
Woolf, Bob PC 1008
Work, John Wesley M 200
Worrall, Arthur J. H 184
Worster, Donald H 548
Wrenn, Tony P. A-A 489
Wright, Austin M. L 669
Wright, Calvin H 1818
Wright, Carroll D. H 839
Wright, Charles R. PC 710
Wright, Conrad R 157
Wright, Elliot R 87
Wright, Erik Olin SOC 509
Wright, Gwendolyn A-A 529, 592
Wright, Helen STM 396
Wright, J. Leitch, Jr. H 1272
Wright, James D. SOC 602, 667
Wright, Louis A-A 145; H 1519
Wright, Louis B. H 185-187
Wright, Luella L 84
Wright, Nathalia L 670
Wright, Paul PS 373
Wright, Roosevelt, Jr. PSY 178
Wright, Sonia R. SOC 602
Wright, Thomas Goddard L 85
Wright, Will PC 642
Wrobel, Paul A-F 165
Wrobel, Sylvia STM 338
Wrong, Dennis PS 67
Wroth, Lawrence C. L 86
Wyatt, David M. L 432
Wyatt-Brown, Bertram H 1520
Wyckoff, Alexander PC 1045
Wyllie, Irving PC 107
Wyrick, Waneen PC 944
Wytrwal, Joseph A. H 1009-1010

Yablonsky, Lewis SOC 327
Yaeger, Mary H 1819
Yaeger, Robert C. PC 1009
Yager, Joseph A. PS 814
Yankelovich, Daniel SOC 19-20
Yans-McLaughlin, Virginia H 1011
Yarmolinsky, Adam PS 405, 815
Yasuba, Yasukichi H 47
Yates, Douglas PS 365
Yates, Gayle Graham SOC 394
Yates, J. Frank PSY 26
Yates, Norris W. PC 304
Yatrakis, Kathryn B. H 825
Yeager, Peter C. SOC 615
Yearley, Clifton K., Jr. H 1644
Yergin, Daniel PS 789, 816

Yin, Robert K. SOC 73
Yoder, Don A-F 468; M 134, 201
Yorburg, Betty SOC 395
York, Herbert STM 397
Young, Alfred F. H 255-256
Young, James Harvey STM 398-399
Young, James Sterling H 1401
Young, Jock PC 650
Young, John A. SOC 603
Young, Oran R. PS 88
Young, Philip L 671
Young, Thomas Daniel L 433-435
Youngblood, Gene PC 643
Youngs, J. William T., Jr. R 67
Yu, Beongcheon L 672

Zablocki, Benjamin SOC 74
Zanzig, Augustus Delafield M 129
Zaretsky, Irving I. R 22
Zasloff, Joseph PS 817
Zaturenska, Marya L 297
Zautzevsky, Cynthia H 1402
Zavarzadeh, Masced L 436
Zeckhauser, Richard J. H 29
Zeidman, Irving PC 406
Zeigler, L. Harmon PS 504-505
Zeitlin, Steven J. A-F 469
Zelinsky, Wilbur A-F 78

Zelizer, Viviana A. Rotman
  SOC 604
Zellman, G. PSY 72
Zelman, Patricia G. H 840
Zerubavel, Eviatar SOC 605
Zheutlin, Barbara PC 644
Zicklin, Gilbert SOC 75
Zieger, Robert H. H 1645
Zietz, Dorothy SOC 768
Ziewacz, Lawrence E. PC 979
Ziff, Larzar L 87, 201-202
Zilbergeld, Bernie PSY 188
Zimilies, Martha A-A 531
Zimilies, Murray A-A 531
Zimmerman, Philip D. A-A 436
Zinberg, Norman E. PSY 189
Zlotnick, Joan L 673
Znaniecki, Florian SOC 228
Zoll, Donald Altwell H 697
Zorbaugh, Harvey W. SOC 247
Zube, Ervin H. A-A 532-533
Zube, Margaret J. A-A 533
Zuck, Barbara Ann M 130
Zucker, Paul STM 400
Zuckerman, Harriet STM 401
Zuckerman, Michael H 188
Zukin, Sharon SOC 76
Zunz, Olivier H 1403
Zur Heide, Karl Gert M 244
Zurier, Rebecca A-A 534

TITLE INDEX

19th-Century America: Furniture and Other Decorative Arts   A-A 426
80 Puerto Rican Families in New York City   A-F 258
110 Livingston Street   SOC 309
110 Livingston Street Revisited   SOC 310
200 Years of American Architectural Drawing   A-A 451
200 Years of American Graphic Art   A-A 271
200 Years of American Sculpture   A-A 240
200 Years of Sport in America   PC 1000
1947: When All Hell Broke Loose in Baseball   PC 922

AFL Attitudes Toward Production, 1900-1932   H 1599
The A.F. of L. from the Death of Gompers to the Merger   H 1636
The A.F. of L. in the Time of Gompers   H 1636
AMA: Voice of American Medicine   STM 57
A.T. & T.: The Story of Industrial Conquest   STM 87
Aaron Burr and the American Literary Imagination   L 171
Abolitionism: A New Perspective   H 386
The Abolitionists   H 287
Abortion in America   STM 255
The Absolute Weapon   PS 591
Abstract and Surrealist Art in America   A-A 216
Abstract Expressionism   A-A 214
Abstract Expressionist Painting in America   A-A 230
Abstract Painting: Background and American Phase   A-A 213
Abstract Painting and Sculpture in America   A-A 113
Abstract Painting and Sculpture in America, 1927-1944   A-A 81
The Absurd Hero in American Fiction   L 280
The Academic Revolution   SOC 286
Academic Women   SOC 521
Academy: The Academic Tradition in American Art   A-A 56
Accounting for Common Costs   H 1810
Accounting for United States Economic Growth, 1929-1969   H 1848
Acculturation in Seven American Indian Tribes   A-F 231
Achievement and Women: Challenging the Assumptions   PSY 110
Achievement in American Poetry, 1900-1950   L 230
Acoma   H 1200
Across the Pacific   PS 681
Across the Tracks   A-F 287
Across the Wide Missouri   H 1441
Action for Children's Television   PC 809
Adjustment to Empire   H 116
Administrative Behavior   PC 384
The Administrative State   PS 396
The Adolescent Passage   PSY 21
Adolescent Sexuality in a Changing American Society   PSY 49
The Adolescent Society   SOC 267
The Adoption of Black Children   SOC 106
Adult Illiteracy in the United States   SOC 284
Advances in Environmental Psychology   PSY 14
Advances in Self Psychology   PSY 83
The Advancing South   H 1483
Adventure in Freedom   H 930
Adventure, Mystery, and Romance   PC 72
Adventures in Medical Research   STM 160
Adventures of a Ballad Hunter   M 169
The Adventurous Decade   PC 311

The Adventurous Muse L 638
The Adversaries: Politics and the Press PC 898
Advertising and Social Change SOC 520
The Advisors: Oppenheimer, Teller, and the Superbomb STM 397
Advocacy & Objectivity: A Crisis in the Professionalism of American Social
    Science, 1865-1905 STM 132
Affairs of Party H 259
Affairs of State: Public Life in Late 19th Century America H 327
Affirmative Discrimination SOC 126
The Affluent Society H 1859
Africa and the United States PS 809
The African Colonization Movement, 1816-1863 H 1083
The African Roots of Jazz M 300
Africans and Creeks H 1188
Africans and Seminoles H 1189
Afro-American Anthropology A-F 197
Afro-American Art and Craft A-A 35
The Afro-American Artist A-A 55
Afro-American Folk Art and Crafts A-F 408
Afro-American Folk Songs M 166
Afro-American Literature L 506
The Afro-American Periodical Press: 1838-1909 PC 848
The Afro-American Tradition in Decorative Arts A-A 428
The Afro-American Woman H 757
After Alienation L 328
After the Clean-Up: Long Range Effects of Natural Disasters SOC 602
After Freedom: A Cultural Study in the Deep South A-F 190
After Innocence L 368
After Secession H 293
After Slavery H 1090
After the Ball M 443
After the Genteel Tradition L 258
After the Hunt A-A 187
After the Lost Generation L 206
After the Revolution L 55
Against Our Will: Men, Women and Rape PSY 32
An Age of Criticism: 1900-1950 L 364
The Age of Energy H 613
The Age of Giant Corporations H 1788
The Age of Jackson H 378
The Age of Reconnaissance H 157
The Age of Reform H 476
The Age of Rock M 380
The Age of Rock, 2 M 381
The Age of Roosevelt H 525-527
The Age of Television (1982) PC 755
The Age of Television (1972) PC 725
The Age of the American Novel L 347
The Age of the American Revolution H 233
The Age of the Avant-Garde A-A 80
Agee on Film PC 409
The Ages of American Law H 1953
Aging PSY 185
Aging and Retirement SOC 409
The Aging Enterprise SOC 407
The Agony of the American Left H 629
Aggressive Political Participation PS 550
Agricultural Exports, Farm Income, and the Eisenhower Administration
    H 1768
Agriculture and the Civil War H 310
Agriculture in the Post-Bellum South H 1439

Ain't No Big Thing A-F 109
The Albuquerque Navajos A-F 217
The Alcoholic Republic H 374
Alcoholism and Human Sexuality PSY 71
Alfred Stieglitz and the Photo-Secession A-A 342
Alien Encounters: Anatomy of Science Fiction PC 252
Alienation and Charisma: A Study of Contemporary American Communes
    SOC 74
The Aliens: A History of Ethnic Minorities in America H 888
Aliens and Linguistics: Language Study and Science Fiction PC 237
The All-American Dollar: The Big Business of Sports PC 936
All American Music, Composition in the Late Twentieth Century M 27
All But the People H 547
All in Color for a Dime PC 315
"All in the Family" PC 712
All Our Kin: Strategies for Survival in a Black Community A-F 192
All that Is Native & Fine H 1514
All the Happy Endings L 172
All the Moves: A History of College Basketball PC 956
All the Years of Popular Music M 384
All Things Are Possible R 273
All You Need Is Love M 421
Alley Life in Washington H 1287
The Alliance: America, Europe, Japan PS 577
Alliance Security PS 788
Almost Persuaded: American Physicians and Compulsory Health Insurance
    1912-1920 STM 271
Alone with America L 316
Along the Color Line H 1063
Altamont M 382
Alternate Worlds PC 227
Alternative Altars R 198
Alternative America PS 62
Alternative Pleasures L 398
Alternative to Extinction H 1254
Altgeld's America H 313
Ambiguous Legacy H 539
Ambition and Attainment PSY 112
The Ambivalent American Jew R 173
America: Images of Empire PS 805
America: Religions and Religion R2
America II SOC 13
America Adopts the Automobile, 1895-1910 STM 127
America and the Image of Europe H 564
America and the World: From the Truman Doctrine to Vietnam PS 742
America and the World: Retreat from Empire PS 743
America and the World Political Economy PS 600
America and Western Europe PS 689
America Arms for a New Century H 415
America as Art A-A 134
America as Utopia L 618
America at the Movies PC 621
America by Design: Science, Technology, and the Rise of Corporate Capi-
    talism STM 269
America Confronts a Revolutionary World H 44
America in Contemporary Fiction L 232
America in Legend A-F 391
America in Our Time H 475
America in Search of Itself H 543
America in the Dark: Hollywood and the Gift of Unreality PC 620
America in the Movies PC 641

America in the Sixties H 558
America in Vietnam PS 718
America, Russia, and the Cold War, 1945-1966 PS 708
America Takes the Stage PC 376
America the Picturesque in Nineteenth-Century Engraving A-A 286
America Through Baseball PC 1004
The American 1890's L 201
The American 1960's L 330
American Abstract Expressionists and Imagists A-A 200
The American Adam L 156
American Agriculture, 1890-1939 H 1653
American and British Technology in the Nineteenth Century STM 148
The American and His Food H 13
The American Animated Cartoon PC 565
American Apocalypse: Yankee Protestants and the Civil War, 1860-1869
    R 288
American Architecture A-A 474
American Architecture, 1607-1976 A-A 526
American Architecture and Urbanism A-A 508
American Architecture Comes of Age A-A 597
The American Architecture of To-day A-A 599
American Architecture Since 1780 A-A 525
American Art A-A 141
American Art: 1750-1800, Towards Independence A-A 409
American Art: Painting, Sculpture, Architecture, Decorative Arts, Photo-
    graphy A-A 29
American Art, a Historical Survey A-A 66
American Art at Mid-century A-A 33
American Art in the Barbizon Mood A-A 180
American Art Nouveau Glass A-A 414
American Art of Our Century A-A 64
American Art of the 20th Century A-A 76
American Art Pottery A-A 387
American Art Since 1900 A-A 114
American Art Since 1945 A-A 19
American Art Theory: 1945-1970 A-A 30
American Art to 1900 A-A 28
The American Artist and His Times A-A 122
American Assassins PS 113
American Autobiography L 480
American Automobile Manufactures, the First Forty Years STM 299
American Balladry from British Broadsides A-F 436
American Baseball PC 1003
American Baseball: From Gentleman's Sport, Vol. 1 PC 1003
American Baseball: From the Commissioners, Vol. 2 PC 1003
American Baseball: From Postwar Expansion, Vol. 3 PC 1003
American Beauty H 702
American Biography L 579
American Black Spiritual and Gospel Songs from Southeast Georgia M 147
American Bridges and Dams STM 400
American Buddhism R 218
American Building A-A 441
American Building, I: The Historical Forces That Shaped It A-A 447
American Building, II: The Environmental Forces That Shaped It A-A 448
American Buildings and Their Architects, I: The Colonial and Neo-classical
    Styles A-A 498
American Buildings and Their Architects, II: Technology and the Pictur-
    esque A-A 583
American Buildings and Their Architects, III: Progressive and Academic
    Ideals A-A 611
American Buildings and Their Architects, IV: The Impact of European Modern-
    ism A-A 612

The American Burlesque Show PC 406
American Business and Foreign Policy 1920-1933 H 546
American Business and Public Policy PS 303
American Business and the Twentieth Century H 1669
The American Business Creed H 1791
American Business History (1967) H 1691
American Business History (1972) H 1736
The American Capital Market, 1846-1914 H 1794
American Catholic Thought on Social Questions R 158
American Catholicism R 164
American Catholics R 171
American Catholics and Social Reform R 179
American Chairs: Queen Anne and Chippendale A-A 394
The American Character SOC 1
The American Children of Krsna A-F 91
American Children Through Their Books, 1700-1835 PC 119
American Christianity R 21
American Churches A-A 472
The American Cinema: Directors and Directions, 1929-1968 PC 592
The American City A-A 439
The American City Novel L 514
American City Planning Since 1890 H 1381
The American Civil Engineer STM 59
The American Civil Engineer, 1852-1974 STM 395
The American Class Structure SOC 474
The American Class Structure: A New Synthesis SOC 460
The American Codification Movement H 1946
The American College and University H 670
American Colonial Architecture A-A 546
The American Colonial Mind and the Classical Tradition L 60
American Colonial Painting A-A 171
The American Colonies in the Eighteenth Century H 155
The American Colonies in the Seventeenth Century H 156
American Communism and Soviet Russia H 447
The American Communist Party H 477
The American Composer Speaks M 46
American Composers on American Music, a Symposium M 51
The American Constitutional System Under Strong and Weak Parties PS 413
American Couples: Money, Work, Sex PSY 23
The American Cowboy PC 275
American Culture: An Anthropological Perspective A-F 35
The American Culture: Approaches to the Study of the United States
    L 475
American Cut and Engraved Glass A-A 415
The American Daguerreotype A-A 331
American Decorative Arts A-A 360
American Decorative Wall Painting, 1700-1850 A-A 157
American Democratic Theories PS 38
American Design Ethic PC 1038
American Diary Literature, 1620-1779 L 64
An American Dilemma: The Negro Problem and Modern Democracy SOC 186
The American Dimension: Cultural Myths and Social Realities A-F 24
American Diner A-A 458
American Diplomacy, 1900-1950 PS 694
American Diplomacy in the Great Depression PS 639
American Disciples of Marx from the Age of Jackson to the Progressive
    Era H 604
The American Disease: Origins of Narcotic Control PSY 139
American Doctors and German Universities STM 34
American Drama Since World War II L 412
The American Dramatist L 592

American Drawings: The 20th Century A-A 288
The American Dream and the National Game PC 995
The American Dream of Success PC 13
American Earthquake L 422
American Economic Growth H 1847
The American Economy H 1889
The American Economy in Transition H 1854
American Education H 573
American Entertainment PC 335
The American Environment STM 264
American Essay Serials from Franklin to Irving L 58
The American Establishment SOC 503
American Ethnic Politics PS 478
American Ethnicity A-F 111
American Evangelicalism R 274
The American Evangelicals, 1800-1900 R 277
The American Eve in Fact and Fiction, 1775-1914 L 496
The American Family in Social-Historical Perspective PSY 86
The American Farmer and the New Deal H 524
American Farmers SOC 540
The American Farmhouse A-A 471
American Fiction: Historical and Critical Essays L 595
American Fiction: The Intellectual Background L 575
American Fiction, 1920-1940 L 215
American Fictions, 1940-1980 L 321
American Figureheads and Their Carvers A-A 245
American Film Exhibition PC 455
American Film Genres PC 501
The American Film Industry PC 416
American Film Now PC 547
The American Firehouse A-A 534
American Flower Painting A-A 146
American Folk Art: From the Traditional to the Naive A-A 317
American Folk Art: The Art of the Common Man in America, 1750-1900
   A-A 291
American Folk Art: The Herbert Waide Hemphill Jr. Collection A-A 292
American Folk Art in Wood, Metal and Stone A-A 311
American Folk Legend A-F 418
American Folk Medicine A-F 419
American Folk Painters A-A 301
American Folk Painters of Three Centuries A-A 314
American Folk Painting A-A 297
The American Folk Scene M 146
American Folk Sculpture A-A 295
American Folk Sculpture: The Work of Eighteenth and Nineteenth Century
   Craftsmen A-A 293
American Folklife A-F 468
American Folklore A-F 392
American Folklore and the Historian A-F 393
American Folksongs of Protest M 157
American Foreign Policy in a Polycentric World PS 729
American Foreign Policy Since World War II PS 784
American Forts A-A 503
The American Frontier A-A 72
American Furniture: Seventeenth, Eighteenth and Nineteenth Century Styles
   A-A 372
American Furniture, 1620 to the Present A-A 382
American Furniture and the British Tradition to 1830 A-A 395
American Furniture in the Henry Francis DuPont Winterthur Museum PC 1032
American Furniture of the Nineteenth Century A-A 411
American Genesis H 178

An American Genius: The Life of Ernest Orlando Lawrence STM 63
American Georgian Architecture A-A 540
American Glass A-A 405
American Gothic: Imagination and Reason PC 196
American Gothic: Its Origins, Its Trials, Its Triumphs A-A 433
American Graphic Art A-A 276
American Growth and the Balance of Payments, 1820-1913 H 1938
The American Health Care System SOC 599
The American Hegelians H 598
The American Heritage History of Notable American Houses A-A 444
The American Heritage History of the Indian Wars H 1267
American Hieroglyphics: The Symbol of the Egyptian Hieroglyphics in the
    American Renaissance L 144
American Historians and European Immigrants, 1875-1925 H 989
The American Historical Novel PC 296
American History/American Film PC 562
American History/American Television PC 799
The American Home: Architecture and Society, 1815-1915 A-A 571
The American House A-A 449
American Humor L 621
The American Humorist PC 304
The American Idea: The Literary Response to American Optimism L 114
The American Idea of Success H 23
The American Ideology of National Science, 1919-1930 STM 373
The American Image of the Old World H 681
American Imagination and Symbolist Painting A-A 152
American Immigration H 945
American Immigration Policy, 1942-1952 H 889
American Impressionism (1974) A-A 181
American Impressionism (1980) A-A 188
The American Indian H 1140
American Indian and White Children A-F 216
American Indian Art A-A 8
American Indian Art: Form and Tradition A-A 1
The American Indian in Urban Society A-F 249
American Indian Leaders H 1131
American Indian Medicine STM 381
American Indian Painting and Sculpture A-A 2
American Indian Poetry L 536
American Indian Policy in Crisis H 1223
American Indian Policy in the Formative Years H 1224
American Indian Policy in the Jacksonian Era H 1237
The American Indian Today A-F 229
American Indians H 1147
American Indians and Christian Missions R 252
American Industry and the European Immigrant, 1860-1885 H 1556
American Inequality H 1940
The American Inquisition H 483
American Interior Design A-A 417
The American Irish: A Political and Social Portrait H 992
American Jazz Music M 295
The American Jeremiad L 41
The American Jew: A Composite Portrait SOC 148
The American Jew: A Reappraisal SOC 149
The American Jew: A Zionist Analysis R 169
American Jewry and the Civil War H 951
American Jews and the Zionist Idea SOC 103
American Jews in Transition SOC 236
American Journalism PC 889
American Judaism R 167
American Judaism: Adventure in Modernity R 177

The American Judicial Tradition H 1981
American Kinship A-F 64
American Labor and Immigration History, 1877-1920s H 1581
American Labor and United States Foreign Policy H 1620
American Labor Songs of the Nineteenth Century M 152
American Landscape and Genre Paintings in the New-York Historical Society
   A-A 156
American Landscapes A-A 351
The American Law of Slavery, 1810-1860 H 1980
The American Law School and the Rise of Administrative Government H 1945
American Lawyers in a Changing Society, 1776-1876 H 1942
The American Left PS 538
American Legal Culture, 1908-1940 H 1966
The American Leonardo: A Life of Samuel F. B. Morse STM 231
American Life: Dream and Reality A-F 74
American Light: The Luminist Movement, 1850-1875 A-A 142
American Literary Criticism 1800-1965 L 22
American Literary Criticism, 1905-1965 L 291
American Literary History: 1607-1830 L 71
American Literary Naturalism L 660
American Literature: The New England Heritage L 596
American Literature and Christian Doctrine L 647
American Literature and the Dream L 472
American Literature and the Experience of Vietnam L 217
American Literature and the Universe of Force L 162
American Literature as an Expression of the National Mind L 2
American Literature in Context, II: 1830-1865 L 138
American Literature in Context, IV: 1900-1930 L 351
American Literature in the Twentieth Century L 399
American Lithographers, 1900-1960 A-A 287
American Locomotives STM 387
The American Lyceum L 99
American Made H 1893
American Master Drawings and Watercolors A-A 275
American Masters A-A 101
American Masters of Sculpture A-A 248
American Medical Education STM 202
The American Medical Profession, 1783-1850 STM 336
American Medical Research, Past and Present STM 339
American Medicine and the People's Health STM 256
American Medicine and the Public Interest STM 358
American Medicine in Transition, 1840-1910 STM 151
American Midwives STM 227
The American Mind H 570
American Minds H 662
American Miniature Case Art A-A 332
American Minimal Music M 91
American Minorities SOC 84
American Modern: Essays in Fiction and Poetry L 409
American Modernity and Jewish Identity SOC 104
American Moderns: From Rebellion to Conformity L 285
The American Monomyth PC 33
The American Monument A-A 238
American Music M 102
American Music: From Storyville to Woodstock M 315
American Music, a Panorama M 19
American Music Since 1910 M 120
American Musical Comedy PC 327
The American Musical Stage Before 1800 PC 364
The American Musical Theater PC 338
American Mysticism: From William James to Zen R 192

The American Myth of Success: From Horatio Alger to Norman Vincent Peale
  PC 105
American Negro Art A-A 51
American Negro Folk-Songs M 197
American Negro Folktales A-F 394
American Negro Slave Revolts H 1013
American Neo-Classic Sculpture A-A 251
The American Newspaperman PC 915
American Newspapers in the 1980s PC 873
The American Newsreel, 1911-1967 PC 465
The American Nightmare: Why Inequality Persists SOC 505
The American Novel, 1789-1939 L 33
The American Novel and Its Tradition L 3
American Novelists in Italy L 670
American Novels of the Second World War PC 299
The American Occupational Structure SOC 522
American Opera and Its Composers M 69
American Operetta: From H.M.S. Pinafore to Sweeney Todd PC 328
American Overture H 921
American Painted Furniture, 1660-1880 A-A 383
American Painting: From the Colonial Period to the Present A-A 163
American Painting: History and Interpretation A-A 148
American Painting: The Eighties A-A 225
American Painting: The Twentieth Century A-A 226
American Painting from Its Beginnings to the Armory Show A-A 162
American Painting from the Armory Show to the Depression A-A 206
American Painting in the 20th Century A-A 210
American Painting of the Nineteenth Century A-A 193
American Painting to 1776 A-A 177
American Paintings in the Metropolitan Museum of Art. Volume III: A
  Catalogue of Works by Artists Born Between 1846 and 1864 A-A 182
American Pantheon L 92
The American Party System PS 423
The American Party System and the American People PS 434
American Patriotic and Political China A-A 396
American Patriots and the Rituals of Revolution L 78
The American People: A Study in National Character A-F 45
The American People and South Africa PS 671
An American Perspective: Nineteenth Century Art from the Collection of
  JoAnn and Julian Ganz, Jr. A-A 143
The American Petroleum Industry: The Age of Energy, 1899-1959 STM 393
The American Petroleum Industry: The Age of Illumination, 1859-1899
  STM 394
American Philanthropy H 9
American Philanthropy Abroad H 14
American Philanthropy in the Near East H 15
American Philosophy H 640
American Philosophy and the Future H 656
American Photographers and the National Parks A-A 321
American Physicians in the Nineteenth Century STM 324
American Physics in Transition STM 262
American Picture Palaces A-A 620
American Picturebooks from Noah's Ark to the Beast Within PC 108
The American Pilgrimage H 80
The American Playhouse in the Eighteenth Century A-A 549
American Pluralism: A Study of Minority Groups and Social Theory
  SOC 188
American Poetry in the Eighteen Nineties L 150
American Poets from the Puritans to the Present L 37
The American Political Novel L 584
American Political Parties PS 432

The American Political Tradition H 21
American Political Writers, 1588-1800 L 40
American Political Writers, 1801-1973 PS 564
American Politics PS 35
American Pop Art A-A 199
American Popular Entertainment PC 44
American Popular Entertainment: Papers and Proceedings of the Conference
    on the History of American Popular Entertainment PC 365
American Popular Song M 444
American Popular Stage Music 1860-1880 PC 387
The American Poor SOC 484
American Portraiture in the Grand Manner, 1720-1920 A-A 164
American Pressed Glass and Figure Bottles A-A 416
American Primitive Painting A-A 312
American Primitives: An Exhibit of the Paintings of Nineteenth Century
    Folk Artists A-A 294
American Printmaking A-A 274
American Prints A-A 270
American Prints and Printmakers A-A 289
American Protestant Thought R 146
American Protestant Women in World Mission R 240
American Protestantism and Social Issues, 1919-1939 R 127
American Protestantism and United States Indian Policy, 1869-82 R 253
American Psychoanalysis PSY 149
American Psychology in Historical Perspective PSY 97
American Psychology Since World War II PSY 79
The American Puritan Imagination L 43
American Puritanism R 40
The American Quest for a Supreme Fiction L 581
The American Radio PC 831
The American Railroad Network, 1861-1890 H 1795
The American Railroad Passenger Car STM 388
American Railroad Politics, 1914-1920 H 1728
American Railroads STM 361
American Railroads and the Transformation of the Antebellum Economy
    H 1685
The American Reading Public PC 98
American Realism L 194
American Realism and the Industrial Age A-A 50
American Realists and Magic Realists A-A 222
American Reformers, 1812-1860 H 403
The American Religious Experience R 153
American Religious Thought R 135
American Renaissance: Art and Expression in the Age of Emerson and Whitman
    L 163
The American Renaissance, 1876-1917 A-A 144
The American Revolution H 193
The American Revolution: Explorations in the History of American Radi-
    calism H 256
American Romantic Painting A-A 165
The American Scene: American Painting of the 1930s A-A 203
American Science and Modern China, 1876-1936 STM 51
American Science in the Age of Jackson STM 88
The American Science of Politics PS 73
The American Scientific Community, 1800-1860 STM 23
American Scientists and Nuclear Weapons Policy STM 136
American Sculpture in Progress, 1930-1970 A-A 253
American Sculpture of the Sixties A-A 266
The American Self: Myth, Ideology, and Popular Culture PC 25
The American Shakers R 197
American Shelter A-A 522

The American Short Story: A Critical Survey L 35
American Short Story: Front Line in the National Defense of Literature
    L 371
American Silent Film PC 457
American Silver: A History of Style, 1650-1900 A-A 390
American Skyline A-A 520
American Slavery, American Freedom H 143
The American Small Town H 1463
American Social Fiction L 360
American Society: A Sociological Interpretation SOC 18
The American Soldier in Fiction, 1880-1963 PC 289
The American Space: Meaning in Nineteenth-Century Landscape Photography
    A-A 336
American Space: The Centennial Years, 1865-1876 A-A 573
The American Spirit in Architecture A-A 459
American Sports, from the Age of Folk Games to the Age of Spectators
    PC 983
American Still-Life Painting A-A 154
American Structuralism A-F 358
American Studies and American Musicology M 52
The American Style H 649
The American Style of Foreign Policy PS 612
American Suffrage from Property to Democracy, 1760-1860 H 694
The American Symphony Orchestra M 118
The American Symphony Orchestra, A Social History of Musical Taste
    M 92
The American System of Manufacturers STM 318
American Television PC 752
American Thought in Transition H 561
American Tradition in Painting A-A 158
The American Tradition in the Arts A-A 91
American Transcendentalism, 1830-1860 H 562
The American University SOC 302
American Values H 594
American Vaudeville PC 344
American Vaudeville as Ritual PC 370
The American View of Death PSY 61
The American Vision L 147
American Visionary Fiction L 126
American Visionary Reality L 659
American Volunteers and Israel's War of Independence PS 670
The American Voter PS 420
American War Literature, 1914 to Vietnam L 411
The American Way in Sport PC 998
American Welfare Capitalism, 1880-1940 H 1831
The American West: Painting from Catlin to Russell A-A 183
The American West on Film PC 537
The American Western Novel PC 273
American Wildlife Painting, 1720-1920 A-A 160
The American Woman H 717
The American Woman in Sport PC 944
The American Woman in Transition H 838
American Women Artists A-A 119
American Women in Jazz M 323
American Women Poets L 295
American Women's Activism in World War I H 823
American Workingclass Culture H 1539
The American Writer and the European Tradition L 486
American Writers in Rebellion L 168
American Writing in the Twentieth Century L 404
American Zionism H 902

American Zionism from Herzl to the Holocaust H 1004
Americanization of the Common Law H 1973
The Americanization of the Synagogue, 1820-1870 R 172
The Americans, 1976 PS 40
The Americans: The Colonial Experience H 60
The Americans: The Democratic Experience H 7
The Americans: The National Experience H 8
Americans and Chinese A-F 50
Americans and Free Enterprise H 1850
Americans and German Scholarship, 1770-1870 H 580
Americans and the California Dream 1850-1915 L 192
Americans and Their Servants H 1635
Americans in Paris L 420
Americans on the Road PC 1011
America's Ascent H 445
America's Ethnic Music M 154
America's Ethnic Politics PS 497
America's Forgotten Architecture A-A 489
America's Frontier Heritage H 1417
America's Great Illustrators A-A 272
America's Humor L 1
America's Immigrant Women H 791
America's Impasse PS 567
America's Jews SOC 219
America's Longest War PS 672
America's Mass Media Merchants PC 681
America's Music from the Pilgrims to the Present M 4
America's Old Age Crisis: Public Policy and the Two Worlds of Aging
    SOC 403
America's Old Masters A-A 173
America's Polish Heritage H 1009
America's Quest for the Ideal Self H 436
America's Quilts and Coverlets A-A 418
America's Rise to World Power, 1898-1954 PS 627
America's Sporting Heritage PC 925
America's Strategy Against Poverty, 1900-1980 H 515
America's Strategy in World Politics PS 787
America's Struggle Against Poverty PS 375
America's Teacher Quality Program SOC 322
America's Wooden Age STM 172
Amerikanuak A-F 93
Amish Society A-F 106
Amoskeag H 1576
Amusements and Sports in American Life PC 1005
Amusing the Million H 1339
The Analysis of Motives: Early American Psychology and Motives L 187
Anarchist Women, 1870-1920 H 783
Anarchy, State, and Utopia PS 49
Anatomy of a Lynching H 1062
Anatomy of Four Race Riots H 1089
The Anatomy of Jazz M 318
The Anatomy of Racial Attitudes SOC 80
Anatomy of the Spy Thriller PC 157
Ancient Wisdom Revived R 195
Ancients and Axioms H 140
And Always a Detective PC 164
And Every Day You Take Another Bite PC 973
And Keep Your Powder Dry SOC 14
And Other Neighborly Names A-F 374
And Still the Waters Run H 1120
And the War Came H 388

Andrew Carnegie and the Rise of Big Business   H 1741
Andrew Johnson and Reconstruction   H 342
Angel Dust   A-F 305
The Anglo-American Connection in the Early Nineteenth Century   H 392
Anglo American Encounters: England and the Rise of American Literature
    L 154
Anglo-American Folksong Scholarship Since 1898   A-F 466
Anglo-American Politics, 1660-1775   H 154
The Anglo American Suburb   A-A 513
Angry Voices   H 4^7
Anishinabe   A-F 236
Annals of Music in America   M 82
Another Part of the Fifties   H 431
Another Part of the Twenties   H 432
Ante-Bellum Southern Literary Critics   L 173
Anthracite People   H 1528
Anthropologists at Home in North America   A-F 18
Anthropology in American Life   A-F 51
Anthropology and Contemporary Human Problems   A-F 31
Anthropology and Modern Life   A-F 30
Anthropology and the Public Interest   A-F 333
The Anthropology of World's Fairs   A-F 27
Anthropology on the Great Plains   A-F 256
Anthropology Towards History   A-F 105
The Anti-Aesthetic: Essays on Postmodern Culture   A-A 57
The Anti-Federalists: Critics of the Constitution, 1787-1788   H 221
Anti-Intellectualism in American Life   H 607
The Antinomian Controversy, 1636-1638   R 31
Antique Country Furniture of North America   A-A 423
The Antiques Guide to Decorative Arts in America, 1600-1875   A-A 424
Antisemitism in the United States   SOC 109
The Antislavery Impulse, 1830-1844   R 91
Anti-slavery Sentiment in American Literature Prior to 1865   L 655
Antitrust and the Oil Monopoly   H 1659
Antitrust in the Motion Picture Industry   PC 441
The Anxious Object: Art Today and Its Audience   A-A 115
Any Old Way You Choose It   M 373
Apache, Navajo and Spaniard   H 1135
Apocalypse and Science Fiction   PC 234
The Apocalyptic Vision in Nineteenth-Century American Fiction   L 160
Apostles of Culture: The Public Librarian and American Society, 1876-
    1920   SOC 544
Apostles of Discord   R 267
Apostles of the Self-Made Man   PC 73
Appalachia on Our Mind   H 677
Appalachian Valley   A-F 104
Appearance and Reality in Politics   PS 13
Apples and Ashes   R 298
Applied Anthropology   A-F 297
Applied Anthropology in America   A-F 304
Approaches to American Economic History   H 1925
Approaches to Popular Culture   PC 2
Apthorp House, 1760-1960   A-A 542
Arapahoe Politics, 1851-1978   H 1138
The Arcadian Landscape: Nineteenth-century American Painters in Italy
    A-A 194
Archetypal Patterns in Women's Fiction   L 609
Architectural Follies in America   A-A 477
The Architectural Heritage of Newport, Rhode Island, 1640-1815   A-A 445
Architecture, Ambition, and Americans   A-A 434
Architecture and the Esthetics of Plenty   A-A 568

Architecture and Town Planning in Colonial Connecticut A-A 543
Architecture in New Jersey A-A 454
Architecture in Old Kentucky A-A 490
Architecture in the United States A-A 460
The Architecture of America A-A 438
The Architecture of Choice A-A 473
The Architecture of Colonial America A-A 539
Architecture of the Old Northwest Territory A-A 491
The Architecture of the Old South A-A 450
The Architecture of the Southwest A-A 507
Architecture Today A-A 610
Architecture USA A-A 616
An Armed America, Its Face in Fiction PC 297
The Armed Vision: A Study in the Methods of Modern Literary Criticism
   L 317
The Armies of the Streets H 872
Arms Control II PS 580
Arms Control and Defense Postures in the 1980s PS 598
The Army and Civil Disorder H 1546
The Army and the Navajo H 1252
Army Exploration in the American West, 1803-1863 H 1454
The Army Gets an Air Force PS 305
The Art and Architecture of German Settlements in Missouri A-A 587
Art and Commerce A-A 280
Art and Culture A-A 67
Art and Life in America A-A 82
Art and Sexual Politics A-A 71
Art and the Future: A History/Prophecy of the Collaboration Between Sci-
   ence, Technology and Art A-A 45
Art-as-Politics A-A 207
Art Chronicles, 1954-1966 A-A 102
Art for the Millions: Essays from the 1930s by Artists and Administrators
   of the WPA Federal Art Project A-A 99
Art in America: A Brief History A-A 92
Art in America: A Critical and Historical Sketch A-A 26
Art in Progress: The Visual Development of a Collage A-A 268
Art in Public Places in the United States A-A 58
Art in the Age of Risk, and Other Essays A-A 31
The Art-Makers of Nineteenth-Century America A-A 88
The Art of Assemblage A-A 264
The Art of Healing: Medicine and Science in American Art A-A 61
The Art of Jazz M 362
The Art of Life: Studies in American Autobiographical Literature L 457
The Art of North America A-A 12
The Art of Ragtime M 334
The Art of Rock and Roll M 370
The Art of Southern Fiction L 309
The Art of the American Folk Preacher A-F 452
The Art of the Moving Picture PC 518
The Art of the Mystery Story PC 152
The Art of the Old South A-A 108
Art of the Pacific Northwest A-A 68
Art of the Real A-A 232
Art on the Edge A-A 116
The Art Presence A-A 124
Art-Song in America, a Study in the Development of American Music M 121
Art Worlds A-A 25
Artful Thunder L 485
Artifacts and the American Past PC 1042
The Artillery of the Press PC 896
Artisans for Independence STM 280

The Artists in American Society A-A 69
Artists in Offices: An Ethnography of an Academic Art Scene SOC 510
Artistic America, Tiffany Glass, and Art Nouveau A-A 358
Artists and Illustrators of the Old West, 1850-1900 A-A 132
Artists in Aprons A-A 299
Artists in Wood A-A 305
The Arts and Architecture of German Settlements in Missouri PC 1044
The Arts and Crafts Movement in America, 1876-1916 A-A 371
The Arts in America: The Colonial Period A-A 145
The Arts in America: The Nineteenth Century A-A 59
Arts of the Pennsylvania Germans A-A 131
Arts of the Young Republic A-A 47
As a City upon a Hill H 1506
As Equals and as Sisters H 733
As Long as the Grass Shall Grow H 1183
As Serious as Your Life M 364
As You Sow A-F 97
Asa Gray, 1810-1888 STM 107
Ascription and Labor Markets: Race and Sex Differences in Earnings
    SOC 575
An Asian Anthropologist in the South A-F 52
The Asian in the West H 958
Asians in America H 967
Asimov on Science Fiction PC 203
Aspects of American Film History Prior to 1920 PC 607
Aspects of American Poetry L 564
Aspects of Early New York Society and Politics H 120
The Assault on Assimilation H 1173
Assault on the Media: The Nixon Years PC 894
Assemblage, Environments & Happenings A-A 259
Assimilation in American Life SOC 134
The Assimilation of Cuban Exiles SOC 203
Asylums A-F 96
The Asymmetric Society SOC 4
At Dawn We Slept PS 753
At East in Zion R 111
At Home: Domestic Life in the Post-Centennial Era A-A 334
At Home and at Work: The Family's Allocation of Labor SOC 277
At Home in America R 176
At Last, the Real Distinguished Thing L 431
At Odds H 725
At the Point of Production H 1545
The Athlete Revolution PC 992
The Atlantic Economy and Colonial Maryland's Eastern Shore H 1840
The Atlantic Migration, 1607-1860 H 934
The Atlantic Slave Trade H 1025
The Atomic Bomb and the End of World War II PS 635
Attack and Die H 344
The Attitudes of the New York Irish Toward State and National Affairs,
    1848-92 H 915
The Authoritarian Personality PS 506
The Authority of Experience: Essays in Feminist Criticism L 488
Autobiography L 520
An Autobiography of Black Jazz M 351
Automobile Age Atlanta H 1368
Automobile Workers and the American Dream SOC 531
Avant-Garde Painting and Sculpture in America, 1910-1925 A-A 74
The Awakening of American Nationalism, 1815-1828 H 281
Axel's Castle L 666

Babel to Byzantium L 263
Babes in Arms: Youth in the Army SOC 414
Back to Work: Determinants of Women's Successful Re-entry SOC 514
The Background Revolution PS 414
Backgrounds of American Literary Thought L 535
Backstage at the Strips PC 320
Backtalk: Press Councils in America PC 900
Backwoods Utopias R 189
Bad Blood: The Tuskegee Syphilis Experiment STM 195
The Badge and the Bullet: Police Use of Deadly Force SOC 653
Ball Four Plus Ball Five PC 927
The Ballad as Song M 136
The Ballad Mongers M 135
Ballots and Fence Rails H 294
Ballots for Freedom H 380
Baltimore in the Nation, 1789-1861 H 1289
Baltimore Painted Furniture, 1800-1840 A-A 379
Baltimore's Music M 76
Bands of America M 432
Bankers and Cattlemen H 1869
Banking and Economic Development H 1837
Banks and Politics in America H 1707
Baptized in Blood R 98
Barefoot in Babylon M 439
The Barn A-A 435
Baseball PC 993
Baseball: America's Diamond Mind, 1919-1941 PC 933
Baseball: The Early Years PC 993-1
Baseball: The Golden Age PC 993-2
Baseball's Great Experiment: Jackie Robinson and His Legacy PC 1001
Basic Family Therapy PSY 10
Basic Issues in Mass Communication PC 655
The Beat Generation L 249
Beating the Bushes PC 935
The Beasts L 213
Beautiful, Also, Are the Souls of My Black Sisters H 794
Becoming a Two-Job Family SOC 283
Becoming a Woman SOC 369
Becoming Americans: Asian Sojourners, Immigrants, and Refugees in the
    Western United States SOC 157
The Beekmans of New York in Politics and Commerce, 1648-1877 H 1812
Been Here and Gone M 326
Been in the Storm So Long R 228
Before Mickey: The Animated Film 1898-1928 PC 443
Before Silent Spring STM 389
Before the Convention PS 408
Before the Ghetto H 1051
The Beginning of Naturalism in American Fiction L 89
The Beginnings of National Politics H 234
Beginnings of Sisterhood H 788
The Beginnings of Unitarianism in America R 157
Behavior in New Environments: Adaptation of Immigrant Populations
    PSY 28
Behavior Modification in Black Populations PSY 172
Behavior Research and Government Policy SOC 568
Behind Closed Doors PC 1008
Behind Closed Doors: Violence in the American Family SOC 318
Behind Every Successful Man: Wives of Medicine and Academe SOC 273
Behind the Front Page PC 836
Belief and Worship in Native North America A-F 218
Beliefs and Self-Help PSY 179

Bell: Alexander Graham Bell and the Conquest of Solitude STM 49
"Benevolent Assimilation" PS 730
Benjamin Franklin and a Rising People H 81
Benjamin West and His American Students A-A 172
Bent's Fort H 1471
Bertolt Brecht in America L 345
The Best Men H 387
The Best of Jazz M 307
The Best of Jazz 2 M 308
The Best Poor Man's Country H 1472
The Best Remaining Seats A-A 604
Bestsellers PC 102
Betrayers of Truth: Fraud and Deceit in the Halls of Science SOC 612
Better City Government H 1313
Better Felt Than Said R 269
Better Foot Forward: The History of American Musical Theater PC 377
The Better Half H 817
A Better Kind of Hatchet H 1229
A Better World—The Great Schism H 659
Between Fact and Fiction: The Problem of Journalism PC 860
Between Money and Love: The Dialectics of Women's Home and Market Work
    SOC 383
Between Two Worlds: The American Novel in the 1960's L 377
Between War and Peace PS 636
Beyond Culture A-F 6
Beyond Democracy PS 43
Beyond Equality H 1606
Beyond Formula: American Film Genres PC 611
Beyond Her Sphere H 758
Beyond Interpretation PSY 76
Beyond Modern Sculpture A-A 256
Beyond Necessity A-F 372
Beyond Rebel: New Directions in Communications PC 672
Beyond Separate Spheres H 803
Beyond Sixty-Five PSY 93
Beyond Suffrage H 832
Beyond the American Housing Dream SOC 66
Beyond the Magic Bullet STM 97
Beyond the Melting Pot SOC 128
Beyond the North-South Stalemate PS 666
Beyond the Wasteland: A Democratic Alternative to Economic Decline PS 516
Beyond the Wasteland: A Study of the American Novel of the Nineteen-
    Sixties L 367
Bias in Mental Testing PSY 104
Bias in the News: Network Television Coverage of the 1972 Election Cam-
    paign PC 768
The Bias of Communication PC 665
The Bias of Pluralism PS 14
Big Bad Wolves: Masculinity in the American Film PC 544
Big Band Jazz M 309
The Big Bands M 435
Big Business and Presidential Power PS 491
The Big Change H 417
Big City Police H 1309
The Big Game: College Sports and American Life PC 929
The Big Little School R 87
Big Road Blues M 212
Big Steel H 1572
Big Story: How the American Press . . . Tet 1968 PC 648
Bilingualism in the Southwest A-F 367
Billion Year Spree: The True History of Science Fiction PC 199
Billy Sunday Was His Real Name R 109

Biocultural Basis of Health A-F 325
Biography of a Small Town SOC 45
Biology in the Nineteenth Century STM 70
Birth Control in America STM 205
The Birth of Talkies PC 473
Birth Rates of the White Population of the United States H 47
A Birthday Offering to Carl Engel M 99
Bishops by Ballot R 63
The Bit Between My Teeth L 423
Bitter Harvest H 1543
Bitter Strength H 844
Bittersweet Encounter: The Afro-American and the American Jew SOC 238
Black Abolitionists H 1072
The Black Aesthetic L 513
Black Alcoholism PSY 177
The Black American in Books for Children PC 124
The Black American in Sociological Thought SOC 169
Black American Literature and Humanism L 582
Black American Music M 25
The Black American Writer L 450
Black Americans in the Roosevelt Era H 1052
Black and Presbyterian R 238
Black and White in School SOC 209
Black Anti-Semitism and Jewish Racism SOC 144
Black Apollo of Science STM 233
The Black Athlete PC 952
Black Ballots H 485
Black Bostonians H 1049
Black Bourgeoisie SOC 119
Black Chicago H 1080
Black Children SOC 140
Black Children/White Children SOC 90
Black Church in the Sixties R 230
Black Consciousness, Identity and Achievement SOC 139
Black Culture and Black Consciousness R 225
Black Detroit and the Rise of the UAW H 1603
Black Diamonds H 1628
Black Drama and the Federal Theater Era L 259
Black Ethos H 1066
The Black Experience in Religion R 227
Black Families in White America SOC 87
The Black Family in Modern Society SOC 208
The Black Family in Slavery and Freedom, 1750-1925 H 1042
Black Fiction L 619
Black Fiction: New Studies in the Afro-American Novel Since 1942 L 558
Black Film as Genre PC 444
Black Folk Art in America, 1930-1980 A-A 315
Black Freemasonry and Middle-Class Realities SOC 241
Black Giants M 329
Black Gods of the Metropolis R 222
Black Humor Fiction of the Sixties L 630
The Black Image in the White Mind H 1035
Black Images in American Films, 1896-1954 PC 556
The Black Jews of Harlem SOC 96
Black Life in Corporate America A-F 174
Black Literature in White America L 598
Black Mafia A-F 182
Black Majority H 1093
The Black Man on Film PC 538
Black Masculinity SOC 385
Black Messiahs and Uncle Toms L 593

Black Metropolis SOC 111
Black Migration and Poverty H 1071
Black Migration in America SOC 150
Black Music M 252
Black Music in America M 29
Black Music in Our Culture M 6
Black Music of the Two Worlds M 26
The Black Muslims in America R 226
Black Nationalism H 1030
Black Nationalism and the Revolution in Music M 301
Black New Orleans, 1860-1880 H 1016
Black Novelists and the Southern Literary Tradition L 600
Black Odyssey H 1050
Black Over White H 1048
Black Parties and Political Power SOC 122
Black Poetry in America L 543
Black Power SOC 99
Black Power/White Control: The Struggle of the Woodlawn Organization
    in Chicago SOC 33
The Black Press, U.S.A. PC 916
Black Psychology PSY 106
Black Religion R 235
Black Religion and American Evangelicalism R 232
Black Religion and Black Radicalism R 239
Black Religions in the New World R 233
Black Representation and Urban Policy SOC 153
Black Rock A-F 433
Black Scare H 412
Black Sects and Cults R 236
Black Separatism in the United States SOC 141
The Black Song, the Forge and the Flame M 227
Black Southerners, 1619-1869 H 1018
Black Street Speech A-F 167
Black Studies and Anthropology A-F 195
Black Talk M 31
Black Theology R 156
Black Time: Fiction of Africa, the Caribbean and the United States
    L 443
The Black Towns A-F 171
The Black Underclass A-F 177
Black Violence SOC 528
The Black Woman in America SOC 386
Black Women in the Labor Force SOC 234
Black Women Novelists L 241
Blacking Up: The Minstrel Show PC 399
Blackout Looting!: New York City, July 13, 1977 SOC 618
Blacks and White TV: Afro-Americans in Television Since 1948 PC 783
Blacks in American Film PC 528
Blacks in Black and White PC 589
Blacks in Blackface PC 390
Blacks in Suburbs A-F 170
Blacks in the Law SOC 211
Blacks in White-Collar Jobs SOC 191
Blacks, Whites, and Blues M 239
Blackways of Kent A-F 118
Black-White Contact in Schools SOC 196
Blaming the Victim PSY 154
The Block SOC 42
Blood of My Blood H 910
Blood Relations H 1753
Bloodstoppers and Bearwalkers A-F 395

Blowing in the Wind PS 620
Blue Collar Community SOC 479
Blue-Collar Marriage SOC 478
Blue-Collar Women H 1642
Bluegrass M 133
Blues M 219
Blues and the Poetic Spirit M 215
Blues Fell This Morning M 230
Blues from the Delta M 213
Blues Music in Arkansas M 218
Blues People M 253
The Blues Revival M 217
The Bluesmen M 206
Body, Boots and Birtches A-F 457
Bohemians and Critics: American Theatre Criticism in the Nineteenth Century L 165
Bonds of Loyalty H 957
The Bonds of Wickedness R 93
The Bonds of Womanhood H 721
Bonnet Brigades H 784
Boogie Lightning M 228
A Book About the Theater PC 366
The Book in America L 10
The Book of American Spirituals M 224
The Book of Clowns PC 396
Books: The Culture and Commerce of Publishing SOC 532
Books for Pleasure PC 79
Boontling A-F 347
Boosters and Businessmen H 1274
The Bootleggers M 245
The Border Economy A-F 269
The Border States H 1489
Born to Lose: The Gangster Film in America PC 581
Boss Cox's Cincinnati H 1359
Boss Tweed's New York H 1351
Bossess, Machines, and Urban Voters H 1276
Boston Capitalists and Western Railroads H 1723
Boston Furniture of the Eighteenth Century A-A 431
Boston Prints and Printmakers, 1670-1775 A-A 277
The Boston Region, 1810-1850 H 1286
The Boston Symphony Orchestra, 1881-1931 M 71
Boston's Immigrants, 1790-1880 H 931
Bourbon Street Black M 254
Boys and Girls at Play SOC 375
Boys in White: Student Culture in Medical School SOC 252
The Boys of Summer PC 960
The Boys on the Bus PC 853
The Bracero Experience M 161
The Brandywine Tradition A-A 106
Brass Bands & New Orleans Jazz M 333
The Brazen Face of History L 632
Breaking Bread R 180
Breaking Out: Feminist Consciousness and Feminist Research SOC 384
The Breaks of the Game PC 948
Bricks and Brownstone A-A 479
The Bride and the Bachelors A-A 136
Bridges to Science Fiction PC 258
Bright Book of Life L 322
Brighter Than a Thousand Suns STM 197
Bringing Aerodynamics to America STM 157
Bringing the Left Back Home PS 61

Bringing the War Home: The American Soldier   PSY 96
British Emigration to British North America   H 874
The British Empire Before the American Revolution   H 106
British Immigrants in Industrial America, 1790-1950   H 852
British Investment in American Railroads, 1834-1898   H 1647
The British Traditional Ballad in North America   A-F 387
The British Traveller in America, 1836-1860   H 849
British Travelers Among the Southern Indians   H 1227
Britons in American Labor   H 1644
Broadcast Regulation and Joint Ownership of Media   PC 779
Broadcasting in the United States   PC 794
Broadcasting Music   PC 357
Broadway   PC 323
Broadway Babies   PC 378
Broadway Musicals   PC 345
Broadway's Greatest Musicals   PC 358
The Broken Connection: On Death   PSY 125
The Broken Covenant: American Civil Religion in Time of Trial   R 292
Broken Promises: How Americans Fail Their Children   PSY 91
Bronzes of the American West   A-A 236
Brooklyn Bridge   H 1390
Brothers in Clay   A-F 381
Brothers of Light   A-F 293
The Brown Decades   A-A 581
The Browns of Providence Plantations: Colonial Years   H 1708
The Browns of Providence Plantations: The Nineteenth Century   H 1709
Buddhism in America   R 208
Buddhism in America: The Social Organization of an Ethnic Religious Insti-
    tution   R 207
Builders of the Bay Colony   H 146
Building a New American State   H 529
Building Early America   A-A 496
The Building of a Club   A-A 572
Building the Dream   H 1400
Building the Organizational Society   H 479
Built in Boston   A-A 519
Built in Texas   A-F 369
Built in USA: Post-War Architecture   A-A 465
Built in USA: Since 1932   A-A 617
Bullets and Bureaucrats   STM 11
The Burden of Southern History   H 1517
Bureaucracy and Foreign Policy   PS 768
Bureaucracy and Social Justice   PS 395
The Bureaucratic Experience   PS 336
Bureaucratic Failure and Public Expenditure   PS 376
Bureaucratic Insurgency   PS 346
Bureaucratic Politics and Foreign Policy   PS 665
Burleycue   PC 395
Burlington Route   H 1762
The Burned-over District   R 70
The Burr Conspiracy   H 257
Bury My Heart at Wounded Knee   H 1105
The Bush Is Burning! Radical Judaism Faces the Pharaohs of the Modern
    Superstate   SOC 235
Business and Government in the Oil Industry   H 1697
Business and Its Environment   H 1917
Business Enterprise and Economic Change   H 1836
Business Enterprise in Early New York   H 1687
Business Enterprise in the American Revolutionary Era   H 1678
Business in American Life   H 1670
Business in Politics   PS 482

Business in the New South H 1414
The Business of Crime H 971
The Business of Sports PC 964
The Business Press in America: 1750-1860 PC 864
The Business Response to Keynes, 1929-1964 PS 310
Businessman and Reform H 544
The Butcher Workmen H 1533
The Butterfly Caste STM 116
Buying the Wind A-F 396
By the Beautiful Sea H 1315
By the Sweat of Their Brow H 981
By What Authority R 128

The CIO Challenge to the AFL H 1565
The Cabinetmakers of America A-A 362
Caging the Bear PS 648
A Calculating People STM 68
The Calculus of Consent PS 71
The California Bungalow A-A 633
The California Progressives H 502
California Rock, California Sound M 390
California's Architectural Frontier A-A 576
The Cambridge History of American Literature L 32
Camerado: Hollywood and the American Man PC 615
Canals and American Economic Development H 1867
Cancer Crusade STM 307
Canones: Values, Crisis, and Survival in a Northern New Mexico Village
    A-F 115
Capital and Credit in British Overseas Trade H 1908
Capital in Agriculture H 1800
Capital in Manufacturing and Mining H 1674
Capital in the American Economy H 1885
Capital Losses: A Cultural History of Washington's Destroyed Buildings
    A-A 453
Capital Transformation, Communications, and Public Utilities H 1802
Capitalism and Freedom PS 28
Capitalism and Human Obsolescence SOC 603
Capitalism and the Welfare State PS 322
Capitalism, Slavery, and Republican Values H 622
Capitalism, Socialism and Democracy H 1914
A Capitalist Romance STM 41
The Car Culture STM 128
Career Change in Midlife SOC 410
Career Patterns in Education SOC 300
Career Women of America, 1776-1840 H 727
Careers and Contingencies: How College Women Struggle with Gender
    SOC 328
Carlos Montezuma and the Changing World of American Indians H 1166
Carnival Strippers PC 372
Carolina Dwelling A-A 515
The Case for Participatory Democracy PS 513
The Case of the University of North Carolina SOC 107
A Casebook on the Beat L 369
Cases in Accountability PS 341
Caste and Class in a Southern Town SOC 455
Castlereagh and Adams H 364
Catalogues and Counters H 1680
Catherine Beecher R 247
Catholic Activism and the Industrial Worker H 1526
Catholic and American Politics PS 483

The Catholic Church and the Knights of Labor   H 1536
Catholic High Schools and Minority Students   SOC 278
The Catholic Indian Missions and Grant's Peace Policy, 1870-1884   H 1226
Catholic Revivalism   R 71
Catholics and Radicals   H 1629
Catholics in Colonial America   R 28
Catholics in the Old South   R 89
The Cattle Kings   H 1410
Cattle, Priests, and Progress in Medicine   STM 333
The Cattle Towns   H 1305
Causal Explanation and Model Building in History, Economics, and the New
     Economic History   H 1896
Causal Factors in American Economic Growth in the Nineteenth Century
     H 1926
Causes and Cures of Welfare   PSY 85
Cavalcade of the American Novel   L 36
Cavalier and Yankee: The Old South and American National Character
     L 652
The Cayuse Indians   H 1232
A Celebration of American Family Folklore   A-F 469
The Celebration of Society   PC 43
Celebrations   PC 49
Celebrity   PC 47
The Celluloid Closet: Homosexuality in the Movies   PC 587
Celluloid Rock: Twenty Years of Movie Rock   PC 494
The Celluloid Sacrifice: Aspects of Sex in the Movies   PC 629
The Celluloid South: Hollywood and the Southern Myth   PC 433
The Celluloid Weapon: Social Comment in the American Film   PC 635
Censorship of the Movies   PC 571
A Centennial History of the American Society of Mechanical Engineers,
     1800-1980   STM 343
Centuries and Styles of the American Chair, 1640-1970   A-A 359
A Century of Ceramics in the United States, 1878-1978   A-A 370
A Century of Chemistry   STM 345
A Century of Jewish Life in Dixie   H 894
A Century of Labor Management Relations at McCormick and International
     Harvester   H 1613
Century of Struggle   H 742
Ceramic Sculpture   A-A 261
Ceramics in America   A-A 413
The Challenge of Change   H 1720
The Challenge of the American Dream: The Chinese in the United States
     SOC 146
Challenges and Innovations in U.S. Health Care   STM 186
Change and Continuity in the 1980 Elections   PS 407
Change in Agriculture   H 283
Change in Public Bureaucracies   PS 358
Change in the Political Agenda   PS 460
Changes in the Industrial Distribution of Employment, 1919-1959   H 1578
Changes in the Land   H 84
Changes in University Organization, 1964-1971   SOC 279
Changing: Essays in Art Criticism   A-A 84
The Changing American Voter   PS 453
Changing Attitudes Toward American Technology   STM 183
Changing Channels   PC 740
The Changing Culture of an Indian Tribe   A-F 233
Changing Cultures, Changing Lives   A-F 113
The Changing Demography of Spanish Americans   SOC 147
The Changing Face of Inequality   H 1403
Changing Ideas About Women in the United States, 1776-1825   H 764
Changing Places: Men and Women in Transitional Occupations   SOC 381

Changing Rural Landscapes A-A 533
Changing the Lawbreaker SOC 625
Channels of Desire PC 20
Channels of Power PC 804
Chant of Saints: A Gathering of Afro-American Literature, Art, and Scholar-
    ship L 524
Chapters of Opera M 78
Character, Community, and Politics PS 11
The Character of the Good Ruler H 62
The Characteristics of American Jews SOC 127
Chariots for Apollo STM 46
Charles E. Merriam and the Study of Politics H 621
Charles Francis Adams, Jr., 1885-1915 H 1730
Charles Proteus Steinmetz STM 155
Charleston Blacksmith A-F 461
Charleston Furniture, 1700-1825 A-A 365
Charleston's Sons of Liberty H 249
Chautauqua PC 379
Cheap Thrills: An Informal History of the Pulp Magazines PC 78
A Cheerful Nihilism L 526
The Cherokee Strip Live Stock Association H 1240
Cherokee Sunset, a Nation Betrayed H 1107
Cherokee Tragedy H 1268
The Chesapeake in the Seventeenth Century H 175
Chesapeake Politics, 1781-1800 H 236
Cheyenne and Arapaho Music M 145
The Cheyenne and Arapaho Ordeal H 1102
The Cheyenne Indians H 1144
Cheyenne Memories H 1186
The Cheyenne Way H 1190
Chicago: Growth of a Metropolis H 1352
Chicago, 1910-1929 STM 72
Chicago, 1930-1970 STM 73
The Chicago Board of Trade 1859-1905 H 1894
Chicago Lawyers SOC 549
The Chicago Pragmatists H 669
Chicago Renaissance L 334
The Chicago Renaissance in American Letters L 265
The Chicago School of Architecture: A History of Commercial and Public
    Building in the Chicago Area, 1875-1925 A-A 564
The Chicago School of Architecture: Early Followers of Sullivan and Wright
    A-A 621
Chicago's Catholic R 184
Chicago's White City of 1893 H 1291
La Chicana A-F 282
The Chicano H 940
Chicano Authors L 467
The Chicano Experience A-F 294
Chicano Intermarriage A-F 284
Chicano Prisoners A-F 263
Chicano Revolt in a Texas Town H 996
The Chicanos: A History of Mexican Americans H 965
The Chicanos: As We See Ourselves A-F 291
Chicanos and the Police A-F 266
Chicanos and Rural Poverty SOC 95
Chicanos in a Changing Society A-F 261
Chief Lawyer of the Nez Perce Indians, 1796-1876 H 1128
Chiefs and Challengers H 1215
Child Analysis and Therapy PSY 82
The Child and the Book PC 135
Child of Conflict PS 610

Child Services PSY 59
Childhood in Contemporary Cultures A-F 322
Childhood and Folklore: A Psychoanalytic Study of Apache Personality
   PSY 25
Childhood and Society PSY 63
Children and Families in the Social Environment PSY 75
Children and Literature PC 116
Children and Politics PS 531
Children and Poverty PSY 81
Children and Puritanism H 99
Children and Television PC 731
Children and Television: Lessons from "Sesame Street" PC 778
Children and the Faces of Television PC 801
Children and Their Organizations A-F 65
Children in Front of the Small Screen PC 797
Children in the New England Mind in Death and Life H 169
Children in Urban Society H 1330
The Children of Aataentsic A-F 246
Children of Bondage A-F 172
The Children of Prosperity: Thirteen Modern American Communes SOC 37
Children of Strangers A-F 188
Children of the Gilded Ghetto: Conflict Resolutions of Three Generations
   of American Jews SOC 159
Children of the Great Depression SOC 269
Children of the People A-F 227
Children, Television and Sex-Role Stereotyping PC 834
Children's Books in England and America in the Seventeenth Century
   PC 133
Children's Riddling A-F 441
Children's Television PC 790
The Child's Construction of Politics PS 525
The Child's First Books PC 123
China Market PS 727
China, Oil, and Asia PS 668
The China Tangle PS 637
Chinatown A-F 164
Chinese Americans SOC 170
Chinese Labor in California, 1850-1880 H 863
Chippewa Music M 145
The Chippewas of Lake Superior H 1119
Choctaw Music M 145
The Choctaws H 1194
Choice of Conscience: Vietnam Era Military and Draft Resisters in Canada
   SOC 662
Choices and Echoes in Presidential Elections PS 456
Cholera STM 377
The Cholera Years STM 314
Choosing the President PS 410
Choosing Sides: Playground and Street Life on the Lower East Side
   SOC 41
Chosen Children: New Patterns of Adoptive Relationships SOC 272
The Chosen People in America R 163
A Christian America R 7
Christians on the Right R 123
A Chronicle of Early American Engineering STM 18
Church and State H 123
Church and State in French Colonial Louisiana R 308
Church and State in the United States R 311
Church History in the Age of Science R 132
Church, State, and Freedom R 309
Church, State, and the American Indians R 250

The Churches and the Indian Schools, 1888-1912 H 1225
The Churches Militant: The War of 1812 and American Religion R 52
The C.I.A. in Guatemala PS 680
Cigarettes SOC 666
Cinema and Sentiment PC 408
The Cinema of Loneliness PC 512
Cinema, Politics and Society in America PC 447
Cinema Strikes Back PC 434
Cinema Verite in America PC 526
The Cinematic Apparatus PC 448
The Cinematic Imagination PC 551
The Circuit Rider Dismounts R 94
The Circus from Rome to Ringling PC 367
Cities and Immigrants H 1394
Cities in a Larger Context A-F 32
Cities in Revolt H 65
Cities in the Commonwealth H 1502
Cities in the Wilderness H 66
Cities of the American West H 1372
Cities of the Prairie H 1306
Cities, Suburbs and Blacks SOC 88
Citizen Politics PS 409
City and Country H 1340
The City and the Grassroots: A Cross-Cultural Theory of Urban Social
   Movement SOC 26
City and Hinterland H 1357
A City and Its Universities H 1302
City and Suburb H 1385
The City as Metaphor L 663
City Building in the New South H 1366
The City Game: Basketball in New York PC 920
City Hospitals STM 99
The City in the American Novel, 1789-1900 L 494
City Life-Cycles and American Urban Policy SOC 55
City Lights: An Introduction to Urban Studies SOC 58
City Scenes: Problems and Prospects SOC 56
City of Words: American Fiction 1950-1970 L 401
City People H 1281
City Scriptures: Modern Jewish Writing L 214
The City, the Immigrant, and American Fiction, 1880-1920 L 125
The Civil War H 301
The Civil War in the Western Territories H 1431
Civil War Nurse Diary and Letters STM 310
The Civil War on the Screen and Other Essays PC 614
Civilities and Civil Rights H 1022
Civilizing the Machine STM 201
Class and Conformity SOC 477
Class and Community H 1549
Class and Politics in the United States SOC 463
Class Awareness in the United States SOC 471
Class, Race and Labor: Working-Class Consciousness in Detroit SOC 49
Class, Sex, and the Woman Worker H 715
Class Structure and Income Determination SOC 509
The Classic American Novel and the Movies PC 566
Classic Americans: A Study of Eminent American Writers from Irving to
   Whitman L 112
Classical America, 1815-1845 A-A 137
Classical Spirit in American Portraiture A-A 37
Classics and Commercials L 424
Clean Air PS 337
The Clergy and the Great Awakening in New England R 53

Clifford W. Beers STM 85
Climb to Greatness: The American Aircraft Industry, 1920-1960 STM 300
Clio's Consciousness Raised H 759
Clio's Cowboys H 1806
Clipped Wings: The American SST Conflict STM 179
Clockwork Worlds: Mechanized Environments in SF PC 221
Close-up: How to Read the American City PC 1017
Closing the Iron Cage: The Scientific Management of Work and Leisure
    SOC 513
The Clouded Vision: The Student Movement in the United States in the
    1960s SOC 324
Clowns PC 402
The Clubwoman as Feminist H 710
Coal Dust on the Fiddle A-F 434
Coal, Iron, and Slaves H 1058
Cobwebs to Catch Flies: Illustrated Books PC 136
The Cocktail Waitress A-F 142
The Code of the West H 1499
Cognitive Styles PSY 185
Cold Dawn PS 735
Cold War Diplomacy, 1945-1960 PS 656
The College Novel in America L 567
Collegiate Women H 744
The Colloquial Style in America L 463
Colonial Connecticut H 176
The Colonial Craftsmen A-A 364
Colonial Craftsmen and the Beginnings of American Industry STM 376
Colonial Delaware H 150
The Colonial House A-A 536
The Colonial Houses of Worship in America A-A 553
Colonial Massachusetts H 124
The Colonial Merchants and American Revolution, 1763-1776 H 241
Colonial North Carolina in the Eighteenth Century H 138
The Colonial Period of American History H 50
The Colonial Physician and Other Essays STM 26
The Colonial Printers L 86
The Colonial Revival A-A 500
The Colonial Silversmith A-A 391
Colonial Women of Affairs H 728
The Colonies in Transition H 82
Colonists in Bondage H 170
The Color of Mood A-A 41
The Columbia Historical Portrait of New York H 1342
The Columbian Exchange H 1117
The Columbian Muse of Comedy L 139
The Commanches H 1264
Combat Films PC 586
Comic Art in America PC 305
The Comic-book Book PC 319
Comic Imagination in American Literature L 625
The Comic Mind PC 532
Comic Relief L 244
The Comic-Stripped American PC 306
Comic Tones in Science Fiction PC 228
The Comics PC 321
The Comics: An Illustrated History of Comic Strip Art PC 318
Comics: Anatomy of a Mass Medium PC 317
Coming Apart H 512
Coming of Age in Samoa A-F 321
Coming of Age in the Ghetto SOC 172
The Coming of the Civil War H 276

Comix: A History of Comic Books in America PC 308
Comment and Criticism on the Work of Henry F. Gilbert, Composer M 47
Commissioned Spirits: The Shaping of Social Motion in Dickens, Carlyle,
    Melville, and Hawthorne L 91
Common Culture and the Great Tradition PC 21
The Common Defense PS 679
Common Landscape of America, 1580-1845 A-A 514
A Common Spring: Crime Novel and Classic PC 138
Commonwealth, a Study of the Role of Government in the American Economy
    H 1870
The Communal Experience SOC 69
Communication Is Power PC 847
Communication, Speech and Politics PS 79
Communications for Tomorrow PC 684
Communications in Modern Society PC 689
Communism, Anti-Communism and the CIO H 1590
Communist Cadre PS 540
The Communist Party and the Auto Workers Union H 1585
Communist Indochina and United States Foreign Policy PS 817
Communists in Harlem During the Depression H 509
Community and Organization in the New Left, 1962-1968 H 427
Community and Social Change in America H 1282
Community in a Black Pentecostal Church R 237
The Community in America SOC 70
A Community in Limbo A-F 126
Community Planning in the 1920s H 1349
Community Power and Political Power PS 101
Community Psychology PSY 132
Community Treatment of Juvenile Offenders SOC 639
The Compact History of the American Newspaper PC 909
Comparing the Work Attitudes of Women and Men SOC 511
The Competent Woman PSY 13
Competition and Coercion H 1047
Composition and Control at Work SOC 550
Competition and Cooperation H 1692
Competition and Regulation H 1819
Complaints and Disorders H 734
Complex Fate: Hawthorne, Henry James and Some Other American Writers
    L 96
Composers, Conductors, and Critics M 100
The Compound Cinemas: The Writings of Harry Alan Potamkin PC 568
Compromised Compliance PS 301
The Compromised Scientist: William James PSY 20
Compulsory Health Insurance STM 273
The Computer from Pascal to von Neumann STM 137
Concentration and the Rate of Change of Wages in the United States, 1950-
    1962 H 1619
The Concept of Equilibrium in American Social Thought STM 326
The Concept of Jacksonian Democracy H 263
The Concept of Representation PS 51
Conceptions of Reality in Modern American Poetry L 262
Concepts of Insanity in the United States, 1789-1865 STM 86
Conceptual Art A-A 262
Concert Life in New York, 1902-1923 M 37
Concise Histories of American Popular Culture PC 31
A Concise History of American Architecture A-A 506
Confederate Music M 68
The Confederate Nation, 1861-1865 H 393
Confession and Community in the Novel L 491
The Confessional Poets L 375
The Confidence Game in American Literature L 658

The Confidence Gap PS 348
The Confidence Man in American Literature L 562
Confidence Men and Painted Women H 317
The Confident Years: 1885-1915 L 102
Conflict and Accommodation H 1610
Conflict and Crisis PS 624
The Conflict Between the California Indian and White Civilization H 1112
Confrontation and Commitment: A Study of Contemporary American Drama,
    1959-1966 L 222
The Congo Cables PS 690
Congress and Arms Control PS 751
Congress Reconsidered PS 118
Congress, the Presidency, and American Foreign Policy PS 785
Congressional Districting PS 435
Congressional Elections PS 437
Congressmen in Committees PS 122
The Connecticut Town H 87
The Connecticut Wits L 61
Connecticut's Music in the Revolutionary Era M 126
Conscience and Convenience: The Asylum and Its Alternatives in Progressive
    America STM 323
Consequences of Party Reform PS 458
Conservation and the Gospel of Efficiency H 469
The Conservative Intellectual Movement in America H 653
Conservative Judaism R 185
Conservative Ordeal: Northern Democrats and Reconstruction, 1865-1868
    H 308
The Conservative Realists' Image of America in the 1920's A-A 220
The Conservative Reformers: German-American Catholics and the Social
    Order R 168
The Conservative Tradition in America L 521
Conserving America's Neighborhoods SOC 73
Constance Rourke and American Culture L 623
The Constitution Between Friends PS 126
The Constitution in Crisis Times 1918-1968 H 1972
Constructive Liberalism H 1873
Contemporary American Composers M 72
Contemporary American Literature L 349
Contemporary American Literature and Religion L 342
Contemporary American Poetry L 361
Contemporary American Realism Since 1960 A-A 65
Contemporary American Theologies R 137
Contemporary Marriage PSY 92
Contemporary Music and Music Cultures M 10
Contemporary Photographers A-A 347
Contemporary Southern Political Attitudes and Behavior, Studies and Essays
    H 1484
Contemporary Suburban America SOC 54
Contemporary Theories About the Family, Vol. I PSY 36
Contemporary Theories About the Family, Vol. II PSY 37
Contested Terrain H 1553
The Continuity of American Poetry L 601
The Contours of American History H 45
Contrasting Approaches to Strategic Arms Control PS 749
Contributions to the Art of Music in America by the Music Industries of
    Boston, 1640-1936 M 2
The Control of the Arms Race PS 596
Controversies in American Voting Behavior PS 454
Controversy in the Twenties: Fundamentalism, Modernism, and Evolution
    R 102
Conversations with the Blues M 231

Conversations with Wallace Stegner on Western History and Literature
   H 1507
Coordinates: Placing Science Fiction and Fantasy PC 259
Coping with Crime SOC 658
Copland on Music M 48
Cops and Bobbies H 1358
CORE SOC 180
Cornerstones of Religious Freedom in America R 300
Corporate Crime SOC 615
Corporate Cultures A-F 300
The Corporate Ideal in the Liberal State H 540
Corporate Profits and Cooption H 1835
The Corporation and the Indians H 1198
The Corporation in Modern Society H 1747
Corporations, Classes and Capitalism SOC 589
Corresponding Motion: Transcendental Religion and the New America
   R 131
Corruption PS 496
The Cost of Human Neglect: America's Welfare Failure SOC 583
The Cost of Living Longer SOC 534
The Cotton Club M 291
Cotton Fields and Skyscrapers H 1320
Cotton Kingdom of the New South H 1423
Cotton Mather STM 20
Council Fires on the Upper Ohio H 1127
Counter Revolution and Revolt PS 45
Countercultural Communes SOC 75
The Counter-Revolution in Pennsylvania 1776-1790 H 198
Counting Sheep H 1750
Country M 192
The Country Blues M 207
The Country Life Movement in America, 1900-1920 H 426
Country Music U.S.A. M 170
The Country Railroad Station in America A-A 456
Country Roots M 156
The Course of American Democratic Thought H 595
The Course of Empire H 89
Court House: A Photographic Document A-A 495
Courtyard Housing in Los Angeles A-A 622
The Cousin Jacks H 985
The Covenant Sealed: The Development of Puritan Sacramental Theology
   R 35
Covering Campaigns PC 851
The Cowboy PC 276
The Cowboy Hero PC 284
The Cox Report on the American Corporation SOC 533
Cradle of the Middle Class H 806
The Craft of Science Fiction PC 209
Crazy Horse H 1236
The Crazy Mirror: Hollywood Comedy PC 453
Creating Media Culture PC 696
Creating the Modern American Novel L 302
Creating the Welfare State SOC 519
Creation by Natural Law: Laplace's Nebular Hypothesis in American Thought
   STM 272
The Creation of the American Republic 1776-1787 H 254
The Creation of the Presidency, 1775-1789 H 246
Creation of Tomorrow: Fifty Years of Magazine Science Fiction PC 212
Creative Differences: Profiles of Hollywood Dissidents PC 644
The Creative Present: Notes on Contemporary American Fiction L 211
Crestwood Heights A-F 139

Crime and Gerontology SOC 431
Crime and Punishment in Colonial Massachusetts 1620-1692 H 163
Crime as Play: Delinquency in a Middle Class Suburb SOC 650
Crime in American Society SOC 641
Crime in Good Company PC 149
Crime Movies PC 439
Criminalization, Victimization and Structural Correlates of Twenty-Six
    American Cities SOC 619
Crisis and Opportunity PS 58
A Crisis for the American Press PC 870
Crisis in Black and White SOC 216
Crisis in Freedom H 227
Crisis in International News PC 897
The Crisis of Confidence H 674
The Crisis of Democratic Theory STM 293
Crisis of Fear H 273
Crisis of the House Divided H 325
Crisis on the Left H 496
Critical Elections and the Mainsprings of American Politics PS 417
Critical Encounters: Writers and Themes PC 251
Critical Essays on American Transcendentalism L 135
Critical Essays on the Western American Novel PC 282
A Critical History of Children's Literature PC 128
A Critical History of Police Reform H 1392
A Critical Introduction to Twentieth Century American Drama: Volume I:
    1900-1940 L 223
Critical Period in American Literature L 151
Critical Perspectives in American Art A-A 215
Critical Social Psychology PSY 180
Critical Studies in American Jewish History H 961
The Croatian Immigrant in America H 979
Cross-Cultural Counseling and Psychotherapy PSY 133
Cross-Cultural Research Methods PSY 27
Crosscurrents Along the Colorado: The Impact of Government Policy on
    the Quechan Indians H 1100
The Cross in the Sand R 30
The Crow Indians A-F 232
Crowd Action in Revolutionary Massachusetts, 1765-1780 H 212
The Crowd-Catchers, Introducing Television PC 813
The Crucial Decade and After H 457
Cruise Missiles and U.S. Policy PS 587
Crusade for Freedom H 782
Crusaders for Fitness PC 1006
Crying for the Carolines M 203
Cuban Americans A-F 227
The Cuban Threat PS 762
The Cult Experience R 217
The Cult Experience: Responding to the New Religious Pluralism R 210
The Cult of the Atom STM 129
Cults of Unreason R 200
Cultural and Economic Reproduction in Education PS 507
Cultural and Natural Areas of Native North America A-F 224
Cultural Conformity in Books for Children PC 125
The Cultural Contradictions of Capitalism PS 510
The Cultural Experience: Ethnography in Complex Society A-F 70
The Cultural Geography of the United States A-F 78
A Cultural History of Religion in America R 16
A Cultural History of the American Revolution L 81
The Cultural Life of the American Colonies, 1607-1763 H 185
The Cultural Life of the New Nation, 1776-1830 H 232
Cultural Pluralism and the American Idea H 619

Cultural Regions of the United States A-F 36
Cultural Relevance and Educational Issues A-F 314
Culture: A Critical Review of Concepts and Definitions STM 215
Culture Against Man A-F 47
Culture and Aging A-F 89
Culture and Agriculture A-F 123
Culture and Community A-F 1
Culture and Democracy A-A 566
Culture and Early Interactions PSY 69
Culture and Environment PSY 4
Culture and Mental Health PSY 142
Culture and Poverty A-F 341
Culture and Technology PC 1
Culture, Behavior, and Education A-F 95
Culture, Behavior, and Personality PSY 123
Culture for the Millions PC 666
Culture in American Education A-F 37
Culture in Crisis H 1253
Culture, Mind and Therapy PSY 172
The Culture of Early Charleston H 61
The Culture of Experience H 638
The Culture of Inequality SOC 483
The Culture of Narcissism H 630
The Culture of Professionalism H 560
Culture on the Moving Frontier H 1519
Cultures in Crisis A-F 301
Curanderismo A-F 275
Curing the Mischiefs of Faction PS 461
The Curious Death of the Novel L 624
The Currency of the American Colonies, 1700-1764 H 1832
The Current Crisis in American Politics PS 418
The Curse H 726
The Curtain and the Veil L 552
Custer and the Epic of Defeat A-F 453
The Cybernetic Imagination in Science Fiction PC 263
The Cycle of American Literature L 25
Cycles of Conquest A-F 242
Czech-American Catholics 1850-1920 H 862

DDT STM 104
The Daguerrotype in America A-A 329
The Daily Newspaper in America PC 880
Damned Indians H 1184
Dan Emmett and the Rise of the Early Negro Minstrelsy PC 382
The Dance Band Era PC 368
The Dangerous Class H 1363
The Danish Americans SOC 189
Danse Macabre PC 176
The Daring Young Men: The Story of the American Pre-Raphaelites
   A-A 46
Dark Ancestor: The Literature of the Black Man in the Caribbean L 481
Dark Ghetto: Dilemmas of Social Power SOC 102
Dark Paradise STM 81
The Darkened Sky: Nineteenth-Century American Novelists and Religion
   L 128
Darwin in America STM 327
Darwinism Comes to America STM 90
Daughters of the Earth H 1203
Daughters of the Promised Land H 818
David Belasco PC 363

David Rittenhouse STM 168
The Day of the Carpetbaggers H 319
Daytop Village A-F 145
Deadlock of Democracy PS 419
Dean Rusk PS 607
The Dear Bought Heritage H 779
The Death and Life of Great American Cities H 1337
The Death and Rebirth of the Seneca A-F 252
Death in America H 38
Death in Early America A-F 382
Death of a Music? M 324
The Death of Tinker Bell L 290
Debacle: The American Failure in Iran PS 714
The Debate Over Slavery H 1057
Debts Hopeful and Desperate H 137
A Decade Later: A Follow-up of Social Class and Mental Illness SOC 488
Decade of Decisions: American Policy Toward the Arab-Israeli Conflict,
    1967-1976 PS 756
Decade of Decision: The Crisis of the American System PS 31
Decade of Disillusionment H 471
The Decade of Elusive Promise H 762
A Decade of Federal Antipoverty Programs PS 331
A Decade of Radio Advertising PC 766
Decades of Discontent H 810
Deciding What's News: A Study of CBS PC 658
Decision for the Democrats PS 426
The Declaration of Cultural Independence in America L 202
The Declaration of Independence: A Study in the History of Political
    Ideas H 555
The Decline and Revival of the Social Gospel R 116
The Decline of Agrarian Democracy H 1748
The Decline of American Gentility L 603
The Decline of Competition H 1834
The Decline of Laissez-Faire, 1897-1917 H 1853
The Decline of Socialism in America, 1912-25 H 541
The Decline of the Californios H 978
The Declining Significance of Race SOC 244
The Decorative Arts of the Forties and Fifties A-A 388
The De-Definition of Art A-A 117
Deep Blues M 236
Deep Down in the Jungle A-F 370
Deep Like the River H 1086
Deep South: A Social Anthropological Study of Caste and Class A-F 173
Deep South Piano M 244
The Deep South States of America H 1489
Defending the National Interest PS 706
The Defense Industry PS 647
Defense Strategies for the Seventies PS 664
The Deindustrialization of America PS 514
Deinstitutionalization and the Welfare State SOC 561
Delinquency and Justice SOC 665
Delinquent Saints H 153
Deliver Us from Evil H 435
Delta: The History of an Airline H 1740
Demagogues in the Depression H 422
The Demands of Justice PS 60
Democracy and the Novel L 189
Democracy in Jonesville A-F 151
The Democratic Art A-A 285
Democratic Humanism and American Literature L 145
Democratic Politics and Sectionalism H 352

1933

Democratic Promise H 316
The Democratic Republic, 1801-1815 H 384
The Democratic-Republicans of New York H 255
The Democratic Vista: A Dialogue on Life and Letters in Contemporary
     America L 473
The Democrats: From Jefferson to Carter H 36
The Democrats: The Years After F.D.R. H 514
Demographic Dimensions of the New Republic H 29
Demography in Early America H 75
The Denigration of Capitalism PS 553
Denominationalism R 20
The Dependency Tragedy: Returning to Each Other in Modern America
     SOC 6
A Deplorable Society H 1827
Depression Decade H 1900
The Depression of the Nineties H 1875
The Derelicts of Company K SOC 655
Desideratum in Washington STM 124
Design in America A-A 377
The Design of the Present: Essays on Time and Form in American Literature
     L 565
Design on the Land A-A 492
Designing for Industry H 1713
Designs of Darkness PC 142
Desperate Faith: A Study of Bellow, Salinger, Mailer, Baldwin, and Updike
     L 298
A Destroying Angel H 183
Detective Fiction PC 168
The Detective in Hollywood PC 624
The Detective Novel of Manners PC 141
The Determinants of Educational Outcomes SOC 260
The Determinants of Public Policy PS 316
Deterrence in American Foreign Policy PS 653
Detroit and the Problem of Order, 1830-1880 H 1380
Developing the American Colonies, 1607-1783 H 1862
Development Anthropology A-F 298
The Development of American Agriculture H 1842
Development of American Architecture, 1783-1830 A-A 574
The Development of American Citizenship, 1608-1870 H 1967
The Development of American Commercial Banking H 1684
The Development of American Literary Criticism L 28
The Development of American Petroleum Pipelines STM 191
The Development of Modern Medicine STM 340
The Development of Sex Differences PSY 128
The Development of the American Glass Industry H 1675
The Development of the American Short Story L 16
The Development of the Detective Novel PC 159
Deviance and Mass Media PC 708
Deviance and Medicalization SOC 617
Deviant Street Networks: Prostitution in New York City SOC 616
The Devil in the Fire L 207
The Devil Wagon in God's Country: The Automobile PC 1013
The Devils and Canon Barham L 425
Diagnosis and Management of Psychological Emergencies PSY 98
Dialogue in American Drama L 245
Dialogues on American Politics PS 536
Did Monetary Factors Cause the Great Depression? H 1927
The Diffusion of Power PS 765
The Dilemma of American Immigration SOC 98
The Dilemma of American Music M 87
Dilemmas of Pluralist Democracy PS 15

The Dime Novel Western PC 278
Dime Novels PC 90
Dimensions in Urban History H 1334
Dimensions of Detective Fiction PC 154
The Dimensions of Quantitative Research in History H 2
Dimity Convictions H 834
Dinosaurs in the Morning M 247
The Diplomacy of Silence PS 615
The Diplomacy of the Dollar, 1919-1932 H 451
Diplomats in Buckskins H 1262
Directions in Sociolinguistics A-F 354
A Directory of American Silver, Pewter and Silverplate A-A 397
Disaster by Decree H 1954
Discovering the Comic L 357
Discovering the News PC 905
The Discovery of the Asylum H 376
Dismantling America PS 391
The Disney Version PC 595
Disorganized Crime SOC 649
Dispensationalism in America R 287
Dispossessing the American Indian A-F 220
Dispute and Conflict Resolution in Plymouth County, Massachusetts, 1725-
    1825 H 1974
The Disruption of American Democracy H 357
Dissent and Conforming on Narragansett Bay H 1436
Dissent in American Religion R 4
The Distant Magnet H 1001
Distribution's Place in the American Economy Since 1869 H 1826
The Divided Academy: Professors and Politics SOC 292
The Divided Heart: Scandinavian Immigrant Experience Through Literary
    Sources L 635
Divided Loyalties: Whistle-Blowing at BART SOC 610
The Divided Mind: Ideology and Imagination in America, 1898-1917 L 246
The Divided Mind of Protestant America, 1880-1930 R 112
Division Street SOC 65
Divorce and After A-F 82
Divorce and Remarriage SOC 249
Divorce in the Progressive Era H 513
Divorce Reform SOC 280
Doctors on the New Frontier STM 176
"Doctors Wanted: No Women Need Apply" SOC 600
Documentary PC 417
The Documentary Conscience PC 579
Documentary Explorations PC 517
Documentary Expression and Thirties America A-A 349
A Documentary History of American Interiors from the Colonial Era to 1915
    A-A 404
A Documentary History of Religion in America R 5
Documentary in American Television PC 724
The Documentary Tradition PC 491
Documents of American Broadcasting PC 770
Does Freedom Work? PS 18
Doing the Ethnography of Schooling A-F 336
Doings and Undoings L 378
Dollars for Research: Science and Its Patrons in Nineteenth-Century
    America STM 251
Domestic Architecture of the American Colonies and of the Early Republic
    A-A 548
Domestic Intelligence PS 360
Domestic Life in New England in the Seventeenth Century H 91
Domestic Sources of Foreign Policy PS 764

The Dominican Diaspora A-F 272
Donald Duck Joins Up: The Walt Disney Studio During World War II
    PC 600
Don't Go Up Kettle Creek A-F 444
Don't You Know There's a War On? H 489
The Double Agent: Essays in Craft and Elucidation L 225
The Double Agent: Essays in Poetry L 226
Doubletalk: The Story of the First Strategic Arms Limitation Talks
    PS 780
Down and Out in the Great Depression H 499
Down the Rabbit Hole PC 121
The Downtown Jews H 988
The Drama Since 1918 L 335
Drama Was a Weapon L 306
The Dramatic Event L 218
Dramatic Soundings L 283
Drawing Down the Moon R 186
Drawing Now A-A 290
The Dream and the Deal H 494
Dream and Thought in the Business Community, 1860-1900 H 625
The Dream Beside Me: The Movies PC 636
Dream Makers: The Uncommon People Who Write Science Fiction PC 247
Dream Makers, Vol. II: The Uncommon Men and Women PC 248
The Dream of Arcadia: American Writers and Artists in Italy, 1760-1915
    L 103
The Dream of Arcady: Place and Time in Southern Literature L 569
The Dream of Prosperity in Colonial America H 186
The Dream of Success: A Study of the Modern American Imagination L 344
The Dream of the Golden Mountains L 253
A Dream of Wings STM 84
Dreamers Without Power A-F 244
Dreaming of Heroes: American Sports Fiction, 1868-1980 PC 298
Dreams and Dead Ends: The American Gangster/Crime Film PC 599
The Dred Scott Case H 1948
Drinking PSY 66
Drinking Behavior Among Southwestern Indians A-F 248
Drinking in America PSY 120
The Drive to Industrial Maturity H 1930
Drugs and Suicide PSY 121
Drugs in America STM 258
Drumbeats, Masks, and Metaphor: Contemporary Afro-American Literature
    L 270
Drumbeats, Masks and Metaphor: Contemporary Afro-American Theatre
    L 269
Drums in My Ears, Jazz in Our Time M 285
Drylongso A-F 178
The Dual Economy H 1825
Duel for the Dunes: Land Use Conflict on the Shores of Lake Michigan
    SOC 34
The Dungeon of the Heart: Human Isolation and the American Novel L 460
The Dusseldorf Academy and the Americans A-A 282
The Dust Bowl: An Agricultural and Social History H 478
The Dust Bowl: Men, Dirt and Depression H 425
Dust Bowl: The Southern Plains in the 1930s H 548
Dutch Calvinistic Pietism in the Middle Colonies R 64
The Dutch in America, 1609-1974 H 881
To Dwell Among Friends: Personal Networks in Town and City SOC 32
The Dwellings of Colonial America A-A 556
Dwight L. Moody R 72
Dwight Macdonald on Movies PC 522
The Dynamic of Business-Government Relations H 1829

The Dynamics of Party Support   PS 424
Dynamics of the Party System   PS 471
Dynamos and Virgins Revisited   STM 375

Eagle Defiant   PS 744
Early American Architecture   A-A 486
Early American Dramatists   L 34
Early American Dress   PC 1045
Early American Furniture, from Settlement to City   A-A 403
The Early American House   A-A 544
Early American Houses   A-A 545
Early American Ironware, Cast and Wrought   A-A 392
Early American Jewry   H 960
Early American Literature: A Collection of Critical Essays   L 57
Early American Literature: A Comparatist Approach   L 39
Early American Mills   A-A 531
Early American Modernist Painting, 1910-1935   A-A 208
Early American Music Engraving and Printing   M 128
The Early American Novel (1971)   L 72
The Early American Novel (1907)   L 158
Early American Painting   A-A 178
Early American Prints   A-A 278
Early American Science   STM 173
Early American Science: Needs and Opportunities for Study   STM 27
Early American Stencils on Walls and Furniture   A-A 429
Early American Wall Paintings, 1710-1850   A-A 170
Early American Wood Carving   A-A 298
Early Americans   H 67
Early Architecture in New Mexico   A-A 437
Early Children's Books and Their Illustration   PC 129
Early Concert Life in America (1731-1800)   M 113
Early Connecticut Silver, 1700-1840   A-A 363
The Early Development of the Motion Picture (1887-1909)   PC 560
The Early Domestic Architecture of Connecticut   A-A 547
Early Downhome Blues   M 243
Early German Music in Philadelphia   M 55
Early Histories of the New York Philharmonic   M 109
Early Jazz   M 335
Early Nantucket and Its Whale Houses   A-A 541
The Early New England Cotton Manufacturer   H 1808
Early New England Potters and Their Wares   A-A 430
Early Opera in America   M 114
Early Pennsylvania Arts and Crafts   A-A 130
Early Potters and Potteries of New York State   A-A 393
Early Stationary Steam Engines in America   STM 294
The Early Temples of the Mormons   A-A 561
The Earnest Men   H 268
Earth Art   A-A 265
East Across the Pacific   H 870
The Eastern Frontier   H 76
Eastern Shore, Virginia Raised-Panel Furniture, 1730-1830   A-A 407
Eating in America   H 35
The Eccentric Design: Form in the Classic American Novel   L 97
The Eccentrics and Other American Visionary Painters   A-A 151
The Eccentric Tradition   PS 669
The Ecology of Freedom   PS 6
Economic Aspects of Television Regulation   PC 798
Economic Aspects of the Second Bank of the United States   H 1918
The Economic Basis of Ethnic Solidarity   SOC 93
Economic Beginnings in Colonial South Carolina, 1670-1730   H 1841

Economic Control of the Motion Picture Industry PC 486
The Economic Crisis and American Society PS 523
Economic Development in the Philadelphia Region, 1810-1850 H 1347
The Economic Effects of Regulation H 1744
The Economic Growth of Seventeenth-Century New England H 1822
Economic History of Virginia in the Seventeenth Century H 72
The Economic Impact of the American Civil War H 1823
Economic Inequality SOC 490
An Economic Interpretation of the Constitution of the United States
    H 1828
The Economic Mind in American Civilization, 1606-1933 H 1851
The Economic Novel in America L 30
Economic Opportunity and White American Fertility Ratios, 1800-1860
    H 18
Economic Policy and Democratic Thought H 602
Economic Policy in the Development of a Western State H 1909
The Economic Prerequisite to Democracy PS 563
Economic Readjustment of an Old Cotton State H 1505
Economic Regulation and the Public Interest H 1922
The Economic Rise of Early America H 1932
An Economic Theory of Democracy PS 78
The Economics of the American Newspaper PC 913
The Economy of Colonial America H 159
Ecstasy at the Onion M 248
Eddie Condon's Treasury of Jazz M 266
The Edge of Friendliness: A Study of Jewish-Gentile Relations SOC 201
Edison STM 196
The Edison Motion Picture Myth PC 482
Educated Lives: The Rise of Modern Autobiography in America L 118
Educating Professional Psychologists PSY 146
Education and Culture A-F 337
Education and the American Indian H 1250
Education and the New America A-F 315
Education in the Forming of American Society H 551
Education in the United States H 569
The Education of American Physicians STM 274
Educational Patterns and Cultural Configurations A-F 330
Edward Jarvis and the Medical World of Nineteenth-Century America
    STM 142
Edward Randolph and the American Colonies H 110
The Effects of Mass Communication PC 37
The Effects of Social Security on Income and Capital Stock H 1845
The Effects of Television Advertising on Children PC 714
The Effete Conspiracy and Other Crimes by the Press PC 838
Efficiency and Uplift STM 149
The Egyptian Revival A-A 563
Eight Lives in Jazz M 257
Eight Men Out PC 918
The Eighth Art PC 814
The Eighth Generation A-F 191
The Eighteenth-Century Houses of Williamsburg A-A 559
Eisenhower and the Cold War PS 621
The Elderly and the Future Economy SOC 435
Electing the President PS 416
Elections and Political Order PS 421
The Electorate Reconsidered PS 457
Electric Children M 194
The Electric-Lamp Industry STM 44
Electric Power in American Manufacturing, 1889-1958 H 1676
Electric Traction on the Pennsylvania Railroad, 1895-1968 STM 28
The Electrical Manufacturers, 1875-1900 H 1766

The Electrical Workers H 1626
Electronic Democracy: Television's Impact PC 808
The Electronic Gospel PC 669
Eli Whitney and the Birth of American Technology STM 139
The Elite Press PC 885
Elitism PS 87
The Elizabethans and America H 166
Elmer Sperry STM 181
Elmtown's Youth and Elmtown Revisited SOC 467
Elmtown's Youth, the Impact of Social Classes on Adolescents SOC 466
The Elusive Republic H 225
Emergence from Chaos L 534
The Emergence of Agricultural Science STM 321
The Emergence of American Political Issues PC 906
The Emergence of an American Art A-A 93
The Emergence of Christian Science in American Religious Life R 203
The Emergence of Conservative Judaism H 880
The Emergence of Industrial America H 1863
The Emergence of Liberal Catholicism in America R 160
The Emergence of Lincoln H 354
The Emergence of Metropolitan America, 1915-1966 H 1354
The Emergence of Multinational Enterprise H 1813
The Emergence of National Economy, 1775-1815 H 1903
The Emergence of Oligopoly H 1679
The Emergence of Professional Social Science STM 162
Emergence of the American University H 686
The Emergent Native Americans A-F 250
An Emerging Independent American Economy, 1815-1875 H 1688
The Emigration Dialectic A-F 279
Eminent Women of the West H 801
Empire and Independence H 248
Empire as a Way of Life H 46
Empire in Wood H 1541
The Empire of Reason H 202
The Empire of the Mother H 807
The Empire's Old Clothes PC 18
Emulation and Invention STM 169
The Enchanted Country: Northern Writers in the South 1865-1910 L 182
An Encore for Freedom H 460
Encyclopedia of American Economic History H 1907
The Encyclopedia of American Religions R 15
The End of American Innocence H 636
The End of an Alliance PS 357
The End of Ideology PS 511
The End of Indian Kansas H 1199
The End of Liberalism PS 488
The End of the American Era SOC 7
The End of the World PC 249
An End to Hierarchy and Competition PS 389
The Endless Day: The Political Economy of Women and Work SOC 517
Endless Experiments: Essays on the Heroic Expatriate in American Romanti-
    cism L 561
Endless Rapture: Rape, Romance, and the Female Imagination PC 189
The Enduring South: Subcultural Persistence in Mass Society SOC 59
The Enduring Struggle H 1216
Energy Future PS 789
Energy in the American Economy, 1850-1975 H 1784
Energy Policy in Perspective PS 323
Energy Transition and the Local Community A-F 332
Engineering American Society, 1850-1875 STM 249
Engines of Democracy STM 53

The Engines of the Night: Science Fiction in the Eighties PC 236
English America and the Restoration Monarchy of Charles II H 172
English America and the Revolution of 1688 H 173
English in Black and White A-F 348
The English Language in America L 555
Enter, Mysterious Stranger L 571
English Radicals and the American Revolution H 196
The Enlightenment in America H 637
Enterprise Denied H 1746
The Enterprise of a Free People H 1752
Enterprise Zones: Greenlining the Inner Cities SOC 527
Entertaining Satan: Witchcraft and the Culture of Early New England
    R 27
Entertainment, Education, and the Hard Sell PC 828
The Entertainment Machine: American Show Business PC 400
The Entertainment of a Nation or Three-Sheets in the Wind PC 380
Entry into the American Labor Force SOC 573
The Environment SOC 500
Environmental Politics PS 364
Environmental Politics and the Coal Coalitions PS 394
The Epidemic That Never Was PS 367
An Episode in Anti-Catholicism R 263
Equal Justice Under Law H 1963
Equalities PS 102
Equality and the Rights of Women SOC 393
The Equitable Life Assurance Society of the United States, 1859-1964
    H 1662
Equity and Energy: Rising Energy Prices and the Living Standards of Lower
    Income Americans SOC 453
Era of Experiment: The Rise of Landscape Photography in the American
    West, 1860-1885 A-A 328
The Era of Good Feelings H 282
The Era of Reconstruction H 389
The Era of the Muckrakers PC 895
The Era of Theodore Roosevelt, 1900-1912 H 503
Erastus Corning H 1758
Erin's Daughters in America H 884
Errand into the Wilderness H 642
An Errand of Mercy R 73
Eskimo Capitalists, Oil Politics and Alcohol SOC 557
Esperanza A-F 260
An Essay on Liberation PS 46
Essays in Nineteenth-Century Economic History H 1467
Essays in Afro-American History H 1033
Essays in American Jewish History H 898
Essays in Early Virginia Literature L 66
Essays in Modern American Literature L 336
Essays in the History of Early American Law H 98
Essays on the American Revolution H 219
Essays on Determinism in American Literature L 556
Essays on Literature and Politics, 1932-1972 L 381
Essays on Moral Development PS 542
Essence of Decision PS 572
The Eternal Adam and the New World Garden L 597
Ethics and the Press PC 886
Ethics in an Age of Pervasive Technology STM 213
Ethics, Morality and the Media PC 703
The Ethics of Intensity in American Fiction L 531
The Ethics of Psychoanalysis PSY 168
Ethnic Alienation: The Italian-Americans SOC 123
Ethnic America H 998

Ethnic Americans SOC 110
Ethnic and Political Attitudes SOC 193
Ethnic and Racial Segregation in the New York Metropolis SOC 152
An Ethnic at Large H 495
Ethnic Conflict and Political Development PS 477
The Ethnic Dimension in American Society H 952
Ethnic Diversity in Catholic America SOC 77
Ethnic Encounters A-F 48
Ethnic Enterprise in America SOC 164
The Ethnic Factor in Family Structure and Mobility SOC 158
The Ethnic Frontier H 938
The Ethnic Imperative A-F 71
Ethnic Leadership in a New England Community SOC 239
Ethnic Medicine in the South West A-F 67
Ethnic Minorities in Urban Areas SOC 232
The Ethnic Myth SOC 226
Ethnic Recordings in America M 131
Ethnic Relations in the United States SOC 177
The Ethnic Southerners H 1509
Ethnicity SOC 129
Ethnicity and Cultural Pluralism in the United States A-F 26
Ethnicity in the United States SOC 137
Ethnicity on the Great Plains A-F 119
Ethnicity, Pluralism, and Race SOC 233
Eugenics STM 154
The Euroepan and the Indian A-F 201
The European Discovery of America H 147
Evaluating and Optimizing Public Policy PS 373
The Evangelical Alliance for the United States of America, 1847-1900
    R 105
The Evangelical Mind and the New School Presbyterian Experience R 275
Evangelicals in the White House R 121
Everyday Life in the Age of Enterprise, 1865-1900 H 402
Everyday Life in Colonial America H 187
Everyday Life in the United States Before the Civil War H 330
Everyday Life in Twentieth Century America H 446
Everything in Its Place A-F 61
Everyone Was Brave H 796
Evolution and Religion STM 206
Evolution and the Founders of Pragmatism H 692
The Evolution of a Tidewater Settlement System H 1677
The Evolution of American Taste A-A 111
The Evolution of American Urban Society H 1296
The Evolution of Management Education H 1786
Evolutionary Thought in America H 663
The Examined Self: Benjamin Franklin, Henry Adams, Henry James L 629
The Executive Privilege PS 111
Executives for Government PS 312
Exile's Return: A Literary Odyssey of the Nineteen Twenties L 254
Exit, Voice and Loyalty PS 534
Exodusters H 1070
Expanded Cinema PC 643
Expansion and American Policy, 1783-1812 H 1159
The Expatriates L 620
Experimental Cinema PC 446
Explaining America H 252
The Exploded Form: The Modernist Novel in America L 358
Exploration and Empire H 1455
The Exploration of North America H 86
Explorations in Chicano Psychology PSY 12
Explorations in Communication PC 649

Explorations in Enterprise   H 1820
Explorations in Psychohistory   H 27
Explorations in the New Economic History   H 1911
Explorer of the Universe   STM 396
Explorers of the Infinite: Shapers of Science Fiction   PC 238
Exploring the Johnson Years   PS 623
The Eye of Conscience   A-A 325
Eyewitness to Space: Paintings and Drawings Related to the Apollo Mission
    to the Moon   A-A 40

F.D.R. and the South   H 454
The FY 1982-86 Defense Program   PS 568
Fables of Fact   PC 293
The Fabulators   L 390
The Fabulous Phonograph   M 8
The Face of the Fox   A-F 214
The Face on the Cutting Room Floor   PC 597
The Faces of Eve: Women in the Ninteenth-Century American Novel   L 129
The Faces of Power   PS 594
Facing the Enlightenment and Pietism   R 59
Facing West: The Metaphysics of Indian-Hating and Empire-Building
    L 492
Fact and Fancy in Television Regulation   PC 780
Fact and Fiction: The New Journalism and the Nonfiction Novel   PC 294
Fact Book on Aging   SOC 416
A Factious People   H 59
Factories in the Field   H 1601
The Facts of Life in Popular Song   M 437
Fads, Follies and Delusions of the American People   PC 57
Failure and Success in America   L 442
The Failure of the NRA   H 421
Fair Game: Inequality and Affirmative Action   SOC 166
Fair Science: Women in the Scientific Community   STM 69
"Faire and Easie Way to Heaven"   R 42
The Fairness Doctrine and the Media   PC 816
Fairy Tales and After   PC 132
Faith in Fiction   L 75
Faithful Magistrates and Republican Lawyers   H 1976
The Faithful Shepherd: A History of the New England Ministry   R 32
The Fall of the First British Empire   H 247
The Fallen Angel: Chastity, Class, and Women's Reading   PC 84
Fame and the Founding Fathers   H 189
Familiar Faces--Hidden Lives   PSY 30
Families Against the City   H 1382
Families in the Military System   PSY 136
Families of Black Prisoners   SOC 319
Families Under the Flag   PSY 101
The Family: America's Hope   PS 554
The Family: Evaluation and Treatment   PSY 100
Family and Class Dynamics in Mental Illness   SOC 489
Family and Community   H 1011
The Family and Public Policy   PSY 58
A Family Business: Kinship and Social Control in Organized Crime
    A-F 112
Family Life and School Achievement   PSY 50
The Family Life Cycle   PSY 41
Family Life in America, 1620-2000   PSY 2
The Family of God   A-F 152
The Family Secret: Domestic Violence in America   SOC 315
Family Systems in America   PSY 151

Family Therapy   PSY 89
Family Violence   SOC 321
The Family's Construction of Reality   SOC 307
The Fantastic in Literature   PC 181
Fantasy: The Literature of Subversion   PC 175
Fantasy Literature   PC 169
The Fantasy Tradition in American Literature   PC 170
The Far Southwest, 1846-1912   H 1469
The Far Eastern Policy of the United States   PS 660
The Far Western Frontier   H 1418
The Faraway Country: Writers of the Modern South   L 386
Farewell to Reform   H 434
Farewell to the Bloody Shirt   H 322
Farewell to the Party of Lincoln   H 1087
Farm to Factory   H 731
Farm Workers, Agribusiness and the State   SOC 564
The Farmer's Age   H 311
Farmers, Bureaucrats, and Middlemen   H 1769
The Farmer's Last Frontier   H 381
Farms and Farmers in an Urban Age   H 473
Fashion for Everyone: The Story of Ready-to-Wear   PC 1029
Fashion Power: The Meaning of Fashion in American Society   SOC 11
Fast Forward: The New Television and American Society   PC 730
Fat Mutton and Liberty of Conscience   H 68
Father and Child   PSY 42
Father-Daughter-Incest   SOC 281
Father of the Man   A-F 299
Fatherhood   SOC 253
Fatherhood and Family Policy   PSY 119
Fathers and Children   H 1231
Fathers and Sons   SOC 327
The Fathers of the Towns   H 78
Fathers Without Partners   SOC 311
Feature Film as History   PC 602
The Federal Antitrust Policy   H 1798
Federal Art Patronage, 1933-1943   A-A 98
Federal Conservation Policy: 1921-1933   STM 368
Federal Indian Relations, 1774-1788   H 1201
The Federal Presence: Architecture, Politics, and Symbols in United States
     Government Building   A-A 442
Federal Relief Administration and the Arts   H 498
Federal Reserve Monetary Policy, 1917-1933   H 1937
The Federal Reserve System   H 1830
The Federal Theatre, 1935-1939   L 353
The Federalist Era, 1789-1801   H 228
The Federalists: A Study in Administrative History   H 250
Federalists in Dissent   H 623
The Federalization of Presidential Primaries   PS 462
Feel Like Going Home   M 398
Female and Male   SOC 389
Female Complaints: Lydia Pinkham and the Business of Women's Medicine
     STM 353
The Female Eunuch   SOC 358
The Female Gothic   PC 187
The Female Laborforce in the United States   H 798
The Female World   SOC 332
The Feminine Eye: Science Fiction and the Women Who Write It   PC 260
The Feminine Fifties   PC 89
The Feminine Mystique   SOC 350
Feminine Spirituality in America   R 244
Feminism and Suffrage   H 732

Feminism and the New Right SOC 340
Feminism in American Politics SOC 352
Feminist Drama L 465
The Feminists H 739
The Feminization of American Culture L 121
Fenian Fever H 976
Fenians and Anglo-American Relations During Reconstruction H 944
The Ferment of Realism: American Literature 1884-1919 L 95
The Fervent Years: The Story of the Group Theatre and the Thirties
    L 242
Festival! M 403
Festivals U.S.A. & Canada PC 374
The Fiction Factory; or from Pulp Row to Quality Street PC 93
Fiction Fights the Civil War L 157
Fiction of the Forties L 268
Fiddle-backs and Crooked-backs A-A 373
A Field Guide to American Architecture A-A 501
The Fifties, Fiction, Poetry, Drama L 272
Fifty Million Acres H 1452
Fifty Years of American Drama, 1900-1950 L 264
Fifty Years of the American Novel L 281
Fighting Infection STM 100
"Fill 'Er Up": An Architectural History of America's Gas Stations
    A-A 631
Fill 'Er Up!: The Story of Fifty Years of Motoring STM 284
Film: An Anthology PC 618
Film: The Democratic Art PC 497
Film and the Liberal Arts PC 584
Film and the Narrative Tradition PC 460
The Film and the Public PC 527
Film Archetypes: Sisters, Mistresses, Mothers and Daughters PC 634
Film as Subversive Art PC 627
Film Before Griffith PC 461
The Film Criticism of Otis Ferguson PC 463
Film/Culture PC 619
Film Culture Reader PC 605
Film Genre PC 475
The Film in History PC 612
Film on the Left PC 410
Film Style and Technology PC 588
Finance and Economic Development in the Old South H 1702
Finance and Enterprise in Early America H 1646
Financial History of the United States (1963) H 1923
A Financial History of the United States (1970) H 1899
Financial Intermediaries in the American Economy Since 1900 H 1864
Financing American Enterprise H 1801
Financing Anglo-American Trade H 1767
The Fine Arts in America A-A 135
Finnish-American Folklore A-F 432
Fire and the Spirits H 1248
Fire in America STM 297
Fire in the Lake PS 640
Fire in the Streets H 536
Fire Music M 246
Firewater Myths A-F 228
The First Amendment Under Seige: The Politics of Broadcast Regulation
    PC 773
The First Americans A-F 49
The First Birth SOC 270
The First Century of American Literature L 17
The First Century of New England Verse L 62

The First Federal Court H 1943
First Flowers of Our Wilderness A-A 174
The First Freedom PC 687
First Freedom: The Responses of Alabama's Blacks to Emancipation and
   Reconstruction H 1055
The First Frontier H 1158
First Majority-Last Majority H 37
The First New Nation SOC 12
The First One Hundred Years of American Geology STM 248
First Person America PC 324
The First South H 190
The Fiscal Crisis of the State PS 369
The Fiscal Revolution in America H 531
Fiscal Stress and Public Policy PS 347
Five Centuries of American Costume PC 1046
The Five Dollar Day H 1604
Five Temperaments L 320
Flashes of Merriment M 408
Flesh of Steel: Literature and the Machine in American Culture L 418
Flight and Rebellion H 1065
Flight Patterns STM 30
Flight to America H 941
Flintlock and Tomahawk H 128
Flood Tide of Empire H 79
The Flowering of American Folk Art, 1776-1876 A-A 313
The Flowering of New England L 104
Flying Dragons, Flowing Streams M 185
Focus on Art A-A 127
Focus on the Horror Film PC 487
Focus on the Science Fiction Film PC 496
Focus on the Western PC 554
Folk and Traditional Music of the Western Continents M 173
Folk Architecture in Little Dixie A-A 482
Folk Art in America A-A 302
Folk Art of Rural Pennsylvania A-A 310
The Folk Arts and Crafts of New England A-A 316
Folk Beliefs of the Southern Negro A-F 450
Folk Housing in Middle Virginia A-A 452
Folk Music and Modern Sound M 150
Folk Music in the United States M 174
The Folk of Southern Fiction L 634
Folk Painters of America A-A 296
Folk Sculpture USA A-A 306
Folk Song of the American Negro M 200
Folklore: From the Working Folk of America A-F 385
Folklore and Folklife A-F 400
The Folklore and Folklife of New Jersey A-F 389
Folklore and the Ethnicity Factor in the Lives of Romanian-Americans
   A-F 456
Folklore Communication Among Filipinos in California A-F 442
Folklore from the Schoharie Hills, New York A-F 412
Folklore Keeps the Past Alive M 162
Folklore in the Writing of Rowland E. Robinson A-F 373
Folklore of the Great West A-F 416
Folklore of the Oil Industry A-F 377
The Folktale A-F 458
Food and Drink in America H 22
Footlights on the Prairie: The Story of the Repertory Tent Players
   PC 375
For God and Country H 924
For Her Own Good: 150 Years of the Experts' Advice to Women SOC 346

Forbidden Fruits: Taboos and Tabooism PC 6
Force Without War PS 590
Forces in American Criticism L 24
Ford: Decline and Rebirth, 1933-1962 STM 268
Ford: Expansion and Challenge, 1915-1933 STM 267
Ford: The Times, the Man, the Company STM 266
The Ford Hunger March H 1634
The Foreground of American Fiction L 299
Foreign Assistance PS 793
Foreign Policy and Congress PS 641
Foreign Policy and the Democratic Dilemmas PS 786
Foreign Policy and the Democratic Process PS 663
Foreign Policymaking and the American Political System PS 73
Foreigners: The Making of American Literature 1900-1940 L 329
Foreigners in the Confederacy H 335
The Forest Ranger PS 339
Forging the Copper Collar H 1538
Forgive and Remember STM 37
Form and Fable in American Fiction L 143
Form and Ideology in Crime Fiction PC 153
The Formal Principle in the Novel L 669
The Formation of the American Medical Profession STM 207
The Formation of the American Scientific Community STM 211
The Forming of an American Tradition R 66
Forms and Functions of History in American Literature L 507
Forms and Functions of Twentieth-Century Architecture A-A 605
Forms of Order H 1689
Forms of Play of Native North Americans A-F 60
Forms upon the Frontier A-F 410
Formula's Fiction: An Anatomy of American Science Fiction, 1930-1940
    PC 213
The Forties L 426
The Forties: Fiction, Poetry, Drama L 273
Forts and Supplies H 1451
Forty Acres and a Mule H 1068
The Forty-Nine Percent Majority: The Male Sex Role PSY 56
Forum for Protest: The Black Press During World War II PC 862
Foul! The Connie Hawkins Story PC 1007
The Foundation of Nativism in American Textbooks, 1783-1860 H 905
Foundations of American Journalism PC 878
Foundations of Political Analysis PS 68
Foundations of Power H 1956
The Founders and the Architects A-A 586
Founding Fathers R 25
The Founding of American Civilization: The Middle Colonies A-A 557
The Founding of American Civilization: The Old South A-A 558
The Founding of Harvard College H 148
The Founding of Maryland H 52
The Founding of New England H 48
Four Anthropologists STM 235
Four Arguments for the Elimination of Television PC 786
Four Centuries of Sport in America: 1490-1890 PC 972
Four Generations H 108
Four Lives in the Bebop Business M 342
Four Spiritual Crises in Mid-Century American Fiction L 487
Fourteen Sculptors A-A 257
The Fourth Branch of Government PC 850
The Fragmented Metropolis H 1310
The Fraktur-Writings or Illuminated Manuscripts of the Pennsylvania Germans
    A-A 318
Frame Analysis A-F 38

The Framed Houses of Massachusetts Bay, 1625-1725   A-A 537
A Framework for Political Analysis   PS 80
The Framing of the Fourteenth Amendment   H 1965
Framing the Artist: A Social Portrait of Mid-American Artists   SOC 582
France and the Chesapeake   H 1776
France in America   H 95
Franklin and Newton   STM 67
Franklin D. Roosevelt and American Foreign Policy 1932-1945   PS 613
Franklin D. Roosevelt and the New Deal   H 486
Freaks   PC 342
Freakshow   M 396
Frederick Law Olmsted and the American Environmental Tradition   H 1308
Frederick Law Olmsted and the Boston Park System   H 1402
Frederick Taylor   STM 198
Frederick Taylor and the Rise of Scientific Management   H 1756
A Free and Responsive Press   PC 839
The Free Black in Urban America 1800-1850   H 1024
Free Negroes in the District of Columbia, 1790-1846   H 1020
Free Soil, Free Labor, Free Men   H 299
Free Speech   PS 54
Free Will and Determinism in American Literature   L 667
Freedom and Culture   A-F 54
Freedom and Fate in American Thought from Edwards to Dewey   L 458
Freedom and Responsibility in the American Way of Life   H 556
Freedom in Constitutional Contract   PS 69
Freedom in the Air   M 148
Freedom of Speech by Radio and Television   PC 821
Freedom's Ferment   H 399
Freedom's First Generation   H 1029
French-Indian Relations on the Southern Frontier, 1699-1762   H 1273
Fresh Starts: Men and Women After Divorce   SOC 265
Freud and Man's Soul   PSY 19
Freud and the Americans   PSY 94
Freudianism and the Literary Mind   L 310
Friend and Foe   H 1168
Friend and Foe in the U.S. Senate   PS 107
The Friendly Circle   H 993
Friendly Facism   PS 533
From a Minyan to a Community   H 986
From Ararat to Suburbia   H 841
From Bauhaus to Our House   A-A 634
From Behind the Veil: A Study of Afro-American Narrative   L 645
From Colony to Country   H 217
From Dr. Mather to Dr. Seuss   PC 122
From ENIAC to UNIVAC   STM 357
From Hayes to McKinley   H 349
From Home to Office   H 804
From Hopalong to Hud: Thoughts on Western Fiction   PC 285
From Immigrant to Inventor   STM 292
From Immigrants to Ethnics   H 972
From Indians to Chicanos   A-F 292
From Jehovah to Jazz   M 17
From King's College to Columbia, 1746-1800   H 214
From Know-How to Nowhere   STM 260
From Main Street to State Street   H 1319
From Mammies to Militants   L 525
From Military to Civilian Economy   PS 353
From Native Roots: A Panorama of Our Regional Drama   L 639
From Obscurity to Oblivion   PS 449
From Parlor to Prison   H 750
From Prairie to Corn Belt   H 1421

From Prescription to Persuasion H 1910
From Private Vice to Public Virtue STM 303
From Puritan to Yankee R 47
From Realism to Reality in Recent American Painting A-A 204
From Resistance to Revolution H 220
From Reverence to Rape: The Treatment of Women in the Movies PC 481
From Ritual to Record PC 447
From Rollo to Tom Sawyer, and Other Papers PC 117
From Sacred to Profane America R 3
From Sambo to Superspade: The Black Experience in Motion Pictures
    PC 515
From Scarface to Scarlett: American Films in the 1930s PC 451
From Self to Society, 1919-1941 H 575
From Sky Girl to Flight Attendant H 792
From Slavery to Freedom H 1034
From Small Town to the Great Community H 1369
From Spark to Satellite: A History of Radio Communication PC 776
From Streetcar to Superhighway H 1312
From Student to Nurse: A Longitudinal Study of Socialization SOC 593
From Suburb to Shtetl: The Jews of Boro Park SOC 175
From Sundown to Sunup H 1075
From the Center: Feminist Essays on Women's Art A-A 85
From the Depths H 10
From the Ground Up A-A 618
From the Old South to the New H 1449
From Tobacco Road to Route 66 L 250
From Versailles to Wall Street, 1919-29 H 1821
From Vietnam to America H 949
From West to East PC 279
From Wilderness to Wasteland L 446
Frontier: American Literature and the American West L 130
The Frontier Against Slavery H 266
Frontier America A-A 54
The Frontier Camp Meeting R 75
The Frontier in American History H 1510
The Frontier in American Literature PC 277
The Frontier Mind H 648
Frontier Musicians on the Connoquenessing, Wabash and Ohio M 125
Frontier on the Rio Grande SOC 469
Frontier Regulars H 1260
The Frontier Spirit and Progress PC 705
Frontier Women H 765
Frontiers of Change H 1671
Frontiers of Jazz M 269
Frontiersmen in Blue H 1511
Fruitland, New Mexico A-F 237
The Fugitive Group L 252
The Fugitives L 233
Fundamentalism and American Culture R 276
The Fundamentalist Controversy, 1918-1931 R 101
The Fungus Fighters STM 14
The Funnies PC 322
The Fur Trade H 1770
Fur Trade and Exploration H 1726
The Fur Trade and the Indian H 1239
The Fur Trade of the American West, 1807-1840 H 1516
Furniture and Its Makers of Chester County Pennsylvania A-A 419
Furniture of the American Arts and Crafts Movement A-A 368
Further Reflections on Ethnicity PS 494
The Future as Nightmare: H. G. Wells PC 229
Future Females PC 205

The Future of American Democracy PS 859
The Future of Eternity PC 225
The Future of Evangelical Christianity R 271
The Future of Marriage SOC 256
The Future of Motherhood SOC 257
The Future of Political Science PS 93
The Future of Strategic Deterrence PS 585
The Future of the Jewish Community in America SOC 215
Future Perfect PC 223
Future Tense: The Cinema of Science Fiction PC 428
The Futurians PC 231

G-Men: Hoover's FBI in Popular Culture PC 52
The GAO PS 361
The Gambling Scene SOC 640
The Game of Disarmament PS 732
The Game of the Impossible: A Rhetoric of Fantasy PC 174
The Game They Played PC 931
Games, Sport and Power PC 100
The Games They Played: Sports in American History, 1865-1980 PC 979
The Gang: A Study of 1,313 Gangs in Chicago SOC 230
The Gangster Film PC 506
Garbage in the Cities H 1356
The Garden and the Wilderness: Religion and Government R 303
Garden Cities for America A-A 625
Gay American History H 24
Gay and Gray: Older Homosexual Men SOC 331
Gay Children Grow Up SOC 361
Gay Men, Gay Selves SOC 392
Gender PSY 113
Gender Advertisements SOC 355
Gender and Sex in Society SOC 344
Gender, Fantasy and Realism in American Literature L 136
A Generation in Motion M 422
A Generation of Women H 775
Generations: An American Family SOC 268
Generational Change in American Politics PS 406
The Genesis of American Patent and Copyright Law H 1944
The Genet Mission H 192
Genetics and American Society STM 229
The Genius of American Painting A-A 169
The Genius of American Politics PS 7
Genre: The Musical PC 412
A Genteel Endeavor H 395
The Genteel Tradition L 627
The Gentleman in America L 109
Gentlemen Freeholders H 244
The Gentlemen Theologians: American Theology in Southern Culture, 1795-
    1860 R 144
The Geography of the Imagination L 482
Geology in the Nineteenth Century STM 141
The Geopolitics of Information PC 695
George Herbert Mead H 641
George Washington A-A 279
George Washington in American Literature, 1775-1865 L 468
The Germ of Laziness STM 117
The German-Americans H 982
German Culture in America H 665
The German Rearmament Question PS 728
German Seed in Texas Soil H 946

Germany and the United States PS 649
Geronimo H 1121
"Get That Nigger Off the Field" PC 991
"Get Your Ass in the Water and Swim Like Me" A-F 423
Getting Saved from the Sixties R 220
Getting Up: Subway Graffiti in New York SOC 27
The Ghetto and Beyond: Essays on Jewish Life in America SOC 205
A Ghetto Takes Shape H 1056
The Ghost Dance Religion and the Sioux Outbreak H 1202
Giants of Jazz M 349
The Gift of Government H 161
The Gilded Age H 350
The Gingerbread Age A-A 578
The Girl Sleuths PC 127
Git Along, Little Dogies M 196
Give Me Yesterday M 409
Give Us Bread but Give Us Roses SOC 539
"Give Us Good Measure" H 1228
The Glass Gaffers of New Jersey and Their Creations from 1739 to the Present A-A 412
The Glass Teat: Essays of Opinion on the Subject of Television PC 753
Global Food Interdependence PS 677
The Glorious Cause H 226
The Glory of Their Times: The Story of the Early Days of Baseball
  PC 988
God, Church, and Flag H 440
God Struck Me Dead R 224
God's Altar: The World and the Flesh in Puritan Poetry L 49
God's Messengers: Religious Leadership in Colonial New England, 1700-
  1750 R 67
God's New Israel R 283
The Gods of Antenna PC 765
The Gold Coast and the Slum: A Sociological Study of Chicago's Near North
  Side SOC 247
The Golden Age of American Anthropology A-F 16
The Golden Age of "B" Movies PC 541
The Golden Age of the Movie Palace PC 1022
The Golden City A-A 499
The Golden Day: A Study in American Literature and Culture L 169
Golden Day, Silver Night A-A 196
The Golden Door: Artist-Immigrants of America, 1876-1976 A-A 89
The Golden Door: Italian and Jewish Immigrant Mobility in New York City
  H 950
Golden Multitudes: The Story of Best Sellers PC 85
The Golden Threads H 766
The Golden Web: A History of Broadcasting in the United States, Volume
  II--1933-1953 PC 718
Gone from Texas A-A 504
Good and Faithful Labor H 1437
Good Company SOC 627
Good Neighbor Diplomacy PS 651
Good News, Bad News PC 656
Good Wives H 830
Goodbye Gutenberg: The Newspaper Revolution of the 1980s PC 908
Gorham Silver, 1831-1981 A-A 367
Gospel Hymns and Social Religion R 77
The Gospel Sound M 221
The Gothic Fiction in the American Magazines (1765-1800) PC 195
The Gothic Flame PC 198
The Gothic Novel PC 190
The Gothic Revival and American Church Architecture A-A 585

The Gothic Tradition in Fiction PC 192
Governing America PS 112
The Governing of Man A-F 320
Government and Labor in Early America H 149
Government and Science STM 290
Government and the Sports Business PC 977
Government by Contract PS 329
Government in Science: The U.S. Geological Survey, 1867-1894 STM 234
Government Promotion of American Canals and Railroads, 1800-1890 H 1866
The Governmental Process PS 500
The Governors-General H 181
Grace Notes in American History M 410
The Grand Domestic Revolution A-A 461
The Grandees H 853
Grass-Roots Socialism H 462
Graven Images: New England Stonecarving and Its Symbols, 1650-1815
    A-A 244
Gravestones of Early New England and the Men Who Made Them, 1653-1800
    A-A 243
The Graying of America: Retirement and Why You Can't Afford It SOC 424
The Great American Amusement Park PC 356
The Great American Degree Machine: An Economic Analysis of the Human
    Resource Output of Higher Education SOC 248
The Great American Desert Then and Now H 1461
The Great American Nude A-A 62
The Great American Popular Singers M 423
Great American Sculptures A-A 249
The Great American Spectaculars: The Kentucky Derby, Mardi Gras PC 971
The Great American Water Cure Craze STM 386
The Great Audience PC 693
The Great Awakening R 55
The Great Awakening in New England R 48
The Great Awakening in Virginia, 1740-1790 R 49
Great Basin Kingdom H 1408
The Great Bridge STM 240
Great Camps of the Adirondacks A-A 470
The Great Circle: American Writers and the Orient L 672
The Great Crash H 1860
The Great Crisis in American Catholic History, 1895-1900 R 174
Great Day Coming M 143
The Great Decade of American Abstraction A-A 34
The Great Departure H 530
Great Expectations: America and the Baby Boom Generation SOC 423
Great Expectations: Marriage and Divorce in Post-Victorian America
    H 786
The Great Experiment in American Literature L 456
The Great Frontier H 1512
The Great Glut: Public Communication in the United States PC 709
Great Men of American Popular Song M 385
The Great Movie Serials PC 480
The Great Pendulum of Becoming L 407
The Great Pierpont Morgan H 1649
The Great Plains H 1513
The Great Rapprochement PS 747
The Great Plains States of America H 1489
The Great Republic H 3
The Great Revival, 1785-1805 R 68
The Great Richmond Terminal H 1733
The Great School Wars H 1371
The Great Sioux Nation H 1207
The Great Television Race PC 829

The Great Time Killer PC 789
The Great Tradition: An Interpretation of American Literature Since the
    Civil War L 529
The Great Tradition of the American Churches R 304
The Great United States Exploring Expedition of 1838-1842 STM 354
The Great War and the Search for a Modern Order H 468
The Great White Way PC 332
Great Women of the Press H 811
Greek-American Folk Beliefs and Narratives A-F 413
Greek Americans SOC 185
A Greek Community in America A-F 147
Greek Revival Architecture in America A-A 570
The Greenback Era H 1929
Greenwich Village, 1920-1930 H 1395
Gregarious Saints: Self and Community in American Abolitionism, 1830-
    1870 R 95
The Grotesque in Photography A-A 322
A Group Called Women A-F 84
Groupthink PS 684
Growing Old in America H 17
Growing Old in Silence SOC 396
The Growing Power of Congress PS 106
Growing Up Absurd: Problems of Youth in the Organized Society SOC 413
Growing Up American SOC 303
Growing Up in the Midwest H 1407
Growing Up on Television PC 792
Growth and Stability of the Postwar Economy H 1874
The Growth of a Refining Region H 1774
The Growth of American Law H 1960
The Growth of American Thought H 576
The Growth of Southern Civilization, 1790-1860 H 1444
The Growth of Southern Nationalism, 1848-1861 H 277
The Growth of the Major Steel Companies, 1900-1950 H 1783
Guide to Life and Literature of the Southwest L 489
A Guide to Old American Houses, 1700-1900 A-A 527
A Guide to the Artifacts of Colonial America PC 1033
The Gunfighter PC 283
Guts and Glory: Great American War Movies PC 617
Gypsies A-F 146
Gypsies in the Cities A-F 98
Gypsy Lifestyles SOC 178
Haida Culture in Custody A-F 245
The Half-Blood L 186
The Half-Way Covenant R 39
Hall Jackson and the Purple Foxglove STM 115
Hallelujah, Amen! M 73
The Hand and the Spirit: Religious Art in America, 1700-1900 A-A 49
Handbook for Mental Care of Disaster Victims PSY 51
Handbook of American Folklore A-F 401
A Handbook of Jazz M 353
A Handbook of Method in Cultural Anthropology A-F 19
Handbook of Political Science PS 92
Handbook of Social and Cultural Anthropology A-F 10
Handicrafts of New England A-F 405
Handicrafts of the Southern Highlands A-F 406
Happenings A-A 77
Hard Hats: The Work World of Construction Workers SOC 581
Hard Living on Clay Street A-F 110
The Hard-Rock Men H 984
The Hardrock Miners H 1594
Hard Times H 534

The Harder We Run H 1045
The Harding Era H 507
Harlem, the Making of a Ghetto H 1067
Harmless Entertainment: Hollywood and the Ideology of Consensus PC 524
Harpers Ferry Armory and the New Technology STM 348
The Harrowing of Eden H 1108
Henry L. Russell and Agricultural Science in Wisconsin STM 21
Harry S. Truman Versus the Medical Lobby STM 287
Harvard Guide to Contemporary American Writing L 308
Harvests of Change: American Literature 1865-1914 L 161
The Hasidic Community of Williamsburg SOC 199
Haven in a Heartless World: The Family Besieged SOC 293
Hawaiian Americans A-F 83
Hawaiian Music and Musicians M 165
Hawthorne and the Historical Romance of New England PC 184
Hawthorne, Melville, and the Novel L 101
The Hazards of Being Male SOC 356
Heads and Headlines H 391
The Healers STM 101
Health and Aging SOC 420
Health and the War on Poverty SOC 454
Health Care and the Elderly SOC 439
Health Care Delivery in the United States STM 193
Health Care in America STM 308
Health in the Mexican-American Culture and Community Study A-F 262
The Health of a Nation STM 8
Health Policy and the Bureaucracy STM 371

The Healthiest City: Milwaukee and the Politics of Health Reform
    STM 220
Hear Me Talkin' to Ya M 336
Hearth and Home: Images of Women in the Mass Media PC 704
Hearth and Home: Preserving a People's Culture A-F 400
The Heart of Jazz M 288
The Heart Prepared: Grace and Conversion in Puritan Spiritual Life
    R 38
Hearts and Crowns A-F 459
The Hearts of Men: American Dreams and the Flight from Commitment
    SOC 345
The Heathen Chinese PS 726
Heaven Is a Playground PC 997
Heavens on Earth: Utopian Communities in America, 1680-1880 R 205
The Heel of Elohim Science and Values in Modern American Poetry L 408
Heiress of All the Ages: Sex and Sentiment in the Genteel Tradition
    PC 104
Hellenes and Hellions L 550
Hell's Cartographers: Some Personal Histories PC 200
Helping America's Families SOC 289
Henry Ford and Grass-Roots America STM 391
Here Lies Virginia A-F 57
Here to Stay: American Families in the Twentieth Century SOC 251
A Heritage of Her Own H 722
The Hero in Transition PC 9
Heroes of Popular Culture PC 10
Heroes, Villains, and Fools PC 36
Heroic Fiction L 343
Heroines in Love, 1750-1974 PC 186
Herspace, Her Place H 787
The Hidden Election PS 433
The Hidden-Hand Presidency H 463
The Hidden Injuries of Class SOC 502
The Hidden Public: The Story of the Book-of-the-Month Club PC 82

High Hopes H 1456
The High Noon of American Films in Latin America PC 450
The Higher Circles: The Governing Class in America SOC 456
Highlights in the History of the American Press PC 859
The Highway and the City A-A 619
Hip Capitalism SOC 560
The Hippie Ghetto A-F 129
Hippies of the Haight A-F 87
His Picture in the Papers: A Speculation on Celebrity in America
    PC 596
Hispanic Folk Music of New Mexico and the Southwest H 186
Hispano Folklife of New Mexico A-F 259
The Historian and the City H 1328
Historians and the American West H 1477
Historic America: Buildings, Structures, Sites A-A 463
Historic Wisconsin Buildings A-A 582
Historical Archaeology A-F 58
Historical Geography of the United States H 1425
A Historical Study of the Academy of Motion Picture Arts and Sciences
    PC 591
A Historical Study of the Development of American Motion Picture Content
    PC 590
History and American Society H 32
History and Bibliography of American Newspapers 1690-1820 PC 844
A History of Accounting in America H 1775
History of Agriculture in the Northern United States, 1620-1860 H 1416
A History of American Art A-A 38
A History of American Art A-A 70
A History of American Art A-A 94
A History of American Art Porcelain A-A 420
History of American Ceramics A-A 378
A History of American Drama L 20
The History of American Electoral Behavior PS 468
A History of American Graphic Humor, Vol. I PC 316
History of American Journalism PC 881
A History of American Labor H 1622
A History of American Law H 1950
A History of American Life H 298
A History of American Literature: 1607-1765 L 82
A History of American Literature Since 1870 L 18
A History of American Magazines PC 86
A History of American Marine Painting A-A 168
The History of American Music (1904) M 57
History of American Music (1908) M 16
A History of American Painting A-A 147
The History of American Painting A-A 155
History of American Pediatrics STM 75
A History of American Pewter A-A 408
A History of American Philosophy H 676
A History of American Physical Anthropology, 1930-1980 STM 352
A History of American Poetry, 1900-1940 L 297
The History of American Sculpture A-A 239
The History of American Wars H 43
History of Behavior Modification PSY 111
A History of Early American Magazines, 1741-1789 L 76
A History of Engineering and Science in the Bell System: The Early Years
    (1875-1925) STM 119
A History of Engineering and Science in the Bell System: National Service
    in War and Peace (1925-1975) STM 120
The History of Ethnology A-F 23
A History of Experimental Psychology PSY 24

History of Humble Oil and Refining Company H 1738
A History of Industrial Power in the United States, 1780-1930
    Volume I: Waterpower in the Century of the Steam Engine STM 184
A History of Jazz in America M 354
History of Journalism in the United States PC 891
History of Labour in the United States H 1544
A History of Maine Agriculture, 1604-1860 H 1438
History of Manufacturers in the United States H 1668
History of Medicine in the United States STM 282
A History of Metals in Colonial America STM 263
A History of Modern Psychology PSY 159
A History of Music in American Life M 5
A History of Musical Americanism M 130
A History of New Mexican-Plains Indian Relations H 1177
A History of Philosophy in America H 591
The History of Popular Culture PC 11
A History of Popular Music in America M 438
The History of Printing in America PC 911
A History of Psychoanalysis in America PSY 141
A History of Public Health in New York City, 1625-1866 H 1303
A History of Public Health in New York City, 1866-1966 STM 103
History of Public Land Law Development H 1951
History of Radio to 1926 STM 10
A History of Recreation PC 19
The History of Rocket Technology STM 111
History of the American Film Industry PC 478
A History of the American Labor Movement H 1527
History of the American Stage Containing Biographical Sketches PC 329
History of the American Theatre L 23
A History of the American Theatre, 1700-1950 L 8
A History of the American Worker H 1608
A History of the Churches in the United States and Canada R 8
A History of the Circus PC 397
A History of the Circus in America PC 330
A History of the Comic Strip PC 307
A History of the Freedman's Bureau H 265
A History of the Indians of the United States H 1122
History of the Jews of Cleveland H 913
History of the Jews of Los Angeles H 1005
History of the Labor Movement in the United States H 1562
A History of the Los Angeles Labor Movement, 1911-1941 H 1617
A History of the Massachusetts Hospital Life Insurance Company H 1811
A History of the Monroe Doctrine PS 748
A History of the Music Festival at Chautauqua Institution from 1847 to
    1957 M 124
A History of the National Resources Planning Board, 1933-1943 H 1934
A History of the Public Land Policies H 1957
A History of the Rockefeller Institute, 1901-1953 STM 80
A History of the Southern Confederacy H 291
History of the United States Army H 40
A History of the United States Atomic Energy Commission. Volume I: The
    New World, 1939-1946 STM 165
A History of the United States Atomic Energy Commission. Volume II:
    Atomic Shield, 1947-1952 STM 166
History of the United States Rubber Company H 1650
History of the Western Movement H 1482
A History of Underground Comics PC 310
A History of Urban America H 1318
History of Water Color Painting in America A-A 269
A History of Women in America H 763
The Hite Report PSY 99

The Hoe and the Horse on the Plains H 1156
Holding on to the Land and the Lord A-F 100
Holding the Line H 416
Holding Their Own H 833
The Holiness Revival of the Nineteenth Century R 272
Hollywood: The Dream Factory PC 569
Hollywood and After PC 622
Hollywood as Historian PC 577
Hollywood Genres PC 594
Hollywood Goes to War: Films and American Society 1939-1952 PC 601
The Hollywood Hallucination PC 625
Hollywood in Fiction PC 613
Hollywood in the Fifties PC 474
Hollywood in the Forties PC 484
Hollywood in the Seventies PC 509
Hollywood in the Sixties PC 422
Hollywood in the Thirties PC 423
Hollywood in the Twenties PC 574
Hollywood in Transition PC 520
The Hollywood Indian PC 561
Hollywood Looks at Its Audience PC 479
The Hollywood Musical (1971) PC 398
The Hollywood Musical (1981) PC 548
The Hollywood Musical (1982) PC 464
The Hollywood Musical Goes to War PC 638
Hollywood Renaissance PC 490
The Hollywood Social Problem Film PC 576
Hollywood Studio Musicians M 388
Hollywood the Movie Colony the Movie Makers PC 585
The Hollywood Writer's War PC 598
Hollywood's Children PC 435
Hollywood's Image of the Jew PC 472
The Holy Barbarians L 338
Home as Found: Authority and Genealogy in Nineteenth-Century American
    Literature L 193
The Home Front PSY 5
The Home Front and Beyond H 760
Home Life in Colonial Days H 93
A Homemade World: The American Modernist Writer L 325
Home Missions on the American Frontier R 74
Home Style PS 123
Home Sweet Home: American Domestic Vernacular Architecture A-A 484
Homeboys: Gangs, Drugs, and Prison in the Barrios of Los Angeles
    SOC 643
The Homes of America A-A 497
The Homes of the Pilgrim Fathers in England and America, 1620-1685
    A-A 535
Homicide in American Fiction, 1798-1860 L 119
The Homosexual Tradition in American Poetry L 573
Homosexuality and Psychotherapy PSY 84
Honkers and Shouters M 240
Honor and the American Dream A-F 274
Hooded Americanism: The History of the Ku Klux Klan R 259
Hookers, Rounders, and Desk Clerks: The Social Organization of the Hotel
    Community SOC 647
Horizons West, Anthony Mann, Budd Boeticher, Sam Peckinpah: Studies in
    Authorship Within the Western PC 510
The Horrors of the Half-Known Life H 704
Horse Sense in American Humor, from Benjamin Franklin to Ogden Nash
    L 451
The Horse, the Gun, and the Piece of Property PC 727

A Host of Tongues: Language Communities in the United States   A-F 349
Hosts and Guests   A-F 140
Hot Jazz   M 321
An Hour with American Music   M 28
The House and Foreign Policy   PS 808
The House at Work   PS 114
A House for All People   H 842
The House of Baring in American Trade and Finance   H 1711
The House of Beadle and Adams and Its Dime and Nickle Novels   PC 81
House of Cards: The Legalization and Control of Casino Gambling
    SOC 659
The House of Hancock   H 1655
Houses of Boston's Back Bay   A-A 562
Househusbands   SOC 330
Housing Market Discrimination   SOC 40
Housing Messages   PC 1010
How Boston Played   PC 949
How Capitalism Underdeveloped Black America   PS 548
How Many Miles to Camelot: The All-American Sport Myth   PC 958
How Much Is Enough?   PS 630
How New York Stole the Idea of Modern Art   A-A 211
How Should the U.S. Meet Its Military Manpower Needs?   PS 614
How the North Won   H 320
How the West Was Drawn   A-A 281
How to Limit Government Spending   PS 398
How to Read Donald Duck   PC 309
How to Talk Back to Your Television Set   PC 769
How We Live   SOC 411
How We Play the Game   PC 965
Howells and the Age of Realism   L 115
The Human Basis of the Polity   PS 541
The Human Cage   A-A 468
Human Nature, Class, and Ethnicity   SOC 135
Human Nature in American Thought   H 577
Human Relations in an Expanding Company   A-F 328
Human Relations in Industry   A-F 308
Human Relations in the Restaurant Industry   A-F 343
Human Rights in American and Russian Political Thought   PS 36
Human Services for Cultural Minorities   PSY 55
Humanistic Psychology   PSY 170
Humbug: The Art of P. T. Barnum   PC 350
A Hundred Years of Music in America   M 89
Hunter's Point   A-F 181
Hunters, Seamen, and Entrepreneurs   A-F 128
Husbandmen of Plymouth   H 167
Hustling and Other Hard Work   A-F 194
Hutterian Brethren   A-F 81
Hutterite Society   A-F 107
The Hutterites in North America   A-F 108
Hyemeoyohsts Storm's "Seven Arrows"   L 374
The Hyphenate in Recent American Politics and Diplomacy   PS 479

I.T.T.   H 1789
I Heard the Old Fisherman Say   A-F 446
I Lost It at the Movies   PC 499
"I Respectfully Disagree with the Judge's Order": The Boston School
    Desegregation Controversy   SOC 206
Icons and Images of the 60s   A-A 32
Icons of Popular Culture   PC 1014
Idea Art: A Critical Anthology   A-A 255

The Idea of a Party System H 608
The Idea of a Southern Nation H 1478
The Idea of Fraternity in America H 639
The Idea of the American South H 658
Ideals and Self-Interest in America's Foreign Relations PS 738
Ideas and the Novel L 576
Ideas in America H 614
The Ideas of the Woman Suffrage Movement, 1890-1920 H 774
Identity and the Life Cycle PSY 64
The Identity Crisis Theme in American Feature Films, 1960-1969 PC 531
Identity, Youth and Crisis PSY 65
The Ideological Origins of the American Revolution H 194
Ideologies and Utopias H 586
Ideology and Myth in American Politics PS 558
Ideology and the Image PC 557
Ideology and the Rise of Labor Theory in America SOC 536
Ideology and Utopia in the United States PS 535
If All We Did Was to Weep at Home H 768
If I Forget Thee O Jerusalem H 997
The Ignoble Savage: American Literary Racism, 1790-1890 L 93
Ill Fares the Land H 1602
I'll Take My Stand: The South and the Agrarian Tradition L 318
The Illegals SOC 143
The Illogic of American Nuclear Strategy PS 685
The Illusion of Equality: The Effect of Education on Opportunity, Inequal-
   ity, and Social Conflict SOC 487
The Illusion of Life: American Realism as a Literary Form L 152
The Illusion of Neutrality PS 622
The Illustrated Book of Baseball Folklore PC 930
The Illustrated History of Country Music M 138
The Illustrated History of Magic PC 331
Illustrious Immigrants H 906
The Image: A Guide to Pseudo-Events in America PC 4
Image and Idea L 612
Image and Influence: Studies in the Sociology of Film PC 623
The Image Decade: Television Documentary, 1965-1975 PC 763
The Image Empire: A History of Broadcasting in the United States,
   Volume III--From 1953 PC 719
The Image of Man in America H 695
The Image of the American City in Popular Literature, 1820-1870 PC 96
Image of the Black in Children's Fiction PC 111
The Image of the City in Modern Literature L 376
The Image of the Indian and the Black Man in America, 1590-1900 A-A 103
The Image of the Jew in American Literature from Early Republic to Mass
   Immigration L 523
The Image of Thomas Jefferson in the Public Eye A-A 43
Images and Enterprise STM 188
Images of Alcoholism PC 442
Images of American Living A-A 455
Images of Healing STM 270
The Images of Life on Children's Television PSY 7
Images of the Mexican American in Fiction and Film PC 281
Images of Women in Fiction L 479
Images of Women in Film PC 414
Imaginary Worlds PC 171
The Imagined Past: Portrayals of Our History in Modern American Literature
   L 315
Imagining America L 248
Imagism L 243
The Immediate Experience PC 632
The Immigrant Church H 890

Immigrant City H 868
Immigrant Destinations H 920
Immigrant Life in New York City, 1825-1863 H 897
Immigrant Milwaukee, 1836-1860 H 871
The Immigrant Press and Its Control PC 890
Immigrant-Survivors: Post Holocaust Consciousness in Recent Jewish American Fiction L 224
The Immigrant Upraised H 983
Immigrants and Religion in Urban America H 969
Immigrants and the City H 899
Immigrants, Baptists, and the Protestant Mind in America H 879
Immigrants in Industrial America H 893
Immigrants in the Ozarks H 914
The Immigrants' Influence on Wilson's Peace Politics H 977
Immigrants to Freedom H 857
Immigration and American History H 869
Immigration and Industrialization H 856
The Immortal Eight A-A 224
The Immortal Storm PC 239
Impact of Air Power STM 112
The Impact of Publicity on Corporate Offenders SOC 623
The Impact of Reapportionment PS 455
The Impact of Victorian Children's Fiction PC 110
The Impact of Work Schedules on the Family SOC 317
The Impending Crisis, 1848-1861 H 368
The Imperfect Diamond: The Story of Baseball's Reserve Systems PC 967
The Imperfect Union: A History of Corruption in American Trade Unions H 1583
The Imperfect Union: School Consolidation and Community Conflict SOC 304
An Imperfect Union: Slavery, Federalism, and Comity H 1949
Imperial America PS 721
Imperial Democracy PS 724
The Imperial Self: An Essay in American Literary and Cultural History L 90
Imperial Texas H 1481
The Imperiled Union H 390
The Imperious Economy PS 599
Implementing Public Policy PS 374
The Impossible Revolution? Black Power and the American Dream: Phase II SOC 154
Impounded People A-F 334
Imprisonment in America SOC 654
Improving Prosecution? PS 397
Improvising M 249
The Impulse of Fantasy Literature PC 178
In a Different Voice: Psychological Theory PSY 80
In Defense of Reason L 667
In English Ways H 49
In Fear of Each Other PSY 53
In Good Taste H 1656
In Her Own Words: Oral Histories of Women Physicians STM 257
In His Image, But . . . : Racism in Southern Religion, 1780-1910 R 268
In Its Own Image: How Television Has Transformed Sports PC 984
In Labor: Women and Power in the Birthplace SOC 379
In Praise of America A-A 374
In Pursuit of Profit H 1763
In Red Man's Land H 1185
In Search of Heresy: American Literature in an Age of Conformity L 208
In Search of the Golden West H 1492
In Search of White Crows R 213

In Search of Wonder: Essays on Modern Science Fiction PC 232
In Struggle PS 522
In the Arresting Eye: The Rhetoric of Imagism L 279
In the Course of Human Events H 224
In the Driver's Seat PC 74
In the Eyes of the Law H 1941
In the Shadow of FDR H 487
In the Shadow of the Enlightenment STM 224
In the Singer's Temple: Prose Fictions of Barthelme, Gaines, Brautigan,
    Piercy, Kesey, and Kosinski L 304
In This Proud Land A-A 350
In Transition: How Feminism, Sexual Liberation and the Search for Self-
    Fulfillment Have Altered America SOC 329
"In Vain I Tried to Tell You" A-F 219
The Inadvertent Epic: From Uncle Tom's Cabin to Roots PC 75
The Inclusive Flame: Studies in Modern American Poetry L 237
Income and Wealth of the United States H 1887
Income Maintenance and Work Incentives SOC 574
Income Support PS 307
The Incompleat Board: The Unfolding of Corporate Governance SOC 572
The Incompleat Folksinger M 191
The Inconstant Savage H 1218
The Incorporation of America H 396
Indefensible Weapons PS 719
The Index of American Design A-A 369
Indian Americans PSY 178
The Indian and the Horse H 1230
Indian and White A-F 206
Indian Art in America A-A 6
Indian Art in North America A-A 16
Indian Art of the United States A-A 7
An Indian Canaan H 1243
The Indian Dispossessed H 1162
Indian Drinking A-F 230
Indian Healing A-F 221
The Indian Heritage of America H 1171
The Indian in America H 1265
The Indian in American Life H 1187
Indian Life H 1241
Indian Life of the Northwest Coast of North America H 1146
Indian Life on the Upper Missouri H 1133
Indian New England Before the Mayflower H 1234
The Indian Office H 1249
Indian Painters and White Patrons A-A 3
Indian Police and Judges H 1148
Indian Removal H 1137
Indian Running A-F 235
The Indian Traders H 1196
Indian Traders on the Middle Border H 1255
Indians and Other Americans H 1134
Indians, Animals, and the Fur Trade H 1181
Indians, Bureaucrats and Land H 1106
Indians of North America (1969) A-F 210
Indians of North America (1979) H 1256
The Indians of the Americas H 1110
Indians of the High Plains H 1163
Indians of the Pacific Northwest H 1233
The Indians of the Southwest H 1118
Indians of the United States A-F 254
Indians of the Woodlands H 1164
Indicators of Change in the American Family PSY 68

Indigenous Psychologies PSY 95
Individual Psychology PSY 131
Individualism and Nationalism in American Ideology H 550
Individuals: Post Movement Art in America A-A 126
Industrial Design H 1710
Industrial Evolution H 1765
Industrial Slavery in the Old South H 1082
Industry and the Photographic Image A-A 344
Industry Comes of Age H 1731
Inequality SOC 472
Inequality and Stratification in the United States SOC 497
Inequality in American Society SOC 496
Inequality in an Age of Decline SOC 449
The Inevitable Americans SOC 5
Inevitable Revolutions PS 709
The Inevitability of Patriarchy SOC 357
The Influence of the Carnegie, Ford, and Rockefeller Foundations on Ameri-
    can Foreign Policy PS 583
The Influence of the Ecole des Beaux-Arts on the Architects of the United
    States A-A 493
The Information Machines PC 646
The Ingenious Yankees STM 135
Inheritance, Wealth, and Society H 568
The Inmate Economy SOC 631
The Inmost Leaf L 323
The Inner American PSY 175
The Inner Civil War H 592
Innovation and Implementation in Public Organizations PS 365
The Inquisition in Hollywood PC 438
Inside Bebop M 273
Inside Bureaucracy PS 313
Inside Jazz M 264
Inside the Bureaucracy PS 363
Inside the Jury SOC 628
Inside the Music Publishing Industry M 379
In Small Things Forgotten A-F 33
Institutional Change and American Economic Growth H 1846
Institutional History of Virginia in the Seventeenth Century H 73
Insull STM 242
Insurance Reform H 1701
The Insurgent Progressives in the United States Senate and the New Deal,
    1933-1939 H 506
Insuring the Nation's Health PS 319
Intellectual America L 238
The Intellectual Crisis in American Public Administration PS 371
Intellectual History in America H 683
Intellectual Life in Jefferson's Virginia, 1790-1830 L 51
Intellectual Life in the Colonial South, 1585-1763 L 50
The Intellectual Life of Colonial New England L 69
The Intellectual Migration, Europe and America, 1930-1960 H 589
Intellectual Origins of American Radicalism H 634
The Intellectual Versus the City H 691
Intellectuals and Other Traitors PS 519
The Intelligence of a People H 566
The Intelligence of Democracy PS 97
The Intemperate Zone PS 634
The Intensive Group Experience PSY 152
Interaction Ritual A-F 39
Interest Groups and Lobbying PS 485
Interest Groups in American Society PS 505
Interest Groups in the United States PS 502

Intergenerational Occupational Mobility in the United States SOC 494
Intergovernmental Perspectives on Canada-U.S. Relations PS 790
Interlocking Directorates SOC 576
Intermarriage in the United States PSY 54
International Conflict in an American City H 999
The International Film Industry PC 477
The Interpretation of Ordinary Landscapes PC 1031
The Interpretation of Otherness L 519
Interpretations of American Literature L 501
The Interpreted Design as a Structural Principle in American Prose
   L 586
Interpreters and Critics of the Cold War PS 794
Interpreting Folklore A-F 402
The Intersection of Science Fiction and Philosophy PC 242
Interstate Express Highway Politics, 1941-1956 STM 311
Intimate Strangers: Men and Women Together SOC 312
Introduction to American Indian Art, the Exposition of Indian Tribal Arts
   A-A 15
Introduction to Chicano Studies A-F 264
An Introduction to Positive Political Theory PS 105
An Introduction to Thanatology SOC 440
An Introduction to the American Underground Film PC 572
The Invaded Universities H 582
The Invasion of America H 1169
Inventing America H 253
Inventing Billy the Kid PC 288
Inventing the American Way of Death, 1830-1920 STM 121
Invention and Economic Growth STM 329
Invention and Innovation in the Radio Industry STM 232
The Invention of the Modern Hospital STM 379
Inventors Behind the Inventor STM 54
The Investigators PS 400
Investment Banking in America H 1663
The Investment Frontier H 1705
Inviolable Voice: History and Twentieth-Century Poetry L 395
The Invisible Alcoholics SOC 652
The Invisible Farmers SOC 587
Invisible Immigrants H 896
Invisible Lives: Social World of the Aged SOC 444
An Invitation to Archaeology PC 1018
Invitation to Struggle PS 609
The Iowa Testing Programs STM 286
The Ioway Indians H 1104
Irish Americans: Identity and Assimilation SOC 115
The Irish and Irish Politicians H 953
The Irish Diaspora in America H 962
The Irish in America H 1007
The Irish in Philadelphia H 864
The Irish in the United States SOC 112
The Irish New Orleans, 1800-1860 H 974
The Irish Relations H 865
Irish-American Fiction L 239
Irish-American Nationalism 1870-1890 H 860
Iron and Steel in 19th-Century America H 1797
The Iron Barons H 1717
Iron Eye's Family H 1143
Iron Frontier H 1805
The Iron of Melancholy L 553
Iron Road to the West STM 362
Iron Works on the Saugus STM 159
Ironmaker to the Confederacy H 286

The Irony of Liberal Reason PS 59
The Irony of Vietnam PS 650
The Iroquois and the New Deal H 1153
The Iroquois in the American Revolution H 1141
The Irreconcilables H 533
Is Liberalism Dead? And Other Essays H 672
Isaac Backus and the American Pietistic Tradition R 62
Isolationism in America, 1935-1941 PS 686
Israel: The Embattled Ally PS 772
Israel as a Factor in Jewish-Gentile Relations in America PS 776
Israel in the Mind of America PS 661
The Issues at Hand: Studies in Contemporary Magazine Science Fiction
    PC 207
It Changed My Life: Writing on the Women's Movement SOC 351
Italian Americans SOC 168
The Italian-Americans H 943
The Italians of Newark SOC 101
Italian or American? The Second Generation PSY 47
An Italian Passage H 858
Italians in Chicago, 1880-1930 H 973
The Italians of San Francisco, 1850-1930 H 927
It's Rock 'n' Roll M 371
It's Too Late to Stop Now H 407
The Ivory and Ebony Towers: Race Relations and Higher Education
    SOC 243

The J.D. Films PC 543
JFK: Ordeal in Africa PS 723
JPL and the American Space Program STM 212
The Jack-Roller at Seventy SOC 660
Jacksonian America H 367
Jacksonian Aristocracy H 347
The Jacksonian Economy H 1928
The Jacksonian Era, 1828-1848 H 401
Jacksonian Jew R 183
The Jacksonian Persuasion H 346
Jam Session M 281
Jamestown H 69
The Japanese American Community SOC 161
Japanese Americans: Changing Patterns of Ethnic Affiliation Over Three
    Generations SOC 182
Japanese Americans: The Evolution of a Subculture SOC 156
Japanese Americans: Oppression and Success SOC 197
Japanese in the United States H 942
The Japanese Influence in America A-A 478
Jay Cooke, Private Banker H 1737
Jay Gould H 1704
Jazz (1926) M 358
Jazz (1960) M 277
Jazz (1963) M 299
Jazz: A History M 350
Jazz: A History of the New York Scene M 263
Jazz: A People's Music M 276
Jazz: Hot and Hybrid M 332
Jazz: Its Evolution and Essence M 296
Jazz: New Perspectives on the History of Jazz M 294
Jazz: The Transition Years, 1940-1960 M 365
Jazz and Blues M 356
Jazz and the White American M 304
Jazz, an Introduction M 303

Jazz Away from Home M 282
The Jazz Book M 255
The Jazz Cataclysm M 311
Jazz Cavalcade M 270
Jazz City M 319
Jazz Dance M 344
The Jazz Experience M 305
Jazz from the Congo to the Metropolitan M 283
Jazz in Perspective M 302
Jazz in the Sixties M 261
Jazz Is M 292
Jazz Journalism PC 841
The Jazz Life M 293
The Jazz Makers M 337
Jazz Masters in Transition, 1957-69 M 360
Jazz Masters of New Orleans M 359
Jazz Masters of the Fifties M 287
Jazz Masters of the Forties M 280
Jazz Masters of the Thirties M 345
Jazz Masters of the Twenties M 289
Jazz Panorama M 363
Jazz People M 313
Jazz Piano M 348
A Jazz Retrospect M 290
The Jazz Story from the '90s to the '60s M 271
Jazz Style in Kansas City and the Southwest M 331
Jazz Styles M 286
The Jazz Text M 316
The Jazz Titans, Including "The Parlance of the Hip" M 328
The Jazz Tradition M 361
Jazz Women at the Keyboard M 355
The Jazz Word M 262
Jazzmen M 327
Jefferson and Civil Liberties H 333
Jefferson and Madison H 218
The Jefferson Crisis H 292
The Jefferson Image in the American Mind H 664
The Jeffersonian Persuasion H 261
The Jeffersonian Republicans in Power H 279
Jesuit and Savage in New France H 1176
The Jet Makers STM 45
Jew and Irish H 916
The Jew in American Politics PS 501
The Jew in American Sports PC 986
The Jewel-Hinged Jaw PC 218
Jewish Agricultural Utopias in America, 1880-1910 H 605
Jewish Americans SOC 131
Jewish Identity on the Suburban Frontier SOC 222
Jewish Labor in the United States H 895
Jewish Life in Twentieth-Century America R 181
The Jewish Woman in America H 705
The Jewish Woman in America: Two Female Immigrant Generations, 1820-1929
   H 917
The Jewish Writer in America L 522
The Jews: Social Patterns of an American Group SOC 221
Jews and Americans L 348
Jews and Blacks SOC 142
Jews and Judaism in a Midwestern Community H 980
The Jews in America H 883
The Jews in American Society SOC 220
Jews in the South H 886
Jews in Suburbia SOC 133

The Jews of California H 918
The Jews of the United States SOC 118
Jews on the Frontier H 995
The Jews on Tin Pan Alley M 405
Jews, Wars, and Communism H 1000
The Jicarilla Apaches H 1145
Jock Culture, USA PC 957
The Jocks PC 994
Joe Scott, the Woodsman-Songmaker A-F 422
John Collier's Crusade for Indian Reform H 1217
John F. Kennedy and the Second Reconstruction PS 110
Joan Roach, Maritime Entrepreneur H 1792
John Ruskin and Aesthetic Thought in America, 1840-1900 H 680
Jonathan Draws the Long Bow A-F 397
Jonathan Edwards R 151
Jonathan Edwards, Pastor R 65
Jonathan Edwards's Moral Thought and Its British Context R 138
Journalism in the United States, from 1690 to 1872 PC 871
Journals and Journeymen PC 845
The Journey Back: Issues in Black Literature and Criticism L 441
The Journey Beyond Tragedy: A Study of Myth and Modern Fiction L 397
The Journey Narrative in American Literature L 648
The Joy of Sports PC 978
Judaism in America: From Curiosity to Third Faith R 159
Judicial Power and Reconstruction Politics H 1969
Jules Henry on Education A-F 312
The Jurisprudence of John Marshall H 1947
The Jury: Its Role in American Society SOC 656
Just Country M 141
Justice Crucified H 907
Justice, Equal Opportunity, and the Family PS 23
Justice, Human Nature, and Political Obligation PS 37

The Kaleidoscopic Lens: How Hollywood Views Ethnic Groups PC 546
The Kalmyk Mongols A-F 134
The Kansas Beef Industry H 1816
Kansas City and the Railroads H 1317
Keepers of the Game: Indian-Animal Relationships and the Fur Trade
    H 1193
Keeping Pace with the New Television PC 785
Keeping the Corporate Image H 1796
Kennedy and the Berlin Wall Crisis PS 601
The Kennedy Crises PC 877
Kentucky Country M 198
Keynesian Economy H 1843
Khaki-Collar Crime: Deviant Behavior in the Military Context SOC 613
Kicked a Building Lately? A-A 607
Killing for Profit SOC 620
Kin and Communities A-F 55
Kindred Spirits: Knickerbocker Writers and American Artists, 1807-1835
    L 111
King Cotton and His Retainers H 1817
King Cotton Diplomacy H 363
King of the Delawares H 1263
King of the Bs Working Within the Hollywood System PC 540
The Kingdom of God in America R 18
Kipling, Auden & Co. L 544
Kiva, Cross and Crown H 1178
The Knights of Labor in the South H 1600
Knowledge and Power: Essays on Science and Government STM 217

The Known and the Unknown: The Iconography of Science Fiction PC 267
Knoxville, Tennessee H 1479
Kremers and Urdang's History of Pharmacy STM 350
The Ku Klux Klan in the City, 1915-1930 H 1336

L.A. in the Thirties, 1931-1941 A-A 600
Labor and Immigration in Industrial America H 1615
Labor and Leisure at Home SOC 255
Labor and the Left H 1588
Labor and Monopoly Capital PS 517
Labor, Church, and the Sugar Establishment H 1523
Labor in a New Land H 113
Labor in American Politics PS 481
Labor in New Mexico H 1587
Labor in the South H 1598
Labor-Management Cooperation SOC 591
Labor Market Segmentation H 1554
The Labor Movement in the United States, 1860-1895 H 1643
Laboring and Dependent Classes in Colonial America H 1584
Labor's Search for Political Order H 1560
Labor's War at Home H 1593
Ladies of the Evening PC 788
The Lady Investigates PC 143
Land and People A-A 588
Land of Savagery, Land of Promise H 559
Land of the Millrats A-F 398
The Land Office Business H 1977
The Land That I Show You H 904
Landlord and Tenant in Colonial New York H 1729
Landlords and Farmers in the Hudson-Mohawk Region, 1790-1850 H 1446
Landmarks of American Writing L 476
The Landrum-Griffin Act H 1521
Landscape: Theory A-A 346
Landscape: Selected Writings of J. B. Jackson A-A 532
Language and Art in the Navajo Universe H 1271
Language in Culture and Society A-F 357
Language in the Inner City A-F 361
Language in the USA A-F 351
Language Loyalty in the United States A-F 352
The Language of Allegory L 611
The Language of American Popular Entertainment PC 403
The Language of Canaan L 68
The Language of Children Reared in Poverty PSY 67
The Language of Native America A-F 208
Language of Politics PS 96
The Language of Puritan Feeling L 67
The Language of Television Advertising A-F 353
The Language of the Night PC 235
Language of the Underworld A-F 364
Languages in Conflict A-F 366
La Raza: Forgotten Americans SOC 207
Last Chapters: A Sociology of Aging and Dying SOC 432
The Last Half-Century: Societal Change and Politics in America SOC 9
The Last Laugh: Form and Affirmation in the Contemporary Comic Novel
    L 410
The Last of the Provincials L 286
The Last Taboo: Sex and the Fear of Death SOC 398
Late Adulthood SOC 425
Late Harvest: Essays and Addresses in American Literature and Culture
    L 640

Late Modern: The Visual Arts Since 1945 A-A 87
Late Nineteenth-Century American Economic Development H 1939
The Latin Image in American Film PC 639
The Latin Tinge M 426
Latino Language and Communicative Behavior A-F 265
Latrobe, Jefferson and the National Capitol A-A 552
Laurel and Thorn: The Athlete in American Literature L 530
La Vida: A Puerto Rican Family in the Culture of Poverty--San Juan and
    New York SOC 162
Law and Authority in Colonial America H 57
Law and Economic Growth H 1962
Law and Identity: Lawyers, Native Americans and Legal Practices
    SOC 567
Law and Order Vs. the Miners H 1597
Law and Society in Puritan Massachusetts H 1968
Law and the Conditions of Freedom in the 19th-Century United States
    H 1961
The Law of the Heart L 289
Law, Society, and Politics in Early Maryland H 126
The Lawless State PS 328
Lawrence and Oppenheimer STM 94
The Lay of the Land: Metaphors as Experience and History in American
    Life and Letters L 554
The Lazzaroni: Science and Scientists in Mid-Nineteenth Century America
    STM 252
Lead Time PS 565
Leadership PS 9
Leadership and Change PS 452
Leadership of the American Zionist Organization, 1897-1930 H 994
League of the Ho-de-no-saw-nee or Iroquois A-F 234
The Lean Years H 1524
Learning from Las Vegas A-A 630
Learning Lessons A-F 323
Learning to Be Militant: Ethnic Identity and the Development of Political
    Militance in a Chicano Community SOC 145
The Left-Leaning Antenna: Political Bias in Television PC 772
The Legacy of Jewish Migration H 848
Legends and Folk Beliefs in a Swedish American Community A-F 429
Legends of the Hasidim A-F 443
Legislated Learning PS 403
Legitimation of the Social Rights and the Western Welfare State PS 27
Leisure and Popular Culture in Transition PC 34
Leisure and Recreation Places PC 12
The Leo Frank Case H 885
The Leopard's Spots: Scientific Attitudes Toward Race in America,
    1815-19 STM 355
The Lesbian Community A-F 163
Lesbian/Woman PSY 134
"Lessons" of the Past PS 725
Let There Be Light. The Electric Utility in Wisconsin, 1881-1955
    STM 243
The Levittowners SOC 36
Liberal America and the Third World PS 745
Liberal Democracy PS 42
Liberal Equality PS 30
The Liberal Imagination L 654
The Liberal Tradition in America PS 34
Liberalism Against Populism PS 103
Liberalism and the Limits of Justice PS 53
The "Liberated" Woman of 1914 H 714
Liberating Women's History H 716

The Liberation of American Literature L 471
The Liberation of Women SOC 360
Liberty and Authority H 130
Liberty's Daughters H 795
The Life: The Lore and Folk Poetry of the Black Hustler A-F 465
Life After Youth: Female Forty SOC 422
The Life and Art of the North American Indian A-A 17
The Life and Death of Tin Pan Alley PC 339
The Life and Decline of the American Railroad STM 363
Life and Labor in the Old South H 1490
Life Imitates Architecture A-A 624
Life in Large Families: Views of Mormon Women SOC 250
The Life Insurance Enterprise, 1885-1910 H 1727
The Life of Benjamin Bannekep STM 24
A Life of George Westinghouse STM 291
The Life of the Mind in America H 643
Life on Television PC 762
Life Science in the Twentieth Century STM 6
Life Styles A-F 34
Life, Work, and Rebellion in the Coal Fields H 1547
Lifelines: Black Families in Chicago A-F 166
Lifeway Leap A-F 37
The Light of Distant Skies A-A 175
The Light of the Common Day L 110
The Light of the Home H 753
The Life of the Self PSY 126
Like a Brother, Like a Lover L 628
Li'l Abner PC 290
Limited War PS 739
Limited War Revisited PS 740
The Limits of Infinity PC 610
The Limits of Legitimacy PS 66
The Limits of Liberty PS 70
The Limits of Power PS 705
The Limits of Progressive School Reform in the 1970s SOC 314
Limners and Likenesses A-A 149
Lincoln and His Generals H 408
Lincoln and His Party in the Secession Crisis H 369
Lincoln and the Indians H 1204
Lincoln and the Radicals H 409
Lincoln and the Tools of War STM 50
The Lincoln Legend L 444
Linguistic Convergence A-F 240
Linguistic Theory in America A-F 365
The Lion and the Honeycomb L 227
Liquor License A-F 88
Listen to the Blues M 211
Literacy in Colonial New England H 133
Literacy in the Open-Access College SOC 308
Literary Culture in Early New England 1620-1730 L 85
Literary Disruptions: The Making of a Post-Contemporary Fiction L 331
A Literary History of Alabama L 198
The Literary History of the American Revolution, 1763-1783 L 83
Literary History of the United States L 26
Literary Influences in Colonial Newspapers, 1704-1750 L 48
The Literary Life of the Early Friends, 1650-1725 L 84
Literary Publishing in America, 1790-1850 L 116
Literary Romanticism in America L 438
The Literary Sculptors A-A 252
The Literary Situation L 255
Literary Swordsmen and Sorcerers PC 172

A Literary Symbiosis: Science Fiction/Fantasy Mystery   PC 246
Literary Transcendentalism L 108
Literary Women PC 193
Literature and Ideas in America   L 499
Literature and the American Tradition L 7
Literature and the Sixth Sense L 613
Literature and the Urban Experience L 548
Literature and Theology in Colonial New England L 70
Literature at the Barricades L 231
Literature in America L 614
The Literature of Fact L 413
The Literature of Memory L 296
The Literature of Terror PC 194
The Literature of the American People L 21
The Literature of the Middle Western Frontier L 184
Literature of the Occult PC 179
The Literature of the United States L 5
The Literature of Virginia in the Seventeenth Century L 63
Literature, Popular Culture and Society PC 41
A Literature Without Qualities L 221
A Little Commonwealth H 88
The Little Community A-F 22
The Little Magazine L 313
Little Smoky Ridge A-F 130
The Liveliest Art PC 511
The Lively Experiment: The Shaping of Christianity in America R 14
Lives After Vietnam PSY 40
Lives in Stress: Women and Depression PSY 16
The Lives of Mentally Retarded People SOC 622
Lives of Mississippi Authors, 1817-1967 L 12
Lives Through the Years PSY 183
Living and Dying at Murray Manor A-F 99
The Living and the Dead A-F 153
Living Cinema PC 529
Living Country Blues M 235
Living in the Shadow of the Second Coming R 290
Living Poorly in America SOC 447
Living-Room War PC 717
Living with Energy Shortfall SOC 68
Lobbying PS 504
Lobbying for the People PS 475
Lobbyists and Legislators PS 484
Local Color A-F 407
Loft Living: Culture and Capital in Urban Change SOC 76
The Log Cabin in America A-A 524
The Log Cabin Myth A-A 554
The Logic of Millennial Thought R 284
Loneliness PSY 144
The Lonely Crowd SOC 17
A Long, Deep Furrow H 1500
Long Island Is My Nation A-A 381
Long Journey Home A-F 460
Long Memory H 1015
Long Steel Rail M 139
Longtime Califon': A Documentary Study of an American Chinatown
   SOC 187
The Look of the Land PC 1023
Looking Away: Hollywood and Vietnam PC 608
A Loose Game PC 932
Lords of the Loom H 361
Los Angeles: The Architecture of Four Ecologies A-A 593

The Los Angeles Barrio, 1850–1890 H 926
Los Angeles Transfer A-A 596
Los Majados H 987
The Losers: Gang Delinquency in an American Suburb SOC 644
A Loss of Mastery H 596
The Lost America of Love L 370
Lost Chords M 392
Lost Highways M 399
The Lost Reform STM 175
The Lost Sisterhood H 802
The Lost Tradition: Mothers and Daughters in Literature L 483
The Lost World of Thomas Jefferson H 565
Lotus Among the Magnolias: The Mississippi Chinese SOC 200
Louis Agassiz STM 230
Love and Death in the American Novel L 503
Love Canal SOC 545
Love-Hate Relations: English and American Sensibilities L 637
Love, Mystery, and Misery: Feeling in Gothic Fiction PC 191
Lovely Americans M 41
Lucifer at Large L 355
Lucifer in Harness L 512
The Lumbee Problem A-F 205
Lunar Impact: A History of Project Range STM 150
Lying-In H 837

M. & M. Karolik Collection of American Paintings, 1815-1865 A-A 179
M. & M. Karolik Collection of American Watercolours and Drawings, 1800-
    1875 A-A 284
Ma Rainey and the Classic Blues Singers M 242
The Machiavellian Moment H 160
The Machine in the Garden: Technology and the Pastoral Ideal L 574
Machines that Built America STM 55
The Madam as Entrepreneur: Career Management in House Prostitution SOC
    629
Made in America A-A 475
Madness in Society STM 312
The Madness in Sports PC 923
The Madwoman in the Attic PC 188
The Mafia in America SOC 606
The Mafia Principle SOC 648
Magic and Myth of the Movies PC 626
Magical Medicine A-F 417
The Maginot Line Syndrome PS 715
Main Currents in American Thought L 15
Main Currents in the History of American Journalism PC 842
Main Street: The Face of Urban America A-A 502
Main Street on the Middle Border H 258
Mainland China, Taiwan, and U.S. Policy PS 796
Maintaining Diversity in Higher Education SOC 258
Major Writers of Early American Literature L 56
The Majority Finds Its Past H 780
The Majority of One PS 632
The Makah Indians H 1111
Making Foreign Economic Policy PS 616
Making It To #1: How College Football and Basketball Teams Get There
    PC 924
Making News PC 912
Making Ocean Policy PS 332
The Making of a Counter Culture PC 56
The Making of a Labor Bureaucrat H 1640

The Making of a Special Relationship PS 678
The Making of an American Community H 1434
The Making of an American Jewish Community H 900
The Making of an Architect, 1881-1981 A-A 494
The Making of an Ethnic Middle Class H 1002
The Making of Jazz M 265
The Making of Modern Advertising H 1771
The Making of the American Theatre L 29
The Making of the Missle Crisis PS 618
The Making of the Monroe Doctrine H 337
The Making of Urban America H 1373
Making Sense of Self: Medical Advice Literature in Late Nineteenth-Century
    America STM 122
Making the Grade A-F 80
Making Tracks M 393
Making Work: Self-Created Jobs in Participatory Organizations SOC 585
Male and Female A-F 56
Male Dilemma PSY 165
Male Homosexuals SOC 391
Man and Beast in American Comic Legend A-F 399
Man in Modern Fiction: Some Minority Opinions on Contemporary American
    Writing L 278
The Man in the Principal's Office A-F 345
Man of High Fidelity STM 223
The Man of Letters in New England and the South L 633
"Man Over Money" H 1906
The Managed Heart SOC 421
Managerial Hierarchies H 1839
Managerial Strategies and Industrial Relations H 1700
Managers and Workers H 1611
Mandan and Hidatsa Music M 145
Manhattan Moves Uptown H 1348
Manhattan Project STM 146
Manifest Destiny and Mission in American History H 30
The Manipulators: America in the Media Age PC 697
Manipulatory Politics PS 89
Manitou and Providence H 1235
Manpower in Economic Growth H 1890
The Manufacture of Madness PSY 168
The Manufacture of News PC 650
Manufacturing Consent: Changes in the Labor Process Under Monopoly Capi-
    talism SOC 523
Manufacturing Green Gold H 1690
Manufacturing the News PC 863
Many Futures, Many Worlds: Theme and Form in Science Fiction PC 214
March of the Iron Men STM 56
The March of Time, 1935-1951 PC 466
From Margin to Mainstream: The Social Progress of Black Americans
    SOC 117
Marginal Workers, Marginal Jobs SOC 597
Marital Separation SOC 323
The Mark and the Knowledge: Social Stigma in Classic American Literature
    L 610
Mark Twain and Southwestern Humor L 159
Market Institutions and Economic Progress in the New South, 1865-1900
    H 1933
Marriage and Work in America PSY 176
Marriage Contracts and Couple Therapy PSY 156
Marriage, Divorce, Remarriage SOC 266
The Marriage-Go-Round: An Exploratory Study of Multiple Marriage
    SOC 274

Married Women and Work SOC 364
Mars and Minerva H 465
The Marshall Plan Revisited PS 807
Martin Van Buren: The Romantic Age of American Politics H 358
Marxian Socialism in the United States H 420
The Marxist Misntrels M 418
The Maryland Germans H 875
Maryland Queen Anne and Chippendale Furniture of the Eighteenth Century
    A-A 380
The Masks of Orthodoxy A-A 241
Mass Communication: A Sociological Perspective PC 710
Mass Communications PC 690
Mass Communications and American Empire PC 688
Mass Culture: The Popular Arts in America PC 54
Mass Culture Revisited PC 55
Mass Leisure PC 39
Mass Media and American Politics PC 660
Mass Media and Communication PC 700
The Mass Media and Modern Society PC 682
Mass Media and the National Experience PC 657
The Mass Media Elections PC 675
The Mass Media, Public Opinion, and Public Policy Analysis PC 701
Mass-Mediated Culture PC 53
Masters of Mystery PC 166
Masters Without Slaves H 373
Material Culture and the Study of American Life PC 1039
The Material Culture of the Wooden Age PC 1024
Material Culture Studies in America PC 1043
The Mathers H 141
The Maturing of American Science STM 200
The Maturing of Multinational Enterprise H 1814
Maules Curse L 668
The Mauve Decade: American Life at the End of the Nineteenth Century
    PC 69
Maximum Feasible Misunderstanding PS 362
Mayday at Yale: A Case Study in Student Radicalism SOC 320
McKinley, Bryan and the People H 314
The McNamara Strategy PS 692
Meaning and Action H 685
Meaning in Anthropology A-F 3
Means and Ends in American Abolitionism H 329
Measures for Progress STM 65
Measuring Outcomes of College SOC 301
The Mechanical Bride: Folklore of Industrial Man PC 673
The Mechanical Engineer in America, 1830-1910 STM 60
The Mechanical God: Machines in Science Fiction PC 220
A Mechanical People H 1631
Mechanics and Manufacturers in the Early Industrial Revolution H 1558
Mechanization Takes Command PC 1021
Media PC 692
Media and the American Mind PC 651
The Media and the Cities PC 652
The Media Are American PC 706
Media Culture PC 48
The Media Environment PC 698
The Media in America PC 702
Media-Made Dixie: The South in the American Imagination PC 668
The Media Moguls PC 910
The Media Monopoly SOC 515
Media Power PC 699
Media, Power, Politics PC 676

Media Sexploitation PC 667
The Media Society PC 654
Media-Speak: How Television Makes Up Your Mind PC 746
Media Unbound PC 777
Mediamerica: Form, Content, and Consequence PC 64
Mediaworld: Programming the Public PC 678
Medical America in the Nineteenth Century STM 42
Medical History STM 194
The Medical Merry-Go-Round A-F 311
The Medical Messiahs STM 399
Medicine and Slavery STM 328
Medicine and Society in America, 1660-1860 STM 341
Medicine in America STM 342
Medicine in Chicago, 1850-1950 STM 35
Medicine in Virginia in the Eighteenth Century STM 33
The Medicine Show STM 40
Medicine Without Doctors: Home Health Care in American History STM 309
Mediums, and Spirit Rappers, and Roaring Radicals L 148
Meeting House and Counting House H 1799
Megatrends: Ten New Directions Transforming Our Lives SOC 15
The Mellons H 1735
Melodrama Unveiled L 6
The Melting Pot and the Altar H 851
Memorials for Children of Change A-A 246
Memories of the Moderns L 337
Memoirs: 1925-1950 PS 695
Men and Volts STM 156
Men and Wealth in the United States, 1850-1970 H 1919
Men and Women in Medical School SOC 368
Men and Women of the Corporation SOC 553
Men at Midlife SOC 408
Men at Work A-F 344
Men, Cities, and Transportation H 1732
Men, Ideas and Politics PS 528
Men, Machines, and Modern Times STM 261
Men of Good Hope H 414
Men of Letters in Colonial Maryland L 65
Men of Popular Music M 386
Men of Science in America STM 187
Men of the Steel Rails H 1551
Men Who Control Women's Health: The Miseducation of Obstetrician-
   Gynecologists SOC 382
The Men Who Make Our Novels L 212
Men, Women, and the Novelist L 149
Menominee Drums H 1214
The Menominee Indians H 1209
Menominee Music M 145
Mental Health and Hispanic Americans PSY 17
Mental Health in the Metropolis A-F 143
The Mental Health of Asian-Americans A-F 338
Mental Illness and American Society, 1875-1940 STM 144
Mental Illness in the Urban Negro Community A-F 189
Mental Institutions in America STM 143
Mental Patients and Social Networks SOC 645
Merchants and Manufacturers H 1773
Merchants, Farmers, & Railroads H 264
Merger Movements in American Industry, 1895-1956 H 1757
Message Dimensions of Television News PC 758
The Messenger's Motives: Ethical Problems of the Mass Media PC 872
Metamorphoses of Science Fiction PC 261
Metamorphosis in the Arts: A Critical History of the 1960's A-A 78

Method and Theory in Historical Archeology A-F 66
Metropolis: Its People, Politics, and Economic Life SOC 23
Metropolitan Corridor: Railroads and the American Scene STM 359
The Metropolitan Opera 1883-1966, a Candid History M 77
Mexican American Artists A-A 110
Mexican Americans SOC 184
Mexican Americans in a Dallas Barrio A-F 257
Mexican-Americans of South Texas A-F 278
The Mexican-American People SOC 136
The Mexican in the United States SOC 92
Mexican Labor in the United States SOC 227
The Mexican War H 383
The Mexicans in America H 963
The Miami Indians H 1095
Michael Augustine Corrigan and the Shaping of Conservative Catholicism
    in America, 1878-1902 R 161
Micmacs and Colonists H 1259
Micro-Macro Political Analysis PS 84
The Mid-Atlantic States of America H 1489
The Middle Distance: A Comparative History of American Imaginative Litera-
    ture: 1919-1932 L 356
The Middle East Problem in the 1980s PS 773
The Middle Passage H 1053
The Middle Way: Puritanism and Ideology in American Romantic Fiction
    L 131
The Middle Western Farm Novel in the Twentieth Century L 14
Middletown: A Study in Contemporary American Culture SOC 50
Middletown Families: Fifty Years of Change and Continuity SOC 263
Middletown in Transition: A Study in Cultural Conflicts SOC 51
Midnight Movies PC 485
A Midrash on American Jewish History R 165
Midwestern Progressive Politics H 511
Migrant A-F 176
Migrants in Urban America SOC 57
The Migration of British Capital to 1875 H 1879
Milestones in American Literary History L 641
The Military Establishment PS 405
Military Music of the American Revolution M 43
Military Policy and National Security PS 693
Mill and Mansion A-A 565
The Millenarian Piety of Roger Williams R 285
Millways of Kent A-F 125
Mimicking Sisyphus PS 581
Mind Cure in New England STM 283
The Mind of America, 1820-1860 H 687
The Mind of the Old South H 585
The Mind of the South H 567
The Miners' Fight for Democracy H 1542
Miners, Millhands, and Mountaineers H 1445
Minimal Art A-A 21
Mining Engineers and the American West STM 351
Mining Frontiers of the Far West, 1848-1880 H 1488
The Mining Industries, 1899-1939 H 1654
Ministers of Reform H 441
The Minister's Wife R 248
Minnesota Farmer-Laborism H 455
A Minor Miracle: An Informal History of the National Science Foundation
    STM 228
Minorities, Gender, and Work SOC 78
Minorities in American Higher Education SOC 81
Minority Education and Caste A-F 326

Minority Mental Health   PSY 105
Minority Migrants in the Urban Community   SOC 214
A Minstrel Town   PC 385
Minstrels of the Dawn   M 187
Minstrels of the Mine Patch   A-F 435
The Minutemen and Their World   H 208
Miracle at Midway   PS 754
The Mirror Dance: Identity in a Women's Community   SOC 365
Mirror for Man   A-F 53
Mirror Image   STM 325
Mirror to the American Past   A-A 167
Mirrors and Windows   A-A 352
The Mismeasure of Man   STM 138
Mispokhe   A-F 124
Mission of Sorrows   H 1179
Missions and the American Mind   H 632
The Mississippi Chinese   H 955
Mississippi Choctaws at Play   A-F 204
Mr. Peale's Museum: Charles Wilson Peale and the First Popular Museum
    of Natural Science and Art   STM 335
Mister, You Got Yourself a Horse   A-F 464
Mitre and Sceptre   R 46
Mixed Families: Adopting Across Racial Boundaries   SOC 160
Mobility and the Small Town, 1900-1930   H 1362
Modern American Criticism   L 400
The Modern American Novel   L 234
The Modern American Novel and the Movies   PC 567
Modern American Painters   A-A 217
The Modern American Political Novel, 1900-1960   L 229
Modern American Sculpture (1968)   A-A 254
Modern American Sculpture (1918)   A-A 258
Modern Art: Nineteenth and Twentieth Centuries   A-A 229
Modern Art: The Men, the Movements, the Meaning   A-A 42
Modern Art in America   A-A 36
Modern Culture and the Arts   PC 27
Modern Diplomacy   PS 752
Modern Economic Growth   H 1886
Modern Homesteaders   A-F 148
Modern Jazz   M 312
Modern Negro Art   A-A 109
The Modern Novel in America 1900-1950   L 311
The Modern Olympic Games   PC 969
Modern Painting and the Northern Romantic Tradition   A-A 227
The Modern Poets   L 384
Modern Political Analysis   PS 74
Modern Psychoanalysis in the Schools   PSY 117
Modern Revivalism: Charles Grandison Finney to Billy Graham   R 278
The Modern Revolution in Poetry   L 650
Modern Science Fiction   PC 210
The Modern Stentors   PC 806
The Modern Tendency in American Painting   A-A 184
The Modernist Impulse in American Protestantism   R 104
Modernizing the Mountaineer   H 1515
Modification in Clinical Psychology   PSY 140
Modus Operandi: An Excursion into Detective Fiction   PC 167
Mody Boatright, Folklorist   A-F 376
The Molding of American Banking   H 1777
The Molly Maguires   H 859
Monarchs of Minstrelsy, from "Daddy" Rice to Date   PC 386
Monarchs of the Mimic World or the American Theatre of the Eighteenth
    Century Through the Managers--The Men Who Make It   L 46

A Monetary History of the United States, 1869-1960   H 1857
Monetary Statistics of the United States   H 1858
Money and Capital Markets in Postbellum America   H 1878
Money at Interest   H 1420
Money, Class, and Party   H 1916
The Money Game: Financing Collegiate Athletics   PC 919
Money in Congressional Elections   PS 438
Money, Sex, and Power   PS 33
The Money Supply of the American Colonies Before 1720   H 1904
Money Talks: Language and Lucre in American Fiction   L 572
Monopoly Capital   PS 509
The Monroe Doctrine and American Expansionism, 1843-1849   H 345
Monumental Washington   H 1374
"Moonies" in America   R 193
Moral Philosophy at Seventeenth-Century Harvard   R 139
The Moral Philosophy of Josiah Royce   H 593
Moral Principles and Political Obligations   PS 57
A Moral Tale   PC 126
Moralism and the Model Home   A-A 592
Moralities of Everyday Life   PSY 155
Morality and Foreign Policy   PS 795
Morals and Markets: The Development of Life Insurance in the United States
    SOC 604
Morals Legislation Without Morality   SOC 624
Moravian Architecture and Town Planning   A-A 551
The Moravian Contribution to American Music   M 90
The Moravian Potters in North Carolina   A-A 361
More Chapters of Opera   M 79
More Equality   SOC 543
More Issues at Hand: Critical Studies in Contemporary Science Fiction
    PC 208
More than Just a Friend: The Joys and Disappointments of Extramarital
    Affairs   SOC 298
More Than News: Media Power in Public Affairs   PC 671
More Than Subsistence: Minimum Wage for the Working Poor   SOC 482
More Work for Mother   STM 82
The Mormon Conflict 1850-1859   H 307
The Mormon Experience   R 188
The Mormon Landscape   A-A 569
Mormon Thunder: A Documentary History of Jedidiah Morgan Grant   R 219
Mormonism and the American Experience   R 204
The Mormons   R 216
Morris R. Cohen and the Scientific Ideal   STM 178
Mortal Consequences: A History from the Detective Story to the Crime
    Novel   PC 165
Most Uncommon Jacksonians   H 1618
Mother Camp   A-F 127
Mother of the Blues   M 226
Mother Was a Lady   PC 118
Mother Wit from the Laughing Barrel   A-F 403
Mothers in Poverty   SOC 291
Motivation and Society   PSY 166
Motown and the Arrival of Black Music   M 417
Mount Allegro   H 959
The Mountain States of America   H 1489
The Movement: A History of the American Left   H 535
The Movement for Indian Assimilation, 1860-1890   H 1139
Movers and Shakers   H 820
The Movie Brats   PC 570
Movie-Made America: A Social History of American Movies   PC 606
The Movie Rating Game   PC 459

Movies PC 637
Movies and Methods PC 558
Movies and Money: Financing the American Film Industry PC 633
Movies Are Better Than Ever PC 452
Movies as Artifacts PC 530
Movies as Mass Communication PC 498
Movies as Social Criticism PC 493
The Movies in Our Midst PC 534
The Movies in the Age of Innocence PC 628
The Movies on Your Mind PC 476
Moving the Masses H 1295
Muckraking PC 867
Mud Show: A Circus Season PC 383
Mudville's Revenge: The Rise and Fall of American Sport PC 1002
Mules and Men A-F 421
Multivalence: The Moral Quality of Form in the Modern Novel L 275
The Municipal Revolution H 1386
Murder for Pleasure: The Life and Times of the Detective Story PC 151
Murder in Space City A-F 120
The Murder Mystique: Crime Writers on Their Art PC 146
Murdering Mothers H 112
Muscles and Morals H 1294
Music: Black, White, and Blue M 36
Music and Bad Manners M 122
Music and Dance of the Tewa Pueblos M 167
Music and Imagination M 49
Music and Musicians in Chicago M 61
Music and Musicians in Early America M 85
Music and Musicians of Maine M 56
Music and Musicians of Pennsylvania M 188
Music and Musket M 95
Music and Politics M 340
Music as a Social Force in America and the Science of Practice M 30
Music at Harvard, a Historical Review of Men and Events M 115
Music Comes to America M 60
Music in a New Found Land M 24
Music in America M 101
Music in America and American Music M 86
Music in American Life M 38
Music in American Life, Present and Future M 129
Music in American Society 1776-1976, from Puritan Hymn to Synthesizer
    M 22
Music in Boston--Readings from the First Three Centuries M 117
Music in Colonial Massachusetts 1630-1820 M 93
Music in Lexington Before 1840 M 44
Music in New Hampshire 1623-1800 M 97
Music in New Jersey 1665-1860 M 75
Music in New Orleans, the Formative Years 1791-1841 M 20
Music in Philadelphia M 65
Music in Texas, a Survey of One Aspect of Cultural Progress M 33
Music in the 1920s M 110
Music in the Air: America's Changing Tastes in Popular Music, 1920-1980
    PC 751
Music in the Cultured Generation M 94
Music in the New World M 9
Music in the United States M 7
Music in the United States: A Historical Introduction M 12
Music Making in America M 442
The Music Merchants M 66
Music of Acoma, Isleta, Cochiti, and Zuni Pueblos M 145
The Music of Black Americans M 32

The Music of George Washington's Time   M 70
Music of Santo Domingo Pueblo, New Mexico   M 145
Music of the Old South   M 116
The Music of the Pilgrims, a Description of the Psalm-Book Brought to
    Plymouth in 1620   M 98
Music on Demand   M 389
Music Publishing in Chicago Before 1871   M 59
The Musical: A Look at the American Musical Theater   PC 355
The Musical: From Broadway to Hollywood   PC 337
Musical Comedy in America: From the Black Crook to Sweeny Todd   PC 394
The Musical Experience of Composer, Performer, Listener   M 105
The Musical Heritage of the United States   M 80
Musical Interludes in Boston, 1795-1830   M 74
Musical Life in the Pennsylvania Settlements of the Unitas Fratrum
    M 53
Musical Nationalism, American Composers' Search for Identity   M 84
Mussolini and Fascism   H 882
"Myne Owne Ground"   H 1019
The Mystery Story   PC 139
Mystery Train   M 412
The Mystery Writer's Art   PC 160
The Mystic Warriors of the Plains   H 1191
Myth and Literature in the American Renaissance   L 177
Myth and the Powerhouse   L 615
The Myth and Reality of Aging in America   SOC 417
The Myth of Masculinity   SOC 376
The Myth of Mental Illness   PSY 169
The Myth of the Family Farm   H 1803
The Myth of the Lost Cause   H 1487
The Myth of the Middle Class   SOC 492
The Myth of the Negro Past   A-F 180
The Mythopoeic Reality: The Postwar American Nonfiction Novel   L 436
Myths and Realities   H 70

Naming Names   PC 555
Narcissus and the Voyeur   L 570
Narrative Rhetorical Devices of Persuasion   A-F 414
The Nashville Sound   M 159
Nathan Appleton   H 1703
Nathaniel William Taylor, 1786-1858   R 150
A Nation of Behavers   R 124
A Nation of Cities   H 1316
A Nation of Strangers   SOC 16
The Nation Takes Shape, 1789-1837   H 278
The Nation Transformed   STM 96
The Nation with the Soul of a Church   R 296
The National Academy of Sciences   STM 66
National Conventions in an Age of Party Reform   PS 430
National Defense   PS 633
The National Football Lottery   PC 974
National Health Insurance   PS 320
The National Music of America and Its Sources   M 58
National Parks and the American Landscape   A-A 139
National Security and Individual Freedom   PS 713
The National Urban League, 1910-1940   H 1088
Nationalism and Religion in America   R 295
Nationalizing Government   PS 349
Native American Art in the Denver Museum   A-A 5
Native American Balladry   M 168
Native American Music   M 160

The Native American People of the East R 249
The Native Americans A-F 241
Native Americans Today A-F 202
Native Arts of North America A-A 10
Native North American Art History A-A 14
Native Sons: A Critical Study of Twentieth Century Negro American Authors
    L 350
Natives and Newcomers H 1326
Natives and Strangers H 887
NATO: The Entangling Alliance PS 741
The Natural History of Alcoholism PSY 174
The Natural Paradise A-A 159
Nature and Culture: American Landscape Painting, 1825-1875 A-A 195
Nature and the American H 612
Nature and the Religious Imagination R 134
Nature in American Literature L 508
The Nature of Prejudice PSY 3
Nature's Nation H 644
The Navajo A-F 223
The Navajo Indians and Federal Indian Policy, 1900-1935 H 1174
The Navajo Nation H 1167
Navajo Roundup H 1175
The Navajos H 1257
The Navajos and the New Deal H 1210
The Navigation Acts and the American Revolution H 204
Neat and Tidy A-A 401
Nebraska Folklore A-F 449
The Necessity for Choice PS 701
The Necessity for Ruins and Other Topics A-A 466
Negative Space: Manny Farber on the Movies PC 458
A Neglected Art M 425
The Negro American SOC 195
The Negro and His Folklore in Nineteenth-Century Periodicals A-F 425
The Negro and His Music M 21
The Negro and His Songs M 176
The Negro Author L 563
The Negro Church in America R 223
The Negro Family in the United States SOC 120
Negro Folk Music U.S.A. M 142
The Negro in American Culture: Based on Materials Left by Alain Locke
    L 470
The Negro in American Fiction L 466
The Negro in Colonial New England, 1620-1776 H 1041
The Negro in Films PC 559
The Negro in Hollywood Films PC 495
The Negro in Literature and Art in the United States L 462
The Negro in the American Theatre L 542
The Negro in the United States SOC 121
Negro Mecca H 1078
Negro Musicians and Their Music M 11
The Negro Novel in America L 459
The Negro Novelist L 541
Negro Playwrights in the American Theater 1925-1959 L 204
The Negro Press in the United States PC 856
Negro Slave Songs in the United States M 151
Negro Voices in American Fiction L 517
Negro Workaday Songs M 177
Negroes and the Great Depression H 1092
The Negro's Church R 229
Neighbor and Kin A-F 122
Neighborhoods That Work: Sources for Visibility in the Inner City
    SOC 62

1979

Neighbors in Conflict H 846
Neither Black nor White H 1027
Neither White nor Black: The Mulatto Character in American Fiction
  L 447
The Nerves of Government PS 76
Netherlanders in America H 956
The Networks PC 805
Networks of Power: Electrification in Western Society, 1880-1930
  STM 182
Never Again PS 759
Never Done H 826
A New Age Now Begins H 243
The New Alchemists STM 158
New Alignments in American Politics PS 487
New American Art Museums A-A 510
The New American Cinema PC 421
The New American Literature 1890-1930 L 19
The New American Painting A-A 223
The New American Political System PS 700
The New American Society: The Revolution of the Middle Class SOC 448
New Americans: The Westerner and the Modern Experience in the American
  Novel L 340
The New Art: A Critical Anthology A-A 22
The New Charismatics II R 280
The New Class War: Reagan's Attack on the Welfare State and Its Conse-
  quences SOC 493
The New Color Photography A-A 338
The New Commonwealth, 1877-1890 H 309
New Complete Book of the American Musical Theater PC 340
The New Country H 1413
The New Deal H 438
The New Deal and American Indian Tribalism H 1251
The New Deal and the Last Hurrah H 1384
The New Deal and the Problem of Monopoly H 1872
The New Deal Art Projects A-A 100
The New Deal for Artists A-A 90
A New Deal for Blacks H 1079
A New Deal in Entertainment PC 575
The New Deal in the Suburbs H 1279
The New Deal Lawyers H 1964
New Deal Policy and Southern Rural Poverty H 500
New Directions in American Architecture A-A 628
New Directions in American Intellectual History H 606
New Directions in Chicano Scholarship A-F 286
New Directions in Political Socialization PS 561
The New Documentary in Action PC 580
The New Economic History H 1824
A New Economic View of American History H 1891
The New Empire: An Interpretation of American Expansion, 1860-1898
  H 331
New England: Indian Summer 1865-1914 L 105
New England Begins: The Seventeenth Century A-A 97
The New England Clergy and the American Revolution R 44
The New England Company, 1649-1776 H 122
New England Dissent, 1630-1833 R 305
New England Frontier H 1261
The New England Girl: Cultural Ideals in Hawthorne, Stowe, Howells, and
  James L 122
New England Glass and Glassmaking A-A 432
New England Meeting House and Church, 1630-1850 A-A 436
The New England Meeting Houses of the Seventeenth Century A-A 538

The New England Merchants in the Seventeenth Century H 54
The New England Mind: From Colony to Province H 645
The New England Mind: The Seventeenth Century H 646
The New England States of America H 1489
New England Textiles in the Nineteenth Century H 1749
A New England Town, the First Hundred Years H 134
The New England Transcendentalists and the Dial L 170
The New Ethnicity: Perspectives from Ethnology A-F 29
The New Feminist Movement SOC 336
The New Heavens and New Earth: Political Religion in America R 24
The New Hollywood: American Movies in the Seventies PC 523
New Horizons, 1927-1950 H 1739
The New Humanism: A Critique of Modern America, 1900-1940 L 307
The New Industrial State H 1861
The New Jews SOC 224
The New Journalism PC 303
The New Journalism: The Underground Press, the Artists of Nonfiction,
   and Changes in the Established Media PC 295
A New Language for Psychoanalysis PSY 157
The New Left and the Origins of the Cold War PS 722
New Liberties for Old H 557
A New Look at Black Families A-F 199
New Maps of Hell: A Survey of Science Fiction PC 201
New Masters: Northern Planters During the Civil War and Reconstruction
   H 371
The New Metropolis H 1383
The New Morality: A Profile of American Youth in the 70s SOC 19
The New Muckrakers PC 857
New Muses: Art in American Culture, 1865-1920 A-A 192
The New Music, 1900-1960 M 50
A New Mythos: The Novel of the Artist as Heroine, 1877-1977 L 646
The New Nation: A History of the United States During the Confederation,
   1781-1789 H 215
The New Nation, 1800-1845 H 411
The New Nightingales: Hospital Workers, Unions and New Women's Issues
   SOC 590
The New Novel in America: The Kafkan Mode in Contemporary Fiction
   L 415
New Orleans and the Railroad H 1778
New Orleans Jazz M 330
New People: Miscegenation and Mulattoes in the United States H 1091
New Perspectives on Prisons and Imprisonment SOC 635
The New Poets: American and British Poetry Since World War II L 385
A New Public Education SOC 285
The New Radicalism in America, 1889-1963 H 631
The New Religions R 214
The New Religious 'Political Right in America R 120
The New Revolution in the Cotton Economy H 1508
New Rules: Searching for Self-Fulfillment in a World Turned Upside Down
   SOC 20
The New Shape of American Religion R 125
A New Social Contract PS 309
New Space for Women A-A 632
The New Suburbanites: Race and Housing in the Suburbs SOC 48
A New System for Public Housing PS 388
New Topographics A-A 345
New Trends of Psychiatry in the Community PSY 160
The New Urban America H 1275
New Urban Immigrants: The Korean Community in New York SOC 155
The New Woman in Greenwich Village, 1910-1920 H 821
The New World Dutch Barn PC 1020

A New World Jerusalem: The Swedenborgian Experience in Community Construc-
tion R 212
New World Metaphysics R 6
New World, New Earth: Environmental Reform in American Literature from
the Puritans Through Whitman L 653
New Worlds for Old: The Apocalyptic Imagination, Science Fiction, and
American Literature PC 230
New York: City and State H 1447
New York 1900 A-A 629
New York Beginnings H 77
New York City, 1664-1710 H 1278
The New York City Opera M 112
New York Jews and the Quest for Community H 922
The New York Money Market H 1754
New York Notes M 250
New York Painting and Sculpture: 1940-1970 A-A 60
The New York Police H 1376
New York Savings Banks in the Ante-Bellum Years, 1819-1861 H 1761
The New York School: A Cultural Reckoning A-A 201
The New York School: The Painters and Sculptors of the Fifties A-A 123
New York School, the First Generation A-A 233
Newcastle's New York H 121
The Newcomers: Negroes and Puerto Ricans in a Changing Metropolis
H 932
News for Everyman: Radio and Foreign Affairs in Thirties America
PC 747
News from Nowhere: Television and the News PC 754
News from the Capital: The Story of Washington Reporting PC 884
The News People PC 875
The Newscasters PC 803
Newsmaking PC 901
The Newsmongers PC 903
Newspaper Crusaders PC 840
Newspapering in the Old West PC 876
The Next Generation A-F 327
Next to Nature A-A 161
The Nez Perces H 1150
The Nez Perce Indians and the Opening of the Northwest H 1172
Night Comes to the Cumberlands: A Biography of a Depressed Area
SOC 28
Night Creatures M 251
Night Riders in Black Folk History A-F 411
The Nightingale's Burden: Women Poets and American Culture Before 1900
L 661
Nine American Film Critics PC 552
Nineteenth Century America: Paintings and Sculpture A-A 75
Nineteenth-Century American Painting A-A 185
Nineteenth-Century American Science STM 91
Nineteenth-Century Cities H 1389
Nineteenth-Century Southern Literature L 178
No Haven for the Oppressed H 908
No Offense: Civil Religion and Protestant Taste R 294
No Other Gods: On Science and American Social Thought STM 315
No Place Else: Explorations in Utopian and Dystopian Fiction PC 250
No Place of Grace H 633
No Room at the Top: Underemployment and Alienation in the Corporation
SOC 524
No Strength Without Union H 1530
Noblesse Oblige H 1353
Nonfiction Film PC 418
Nonfiction Film Theory and Criticism PC 419

Nonproliferation and U.S. Foreign Policy PS 814
Nootka and Quileute Music M 145
Normal Psychology of the Aging Process PSY 188
Norman Street: Poverty and Politics in an Urban Neighborhood SOC 64
North America from Earliest Discovery in First Settlements H 164
North American Indian Art A-A 11
North American Indian Musical Styles M 175
North from Mexico H 964
North of Slavery H 1060
The Northern Colonial Frontier, 1607-1763 H 129
Northern Plainsmen: Adaptive Strategy and Agrarian Life A-F 28
Northern Ute Music M 145
Northernizing the South H 1433
Norway to America H 991
The Norwegian-Americans H 843
The Norwegian Language in America A-F 355
Norwegian Migration to America H 855
Not Free to Desist H 867
The Not So Solid South A-F 59
Not to Be Broadcast: The Truth About the Radio PC 728
Notes (8 Pieces) Source a New World Music M 341
Notes and Tones M 347
Notes on Music in Old Boston M 62
Nothing but Freedom H 1032
The Notorious Triangle H 1023
Novel of Manners in America L 656
The Novel of the American West PC 280
The Novel of Violence in America: 1920-1950 L 276
Novel vs. Fiction: The Contemporary Reformation L 478
Novelist's America: Fiction as History, 1910-1940 L 228
The Novels of the Harlem Renaissance L 394
Nuclear Arms Control Choices PS 593
The Nuclear Delusion PS 696
Nuclear Navy, 1946-1962 STM 167
Nuclear Proliferation PS 659
Nuclear Weapons in Europe PS 750
Numismatic Art in America A-A 427
Nursing History M 776

O Strange New World, American Culture H 615
The Oak Park Strategy: Community Control of Racial Change SOC 132
Object Relations in Psychoanalytic Theory PSY 90
Objectivity and the News PC 904
Objects of Special Devotion PC 7
The Oblique Light: Studies in Literary History and Biography L 642
The Obsession: Reflections on the Tyranny of Slenderness SOC 338
Obsessive Images: Symbolism in Poetry of the 1930s and 1940s L 216
Occupations and Social Status SOC 579
Odd Jobs: The World of Deviant Work SOC 570
Of Mice and Magic: A History of American Animated Cartoons PC 525
Of Poetry and Poets L 267
Of the Press, by the Press, for the Press (and Others Too) PC 837
Of Time, Work, and Leisure PC 17
Of Worlds Beyond: The Science of Science Writing PC 222
Oglala Religion H 1221
Ohio Canal Era H 1782
Oil, Land, and Politics H 1716
Oil, War, and American Security H 532
Old Age in the New Land STM 2
Old as the Hills M 182

Old Houses of New England A-A 550
The Old Northwest H 1428
Old People as People SOC 426
The Old Religion in the Brave New World R 297
The Old Republicans H 372
The Old South A-A 558
Old Values in a New Town A-F 296
Olden-Time Music M 40
Older Mexican Americans SOC 173
On Equal Terms: Jews in America, 1881-1981 R 162
On Moral Fiction L 282
On Native Grounds: An Interpretation of American Prose Literature
    L 324
On Reagan PS 119
On the Autonomy of the Democratic State PS 48
On the Cable: The Television of Abundance PC 819
On the Edge of the World A-A 577
On the Rise A-A 602
On the Road for Work: Migratory Workers on the East Coast of the United
    States SOC 506
On the Small Screen PC 767
On the Take: From Petty Crooks to Presidents SOC 614
On the Trail of Negro Folk-Song M 190
On the Verge of Revolt: Women in American Films PC 468
On Thermonuclear War PS 688
On with the Show: The First Century of Show Business in America PC 401
A Once Charitable Enterprise H 1378
Once Upon a Stage: The Merry World of Vaudeville PC 391
The One and the Many H 28
One Half the People H 815
One Hundred Million Acres H 1180
One Hundred Years of Music in America M 83
One Kind of Freedom H 1074
One Nation Divisible H 517
One Potato, Two Potato . . . A-F 430
One Third of a Nation L 341
Oneida: Utopian Community to Modern Corporation R 196
Only a Miner M 155
Only Connect: Readings on Children's Literature PC 114
The Only Game in Town: An Illustrated History of Gambling PC 373
The Only Good Indian . . .: The Hollywood Gospel PC 471
The Only Land I Know H 1125
The Only Land They Knew H 1272
Only the Ball Was White PC 981
The Only Proper Style A-A 480
Open Marriage SOC 299
Opening Up the Suburbs SOC 29
Operation Wetback H 912
The Opinionmakers PC 899
Options for U.S. Policy Toward Africa PS 704
The Oral Tradition in the South H 1422
Ordeal by Fire H 343
Ordeal of the Union H 355
Ores to Metals H 1683
The Organ in New England M 96
The Organization Man SOC 601
The Organization of American Culture, 1700-1900 H 601
The Organization of Interests PS 493
The Organization of Knowledge in Modern America, 1860-1920 STM 279
The Organizational Society PS 556
Organized for Action: Commitment in Voluntary Associations SOC 558

Organized German Settlement and Its Effects on the Frontier of South-
   Central Texas A-A 590
Organized Labor and the Black Worker, 1619-1971 H 1563
Organized Medicine in the Progressive Era STM 58
Organizing Dixie H 1637
Organizing Women Office Workers: Dissatisfaction, Consciousness and Action
   SOC 546
The Oriental Americans H 968
The Oriental Religions and American Thought R 206
Originals: American Women Artists A-A 96
The Origins and Resolution of an Urban Crisis H 1277
The Origins of American Critical Thought: 1810-1835 L 117
The Origins of American Film Criticism, 1909-1939 PC 519
The Origins of American Intervention in the First World War H 464
The Origins of American Politics H 55
Origins of the American Indians H 1160
The Origins of the Cold War in the Near East PS 707
The Origins of the Equal Rights Amendment H 707
Origins of the Fifth Amendment H 1971
The Origins of the Korean War PS 611
The Origins of the Marshall Plan PS 654
Origins of the Modern American Peace Movement, 1915-1929 H 443
The Origins of the National Recovery Administration H 474
Origins of the New South H 1518
The Origins of the Turbojet Revolution STM 77
Origins of the Urban School H 1346
The Ornamented Chair A-A 400
Orpheus in the New World, the Symphony Orchestra as an American Cultural
   Institution M 67
Orthodoxy in Massachusetts 1630-1650 H 142
The Other America H 1871
The Other Bostonians H 1388
The Other Californians A-F 103
Other Criteria: Confrontations with Twentieth-Century Art A-A 129
The Other South H 285
Other Voices: The New Journalism in America PC 855
Other Voices: The Style of a Male Homosexual Tavern SOC 377
Other Worlds: The Fantasy Genre PC 182
Our American Music M 14
Our American Sisters H 748
Our Brother's Keeper A-F 207
Our Crowd H 854
Our Gang H 947
Our Landed Heritage H 34
Our Last First Poets L 363
Our Living Traditions A-F 384
Our Movie Made Children PC 467
Our Selves/Our Past PSY 33
Our Way A-F 165
Out of Our Past H 16
Out of the Bleachers: Writings on Women and Sports PC 999
Out to Work H 771
Outcasts from Evolution STM 152
The Outdoor Amusement Industry H 1745
Outlaw Blues M 445
Outposts of the Forgotten: Socially Terminal People in Slum Hotels and
   Single Room Occupancy Tenements SOC 63
Output, Employment, and Productivity in the United States After 1800
   H 1844
The Output of Manufacturing Industries, 1899-1937 H 1682
The Over-Educated American SOC 541

Over Here H 481
Over the Wire and on TV: CBS and UPI in Campaign '80 PC 685
Owners Versus Players: Baseball and Collective Bargaining PC 938
The Oxford History of the American People H 31

The Pabst Brewing Company H 1672
The Pacific Slope H 1491
The Pacific States of America H 1489
Pacifying the Plains H 1097
The Painters' America A-A 191
Painters of the Humble Truth A-A 153
Painting in America A-A 166
The Palace or the Poorhouse A-A 440
Pamela's Daughters PC 197
Papa Jack: Jack Johnson and the Era of White Hopes PC 989
Papago Music M 145
Paper Lion PC 982
The Paperbound Book in America PC 94
The Papers of Joseph Henry, Vol. I: December 1797–October 1832 STM 163
The Papers of Joseph Henry, Vol. II: November 1832–December 1835
   STM 164
The Parade of Heroes A-F 386
Parade of Pleasure: A Study of Popular Iconography in the USA PC 63
The Parade's Gone By . . . PC 429
The Paradox of Control: Parole Supervision of Youthful Offenders
   SOC 634
The Paradox of Progressive Education H 1297
The Paradox of Progressive Thought H 655
Paradoxes of Power PS 815
Paradoxical Resolutions: American Fiction Since James Joyce L 416
The Paranoid Style in American Politics and Other Essays H 609
Pare Lorentz and the Documentary Film PC 609
Part of Nature, Part of Us L 406
Participation in America PS 472
Parties and Politics in the Early Republic, 1789–1815 H 197
Parties, Interest Groups, and Campaign Finance Laws PS 489
The Partnership: A History of the Apollo-Soyez Test Project STM 118
Party and Ideology in the United States PS 467
Party Coalitions in the 1980s PS 448
Party Dynamics PS 463
The Party of Eros H 624
The Party's Choice PS 441
Pascua H 1246
Passages: Predictable Crisis of Adult Life PSY 161
The Passages of Thought: Psychological Representation in the American
   Novel 1870-1900 L 195
Passing On A-F 144
The Past Has Another Pattern PS 576
The Past in the Present: A Thematic Study of Modern Southern Fiction
   L 433
The Path Between the Seas STM 241
Paths of American Thought H 675
Paths to Political Reform PS 427
Paths to the American Past H 666
Patricide and the House Divided H 302
Patriotic Gore: Studies in the Literature of the American Civil War
   L 200
Patronage and Poverty in the Tobacco South H 1503
Patrons and Patriotism: The Encouragement of the Fine Arts in the United
   States, 1790-1860 A-A 95

Pattern in the Material Folk Culture of the Eastern United States
A-F 415
Pattern of Nationality: Twentieth-Century Literary Versions of America
L 396
Patterns of Culture A-F 4
Patterns of Wealth-Holding in Wisconsin Since 1850 H 1920
Patterns of Time in Hospital Life SOC 605
Paved with Good Intentions PS 769
Pawnee Music M 145
Pawns of Yalta PS 628
The Peace Makers H 230
The Peace Reform in American History PS 526
Peace, War, and Numbers PS 770
Peaceable Kingdom H 188
Pearl Harbor PS 810
Peasants and Strangers H 845
The Peculiar Institution H 1081
Peltries or Plantations H 1651
Penn's Great Town A-A 517
Pennsylvania Dutch: American Folk Art A-A 308
Pennsylvania Folk-Art A-A 319
The Pennsylvania Germans: A Celebration of Their Arts, 1683-1850
A-A 385
Pennsylvania Spirituals M 201
Pentagon Capitalism PS 354
The Pentagon Papers PS 777
The Pentecostal Movement in the Catholic Church R 279
A People Among People R 57
The People Called Shakers R 187
A People in Revolution H 203
The People Look at Radio PC 775
The People Look at Television PC 825
People of Paradox H 620
People of Plenty H 33
The People of Puerto Rico A-F 290
People of Rimrock A-F 73
People of the Sacred Mountain H 1219
People Space: The Making and Breaking of Human Boundaries A-F 25
The People's Architecture A-A 505
The People's Films PC 521
The Peoples of Philadelphia H 878
Perceptions of the Spirit in Twentieth-Century Art A-A 48
Performing Arts—The Economic Dilemma PC 326
The Performing Self: Compositions and Decompositions in the Languages
of Contemporary Life L 606
A Peril and a Hope: The Scientists Movement in America: 1945-47
STM 346
The Perils of Prosperity, 1914-1932 H 488
Period Influences in Interior Decoration A-A 425
The Periodicals of American Transcendentalism L 133
Perish the Thought H 720
Perjury: The Hiss-Chambers Case H 538
Persistent Peoples A-F 85
Personal Politics: The Roots of Women's Liberation in the Civil Rights
Movement and the New Left SOC 349
Personality Development in Two Cultures A-F 313
Personality in Nature, Society, and Culture PSY 118
Perspectives in American Culture Change A-F 243
Perspectives in Vernacular Architecture A-A 523
Perspectives on American Composers M 39
Perspectives on American English A-F 350

Perspectives on American Folk Art A-F 451
Perspectives on Technology STM 316
Petroleum Pipelines and Public Policy, 1906-1959 H 1721
Petroleum Progress and Profits STM 117
Pewter in America A-A 399
The Peyote Cult A-F 225
The Peyote Religion Among the Navajo A-F 200
Philadelphia: Three Centuries of Art A-A 104
Philadelphia: Work, Space, Family, and Group Experience in the Nineteenth
    Century H 1331
Philadelphia and the China Trade, 1682-1846 H 1699
Philadelphia Georgian A-A 555
Philadelphia Printmaking A-A 283
The Philadelphia Riots of 1844 H 903
Philadelphia's Philosopher Mechanics: A History of the Franklin Institute
    1824-1865 STM 344
Philharmonic--A History of New York's Orchestra M 108
Philosophy and Social Issues PS 65
The Philosophy of the American Revolution H 251
Philosophy, Politics and Society PS 41
The Phonograph and Our Musical Life M 13
Photo-Realism A-A 221
Photography and the American Scene A-A 333
Photography as a Fine Art A-A 326
Photography in America A-A 324
Photography in America: The Formative Years, 1839-1900 A-A 335
Photography of the Fifties A-A 339
Photography Rediscovered A-A 353
Phrenology, Fad and Science STM 93
The Physician and Sexuality in Victorian America STM 153
"The Physician's Hand": Work, Culture and Conflict in American Nursing
    STM 247
The Physicists: The History of a Scientific Community in Modern America
    STM 208
Physics, Patients, and Politics: A Biography of Charles Grafton Page
    STM 289
Pickets at the Gates A-F 307
Pictorial Folk Art A-A 304
A Pictorial History of the American Carnival PC 369
The Pictorial Mode: Space and Time in the Art of Bryant, Irving, and
    Cooper L 179
Picture PC 582
A Piece of the Pie: Blacks and White Immigrants Since 1880 SOC 163
Pieced Quilt A-A 389
Pierre S. DuPont and the Making of the Modern Corporation H 1667
Piety and Power H 1003
Piety Versus Moralism R 143
Pilgrim Colony H 127
Pilgrims Through Space and Time PC 204
The Pill, John Rock, and the Church STM 245
Pillars of the Republic H 618
Pink Collar Workers: Inside the World of Women's Work SOC 362
Pioneering in Big Business 1882-1911 H 1712
Pioneering in Industrial Research STM 31
Pioneers and Caretakers: A Study of 9 American Women Novelists L 440
Pioneers and Profits H 1793
Pioneers of Modern Art in America: The Decade of the Armory Show, 1910-
    1920 A-A 63
A Place Called Home H 1335
The Place of Houses A-A 483
Place Over Time H 1440

The Plain People of Boston 1830-1860 H 1341
The Plain People of the Confederacy H 407
Plainville Fifteen Years Later A-F 94
Plainville, U.S.A. A-F 161
Plains Families SOC 53
Planning a Tragedy PS 584
Plantation County A-F 136
The Plantation Mistress H 719
Play, Games and Sports in Cultural Contexts PC 950
The Play Movement in the United States PC 91
Playful Fictions and Fictional Players PC 291
Playing Hardball: The Dynamics of Baseball Folk Speech PC 942
Plow Women Rather Than Reapers H 813
The Plug-In Drug PC 832
Plural Society in the South-West A-F 68
Pluralism and Personality: William James and Some Contemporary Cultures
    of Psychology PSY 31
The Poet and the Gilded Age PC 103
The Poetics of Indeterminancy L 372
The Poetics of Murder: Detective Fiction and Literary Theory PC 158
Poetry and Repression: Revisionism from Blake to Stevens L 453
Poetry and the Age L 545
Poetry in America L 493
Poetry of American Women from 1632 to 1945 L 662
Poetry of the Blues M 208
Poet's Prose L 511
Points of View: The Stereograph in America A-A 327
Poison Penmanship: The Gentle Art of Muckraking PC 888
Poker Faces: The Life and Work of Professional Card Players SOC 548
Poles in American History and Tradition H 1010
The Police Procedural PC 144
The Politics of Agricultural Research PS 326
Policing the City H 1343
Policy Implementation in the Federal System PS 393
The Policy Predicament PS 317
Polish Americans SOC 167
Polish-American Politics in Chicago, 1888-1940 H 948
The Political Behavior of American Jews H 909
The Polish Peasant in Europe and America SOC 228
The Political Character of Adolescence PS 537
Political Crime in the United States SOC 651
The Political Crisis of the 1850s H 323
The Political Culture of American Whigs H 324
Political Ecology PS 524
Political Economics PS 2
The Political Economy of Aging SOC 434
The Political Economy of Slavery H 1036
The Political Economy of the Cotton South H 1818
Political Issues in United States Population Policy PS 324
Political Language PS 83
Political Leadership and Collective Goods PS 88
Political Man PS 546
Political Organization of Native North Americans A-F 239
Political Organizations PS 503
Political Parties PS 431
Political Parties Before the Constitution H 222
Political Parties in a New Nation H 200
Political Parties in the American System PS 470
Political Pilgrims H 610
Political Power: USA/USSR PS 595

Political Power in Birmingham, 1871-1921 H 1329
Political Process and the Development of Black Insurgency, 1930-1970
    SOC 176
The Political Psychology of Appeasement PS 711
Political Realism in American Thought PS 12
Political Satire in the American Revolution, 1763-1783 L 59
Political Science and Public Policy PS 380
The Political Socialization of Black Americans PSY 1
The Political Stage: American Drama and Theater of the Great Depression
    L 292
The Political System PS 81
Political Theory and Public Policy PS 90
The Political Web of American Schools PS 402
The Political World of American Zionism H 929
The Politicization of Society PS 521
Politics: Who Gets What, When, How PS 94
Politics and Economics, and Public Welfare SOC 538
Politics and Force Levels PS 575
Politics and Poverty SOC 44
Politics and Ideology in the Age of the Civil War H 300
Politics and Power H 377
Politics and Power in a Slave Society H 394
Politics and Television PC 774
Politics and the Social Sciences PS 99
Politics as Communication PS 100
The Politics at God's Funeral PS 32
Politics, Economics, and Welfare PS 75
The Politics of a Poverty Habitat A-F 316
The Politics of Abundance H 521
The Politics of Agricultural Research SOC 547
The Politics of American Science 1939 to the Present STM 285
Politics of Arms Control PS 603
The Politics of Black America H 1064
The Politics of Business in California, 1890-1920 H 1658
The Politics of Clean Air PS 330
The Politics of Congressional Elections PS 439
The Politics of Displacement: Racial and Ethnic Transition in Three Ameri-
    can Cities SOC 114
The Politics of Domesticity H 737
The Politics of Efficiency H 1379
The Politics of Indian Removal H 1142
The Politics of Justice H 1955
Politics of Literary Expression L 516
The Politics of Loyalty H 467
The Politics of Lying PS 404
The Politics of Medicare PS 352
The Politics of Moralism: The New Christian Right in American Life
    R 122
The Politics of National Party Conventions PS 429
The Politics of Oil PS 318
The Politics of Park Design A-A 443
The Politics of Prejudice H 877
The Politics of Privacy PS 559
The Politics of Provincialism H 430
The Politics of Pure Science STM 140
The Politics of Rational Man PS 91
The Politics of Reconstruction, 1863-1867 H 289
The Politics of Recovery H 520
The Politics of Regulation PS 401
The Politics of Reproduction PS 50
The Politics of Rescue H 901

The Politics of Science STM 265
The Politics of Soft Coal H 1724
The Politics of TV Violence PC 807
The Politics of Taxing and Spending PS 383
The Politics of Technology Assessment PS 368
The Politics of the Budgetary Process PS 399
The Politics of U.S. Labor H 1605
The Politics of Women's Liberation H 746
Politics, Principle, and Prejudice H 275
Politics, Science, and Dread Disease: A Short History of United States
    Medical Research Policy STM 366
Politics, Values, and Public Policy PS 321
Politics Without Power PS 425
Polyarchy PS 16
"Poor Carolina" H 96
The Poor Pay More: Consumer Practices of Low Income Families SOC 450
Poor People's Lawyers in Transition SOC 475
Poor Pearl, Poor Girl A-F 388
A Poor Sort of Heaven, a Good Sort of Earth A-A 356
Pop Art (1966) A-A 86
Pop Art (1965) A-A 120
Pop Art Redefined A-A 121
Pop Culture in America PC 65
The Pop Culture Tradition PC 67
Pop Music and Blues M 229
The Pop Process M 411
Popcorn Venus: Women, Movies and the American Dream PC 578
The Popular American Novel, 1865-1920 PC 97
Popular Architecture A-A 446
The Popular Arts: A Critical Guide to the Mass Media PC 28
The Popular Arts: A Critical Reader PC 16
The Popular Arts in America: A Critical Reader PC 29
The Popular Book PC 80
Popular Culture: Mirror of American Life PC 66
Popular Culture and American Life PC 38
Popular Culture and High Culture PC 23
Popular Culture and Industrialism, 1865-1900 H 385
Popular Culture and the Expanding Consciousness PC 8
The Popular Culture Reader PC 24
Popular Education and Democratic Thought in America H 688
Popular Literature in America PC 68
The Popular Mood of Pre-Civil War America L 185
Popular Religion: Inspirational Books in America PC 95
Popular Religion in America A-F 77
Popular Songs and Youth Today M 430
The Popular Theater PC 381
The Popular Western PC 272
Population History of New York City H 1377
Population, Labor Force, and Long Swings in Economic Growth H 1852
The Population of the British Colonies in America Before 1776 H 182
The Population of the South H 1494
Population Patterns in the Past H 26
Population Redistribution and Economic Growth H 1888
The Popultist Revolt H 321
The Port of New York STM 74
Portal to America H 990
The Potawatomis H 1130
The Portland Longshoremen A-F 131
The Portrait Extended A-A 337
Portrait of a Decade A-A 343
Portrait of an American City L 673

A Portrait of the Artist as a Young Woman L 540
Portraits of "the Whitemen" A-F 203
Portraying the Media: The White House and the News Media PC 662
The Portuguese Americans SOC 192
The Positive Thinkers PC 83
Positively Black A-F 371
The Post-Darwinian Controversies R 110
The Post-Imperial Presidency PS 117
Post-Minimalism A-A 105
Postmodern American Poetry L 354
The Pottery and Porcelain of the United States and Marks of American
    Potters A-A 357
The Pound Era L 326
Poverty and Progress H 1387
Poverty and Social Change SOC 462
Poverty in America SOC 501
Poverty in New York 1783-1825 H 1361
Poverty in Rural America A-F 306
Poverty U.S.A. A-F 310
Power: Its Forms, Bases and Uses PS 67
Power and Crisis in the City: Cooperations, Unions and Urban Policy
    SOC 35
Power and Culture PS 682
Power and Morality H 1681
Power and Powerlessness: Quiescence and Rebellion in an Appalachian Valley
    SOC 38
Power and Order: Henry Adams and the Naturalist Tradition in American
    Fiction L 146
Power and Personality PS 544
Power and Society H 1327
Power and the Pulpit in Puritan New England L 52
The Power Broker H 1293
The Power Elite SOC 485
Power in Committees PS 108
The Power of Blackness: Hawthorne, Poe, Melville L 155
The Power of Money PS 518
Power on the Left H 484
The Power Structure: Political Process in American Society SOC 586
The Power to Inform; Media: The Information Business PC 694
Powerline: The First Battle of America's Energy War SOC 530
The Powers That Be PC 664
Practical Musical Criticism M 119
The Practice of Fiction in America L 332
The Practice of Piety R 33
The Practice of Political Authority PS 25
The Practice of Rights PS 26
The Pragmatic Movement in American Philosophy H 650
Pragmatic Naturalism H 583
The Pragmatic Revolt in American History H 682
Pragmatism and the American Mind H 689
The Prairie and the Making of Middle America L 490
Prairie Fires and Paper Moons A-A 348
Prairie Grass Dividing H 891
The Prairie People A-F 209
The Prairie School: Frank Lloyd Wright and His Midwest Contemporaries
    A-A 595
Prairie Voices: A Literary History of Chicago from the Frontier to 1893
    L 199
Pratt, the Red Man's Moses H 1129
Preaching in the First Century of New England History H 132
The Precisionist View in American Art A-A 209

A Preface to Democratic Theory   PS 17
Prehistoric Architecture in the Eastern United States   A-A 485
Prelude to Civil War   H 305
Prelude to Greatness H 295
Prelude to Populism   H 1935
Premarital Sexuality   SOC 342
Presbyterian Women in America   R 241
Presbyterians and the Negro   R 264
Present at the Creation   PS 570
Present History   PS 626
The Presentation of Self in Everyday Life   A-F 40
The Presidencies of James A. Garfield and Chester A. Arthur   H 288
The Presidency and the Mass Media in the Age of Television   PC 823
The Presidency of Andrew Jackson   H 332
The Presidency of Thomas Jefferson   H 341
President Wilson Fights His War   H 444
The Presidential Advisory System   PS 116
Presidential Campaign Politics   PS 442
The Presidential Character   PS 109
Presidential Decision-Making   PS 379
Presidential Decision-Making in Foreign Policy   PS 652
The Presidential Election Game   PS 415
The Presidential Game   PS 451
Presidential Influence in Congress   PS 120
Presidential Spending Power   PS 127
Presidential Television   PC 791
The Presidents and the Press   PC 892
The Presidents and the Press: Truman to Johnson   PC 893
Presidents, Bureaucrats and Foreign Policy   PS 617
The President's Cabinet   PS 124
The Press   PC 882
The Press and America   PC 858
The Press and Foreign Policy   PC 852
Press and Public   PC 843
The Press and the American Revolution   H 195
The Press as Guardian of the First Amendment   PC 883
The Press in Perspective   PC 849
Press, Party, and Presidency   PC 686
Pressure on the Press   PC 879
Prestige and Association in an Urban Community   SOC 480
The Pretend Indians   PC 420
A Pretty Good Club   PS 806
A Pre-View of Policy Sciences   PS 95
Previous Convictions   L 247
The Price of Power   PS 673
Primacy or World Order   PS 675
The Primal Mind: Vision and Reality in Indian America   H 1155
Prime-Time America   PC 817
Prime Time Preachers   PC 663
Prime-Time Television   PC 734
Primers for Prudery   STM 384
Primitivism and Decadence: A Study of American Experimental Poetry
    L 430
Printers Face Automation   SOC 584
Printing in the Americas   L 599
Prints in and of America to 1850   A-A 273
Prison and Plantation   H 1958
Prison Homosexuality   SOC 646
Prisoners of Culture   A-F 62
Privacy in Colonial New England   H 97
The Private City   H 1396

The Private Lives and Professional Identity of Medical Students SOC 261
Private Power and American Democracy PS 490
Private Screenings PC 603
Privilege and Creative Destruction H 1970
Privileged Ones SOC 452
Pro Sports: The Contract Game PC 943
The Problem of Authority in America PS 19
The Problem of Slavery in the Age of Revolution H 1026
Problems in Applied Educational Sociolinguistics A-F 309
The Process and Effects of Mass Communication PC 691
The Process of Government Under Jefferson H 280
Prodigal Sons: A Study in Authorship and Authority L 432
Prodigals and Pilgrims H 590
Production in the United States, 1860-1914 H 1856
The Production of Culture PC 51
Productivity Trends in the United States H 1883
The Professional Altruist H 1742
Professional Amateur STM 38
Professional Lives in America SOC 529
Professionals in Search of Work SOC 555
Professionals Out of Work SOC 563
A Profile of the Negro American SOC 198
Profiles in Belief: The Religious Bodies of the United States and Canada
    R 19
Profits Without Production PS 355
Progress and Pragmatism H 635
Progress and Privilege: America in the Age of Environmentalism SOC 507
The Progressive Case and National Security STM 95
Progressive Cities H 1375
The Progressive Presidents H 423
The Progressives and the Slums H 1350
Progressivism and the Open Door PS 683
Progressivism in America H 450
Prohibition H 433
Prologue to Conflict H 318
Prologue to War H 365
Promise and Performance PS 351
The Promise of Power H 1952
The Promised City: New York's Jews, 1870-1914 R 182
Promiseland: A Century of Life in a Negro Community A-F 169
The Pronunciation of English in New York City A-F 356
Propaganda and Aesthetics: The Literary Politics of Afro-American Maga-
    zines in the Twentieth Century L 319
The Prophetic Tradition in American Poetry, 1835-1900 L 153
Prophetic Waters: The River in Early American Life and Literature
    L 77
Proportional Representation in Presidential Nominating Politics PS 428
Proprietary Capitalism H 1915
Prosperity Decade H 1921
Protest: Sacco-Vanzetti and the Intellectuals H 452
Protest and Prejudice: A Study of Belief in the Black Community
    SOC 174
Protest at Selma SOC 125
Protest Songs in America M 189
Protestant and Catholic SOC 67
Protestant-Catholic-Jew R 118
Protestant Church Music in America M 54
Protestant Church Music in America: A Short Survey of Men and Movements
    from 1564 to the Present M 34
Protestant Churches and Industrial America, 1865-1915 R 108

The Protestant Crusade, 1800-1860 R 258
The Protestant Establishment: Aristocracy and Caste in America   SOC 446
Protestant Search for Political Realism, 1919-1941 R 126
The Protestant Temperament R 51
Protestants in an Age of Science R 133
Prudence Crandall H 306
The Psychiatric Hospital as a Small Society A-F 86
Psychiatry Between the Wars, 1918-1945 PSY 29
Psychoanalysis: The Impossible Profession PSY 130
Psychoanalysis and American Medicine, 1894-1918 PSY 35
Psychoanalysis and Literature L 589
Psychoanalysis, Psychotherapy and the New England Medical Scene, 1894-
   1944 PSY 78
Psychoanalytic Explorations of Technique PSY 22
The Psychological Consequences of Being a Black American PSY 181
The Psychological Frontiers of Society A-F 13
Psychological Needs and Political Behavior PS 557
Psychology and History PSY 11
Psychology in Social Context PSY 38
The Psychology of Individual and Group Differences PSY 182
Psychology of Language and Learning PSY 138
The Psychology of Political Control PS 530
The Psychology of Radio PC 735
The Psychology of Rollo May PSY 150
The Psychology of Sex Differences PSY 129
The Psychology of Social Classes PSY 43
The Psychology of the Afro-American PSY 103
The Psychology of Women: A Psychoanalytic Interpretation PSY 60
Psychology of Women: A Study of Bio-Cultural Conflicts PSY 8
Psychology's Crisis of Disunity PSY 164
Psychopathology and Politics PS 545
The Psychotic Process PSY 73
The Public and American Foreign Policy, 1918-1978 PS 716
The Public Arts PC 58
The Public Buildings of Williamsburg, Colonial Capital of Virginia
   A-A 560
Public Entrepreneurship H 1892
Public Health and the State STM 319
Public Health in the Town of Boston, 1630-1822 STM 32
The Public Image of Big Business in America, 1800-1940 H 1693
The Public Lands H 11
Public Lands Politics PS 476
Public Opinion PS 543
Public Opinion, the President and Foreign Policy PS 655
Public Religion in American Culture R 299
Public Representation in Environmental Policy-Making PS 338
A Public Trust: The Report of the Carnegie Commission PC 736
The Public's Impact on Foreign Policy PS 606
Publishers for Mass Entertainment in Nineteenth Century America PC 99
Pueblo A-A 509
Pueblo Indian Religion H 1211
The Puerto Rican Journey: New York's Newest Migrants SOC 181
The Puerto Rican in New York City SOC 100
The Pulitzer Prize Novels PC 101
Pullman H 1537
The Pulse of Politics: Electing Presidents in the Media Age PC 647
The Pure Experience of Order PC 1037
Puritan Boston and Quaker Philadelphia H 552
The Puritan Conversion Narrative L 47
The Puritan Dilemma H 144
The Puritan Ethic and Woman Suffrage H 755

The Puritan Experiment H 64
The Puritan Family H 145
Puritan Influences in American Literature L 57
Puritan New England H 179
The Puritan Origins of the American Self L 42
Puritan Village H 162
The Puritan Way of Death H 174
Puritanism and the American Experience H 136
Puritanism in America L 87
Puritanism in Seventeenth-Century Massachusetts H 109
Puritans Among the Indians R 257
Puritans and Adventurers H 63
The Puritans and Music in England and New England M 104
Puritans and Pragmatists H 571
Puritans and Yankees H 92
Puritans, Indians, and Manifest Destiny R 255
Purity Crusade H 800
The Purposes of American Power PS 800
The Pursuit of a Dream H 1046
The Pursuit of Crime PC 162
The Pursuit of Equality in American History H 667
The Pursuit of Happiness H 616
The Pursuit of Knowledge in the Early American Republic STM 278
The Pursuit of Loneliness PSY 162
The Pursuit of Science in Revolutionary America 1735-1789 STM 170
Pursuits of Happiness: The Hollywood Comedy of Remarriage PC 437

The Quaker Influence in American Literature L 532
Quakers and Politics H 151
Quakers and Slavery in America R 92
The Quakers in the American Colonies H 119
Quakers in the Colonial Northeast H 184
The Quality of American Life PSY 39
Quantification and Psychology PSY 88
Quantification in History H 1
The Quapaw Indians H 1098
The Quest for Completeness PS 334
The Quest for Nationality L 191
The Quest for Paradise: Europe and the American Moral Imagination
   L 644
The Quest for Power H 107
Quest in Modern American Poetry L 382
A Question of Quality: Popularity and Value PC 77

R. G. Dun & Co., 1841-1900 H 1760
Race H 599
Race and Class in the Southwest SOC 83
Race and Economics PS 562
Race and Ethnic Relations in America SOC 179
Race and Manifest Destiny H 611
Race and Politics in North Carolina, 1872-1901 H 1012
Race Awareness in Young Children A-F 44
Race, Color, and the Young Child A-F 76
Race, Culture, and Evolution STM 360
Race Differences in Intelligence PSY 127
Race Relations in the Urban South, 1865-1890 H 1073
Race Riot at East St. Louis, July 2, 1917 H 1077
Racial and Ethnic Relations in America SOC 179
Racial Justice SOC 231

Racial Oppression in America   SOC 91
Racism and Privilege   SOC 245
Racism and Sexism in Corporate Life   SOC 116
The Radical Center: Middle Americans and the Politics of Alienation
    SOC 508
The Radical Future of Liberal Feminism   PS 21
Radical Heritage   H 1627
Radical Innocence: Studies in the Contemporary American Novel   L 300
The Radical Novel in the United States, 1900-1945   L 383
The Radical Persuasion, 1890-1917   H 627
Radical Principles   PS 63
The Radical Republicans   H 398
The Radical Right   PS 512
Radical Sects of Revolutionary New England   R 61
Radical Sophistication: Studies in Contemporary Jewish-American Novelists
    L 631
Radical Visions and American Dreams   H 516
Radio and Poetry   PC 771
Radio Comedy   PC 830
Radio in the Television Age   PC 757
Radio Programming in Action   PC 826
Radio, Television and American Politics   PC 741
Radio, Television and Society   PC 815
Radioactivity in America   STM 12
Rags and Ragtime   M 298
Ragtime   M 256
The Railroad and the City   H 1298
The Railroad and the Space Program   STM 238
Railroad Leaders, 1845-90   H 1673
The Railroad Mergers and the Coming of Conrail   H 1781
The Railroad Station   A-A 580
Railroads and American Economic Growth   H 1686
Railroads and Land Grant Policy   H 1898
Railroads and Regulation 1877-1916   H 1734
Railroads, Freight, and Public Policy   H 1882
The Railroads of the South, 1865-1900   H 1790
The Ramapo Mountain People   A-F 90
The Range Cattle Industry   H 1435
Ransom Kidnapping in America, 1874-1974   SOC 609
The Rapid Deployment Force and U.S. Military Intervention in the Persian
    Gulf   PS 760
Rappaccini's Children   L 80
Rappin' and Stylin' Out   A-F 359
Rascals at Large, or, the Clue in the Old Nostalgia   PC 130
Rationale of the Dirty Joke   A-F 439
The Raven and the Whale   L 164
Raymond Chandler Speaking   PC 147
Reaching Out: Sensitivity and Order in Recent American Fiction by Women
    L 359
Reactionary Essays on Poetry and Ideas   L 403
Read This Only to Yourself   L 137
A Reading of Modern Art   A-A 202
Reading, 'Riting, and Reconstruction   H 351
Reading, Writing, and Resistance: Adolescence and Labor in a Junior High
    School   SOC 271
Readings About Children's Literature   PC 131
Readings from the New Book on Nature   L 362
Readings in Technology and American Life   STM 295
Readings on La Raza   H 966
Readings on the Psychology of Women   PSY 9
The Reagan Experiment   PS 372

The Real Jazz M 322
The Real Majority PS 466
Real Security PS 578
Real Wages in Manufacturing 1890-1914 H 1624
Realism and Idea in the Early American Novel L 141
Realism and Naturalism in Nineteenth-Century American Literature L 174
Realism in Modern Literature L 445
Reapportionment in the 1970s PS 459
Re-Appraisals: Some Commonsense Reading in American Literature L 518
Reasoning About Discrimination: The Analysis of Professional and Executive
   Work in Federal Antibias Programs SOC 562
Rebels: The Rebel Hero in Films PC 549
Rebels and Ancestors: The American Novel, 1890-1915 L 287
Rebels and Reformers: Biographies of Four Jewish Americans SOC 113
Recapitalizing America: Alternative to the Corporate Distortion of
   National Policy PS 359
Recent Conservative Political Thought PS 29
Recent Developments in the Study of Business and Economic History H 1694
Reconstruction H 304
Reconstruction and Redemption in the South H 362
The Recruiting Game PC 990
The Red and the Black H 1157
Red Cloud and the Sioux Problem H 1206
Red Cloud's Folk H 1165
The Red Decade H 493
Red Harvest H 449
The Red Man in the New World Drama H 1270
Red Man's America H 1258
Red Man's Land, White Man's Law H 1266
Red Man's Religion A-F 247
Red Over Black: Black Slavery Among the Cherokee Indians H 1151
Red Scare H 508
Red, White, and Black H 152
Redeem the Time: The Puritan Sabbath in Early America R 41
Redeemer Nation: The Idea of America's Millennial Role R 289
Rediscoveries H 1424
The Rediscovery of American Literature L 389
The Rediscovery of the Frontier L 100
Reflections on the Musical Life of the United States M 106
Reform and Continuity PS 412
Reform in Detroit H 1333
Reformed America: The Middle and Southern States 1783-1837 R 83
The Reformers and the American Indian H 1192
Reforming the Reforms PS 422
Refrigeration in America STM 9
Refugees from Militarism: Draft-Age Americans in Canada SOC 638
Regeneration Through Violence: The Mythology of the American Frontier,
   1600-1860 L 636
Region, Race, and Reconstruction H 1468
Regional Concept H 1443
Regional Diversity H 1462
The Regional Imagination H 1457
Regionalism and the Pacific Northwest H 1497
Regionalism in America H 1464
The Regionalists A-A 212
Regulating Business by Independent Commission H 1657
Regulating the Poor PS 378
Regulation and Its Reform PS 306
The Regulation and Reform of the American Banking System, 1900-1929
   H 1936
Regulation in Perspective H 1897

Rehearsal for Reconstruction H 375
Rehearsal for Republicanism H 339
The Reign of Wonder: Naivety and Reality in American Literature L 651
Reinhold Niebuhr R 148
The Reinterpretation of American Economic History H 1855
The Reinterpretation of American History H 58
Reinterpretation of American History and Culture H 12
Reinventing Anthropology A-F 12
The Relation of Nature to Man in Aboriginal America A-F 255
Relations in Public A-F 41
Relative Deprivation and Working Women SOC 341
The Relevance of Liberalism PS 8
Religion and America R 117
Religion and Politics in the South H 1411
Religion and Sexuality R 201
Religion and the American Mind R 54
Religion and the Rise of the American City R 90
Religion in America R 11
Religion in American History R 17
Religion in Colonial America R 43
Religion in Film PC 536
Religion in the Development of American Culture, 1765-1840 R 79
Religion in the Old South R 88
Religion in the Southern States R 9
Religion in 20th Century America R 129
Religion, the Courts and Public Policy R 302
The Religious Architecture of New Mexico in the Colonial Period and Since
    the American Occupation A-A 476
Religious Assortative Marriage in the United States SOC 287
Religious and Spiritual Groups in Modern America R 199
Religious Enthusiasm and the Great Awakening R 60
Religious Folk Art in America A-A 300
A Religious History of the American People R 1
The Religious Investigations of William James R 149
Religious Liberty in America R 306
Religious Liberty in the United States R 310
Religious Movements in Contemporary America R 221
Religious Perspectives in American Culture R 22
The Religious Press in America PC 854
The Religious Thought of H. Richard Niebuhr R 147
The Reluctant Patron PS 345
The Reluctant Reformation: On Criticizing the Press in America PC 846
Remaking Foreign Policy PS 573
"Remember the Ladies" H 749
The Remembered Gate H 708
Remembering Song M 352
Remote Control: Television and the Manipulation of American Life
    PC 787
The Removal of the Choctaw Indians H 1124
Render Them Submissive H 191
Renderings: Critical Essays on a Century of Modern Art A-A 79
Rendezvous with Destiny H 458
Report on Blacklisting: Volume I--The Movies PC 440
Report on Blacklisting: Volume II--Radio-Television PC 742
The Reporter as Artist PC 914
Reporters and Officials: The Organization and Politics of Newsmaking
    PC 907
Representative Bureaucracy PS 343
Representative Bureaucracy and the American Political System PS 344
Representative Democracy PS 308
Representative Government and Environmental Management PS 327

Representatives and Their Constituencies PS 125
The Republic in Peril H 270
The Republic of Letters: A History of Postwar American Literary Opinion
    L 414
Republic of Technology STM 36
Republican Ascendancy 1921-1933 H 472
The Republican Era, 1869-1901 H 405
Republican Foreign Policy, 1921-1933 PS 629
Republicans and Labor 1919-1929 H 1645
The Rescue and Romance: Popular Novels Before World War I PC 92
Rescuing the American Dream: Public Policies and the Crisis in Housing
    SOC 39
Research Directions of Black Psychologists PSY 26
The Reserve Mining Controversy PS 302
The Reshaping of Plantation Society H 404
Residential Crowding in Urban America SOC 21
The Resisted Revolution H 1299
The Resisting Reader: A Feminist Approach to American Fiction L 502
Response to Imperialism H 542
The Response to Industrialism 1885-1914 H 470
Response to Innovation: A Study of Popular Argument About Mass Media
    PC 653
The Responsible Electorate PS 443
Responsibility in Mass Communication PC 810
Responsibility in Mass Communication, Rev. Ed. PC 683
The Responsibility of the Mind in a Civilization of Machines H 647
The Responsive Chord PC 811
A Restless People H 209
The Restricted Revolution H 1299
The Resurgence of Race H 1084
Retreat from Reconstruction H 312
The Return of the Vanishing American L 504
A Return to Moral and Religious Philosophy in Early America R 136
Return to the Fountains: Some Classical Sources of American Criticism
    L 176
Reunion and Reaction H 413
Reunion Without Compromise H 366
Revealed Masters A-A 189
Revealed Religion: Benjamin West's Commissions for Windsor Castle and
    Fonthill Abbey A-A 176
Reversing the Trend Toward Early Retirement SOC 402
Revisiting Blassingame's The Slave Community H 1038
Revivalism and Separatism in New England, 1740-1800 R 50
Revivalism and Social Reform in Mid-Nineteenth-Century America R 78
Revivalism, Social Conscience, and Community in the Burned-Over District
    H 1406
Revivals, Awakenings, and Reform R 13
Revolt Against Chivalry H 756
Revolt Against Regulation PS 377
The Revolt from the Village 1915-1930 L 305
The Revolt of the Black Athlete PC 939
The Revolt of the Engineers STM 218
Revolt of the Rednecks, Mississippi Politics H 1466
Revolution and Romanticism H 617
Revolution and Tradition in American Painting A-A 205
Revolution in the Wasteland: Value and Diversity in Television PC 737
The Revolution Is Now Begun H 240
The Revolution of American Conservatism H 297
The Revolution of the American Economy H 1912
The Revolutionary Histories H 201
A Revolutionary People at War H 239

The Revolutionary Spirit in France and America H 205
The Revolutionary War in the South H 211
Revolutionary Writers L 53
Revolutions in Americans' Lives H 41
Revue: The Great Broadway Period PC 325
Rhetoric and American Poetry of the Early National Period L 45
The Rhetoric of Conservatism H 1426
The Rhetoric of the Contemporary Lyric L 314
Rhythm and Blues M 415
Rice and Slaves H 1059
The Rich Get Richer and the Poor Get Prison: Ideology, Class, and Criminal
    Justice SOC 495
The Rich Who Won Sports PC 962
Richmond's Jewry, 1769-1976 H 850
Riding on a Blue Note M 279
Right On: From Blues to Soul in Black America M 220
The Right of Mobility SOC 470
The Right Promethean Fire L 301
The Right to Be Indian A-F 238
The Right to Manage H 1577
Right Versus Privilege: The Open-Admissions Experiment at the City Uni-
    versity of New York SOC 295
Righteous Empire: The Protestant Experience in America R 12
The Righteous Remnant H 453
Rights, Justice, and the Bounds of Liberty PS 22
The Rights of Man in America 1606-1861 H 660
Ring Bells! Sing Songs! Broadway Musicals of the 1930s PC 348
Rip Off the Big Game: The Exploitation of Sports by the Power Elite
    PC 954
Ripping and Running: A Formal Ethnography of Urban Heroin Addicts
    SOC 607
The Rise and Fall of American Humor L 448
The Rise and Fall of National Test Scores PSY 6
The Rise and Fall of the Plantation South H 336
The Rise and Fall of the "Soviet Threat" PS 812
The Rise and Repression of Radical Labor USA—1877-1918 H 1564
The Rise of American Civilization H 4
The Rise of American Philosophy, Cambridge, Massachusetts, 1860-1930
    H 628
The Rise of an American Architecture A-A 575
The Rise of Anthropological Theory A-F 8
The Rise of Big Business, 1860-1910 H 1772
The Rise of Children's Book Reviewing in America, 1865-1881 PC 112
The Rise of New York Port, 1815-1860 H 1648
The Rise of Political Consultants PS 464
The Rise of Robert Millikan STM 199
The Rise of Sports in New Orleans: 1850-1900 PC 996
The Rise of Surgery STM 385
The Rise of Teamster Power in the West H 1566
The Rise of the American Chemistry Profession, 1850-1900 STM 22
The Rise of the American Film PC 492
The Rise of the American Novel L 4
The Rise of the Computer State PS 520
The Rise of the Dairy Industry in Wisconsin H 1470
The Rise of the Jewish Community of New York, 1654-1860 H 925
The Rise of the Midwestern Meat Packing Industry H 1807
The Rise of the National Trade Union H 1638
The Rise of the Social Gospel in American Protestantism R 103
The Rise of the Unmeltable Ethnics: Politics and Culture in the Seventies
    SOC 190
The Rise of Urban America H 1323

The Rise to Globalism PS 574
The Rising American Empire H 400
The Rising of the Women H 827
Risk and Technological Innovation STM 364
Rites of Passage PSY 114
The Rites of Passage in a Student Culture A-F 319
The Road: Indian Tribes and Political Liberty H 1099
The Road and the Car in American Life STM 301
The Road to Disappearance H 1123
The Road to Pearl Harbor PS 638
Road to the White House PS 473
Roads, Rails, and Waterways H 1714
The Robber Barons H 1725
The Robe and the Sword R 106
Robert A. Heinlein PC 224
Robert Fuller STM 259
Robert J. Livingston, 1654-1728, and the Politics of Colonial New York
    H 131
Robert Oliver, Merchant of Baltimore, 1783-1819 H 1660
Robert Oppenheimer, Letters and Recollections STM 347
Rock and Roll Will Stand M 413
Rock from the Beginning M 374
A Rock in a Weary Land R 234
Rock Is Rhythm and Blues M 238
Rock Music M 431
Rock 'n' Roll M 427
Rock 'n' Roll Is Here to Pay M 372
Rock 'n' Roll Lady M 419
The Rock Story M 404
Rockdale STM 383
Rockefeller Center A-A 613
Rockefeller Medicine Men STM 47
Rockets, Missiles, and Men in Space STM 226
The Rockin' 50s M 433
The Rocky Mountains: A Vision for Artists in the Nineteenth Century
    A-A 138
Rodeo A-F 117
The Roeblings: A Century of Engineers, Bridge-Builders, and Industrialists
    STM 332
Roger Sessions on Music M 107
Roger Williams R 307
The Role of the Immigrant Women in the U.S. Labor Force, 1890-1910
    H 729
Role Transitions in Later Life SOC 412
Roll, Jordan, Roll H 1037
The Rolling Stone Illustrated History of Rock and Roll M 416
Rolling Thunder PS 791
Roman Catholicism and the American Way of Life R 175
The Romance PC 183
Romance and Realism in Southern Politics H 410
The Romance in America L 175
Romantic Revision A-A 197
Romanticism and American Architecture A-A 567
Romanticism and Nationalism in the Old South H 1485
Romanticism in American Theology R 152
Roosevelt and Churchill, 1939-1941 PS 712
Roosevelt and the Isolationists, 1932-1945 H 437
The Roots of American Bureaucracy, 1830-1900 H 353
The Roots of American Communism H 448
The Roots of American Culture and Other Essays L 622
The Roots of American Economic Growth, 1607-1861 H 1833

Roots of Black Music M 18
The Roots of Black Poverty H 1061
The Roots of Dependency A-F 253
The Roots of Fundamentalism R 282
Roots of Resistance H 1208
Roots of Soul PSY 143
The Roots of Southern Populism H 1459
Roots of the American Working Class H 1580
Roots of Tragedy PS 763
Roughneck, the Life and Times of Big Bill Haywood H 1540
Royal Government in America H 125
Royce on the Human Self H 572
Ruined Eden of the Present L 196
The Run of the Mill STM 105
The Runaways: Children, Husbands, Wives, and Parents SOC 259
Runnin' Down Some Lines A-F 175
Running Away from Myself PC 449
Running Hot: Structure and Stress in Ambulance Work SOC 569
Running Time: Films of the Cold War PC 593
Rural Psychology PSY 48
Rx: Spiritist as Needed A-F 270
Rx Television: Enhancing the Preventive Impact on TV PSY 163

SDS H 523
SF: The Other Side of Realism; Essays on Modern Fantasy and Science
    Fiction PC 215
The Sabbath in Puritan New England H 94
The Saco-Lowell Shops H 1695
The Sacred Cause of Liberty: Republican Thought and the Millennium in
    Revolutionary New England R 286
Sacred Circles: Two Thousand Years of North American Indian Art
    A-A 4
Sacred Sands: The Struggle for Community in the Indiana Dunes SOC 31
A Sad Heart at the Supermarket L 546
Safeguarding the Public Health: Newark, 1895-1918 STM 133
Saga of American Sport PC 970
The Saga of Coe Ridge A-F 445
Saint with a Gun: The Unlawful American Private Eye PC 163
Saints and Secretaries H 56
Saints and Shrews: Women and Aging in American Popular Film PC 616
Saints in the Valleys A-A 303
Saints of Sage and Saddle A-F 409
Sakada: Filipino Adaptation in Hawaii A-F 79
Salem, Massachusetts 1626-1683 H 105
Salem Possessed R 26
The Saloon H 1304
SALT PS 811
The SALT Experience PS 813
The SALT II Treaty PS 803
Salutary Neglect H 111
The Salvage A-F 339
Salvation and the Savage R 251
Salvation in the Slums R 107
Samuel Hopkins and the New Divinity Movement R 81
San Cipriano A-F 276
The San Francisco Irish, 1848-1880 H 861
The San Francisco Stage PC 343
Santa Fe and Taos, 1898-1942 H 1496
The Santa Fe and Taos Colonies H 1453
Santos: The Religious Folk Art of New Mexico A-A 320

Savages and Naturals: Black Portraits by White Writers in Modern American
    Literature L 477
Savages and Scientists STM 174
The Savages of America: A Study of the Indian and the Idea of Civilization
    L 602
Savagism and Civility R 256
Savagism and Civilization H 1212
Savannah Syncopators M 232
Saving the Prairies STM 374
Scandalize My Name M 378
Scandinavian Immigrant Literature L 594
School Desegregation and Defended Neighborhoods SOC 97
School of the Prophets H 180
Schools on Trial: An Inside Account of the Boston Desegregation Case
    SOC 108
The School Upon a Hill H 53
Schooled to Order H 652
Schooling in the Cultural Context A-F 331
Science, Agriculture and the Politics of Research SOC 525
Science and Justice H 101
The Science and Politics of I.Q. PSY 107
Science and Religion in America, 1800-1860 STM 180
Science and Sentiment in America R 155
Science and Society in the United States STM 378
Science and the Ante-Bellum American College STM 147
Science and the Federal Patron PS 381
Science and the Nation STM 106
Science at the Bedside STM 161
Science at the White House STM 52
Science Fiction: A Collection of Critical Essays PC 253
Science Fiction: A Critical Guide PC 245
Science Fiction: Contemporary Mythology PC 264
Science Fiction: History-Science-Vision PC 256
Science Fiction and the New Dark Age PC 206
Science Fiction at Large PC 243
Science Fiction Dialogues PC 268
The Science Fiction Novel PC 257
Science-Fiction Studies PC 241
Science Fiction, Today and Tomorrow PC 211
Science in America Since 1820 STM 304
Science in American Society STM 89
Science in Nineteenth-Century America STM 305
Science in the British Colonies of America STM 356
Science in the Federal Government STM 108
Science, Technology, and National Policy STM 216
The Sciences in the American Context STM 306
Scientific Elite STM 401
Scientific Interests in the Old South STM 192
Scientific Management and the Unions, 1900-1932 H 1609
Scientific Societies in the United States STM 17
A Scientist at the White House STM 210
Scientists Against Time STM 19
Scientists in Politics: The Atomic Scientists Movement, 1945-46
    STM 365
The Scotch-Irish H 954
Scott Joplin and the Ragtime Era M 278
Screen and Society PC 745
Screening the Blues M 233
Sculpture in America A-A 237
Sculpture in Modern America A-A 263
Seabrook and the Nuclear Regulatory Commission PS 386

The Search for an American Indian Identity H 1154
Search for Consensus H 19
The Search for Help: A Study of the Retarded Child in the Community
    SOC 636
The Search for Order, 1877-1920 H 545
A Search for Power H 773
In Search of Excellence: Lessons from America's Best-Run Companies
    SOC 577
In Search of the New Old: Redefining Old Age in America, 1945-1970
    SOC 400
Seascape and the American Imagination A-A 128
Season of Youth H 216
Seasonable Revolutionary: The Mind of Charles Chauncy R 58
The Seasons of a Man's Life PSY 124
Seasons of Shame: The New Violence in Sports PC 1009
The Second American Party System H 340
The Second Black Renaissance L 449
A Second Circle H 587
A Second Flowering: Works and Days of the Lost Generation L 256
The Second Skin: An Interdisciplinary Study of Clothing PC 1025
Secrecy A-F 72
The Secret City H 1040
The Secretary of Defense PS 340
The Sectional Crisis and Northern Methodism R 96
Securing the Revolution H 199
Security in the Nuclear Age PS 687
Seeds of Extinction H 1245
Seeds of Liberty H 673
Seedtime in the Republic H 238
Seeing and Being: The Plight of the Participant Observer in Emerson,
    James, Adams, and Faulkner L 608
Seeing Is Believing: How Hollywood Taught Us to Stop Worrying and Love
    the Fifties PC 425
Seekers of Tomorrow: Masters of Modern Science Fiction PC 240
The Segmented Society H 42
Segmented Work, Divided Workers H 1568
The Segregated Covenant: Race Relations and American Catholics R 265
Selected Papers from American Anthropologists A-F 5
Selections from the Scientific Correspondence of Elihu Thomson STM 1
The Self-Begetting Novel L 551
Self-Help in the 1890s Depression H 1868
The Self-Made Man in America PC 107
Seminole Music M 145
The Semisovereign People PS 498
Send These to Me H 936
Sense and Sensibility in Modern Poetry L 365
The Sense of Life in the Modern Novel L 587
The Sense of Society: A History of the American Novel of Manners L 585
A Sense of Story: Essays on Contemporary Writers for Children PC 134
The Sense of Well-Being in America SOC 2
Sentimental Imperialists PS 792
The Sentimental Novel in America, 1789-1860 PC 70
Separation-Individuation Theory and Application PSY 62
Separation of Church and State R 301
The Sephardic Jewish Community of Los Angeles A-F 454
Serious Music--And All That Jazz! M 325
The Servants of Power STM 16
Serving the Few PS 325
Setmar: An Island in the City A-F 135
Settlement and Unsettlement in Early America H 135
Settling with the Indians H 1182

Seven American Utopias A-A 462
Seven Days a Week H 767
The Seven Lively Arts PC 59
Seven Women H 793
Seventeenth Century in America H 171
The Sewing Machine STM 78
The Sex Offender and the Criminal Justice System SOC 632
Sex Roles in Contemporary American Communes SOC 390
Sex Roles, Life styles, and Childbearing SOC 313
Sex Stratification: Children, Housework, and Jobs SOC 363
Sexism and Youth PSY 77
Sexual Assault Among Adolescents SOC 608
Sexual Fiction L 240
Sexual Harassment of Working Women SOC 370
Sexual Identity SOC 395
Sexual Politics, Sexual Communities: The Making of a Homosexual Minority
    in the United States, 1940-1970 SOC 343
Sexual Stratagems: The World of Women in Film PC 456
Sexual Suicide SOC 354
Sexuality in the Movies PC 413
The Shadow in the Cave: The Broadcaster, His Audience and the State
    PC 822
Shadows of the Indian H 1247
Shaker Furniture A-A 355
Shaker Furniture and Objects from the Faith and Edward Deming Andrews
    Collections A-A 422
Shaker Music M 140
The Shaker Spiritual M 180
Shaker Textile Arts A-A 386
The Shape of Books to Come L 205
The Shape of Time: Remarks on the History of Things PC 1028
The Shaping of American Religion R 23
The Shaping of Art and Architecture in Nineteenth-Century America
    A-A 125
Sharing Caring: The Art of Raising Kids in Two-Career Families SOC 325
Shattered Peace PS 816
The Shattered Silents: How the Talkies Came to Stay PC 630
The Shattered Synthesis H 118
The Shawnee H 1109
Shay's Rebellion H 245
The Shingle Style and the Stick Style A-A 584
The Shingle Style Today A-A 626
Shingling the Fog and Other Plains Lies A-F 463
Shining Trumpets M 258
Shipcarvers of North America A-A 242
Shipping, Maritime Trade and the Development of Colonial America H 1787
The Shock of Recognition: The Development of Literature in the United
    States, Recorded by the Men Who Made It L 38
Shock, Physiological Surgery, and George Washington Crile STM 113
A Shopkeeper's Millennium R 76
The Shores of Light: A Literary Chronicle of the Twenties and Thirties
    L 427
A Short History of American Poetry L 27
A Short History of Music in America M 15
A Short History of the Movies PC 533
The Short Story in America, 1900-1950 L 417
The Show and Tell Machine: How Television Works and Works You Over
    PC 761
Show Biz from Vaude to Video PC 347
Showboats PC 346
Showdown: Confronting Modern America in the Western Film PC 516

Showing Off in America, from Conspicuous Consumption to Parody Display
  PC 5
The Shrine of Party H 382
The Shrinking of America: Myths of Psychological Change PSY 187
Shuckin' and Jivin' A-F 390
Shutdown at Youngstown: Public Policy for Mass Unemployment SOC 526
Sickness and Health in America STM 275
Side-Saddle on the Golden California Pacific Palisades PC 40
Sight, Sound, and Society: Motion Pictures and Television in America
  PC 707
The Sign of Three: Dupin, Holmes, Peirce PC 145
Sign Off: The Last Days of Television PC 749
Signs and Meaning in the Cinema PC 640
The Silent Language A-F 7
Silent Spring STM 61
The Silversmiths of Virginia Together with Watchmakers and Jewelers, from
  1694-1850 A-A 373
Simon Says M 339
The Simplification of American Life: Hollywood Films of the 1930s
  PC 563
Sinful Tunes and Spirituals M 149
Sing a Song of Social Significance M 144
Singers of an Empty Day M 375
Singing Cowboys and All That Jazz M 429
Singing for Power M 193
The Singing Sixties M 158
The Single Vision: The Alienation of American Intellectuals L 266
Singles: Myths and Realities SOC 264
The Sioux H 1152
Sit-Down H 1159
Six Cultures A-F 342
The Six-Gun Mystique PC 270
Sixguns and Society: A Structural Study of the Western PC 642
Sixteenth-Century North America H 1238
The Skyscraper A-A 603
Skyscraper Primitives A-A 133
Skyscraper Style A-A 623
The Slave Community H 1017
Slave Religion R 231
Slave Songs of the United States M 202
Slavery, a Problem in American Institutional and Intellectual Life
  H 1028
Slavery and Freedom H 1076
Slavery and Methodism R 97
Slavery and the Evolution of Cherokee Society, 1540-1866 H 1213
Slavery and the Numbers Game H 1043
Slavery in the Americas H 1054
Slavery in the Cities H 1085
Slavery in the Structure of American Politics, 1765-1820 H 237
The Slavery of Sex H 761
Slaves Without Masters H 1014
The Slavic Community on Strike H 1571
Sleepy Hollow Restorations A-A 366
Slow Fade to Black: The Negro in American Film, 1900-1942 PC 445
Small Business in American Life H 1661
Small Town America H 1473
The Small Town in American Literature L 528
The Snapshot A-A 340
So Far Disordered in Mind STM 131
So Shall Ye Reap H 1595
So This Is Jazz M 317

Social Amnesia: A Critique of Conformist Psychology from Adler to Laing
  PSY 102
Social Anthropology of the North American Tribes A-F 211
The Social Basis of American Communism H 456
Social Change and the Aged SOC 437
Social Class and Mental Illness SOC 468
Social Class in American Sociology SOC 461
Social Concepts of Health, Illness, and Patient Care STM 253
The Social Consequences of Long Life SOC 443
Social Control in the Colonial Economy H 1876
Social Darwinism STM 15
Social Darwinism in American Thought STM 177
Social Documentary Photography in the USA A-A 323
The Social Gospel and Reform in Changing America R 114
The Social Gospel in America, 1870-1920 R 141
The Social Gospel in the South H 1480
A Social History of Rock Music M 397
A Social History of the Bicycle STM 349
The Social History of the Machine Gun STM 109
The Social Ideas of American Educators H 578
The Social Impact of the Telephone STM 288
Social Justice in the Liberal State PS 1
The Social Life of a Modern Community A-F 156
Social Life of Virginia in the Seventeenth Century H 74
The Social Novel at the End of an Era L 271
The Social Organization of Early Industrial Capitalism H 1881
The Social Organization of Leisure in Human Society SOC 3
Social Origins of the New South H 406
Social Patterns in Normal Aging SOC 436
Social Problems in Corporate America A-F 63
Social Realism A-A 231
The Social Reality of Death SOC 401
The Social Responsibility of the Press PC 865
Social Science and Public Policy in the United States PS 333
Social Standing in America: New Dimensions of Class SOC 451
The Social Stratification of English in New York City A-F 362
The Social Structure of Revolutionary America H 223
The Social System of the Modern Factory A-F 155
The Social Systems of American Ethnic Groups A-F 158
Social Thought in America H 690
Social Welfare or Social Control PS 392
The Social World of Old Women SOC 373
Socialism and American Art in the Light of European Utopianism, Marxism,
  and Anarchism A-A 53
Socialization and Social Class SOC 476
Socialization to Politics PS 527
Society and Children's Literature PC 115
Society and Culture in America, 1830-1860 H 360
A Society Ordained by God H 115
Sociocultural Changes in American Jewish Life as Reflected in Selected
  Jewish Literature H 866
Sociolinguistic Patterns A-F 363
Sociology and Everyday Life PC 61
Sociology of the Black Experience SOC 229
Sociology of Sport PC 940
The Sociology of Urban Education SOC 326
The Sod-House Frontier, 1854-1890 H 1442
Sod Walls A-A 589
Soho: The Artist in the City SOC 592
Sojourners and Settlers: Chinese Migrants in Hawaii SOC 130
Soldier Groups and Negro Soldiers A-F 187

Soldiers and Society SOC 554
Soldiers, Statesmen, and Cold War Crises PS 586
Solid Gold M 376
Some Americans: A Personal Record L 405
Some Aspects of the Religious Music of the United States Negro M 184
Some Time in the Sun L 260
"Somebody's Calling My Name" M 195
Song from the Earth: American Indian Painting A-A 13
Songs Along the Mahantongo M 134
Songs of the Teton Sioux M 178
Songs of the Yokutes and Paiutes M 181
Sons of Sam Spade PC 148
Sons of Science STM 277
Sons of the Fathers: The Civil Religion of the American Revolution
    R 291
A Sort of Utopia H 1486
The Soul Book M 222
Soulside A-F 179
Sound and the Cinema PC 432
Sound Effects M 391
The Sound of Our Time M 406
The Sound of Soul M 214
A Sound of Strangers M 35
The Sound of the City M 394
Soundpieces M 64
The Sounds of People and Places M 3
The Sounds of Social Change M 377
A Source Book for the Study of Personality and Politics PS 532
The Sources of Economic Growth in the United States and the Alternatives
    Before Us H 1849
The Sources of Increased Efficiency H 1715
The Sources of Invention STM 190
South Africa and the United States PS 588
The South and Film PC 470
The South and the North in American Religion R 10
The South and the Sectional Conflict H 370
The South and Three Sectional Crises H 1448
The South in American Literature: 1607-1900 L 537
South Italian Folkways in Europe and America A-F 467
The South Returns to Congress H 379
South to Louisiana M 204
South-Watching H 1460
The Southeastern Indians H 1161
Southeastern Indians Since the Removal Era H 1269
Southern Anglicanism R 45
Southern Architecture A-A 511
The Southern Cheyennes H 1103
Southern Churches in Crisis R 119
The Southern Colonies in the Seventeenth Century H 83
The Southern Common People H 1475
The Southern Dream of a Caribbean Empire 1854-1861 H 338
The Southern Enigma H 1450
Southern Enterprise: The Work of National Evangelical Societies in the
    Antebellum South R 85
Southern Evangelicals and the Social Order 1800-1860 R 86
The Southern Federalists, 1800-1816 H 269
The Southern Frontier: 1670-1732 H 1115
Southern Honor H 1520
The Southern Indians H 1113
Southern Indians in the American Revolution H 1205
The Southern Lady H 814

Southern Life in Fiction L 538
Southern Music, American Music M 171
Southern Politics in State and Nation PS 444
Southern Progressivism H 1458
The Southern Redneck SOC 61
A Southern Renaissance: The Cultural Awakening of the American South,
    1930-1955 L 327
Southern Renascence: The Literature of the Modern South L 388
Southern War Poetry of the Civil War L 123
Southern White Protestantism in the Twentieth Century R 115
Southern Workers and Their Unions, 1880-1975 H 1623
Southern Writers and the New South Movement, 1865-1913 L 167
Southerners SOC 60
Southwestern Indian Ritual Drama A-F 212
Sovereign States in an Age of Uncertainty H 213
Sovereignty at Bay PS 804
Soviet-American Relations, 1917-1920: The Decision to Intervene PS 698
Soviet-American Relations, 1917-1920: Russia Leaves the War PS 697
Soviet Criticism of American Literature in the Sixties L 379
Space, Style and Structure A-A 521
Space, Time, and Architecture A-A 601
Spaces A-A 260
Spain in America H 104
The Spanish-Americans of New Mexico A-F 267
The Spanish Borderlands Frontier, 1513-1820 H 1412
Spanish Colonial Tuscon A-F 92
Spanish Folk-Poetry in New Mexico M 137
Spanish Harlem SOC 213
Spanish-Speaking People in the United States A-F 271
Spartan Seasons: How Baseball Survived the Second World War PC 946
Speaking for Nature: How Literary Naturalists from Henry Thoreau to Rachel
    Carson Have Shaped America L 464
Spearheads for Reform H 1300
The Speculator H 1785
Spheres of Justice PS 64
The Spirit and the Flesh: Sex in Utopian Communities SOC 294
The Spirit of American Literature L 13
The Spirit of American Philosophy R 154
The Spirit of American Sculpture A-A 235
The Spirit of Liberalism PS 44
Spirits in Rebellion: The Rise and Development of New Thought R 190
Spiritual Autobiography in Early America L 79
The Spiritual Crisis of the Gilded Age R 100
The Spirituals and the Blues M 210
The Spoilage A-F 340
The Spoken Seen: Film and the Romantic Imagination PC 542
Spokesman L 419
The Sponsor: Notes on a Modern Potentate PC 720
Sport PC 928
Sport and American Mentality: 1880-1910 PC 976
Sport and Social Order PC 921
Sport and the Spirit of Play in American Fiction L 580
Sport, Culture and Society PC 968
Sport in Contemporary Society PC 941
Sport in the Socio-Cultural Process PC 951
Sportin' House M 306
The Sporting Myth and the American Experience L 657
The Sporting Spirit: Athletes in Literature and Life PC 953
The Sporting Woman SOC 334
The Sports Factory PC 937
Sports in America PC 975

Sports Violence PC 945
Sports World PC 966
Sportsmen and Gamesmen PC 934
Spreading the American Dream H 522
Sprout Spring A-F 185
Sputnik, Scientists, and Eisenhower STM 209
The Stages of Economic Growth H 1913
The Stamp Act Crisis H 229
The Standard of Living in 1860 H 1895
Standard Oil Company (Indiana) H 1696
Standards of Excellence: Studies on Modern English and American Poets
    L 210
Star-Marking Machinery M 440
Stardom PC 631
Stars (R. Dyer, 1979) PC 454
The Stars (E. Morin, 1960) PC 550
Stars and Strikes PC 583
Stars of Country Music M 172
The State and Human Services PS 350
The State and the Mentally Ill STM 145
State Government and Economic Development H 1902
The State of the Presidency PS 115
The State, the Investor, and the Railroad H 1780
The Status Seekers SOC 491
The Status System of a Modern Community A-F 157
The Steam Locomotive in America STM 48
Steam Power on the American Farm STM 392
Steamboat Come True STM 126
Steamboats on Western Rivers STM 185
Steelmasters and Labor Reform, 1886-1923 H 1555
Steelworkers in America H 1534
Step Right Up: An Illustrated History of the American Medicine Show
    PC 371
Steppin' Out: New York Nightlife and the Transformation of American Cul-
    ture, 1890-1930 H 1307
The Stereotype of the Single Woman in American Novels L 484
Sticks and Stones A-A 488
Stigma: Notes on the Management of Spoiled Identity A-F 42
Still Rebels, Still Yankees and Other Essays L 261
Stilwell and the American Experience in China, 1911-1945 PS 799
Stoney Knows How: Life as a Tatoo Artist SOC 595
Storms Brewed in Other Men's Worlds H 1170
The Story of American Folk Song M 132
The Story of American Letters L 31
The Story of American Literature L 11
The Story of American Painting A-A 150
The Story of America's Musical Theater PC 341
The Story of Architecture in America A-A 516
The Story of Identity: American Fiction of the Sixties L 380
The Story of Jazz M 343
The Story of Monopoly, Silly Putty, Bingo, Twister, Frisbee, Scrabble,
    et Cetera PC 354
The Story of Our National Ballads M 42
The Story of Rock M 368
The Story of the Blues M 234
The Story of the Original Dixieland Jazz Band M 260
The Story of the Red Man H 1244
Stranded M 414
The Strands Entwined: A New Direction in American Drama L 220
The Strange Career of Jim Crow H 1094
The Strange Career of Marihuana SOC 630

Strange Gods: The Great American Cult Scare R 194
Strange Ways and Sweet Dreams A-F 462
Stranger and Friend A-F 21
Stranger at Home: "The Holocaust," Zionism, and American Judaism R 178
Strangers at the Door H 975
Strangers in the Land: Patterns of American Nativism, 1860-1925 R 262
Strangers Next Door: Ethnic Relations in American Communities SOC 242
Strangers to This Ground: Cultural Diversity in Contemporary American
   Writing L 277
Strangers Within the Gate City H 935
Strategic Implications of the All-Volunteer Force PS 605
Strategic Interaction A-F 43
Strategic Studies and Public Policy PS 657
Strategic Styles: Coping in the Inner City SOC 52
Strategies for Change PS 469
Strategies of Containment PS 645
Strategies of Political Emancipation PS 5
Strategy and Arms Control PS 775
Strategy and Choice in Congressional Elections PS 440
Strategy and Structure H 1665
Strategy and the MX PS 658
The Strategy of Foreign Aid PS 589
Strategy, Structure, and Economic Performance H 1779
Stratification Among the Aged SOC 405
A Streak of Luck STM 76
A Streamlined Decade PC 1016
Street Art M 367
Street Corner Society: The Social Structure of an Italian Slum SOC 240
Street Ethnography A-F 160
Street Signs Chicago: Neighborhood and Other Illusions of Big-City Life
   SOC 24
The Street That Never Slept M 338
Streetcar Suburbs H 1397
The Strenuous Age in America Literature L 333
Stress Disorders Among Vietnam Vets PSY 70
Stress, Health, and Psychological Problems in the Major Professions
   PSY 148
Strikes in the United States H 1552
Structural Change in the American Economy H 1838
Structural Fabulation: An Essay on the Fiction of the Future PC 255
Structure and Change in Economic History H 1905
The Structure of American Medical Practice, 1875-1941 STM 313
The Structure of the Cotton Economy of the Antebellum South H 1764
The Structure of the Popular Music Industry M 402
Structures of Custodial Care A-F 137
The Struggle for Social Security 1900-1935 H 492
Struggles Past and Present A-F 283
Student Politics in America H 418
Studies in American Historical Demography H 39
Studies in Classic American Literature L 557
Studies in Italian American Social History H 873
Studies in Judaica Americans H 919
Studies in Literary Types in Seventeenth-Century America (1607-1710)
   L 73
Studies in New England Transcendentalism L 132
Studies in Religion in Early American Literature L 568
Study in Power H 1759
The Study of American Folklore A-F 379
The Study of Culture at a Distance A-F 17
The Study of Games A-F 2
A Study of Jazz M 346

The Study of Literate Civilizations A-F 11
A Study of Saving in the United States H 1865
The Study of Social Dialects in American English A-F 368
Studying Personality Cross-Culturally PSY 108
Studying the Presidency PS 121
Stuff of Sleep and Dreams L 497
The Subjective Side of Science STM 254
Subliminal Politics PS 551
The Subordinate Sex PSY 34
The Subsidized Muse PS 366
Suburb: Neighborhood and Community in Forest Park, Ohio 1935-1976
    H 1360
Suburban Youth in Cultural Crisis SOC 427
Success in America PC 71
Successful Schools and Competent Students SOC 276
Such a Pretty Face: Being Fat in America SOC 642
Suffragists and Democrats H 790
Sugar Country H 1504
Suicidal Adolescents SOC 404
Suicide A-F 133
Suiting Everyone: The Democratization of Clothing in America PC 1027
The Summer Game PC 917
The Summer of Love M 366
The Sun Dance Religion A-F 222
Sun Records M 383
Sunbelt Cities H 1284
Sunshine Muse: Contemporary Art on the West Coast A-A 107
The Sunshine Windows: Adapting to Sudden Bereavement SOC 418
Super Realism A-A 23
Super Spectator and the Electric Lilliputians PC 959
Superculture: American Popular Culture and Europe PC 3
Superman and Common Man PS 4
Supermannerism A-A 627
Supernatural Horror in Literature PC 177
The Supernatural in Fiction PC 180
Surgeons to the Poor STM 237
Surpassing the Love of Men H 740
Surrealism and American Art, 1931-1947 A-A 234
Surrealism and American Feature Films PC 535
The Survival of American Innocence: Catholicism in an Era of Disillusion-
    ment, 1920-1940 R 170
Swedes in America 1638-1938 H 847
The Swedish Immigrant Community in Transition H 892
Sweet as the Showers of Rain M 209
Sweet Medicine H 1220
Sweet Songs for Gentle Americans M 441
Swing Out M 274
Symbol and Conquest A-F 268
Symbolism and American Literature L 506
Symbols of American Community, 1735-1775 H 139
Symphony and Song M 123
Synagogue Architecture in the United States A-A 528
Synagogue Life A-F 102
Synchromism and American Color Abstraction, 1910-1925 A-A 218
Synchromism and Color Principle in American Painting, 1910-1930 A-A 198
Syntony and Spark STM 3
Systems Analysis for Social Scientists PS 72
A Systems Analysis of Political Life PS 82
Systems of North American Witchcraft A-F 251

The TFX Decision PS 300
TV: The Most Popular Art PC 796
TV & Teens PC 812
TV as Art PC 764
The TV Establishment PC 827
The TV-Guided American PC 723
The TV Ritual: Worship at the Video Altar PC 760
TV Violence and the Child PC 739
TVA and the Grass Roots PS 382
TVA and the Power Fight, 1933-1939 STM 244
Take Me Home M 183
Take Me Out to the Ball Park PC 985
Taking Rights Seriously PS 20
Taking Your Medicine STM 370
The Tale of Terror: A Study of the Gothic Romance PC 185
The Tale of the Tribe: Ezra Pound and the Modern Verse Epic L 219
A Tale of Two Cities M 420
Talking Back: Citizen Feedback and Cable Technology PC 680
The Talladega Story A-F 114
Tally's Corner A-F 186
Tambo and Bones: A History of the American Minstrel Stage PC 405
Tammany H 1365
The Tarnished Dream: The Basis of American Anti-Semitism R 260
Tarzan and Tradition: Classical Myth in Popular Literature PC 173
The Tasteful Interlude A-A 421
The Taste Makers A-A 481
The Taxicab H 1698
Taylorism and the Watertown Arsenal STM 4
Teachers Versus Technocrats A-F 346
Teaching and Learning in City Schools A-F 318
Teaching Science Fiction PC 265
Teamster Rank and File SOC 542
Teapot Dome H 510
Technical Choice, Innovation, and Economic Growth STM 92
Technocracy and the American Dream STM 5
The Technocrats STM 110
Technological Innovation STM 204
Technological Innovation and the Decorative Arts STM 298
Technology and American Economic Growth STM 317
Technology and Change STM 331
Technology and Civility PS 85
Technology and Social Change in America STM 219
Technology and Women's Work H 701
Technology in America STM 296
Technology in Early America STM 171
Technology in Western Civilization. Vol. II, Technology in the Twentieth
   Century STM 214
Technology, Management and Society PS 529
Teenage Tyranny SOC 419
Television: The Business Behind the Box PC 729
Television: The Critical View PC 795
Television: A Selection of Readings from TV Guide Magazine PC 743
Television: Ethics for Hire? PC 715
Television and Aggression PSY 137
Television and Aggression: An Experimental Field Study PC 756
Television and Human Behavior PSY 52
Television and Presidential Politics PC 759
Television and Social Behavior: Beyond Violence and Children PC 833
Television and Socialization of the Minority Child PSY 18
Television and the News: A Critical Appraisal PC 818
Television and the Presidential Elections PC 781

Television and the Public PC 726
Television as a Cultural Force PC 713
Television as a Social Force PC 738
Television Coverage of the 1980 Presidential Campaign PC 711
Television Economics PC 800
Television Fraud PC 716
Television in America PC 744
Television in the Corporate Interest PC 733
Television in the Lives of Our Children PSY 158
Television Programming for News and Public Affairs PC 835
Television Today: The End of Communication PC 824
Television's Child PC 793
Television's Transformation: The Next 25 Years PC 748
Temples of Democracy A-A 464
The Tenacity of Prejudice: Anti-Semitism in Contemporary America
    SOC 212
Tenement Songs M 436
Tennessee Strings M 199
The Tennessee Valley Authority STM 281
Tennessee Writers L 434
The Tenth Muse: The Psyche of the American Poet L 515
Terminal Visions: The Literature of Last Things PC 262
The Territories and the United States, 1861-1890 H 1493
The Territory Ahead: Critical Interpretations in American Literature
    L 591
The Terror That Comes in the Night A-F 420
Teton Sioux Music M 145
Texas Graveyards A-F 428
Texas Log Buildings A-A 469
A Texas-Mexican "Cancionero" M 179
Texas Shrimpers SOC 565
That Most Distressful Nation H 923
That Wilder Image A-A 186
A Theater Divided: The Postwar American Stage L 294
The Theater in Colonial America L 74
Theater in the Ante Bellum South, 1815-1861 L 120
The Theater of the Golden Era in California PC 361
Theatre in a Tent: The Development of a Provincial Entertainment PC 392
Theatre of the Crossroads: Plays and Playwrights of the Mid-Century Ameri-
    can Stage L 284
The Theatre on the Frontier: The Early Years of the St. Louis Stage
    L 113
The Theatrical Twenties PC 333
Theft by Employees SOC 631
Their Brothers' Keepers: Moral Stewardship in the United States, 1800-
    1865 R 82
Their Sisters' Keepers H 745
Their Solitary Way H 100
Theirs Be the Power H 1429
The Theme of Loneliness in Modern American Drama L 495
Theodore Roosevelt and the Progressive Movement H 504
Theodore Roosevelt and the Rise of America to World Power H 419
Theology and Modern Literature L 421
Theology in America R 130
Theories of Authorship PC 436
Theories on Drug Abuse PSY 122
Theory and Practice in American Medicine STM 43
Theory and Research on the Causes of War PS 755
The Theory of American Literature L 9
The Theory of Democratic Elitism PS 3
A Theory of Justice PS 52

The Theory of Political Coalitions PS 104
A Theory of the Labor Movement H 1616
The Therapeutic Revolution STM 380
There Is a River H 1044
There Must Be a Lone Ranger: The American West in Film and in Reality
  PC 431
These Also Believe: A Study of Modern Cults and Minority Religious Move-
  ments R 191
They All Played Ragtime M 259
They All Sang on the Corner M 216
They and We: Racial and Ethnic Relations in the U.S. SOC 204
They Came Here First H 1195
They Shall Take Up Serpents A-F 116
Things in the Driver's Seat: Readings in Popular Culture PC 30
Things That Go Bump in the Night A-F 426
Think Back on Us: A Contemporary Chronicle of the 1930s by Malcolm Cowley
  L 257
Thinkers and Tinkers STM 25
Thinking About National Security PS 592
Thinking About Women L 498
A Thinking Man's Guide to Baseball PC 961
The Third Book of Criticism L 547
The Third Century PS 547
The Third Election System, 1853-1892 H 328
Third Parties in Presidential Elections PS 450
The Third World and United States Foreign Policy PC 767
Thirteen Days PS 699
The Thirties L 428
The Thirites: Fiction, Poetry, Drama L 274
Thirty Years of Change in Puerto Rico SOC 94
This Almost Chosen People H 657
This Hallowed Ground H 272
This High Man: Life of Robert Goddard STM 222
This Is Ragtime M 357
This Land, This South H 1432
This New Ocean: A History of Project Mercury STM 369
This Remarkable Continent PC 1041
This Sacred Trust H 651
This Sheba, Self H 85
This Species of Propriety H 1069
This Was Burlesque PC 334
Thomas Alva Edison STM 382
Thomas Hunt Morgan: Pioneer of Genetics STM 338
Thomas Hunt Morgan: The Man and His Science STM 7
Thoreau and the American Indians H 1242
Those Fabulous Philadelphians, the Life and Times of a Great Orchestra
  M 81
Those Who Can: A Science Fiction Reader PC 266
The Thought of Reinhold Niebuhr R 142
A Thousand Days H 528
A Thousand Golden Horns M 275
Three Bags Full L 671
Three Centuries of American Antiques A-A 376
Three Centuries of American Furniture A-A 384
Three Centuries of American Hymnody M 63
Three Centuries of Microbiology STM 221
Three Eyes on the Past A-F 427
The Three Neophites A-F 438
Three Tomorrows: American, British and Soviet Science Fiction PC 226
Thrillers PC 161
Through the Custom House L 183

Through the Looking Glass PS 86
Thursday's Child: Trends and Patterns in Contemporary Children's Litera-
    ture PC 113
A Tide of Discontent PS 465
Tidewater Towns H 165
The Timber Economy of Puritan New England H 1664
Time for Reason: About Radio PC 732
Time on the Cross H 1031
A Time to Mourn: Expressions of Grief in Nineteenth Century America PC
    1036
Time to Murder and Create L 209
The Times of Melville and Whitman L 106
The Tin Kazoo: Television, Politics, and the News PC 750
Tin Pan Alley M 434
Tin Pan Alley: A Chronicle of American Popular Music M 395
To Be a Woman in America 1850-1930 H 706
To Be or Not to Bop M 287
To Build a Canal H 1301
To Cut, Piece and Solder A-A 398
To Die Game H 1132
To Empower People PS 304
To Find an Image: Black Films PC 553
To Irrigate a Wasteland: The Struggle to Shape a Public Television System
    in the United States PC 784
To Kill a Messenger: Television News and the Real World PC 820
To Live on This Earth A-F 213
To Make a Poet Black L 616
To Move a Nation PS 674
To See Ourselves A-F 75
To Set the Law in Motion H 1975
To the Farewell Address H 207
To the Hartford Convention H 260
To Work and to Wed H 809
The Toadstool Millionaires: A Social History of Patent Medicine in America
    Before Federal Regulation STM 398
Today's Disease: Alcohol and Drug Dependence SOC 664
Tom Paine and Revolutionary America H 206
Tom Swift & Company PC 292
Tomorrow a New World H 439
Tomorrow Is Another Day: The Woman Writer in the South, 1859-1936
    L 54
Tomorrow's Tomorrow: The Black Woman SOC 366
Toms, Coons, Mulattos, Mammies, and Bucks PC 426
Too Many Women? The Sex Ratio Question SOC 359
Too Old, Too Sick, Too Bad: Nursing Homes in America SOC 433
Topics in American Art Since 1945 A-A 18
Tort Law in America H 1982
Touching Base: Professional Baseball and American Culture in the Progres-
    sive Era PC 987
Tough Guy Writers of the Thirties L 346
The Tourist A-F 121
The Tourist Business H 1743
Toward a Definition of the American Film Noir, 1941-1949 PC 505
Toward a New American Literary History L 469
Toward a New Past H 5
Toward a Planned Society H 461
Toward a Response to the American Crises PS 55
Toward a Theory of Popular Culture M 369
Toward an Urban Vision H 1283
Toward Standards: A Study of the Present Critical Movement in American
    Letters L 509

Towards a New Cold War PS 602
Towards a New Historicism L 590
The Tower and the Bridge STM 29
A Tower in Babel: A History of Broadcasting in the United States,
   Volume I--to 1933 PC 721
Town Hall Tonight PC 352
Town into City H 1314
Tradition and Innovation in New Deal Art A-A 39
The Tradition of the New A-A 118
The Traditional and the Anti-Traditional L 366
A Traditional Model of Educational Excellence SOC 288
Traditions in the Twentieth Century American Literature L 392
Tragedy in Dedham H 1979
The Tragedy of Lyndon Johnson H 459
The Tragic Mode in Children's Literature PC 120
Trails to Texas H 1465
The Trans-Appalachian Frontier H 1498
Transatlantic Industrial Revolution H 1719
Transatlantic Mirrors: Essays in Franco-American Literary Relations
   L 461
Transatlantic Revivalism R 69
Transcendentalism as a Social Movement, 1830-1850 L 180
Transcendentalism in America H 626
Transcendentalism in New England R 140
The Transcendentalist Constant in American Literature L 439
The Transcendentalist Ministers R 84
The Transfiguration of the Commonplace: A Philosophy of Art A-A 44
The Transformation of American Foreign Relations, 1865-1900 H 271
The Transformation of American Law, 1780-1860 H 1959
The Transformation of Political Culture H 303
The Transformation of the School H 574
The Transformation of Virginia, 1740-1790 R 56
Transformations PSY 87
Transformations of the American Party System PS 447
Transitions in American Literary History L 474
The Transmission of American Culture A-F 335
The Transportation Industries 1889-1946 H 1652
The Transportation Revolution 1815-1860 H 1924
Transracial Adoption SOC 217
Transracial Adoption: A Followup SOC 218
Treasury of American Design PC 1026
Treating the Mentally Ill PSY 15
The Treatment Techniques of Harry Stack Sullivan PSY 44
Trends in American Electoral Behavior PS 436
The Trial of the Assassin Guiteau H 1978
Trial and Error: The Detroit School Segregation Case SOC 246
The Triangle Fire H 1632
Tried as by Fire R 113
The Triple Revolution: Social Problems in Depth PSY 145
Trips M 428
The Triumph of American Painting A-A 228
The Triumph of Conservatism H 482
The Triumph of Evolution STM 83
The Triumph of Sectionalism H 1476
Trivializing America PC 15
Trouble in Our Backyard PS 619
The Troubled Alliance PS 643
The Troubled Crusade: American Education, 1945-1980 SOC 306
The Troubled Partnership PS 702
Troupers of the Gold Coast, or the Rise of Lotta Crabtree PC 388
Trouping: How the Show Came to Town PC 360

The Truants H 554
True Love and Perfect Union H 777
The Truman Doctrine and the Origins of McCarthyism PS 644
Truman, the Jewish Vote, and the Creation of Israel PS 781
Trumpets of Jubilee L 181
Tube of Plenty: The Evolution of American Television PC 722
The Tumultuous Years PS 625
Tune In, America M 88
The Turbulent Era: Riot and Disorder in Jacksonian America H 296
Turbulent Years H 1525
Turn-of-the-Century America A-A 73
Turning Points: Essays on the Art of Science Fiction PC 233
The Tweed Ring H 1292
Tweed's New York H 1332
Twelve Against Empire H 262
Twelve Great American Novels L 588
Twelve Photographers of the American Social Landscape A-A 354
The Twenties: American Writing in the Post-War Decade L 312
The Twenties, from Notebooks and Diaries of the Period L 429
Twentieth Century Limited: Industrial Design in America, 1925-1939
    H 1751
Twentieth-Century American Folk Art and Artists A-A 307
The Twentieth-Century Mind H 697
Twentieth-Century Populism H 1501
Twenty-Five Years of the Philadelphia Orchestra M 127
Twice a Minority A-F 280
Twigs for an Eagle's Nest PS 387
The Twilight of Authority PS 552
The Twilight of Federalism H 334
The Twilight of Splendor A-A 615
The Two-Career Family SOC 282
Two Centuries of Black American Art A-A 52
Two Cheers for Capitalism PS 39
Two Chicago Architects and Their Clients A-A 598
Two Cultures of Policing SOC 580
Two Hundred Years of American Blown Glass A-A 406
Two Hundred Years of American Foreign Policy PS 597
Two Hundred Years of Geology in America STM 330
Two Hundred Years of North American Indian Art A-A 9
The Two-Paycheck Marriage SOC 333
The Two Rosetos A-F 375
Two Towns: Concord and Wethersfield, a Comparative Exhibition of Regional
    Culture 1635-1850 PC 1012
The Two Worlds of American Art PC 62
Two Worlds of Childhood: U.S. and U.S.S.R. SOC 262
Typology and Early American Literature L 44
Tyranny and Legitimacy PS 24

U.S. Arms Sales PS 579
U.S. Defense Planning PS 608
U.S. Foreign Policy PS 720
A U.S. Foreign Policy for Asia PS 731
U.S. Foreign Policy and Asian-Pacific Security PS 798
U.S. Foreign Policy and the Law of the Sea PS 676
The U.S. Health System STM 302
U.S. Intelligence and the Soviet Strategic Threat PS 642
U.S. Interests in Africa PS 802
U.S. International Broadcasting and National Security PS 801
U.S. International Monetary Policy PS 737
The U.S. Machine Tool Industry, from 1900 to 1950 H 1804

U.S. Troops in Europe PS 736
Ultimately Fiction: Design in Modern American Literary Biography L 373
Unbuilt America A-A 512
The Uncertain Giant, 1921-1941 PS 571
Uncertain Glory A-F 383
The Uncertain Profession H 668
The Unchanging Arts PC 26
Uncle Sam: The Man and the Legend PC 35
Uncle Sam Presents: A Memoir of the Federal Theatre, 1935-1939 L 236
Uncle Sam's Stepchildren H 1222
Under the Gun: Weapons, Crime, and Violence in America SOC 667
The Underclass SOC 445
Underemployed Ph.D's SOC 594
Underemployment Insurance and the Older American SOC 415
The Underground Press in America PC 866
Unequal Americans: Practices and Politics of Intergroup Relations
   SOC 223
Understanding Jazz M 320
Understanding Media PC 45
Understanding the New Religions R 215
Understanding the Rape Victim PSY 109
Underworld U.S.A. PC 539
The Unembarrassed Muse: The Popular Arts in America PC 50
The Unexpected Minority: Handicapped Children in America SOC 626
The Ungentlemanly Art PC 869
Union Democracy PS 486
Unionism and Relative Wages in the United States H 1591
Unions and Universities SOC 537
The Unitarian Conscience R 145
United Artists PC 415
The United States and the Origins of the Cold War, 1941-1947 PS 646
The United States and World War II H 429
The United States and the Caribbean 1900-1970 PS 710
The United States and Iran PS 758
The United States and the Jewish State Movement PS 774
United States-Comanche Relations H 1149
The United States Economy in the 1950s H 1931
United States Foreign Policy and the Third World PS 667
The United States in the Middle East PS 797
The United States in the World Arena PS 766
The United States in the World Economy PS 582
United States Oil Policy, 1890-1964 H 1755
The Universe Makers: Science Fiction Today PC 269
The Unknown Shore: A View of Contemporary Art A-A 20
Unplanned Careers: The Working Lives of Middle-Aged Women SOC 442
The Un-Politics of Air Pollution PS 311
Unrecognized Patriots H 235
The Unseeing Eye: The Myth of Television Power in National Politics
   PC 802
The Unseen Elderly SOC 406
Unsettled People H 6
The Unsounded Centre: Jungian Studies in American Romanticism L 98
Unsung: A History of Women in American Music M 1
Unwanted Mexican Americans in the Depression H 937
The Unwelcome Immigrant H 970
The Unwritten War: American Writers and the Civil War L 88
Up from Communism H 581
Up from Puerto Rico A-F 285
The Uprooted: The Epic Story of the Great Migrations that Made the Ameri-
   can People H 933
Urban America H 1322

The Urban American Indian SOC 225
Urban Anthropology in the United States A-F 69
Urban Blues M 225
Urban Capitalists H 1311
The Urban Crucible H 231
Urban Decline and the Future of American Cities SOC 25
The Urban Elderly SOC 397
Urban Elites and Mass Transportation SOC 71
The Urban Environment System PS 335
The Urban Establishment H 1338
The Urban Ethos in the South H 1290
The Urban Experience and Folk Tradition A-F 448
Urban Folklore from the Paperwork Empire A-F 404
The Urban Frontier H 1391
Urban Growth and City Systems in the United States, 1840-1860 H 1367
Urban Growth in the Age of Sectionalism H 1321
The Urban Idea in Colonial America H 102
The Urban Impact on American Protestantism, 1865-1900 R 99
Urban Masses and Moral Order in America, 1820-1920 H 1288
The Urban Nation, 1920-1960 H 505
The Urban Poor of Puerto Rico A-F 288
Urban Poverty in a Cross-Cultural Perspective A-F 302
The Urban Prospect H 1364
The Urban Real Estate Game SOC 31
Urban Renegades A-F 215
The Urban School A-F 329
Urban Slavery in the American South, 1820-1860 H 1039
Urban Social Space SOC 47
Urban Sociology SOC 72
Urban Village H 1399
The Urban Villagers: Group and Class in the Life of Italian-Americans
    SOC 124
The Urban West at the End of the Frontier H 1345
The Urban Wilderness H 1398
The Urbanization of America, 1860-1915 H 1355
The Urbanized Northeastern Seaboard of the United States SOC 43
The Urgent West: The American Dream and Modern Man L 437
Usable Knowledge: Social Science and Social Problem Solving PS 98
Use of the Mass Media by the Urban Poor PC 661
The Uses of Enchantment PC 109
The Uses of Gothic A-A 594
The Uses of the Media by the Chicano Movement PC 670
Utilitarianism and Beyond PS 56

V Was for Victory H 424
The Valiant Knights of Daguerre A-A 341
Valley City A-F 159
Valley of Discord: Church and Society Along the Connecticut River, 1636-
    1725 R 36
Values and the Future STM 13
Values, Ethics, and the Practice of Policy Analysis PS 314
Values in America H 553
Vanguard American Sculpture, 1913-1939 A-A 267
The Vanishing Adolescent SOC 275
The Vanishing American H 1126
The Vanishing Americans: The Decline and Fall of the White Anglo Saxon
    Protestant SOC 210
The Vanishing Hitchhiker A-F 380
Variations in Value Orientations A-F 14
Varieties of Civil Religion R 293

Variety Entertainment and Outdoor Amusements PC 404
Vaudeville PC 359
Vaudeville U.S.A. PC 336
The Vaudevillians PC 393
Vendetta H 911
The Veracious Imagination L 649
Versions of the Past: The Historical Imagination in American Fiction
    L 527
The Vertical Structure of the Television Broadcasting Industry PC 782
Veterans in Politics H 284
Viable Democracy PS 47
The Vice Lords A-F 183
The Victim as Criminal and Artist L 510
The Victim of Rape SOC 633
Victims: Textual Strategies in Recent American Fiction L 235
Victims of the System: Crime Victims and Compensation in American Politics
    and Criminal Justice SOC 621
The Victorian Home in America A-A 579
The Victorian Mode in American Fiction 1865-1885 L 124
Victorian Resorts and Hotels A-A 591
Video Art A-A 140
Vietnam on Film PC 407
The Vietnam Trauma in American Foreign Policy PS 691
Vietnamese Americans SOC 183
The View from Sunset Boulevard PC 60
Village and Seaport H 117
The Village Indians of the Upper Missouri H 1197
Villains Galore . . . the Heyday of Popular Story Weekly PC 87
The Vineyard of Liberty PS 10
Violence and Culture in the Antebellum South H 1427
Violence and Religious Commitment R 209
Violence in Recent Southern Fiction L 293
Violent America: The Movies 1946-1964 PC 411
Violent Criminal Acts and Actors SOC 611
Violent Death in the City H 1344
Virgin Land: The American West as Symbol and Myth L 190
Virginia, 1705-1786 H 71
Virgins, Vamps, and Flappers PC 483
The Visible Hand H 1666
Visible Saints: The History of a Puritan Idea R 37
Vision of the Disinherited: The Making of American Pentacostalism
    R 270
Visionary Film PC 604
Visions of America L 566
Visions of War: Hollywood Combat Films of World War II PC 502
Visions of Yesterday PC 573
The Vital Few H 1877
The Voice of the Folk: Folklore and American Literary Theory L 455
Voices for the Future, Volume I PC 216
Voices for the Future, Volume II PC 217
Voices from the Great Black Baseball Leagues PC 955
Voices Protest H 428
Vortex: Pound, Eliot, and Lewis L 352
Voting PS 411
Voting in Provincial America H 90
Votive Offerings Among Greek Philadelphians A-F 455
Voyages to the Moon PC 244

Wage-Earning Women H 828
Wages and Earnings in the United States, 1860-1890 H 1596

Wages and Hours H 1633
Wages in Practice and Theory H 1614
The Wagon and the Star A-F 15
Wait Until Dark M 314
Waiting for the 5:05 A-A 457
Waiting for the End L 505
Wake Up Dead Man A-F 424
Wake Up Dead Men M 163
Waking Their Neighbors Up L 435
Walk in the White Line A-F 303
Walking to New Orleans M 205
Wall Street in the American Novel L 665
Wall-to-Wall America A-A 219
Wallace Stevens L 454
Wallpaper in America A-A 402
Walter Reuther and the Rise of the Auto Workers H 1522
War and American Thought H 684
War and Society H 518
The War at Home PS 555
The War Economy of the United States PS 356
The War Film PC 500
The War for the Union H 356
War, Foreign Affairs and Constitutional Power PS 782
The War Industries Board H 442
The War of 1812 H 274
The War of American Independence H 210
War on Film PC 488
The War Over the Family SOC 254
War, Politics, and Revolution in Provincial Massachusetts H 158
War Powers of the President and Congress PS 761
The War, the West, and the Wilderness PC 430
The War with Spain, 1898 H 397
The War Within: From Victorian to Modernist Thought in the South, 1919-
    1945 L 393
Warrior in Two Camps H 1096
Warriors at Suez PS 734
Warriors of the Colorado H 1136
The Wars of America H 25
Wartime Strikes H 1567
Wartime Women H 699
The Wary Fugitives: Four Poets and the South L 387
Washington: Capital City 1879-1950 H 1325
Washington: Village and Capital, 1800-78 H 1324
The Washington Community, 1800-1828 H 1401
The Washington Correspondents PC 902
The Washington Lobbyists PS 492
The Washington Reporters PC 868
Wasteland: Building the American Dream A-A 614
Water for the Cities H 1285
Water Shortage: Lessons in Conservation from the Great California Drought,
    1976-1977 SOC 22
Water Witching U.S.A. A-F 149
Watermelon Wine M 153
Wayne County A-A 467
Wayward Puritans: A Study in the Sociology of Deviance R 29
We Call it Culture--The Story of Chautauqua M 45
We Shall Be All H 1550
We Shall Not Overcome H 1531
"We the People" and Others: Duality and America's Treatment of Its Racial
    Minorities SOC 202
We Were There H 836

We Who Built America H 1008
Wealth and Power in America PS 342
The Wealth of a Nation to Be H 1880
The Weapon Makers: Personal and Professional Crisis During the Vietnam
    War SOC 588
Weapons of Criticism: Marxism in America and the Literary Tradition
    L 626
Weasel Words: The Art of Saying What You Don't Mean PC 677
Weathering the Storm H 738
Welcome Joy H 103
The Welfare Industry SOC 596
The Welfare Mothers Movement SOC 464
Welfare of the Poor SOC 499
Welfare Policy and Industrialization in Europe, America, and Russia
    H 519
The Well-Tempered Lyre M 387
We're Being More Than Entertained PC 14
We're in the Money: Depression America and Its Films PC 424
The West and Reconstruction H 1415
The West as Romantic Horizon A-A 190
The Western: A Collection of Critical Essays PC 274
The Western: From Silents to the Seventies PC 462
The Western Alliance PS 662
The Western Hero in Film and Television PC 564
The Western Hero in History and Legend PC 287
Western Indians SOC 151
Western Lands and the American Revolution H 1405
The Western Peace Officer H 1495
Western River Transportation H 1706
The Western Story PC 271
Western Views and Eastern Visions A-A 330
Westerns PC 469
The Westward Enterprise H 51
Westward Expansion H 1419
Westward the Way A-A 112
What Is Cinema Verite? PC 489
What Jazz Is All About M 272
What Manner of Woman L 643
What Price Vigilance? PS 771
What Was Literature? Class Culture and Mass Society PC 76
What Will Have Happened PC 140
What Women Want SOC 394
What's Fair? American Beliefs About Distributive Justice SOC 465
What's Happening to the American Family SOC 296
What's News PC 645
When Harlem Was Jewish H 928
When the Eagle Screamed H 315
When the Music Mattered M 424
When Workers Fight H 1621
Where Have All the Voters Gone PS 446
Where the Sky Began H 1474
Which Side Are You On? The Brookside Mine Strike in Harlan County
    H 1557
Which Side Are You On?: The Harlan County Coal Miners 1931-39 H 1579
Which Side Were You On? H 480
Which Way Did He Go? The Private Eye PC 156
While Six Million Died H 501
White and Negro Spirituals, Their Life Span and Kinship M 223
White Collar: The American Middle Classes SOC 486
White Collar Crime SOC 663
White-Collar Unionism SOC 578

The White Ethnic Movement and Ethnic Politics SOC 237
White Hopes and Other Tigers PC 963
The White House Years PS 703
The White Man's Indian H 1101
White Protestant Americans SOC 79
White Protestantism and the Negro R 226
White, Red, and Black: The Seventeenth-Century Virginian H 1116
White Sects and Black Men in the Recent South R 261
White Spirituals in the Southern Uplands M 164
White Southerners SOC 46
White Teacher, Black School SOC 194
White Towers A-A 606
Who Are the Major American Writers? L 539
Who Commits Crimes PSY 147
Who Gets Ahead?: The Determinants of Economic Success in America
    SOC 473
Who Is in the House? A Psychological Study of Two Centuries of Women's
    Fiction in America, 1795 to the Present L 578
Who Really Rules? PS 77
Who Rules America? SOC 457
Who Rules America Now? A View for the '80s SOC 458
Who Rules the Joint? The Changing Political Culture of Maximum Security
    Prisons in America SOC 661
Who Voted? PS 445
Who Votes? PS 474
The Whole World Is Watching: Mass Media in the Making & Unmaking of the
    New Left PC 659
Who's Running America PS 315
Why Art? Casual Notes on the Aesthetics of the Immediate Past A-A 24
Why Can't They Be Like Us?: America's White Ethnic Groups SOC 138
Why Survive? Being Old in America SOC 399
Why Teachers Organized H 1639
Why the North Won the Civil War H 290
Widowhood in an American City SOC 429
The Wild West PC 389
Wilderness and the American Mind H 654
Will They Ever Finish Bruckner Boulevard? A-A 608
William Carlos Williams and the American Scene 1920-1940 L 402
William H. Welch and the Rise of Modern Medicine STM 125
William Penn's Legacy H 177
William Tecumseh Sherman and the Settlement of the West H 1409
Wilson the Diplomatist H 490
Windows on the World: Essays on American Social Fiction L 533
The Windsor Chair A-A 410
The Winged Gospel STM 79
The Winning of the Midwest H 326
Winthrop Aldrich H 1722
Winthrop's Boston H 168
The Wire That Fenced the West STM 239
Wiring a Continent: The History of the Telegraph Industry in the United
    States, 1832-1866 STM 372
Wisconsin Medicine STM 276
The Wisdom of Words: Language, Theology, and Literature in the New England
    Renaissance L 134
Witchcraft at Salem R 34
Witchcraft in the Southwest A-F 289
Witches, Mid Wives, and Nurses H 735
"With Bodilie Eyes" A-A 247
"With His Pistol in His Hand" A-F 447
With Shield and Sword H 20
With the Ears of Strangers: The Mexican in American Literature L 617

Witnesses to a Vanishing America L 166
Witnessing Slavery L 188
The Wolf by the Ears H 348
The Woman Citizen H 778
The Woman in American History H 781
The Woman Movement H 797
The Woman Question in American History H 835
Womanhood in America H 808
Woman's Body, Woman's Right H 751
Woman's Fiction L 94
Woman's Legacy H 700
Woman's Place: Options and Limits in Professional Careers SOC 347
Woman's Place Is at the Typewriter H 723
Woman's Proper Place H 805
Woman's Worth: Sexual Economics and the World of Women SOC 367
Women: A Feminist Perspective H 747
Women: Dependent or Independent? PSY 173
Women and Achievement SOC 374
Women and American Socialism, 1870-1920 H 713
Women and American Trade Unions H 1586
Women and Crime SOC 657
Women and Equality H 718
Women and Film PC 503
Women and Language in Literature and Society PSY 135
Women and Madness PSY 45
Women and Medicine STM 225
Women and Men Midwives STM 98
Women and Religion in America R 246
Women and Sex Roles PSY 72
Women and Social Change in America SOC 371
Women and Sport PC 980
Women and Temperance H 712
Women and the American City H 825
Women and the American Labor Movement H 743
Women and the Cinema PC 508
Women and the Future: Changing Sex Roles in Modern America SOC 353
Women and the News PC 861
Women and the Social Costs of Economic Development A-F 324
Women and the Workplace H 711
Women and Their Sexuality in the New Film PC 545
Women and Western American Literature PC 286
Women and Work in America H 819
Women as Widows SOC 430
Women at Work H 730
Women, Ethnics, and Exotics: Images of Power in Mid-Nineteenth-Century
    American Fiction L 140
Women for Hire: A Study of the Female Office Worker SOC 566
Women Have Always Worked H 772
Women in America H 698
Women in American Architecture A-A 518
Women in American Religion R 243
Women in Crisis PSY 153
Women in Film Noir PC 504
Women in Law SOC 348
Women in Modern America H 703
Women in Stuart England and America H 829
Women in the American Revolution H 736
Women in White STM 236
Women, Money, and Power PSY 46
Women of a Certain Age SOC 441
Women of Steel: Female Blue-Collar Workers in the Basic Steel Industry
    SOC 535

The Women of the Confederacy H 816
Women of the Republic H 769
Women of the West H 752
Women of Wonder: Science Fiction Stories by Women About Women PC 254
Women on the Job SOC 512
Women on Words and Images PC 137
Women, Race and Class H 724
Women Scientists in America STM 322
Women, Sex, and Race SOC 335
Women, War and Work H 754
Women Who Embezzle or Defraud SOC 768
Women, Women Writers, and the West L 559
Women, Work, and National Policy H 840
Women Writers of the Short Story L 577
Womenfolks, Growing Up Down South H 1404
Women's America H 770
Women's Career Patterns SOC 372
Women's Diaries of the Westward Journey H 812
The Women's Health Movement SOC 380
Women's Life and Work in the Southern Colonies H 822
The Women's Movement: Political, Socioeconomic, and Psychological Issues
    PSY 57
The Women's Movement: Social and Psychological Perspectives PSY 186
The Women's Movement in Community Politics in the U.S. SOC 388
Women's Pictures: Feminism and Cinema PC 513
Women's Reflections: The Feminist Film Movement SOC 378
Women's Sexual Development PSY 115
Women's Sexual Experience PSY 116
Women's Voices: An Untold History of the Latter-Day Saints, 1830-1900
    R 242
Women's Work and Family Values, 1920-1940 H 831
Women's Work, Women's Health H 824
The Wood-Carvers of Cordova, New Mexico A-F 378
Wood Carvings: North American Folk Sculptures A-A 309
Woodrow Wilson and the Progressive Era, 1910-1917 H 491
Woodrow Wilson and World Politics PS 717
A Word Geography of the Eastern United States A-F 360
The Word War PS 783
Work and Family in the United States SOC 290
Work and Personality SOC 559
Work and Retirement SOC 438
Work and Satisfaction in the Public Sector SOC 551
Work and the Family System SOC 305
Work and the Helpless Self: The Social Organization of a Nursing Home
    SOC 552
Work, Culture, and Society in Industrializing America H 1574
The Work Ethic in Industrial America, 1850-1920 H 1625
Work Without Salvation H 597
Worker City, Company Town H 1641
Worker in the Cane A-F 281
Workers and Allies H 799
Workers and Utopia H 1573
Workers' Compensation and Work-Related Illnesses and Diseases SOC 516
Workers' Control in America H 1607
Workers in Industrial America H 1535
Workers' Struggles, Past and Present H 1570
Workers' World H 1529
Working SOC 598
Working Class Community in Industrial America H 1548
Working Class Hero PS 508
Working-Class Life H 1630

The Working Class Majority SOC 481
Working for the Railroad H 1592
The Working Girls of Boston H 839
Working People of Philadelphia, 1800-1850 H 1589
The Working Population of Manchester, New Hampshire, 1840-1886 H 1575
Working with Structuralism L 339
Working Women and Families H 741
Workingmen's Democracy H 1561
Workshops in the Wilderness STM 123
A World Destroyed: The Atomic Bomb and the Grand Alliance STM 337
A World Elsewhere: The Place of Style in American Literature L 607
The World Encyclopedia of Cartoons PC 313
The World Encyclopedia of Comics PC 314
The World from Brown's Lounge A-F 168
The World in a Frame: What We See in Films PC 427
The World in Depression, 1929-30 H 1884
The World of Antiques, Art, and Architecture in Victorian America
   A-A 27
The World of Big Bands M 297
The World of Black Singles SOC 387
The World of Carnegie Hall M 103
The World of Fanzines PC 106
The World of John Cleaveland H 114
World of Laughter: The Motion Picture Comedy Short, 1910-1930 PC 514
The World of Melodrama PC 384
A World of Men PS 631
The World of Musical Comedy PC 349
World of Our Fathers H 939
The World of Science Fiction, 1929-1976 PC 219
The World of Soul M 241
A World of Strangers SOC 428
The World of Swing M 267
The World of the Thriller PC 150
The World of the Urban Working Class SOC 459
The World of the Worker H 1569
The World of Washington Irving L 107
A World on Film PC 507
World Power Trends and United States Foreign Policy in the 80s PS 604
World War I and the American Novel L 251
The World We Imagine L 391
The Worldly Evangelicals R 281
Worlds Apart: Relationships Between Families and Schools SOC 297
Worlds from Words: A Theory of Language in Fiction L 604
The World's Great Dailies PC 887
Worlds of Music M 111
Worlds of Pain: Life in the Working-Class Family SOC 498
The Wound in the Heart H 466
Wrestlin' Jacob: A Portrait of Religion in the Old South R 80
The Wright Brothers STM 203
Writers in Crisis: The American Novel, 1925-1940 L 288
Writers on the Left L 203
Writings in Jazz M 268

Xenophobia and Immigration H 876

Yankee City A-F 154
Yankee Science in the Making STM 367
Yankee Stonecutters A-A 250
Yankee Theatre L 142

Year by Year in the Rock Era   M 401
Years of Infamy   H 537
Years of Upheaval   PS 703
Yesterdays   M 400
Yesterday's Tomorrows: A Historical Survey of Future Societies   PC 202
You Gotta Deal with It   A-F 184
You Owe Yourself a Drunk   A-F 141
The Young Rebel in American Literature   L 457
Your Ancients Revisited: A History of Child Development   STM 334
Youth Culture   A-F 138
Yuman and Yaqui Music   M 145

Zen and American Thought   H 549
The Zero-Sum Society   PS 499
Zion in America: The Jewish Experience from Colonial Times to the Present
     R 166
The Zunis of Cibola   H 1114

Abolition and Abolitionism: H 287, 329, 380, 386, 761, 782, 1072; R 91-92, 95, 97. See also Blacks; Civil War; Slavery.

Abortion: see Birth Control and Abortion.

Abstract Art: A-A 33, 81, 113, 200, 207, 211, 213-216, 218, 223, 228, 230

Absurd (Literature and Drama): L 280, 322, 377, 526.

Acculturation: A-F 21, 244, 250, 271, 366; H 873, 926-927, 1009, 1143, 1148, 1162, 1187, 1212, 1216, 1246, 1248, 1250, 1257, 1263, 1268, 1395; M 35; PSY 47; R 185, 251-252; SOC 110, 223. See also: Assimilation of Ethnic, Religious and National Groups.

Actors and Acting: L 8, 23, 24, 259, 592; PC 47, 324, 388, 392, 435, 454, 550, 583, 596, 631. See also: Film; Theater.

Adolescence: A-F 138; PS 537; PSY 21, 49, 114; SOC 270, 275. See also: Youth.

Advertising: A-A 271; A-F 353; H 1771; PC 714, 720, 766; SOC 520. See also: Graphic Arts; Illustration; Radio; Television.

Aerospace Industry: STM 455, 77, 157, 179, 226, 300. See also: Aircraft.

Aesthetics: A-A 24, 111, 466-467, 481; H 600; L 413, 421; PC 5, 42. See also: Art--Theory and Criticism.

Affirmative Action, Equal Employment Opportunity: SOC 166, 216; STM 69.

African Religion and Religions: R 231. See also: Blacks--Religion and Religions.

Afro-Americans: see Blacks.

Aged: A-F 89; H 17; SOC 331, 373, 396-397, 399-400, 403, 405-407, 409, 415, 424-426, 431, 433-435, 437-439, 444, 534; STM 2. See also: Medicare and Medicaid; Old Age; Social Security.

Agrarianism (Southern): H 1320; L 318, 387, 403, 434-435, 564, 569. See also: South--Literature.

Agriculture: A-F 79, 97, 123; H 35, 37, 283, 310-311, 381, 1299, 1416, 1438-1439, 1470, 1503-1504, 1595, 1653, 1690, 1748, 1768-1769, 1800, 1803, 1842; PS 326; SOC 525; STM 21, 321. See also: Farms and Farming; Pesticides; Sciences.

Air Force: PS 305. See also: Military.

Air Pollution: see Pollution (Environment).

Aircraft: H 1740; PC 1; STM 30, 71, 79, 83-84, 112, 157, 203. See also: Aerospace Industry.

Alcohol and Alcoholism: A-F 88, 228, 230, 248; H 22, 35, 374, 1304; PC 442; PSY 66, 71, 120, 175, 178; SOC 652, 664. See also: Prohibition; Temperance Societies and Movements.

Alienation and Loneliness: H 597, 953; SOC 16-17, 74, 123, 508.

Aliens: see Immigration.

America--Discovery and Exploration: see North America--Discovery and Exploration.

American Dream: A-A 614; H 522, 1024, 1046, 1400; L 344, 437, 472; PC 578, 613; PS 469; R 3, 298; SOC 146, 154; STM 5.

American English: A-F 350-351, 356, 368. See also: Blacks--Language; Dialects; Language; Linguistics; Slang.

American Renaissance (Literature): L 11, 108, 134, 163, 202, 262, 469.

American Revolution: see War of Independence.

American Telephone & Telegraph Co.: STM 10, 87.

Amish: A-F 106.

Amusement Parks, Fairs, Etc.: H 1339, 1745; PC 356, 362, 369, 374, 404, 971.

Anarchism: PS 4, 49.

Anglican Church: R 45-46. See also: Episcopal Church.

Anthropology: A-F 8-10, 12, 16-19, 21, 31, 297-298, 301, 304, 314, 333, 337; H 53; L 166; M 9; PC 43; PSY 25, 27, 69, 95, 108, 123, 180; R 237; SOC 5; STM 174, 215, 235, 352, 360, 383.

Anti-Catholicism: R 258, 262-263. See also: Nativism.
Antinomianism: H 56; R 29, 31, 42.
Anti-Semitism: H 885, 936; R 169, 178, 260; SOC 109, 144, 212.
Appalachia: A-F 104, 130; H 677, 1445, 1479, 1515; R 269; SOC 28, 38.
    See also: Poor and Poverty.
Archaeology: A-F 33, 57-58, 66; PC 1018-1019, 1033-1035. See also:
    Indians (American).
Architecture: A-A 433-634. See also: Farms and Farming--Buildings;
    Neo-Classical and Colonial Style Architecture; Public Buildings;
    Revival Architecture; Urban Architecture; Vernacular Architecture.
  Design: A-A 451, 461, 473, 488, 501, 512, 525; STM 29.
  History: A-A 29, 445, 453-455, 459-460, 463, 474, 486, 488, 490, 501,
    506, 516, 525-526.
    17th-18th Centuries: A-A 353-560.
    19th Century: A-A 27-28, 125, 561-592.
    20th Century: A-A 76, 465, 593-634; H 1713; PC 1016.
Armed Forces: see Military.
Arms and Armament: PS 596, 678, 693; SOC 588, 698; STM 11, 19, 50, 111,
    209, 222, 337, 397. See also: Defense; Department of Defense;
    Disarmament; Gun Control; Guns; Military; Nuclear Weapons; Rockets.
Arms Control and Arms Race: PS 596, 598, 603, 735, 749, 751, 775, 780,
    803, 811, 813; PSY 145. See also: Defense; Department of Defense;
    Disarmament; Foreign Relations; Military; Nuclear Weapons.
Army: H 20, 39, 872, 1454, 1511, 1546; PS 305; STM 11. See also Military.
Art: PC 26; PSY 143. See also: Abstract Art; Decorative Arts; Folk
    Art; Graphic Arts; Happenings, Performance Art, Etc.; Illustration;
    Minimal Art; Pop Art; Portraits; Realism (Art); Religious Art;
    Sculpture; Surrealism (Art); Symbolism (Art).
  History: A-A 29, 38, 58, 66, 70, 82, 91-92, 94, 104, 128, 134-135,
    141, 147-169.
    17th-18th Centuries: A-A 47, 49, 95, 97, 130, 145, 170-178.
    19th Century: A-A 26-28, 41, 43, 46-47, 49-50, 56, 59, 70, 73, 75,
    88-89, 93, 95, 112, 122, 124-125, 137-138, 142-144, 179-197, 229.
    20th Century: A-A 39, 42, 45, 48, 50, 56, 63-64, 73-74, 76, 81, 89-90,
    93, 96, 98-101, 106, 114, 122, 124, 126-127, 129, 133, 136, 144,
    198-234; PC 27; SOC 510, 592.
    1940s-1980s: A-A 18-25, 30-34, 36, 40-41, 57, 60, 65, 68, 77-80,
    83-87, 102, 105, 107, 123, 140, 209, 225, 233; L 111; M 367.
  Theory and Criticism: A-A 30, 44, 67, 79, 84, 115-118, 129.
Art and Government: A-A 98-100, 219, 231; H 498; L 55; M 23; PS 345,
    366, 387.
Art Patronage: see Patronage.
Artists: A-A 69; L 55, 111, 420, 620; SOC 510, 582, 592. See also:
    Women--Art.
Asia: L 672.
Asian-Americans: A-F 83, 134, 338; H 958, 967-968; PSY 18, 54-55, 105,
    133, 167; SOC 93, 157. See also: Chinese-Americans; Japanese-
    Americans; Korean-Americans; Vietnamese.
Assimilation of Ethnic, Religious and National Groups: A-F 111; H 851,
    870, 873, 923, 935, 1129, 1139, 1173, 1214, 1252, 1395; R 165,
    168-169, 172-173, 175, 183, 254; SOC 110, 112, 134, 177, 179,
    203, 214. See also: Acculturation; Ethnic Groups.
Astronomy: STM 24.
Asylums: see Hospitals and Asylums.
A.T. & T.: see American Telephone & Telegraph Co.
Atomic Bomb: see Nuclear Weapons.
Automation and Mechanization: PC 1021; SOC 584. See also: Industriali-
    zation; Machines and Machinery.
Automobiles and Automobile Industry: H 1280, 1319, 1368, 1370, 1604,
    1698, 1809; PC 74, 1011, 1013; SOC 531; STM 127-128, 130, 250,
    266-267, 284, 299, 301, 391. See also: Transportation.

Aviation: see Aircraft.

Ballads: A-F 387-388, 436-437; M 42, 135-136, 164, 168-169.
Bands: M 267, 274, 297, 309-310, 339, 432, 435. See also: Dance Music;
     Girl Groups (Music).
Banks and Banking: H 1646, 1663, 1684, 1707, 1711, 1754, 1761, 1777,
     1801, 1837, 1864-1865, 1869, 1878, 1918, 1936. See also: Business;
     Federal Reserve System.
Baptists: R 50, 61-62, 111, 113, 305.
Baseball: PC 917-918, 922, 927, 930, 933, 935, 938, 942, 946, 955, 960-961,
     967, 981, 985, 987-988, 991, 993, 995, 1001, 1003-1004.
Basketball: PC 920, 924, 931-932, 948, 956, 996, 1007.
Basque-Americans: A-F 93.
Beat Generation: L 213, 249, 338, 369.
Beatniks and Hippies: A-F 87, 129.
Berlin Crisis: PS 601.
Bicycles: STM 349.
Big Band Era: see Bands.
Bilingualism: A-F 366-367. See also: Language; Linguistics.
Bill of Rights: PS 287; R 301, 303. See also: Constitution.
Bimetalism (1870s): H 314.
Biology: STM 6-7, 90, 233, 338, 374.
Birth: see Childbirth.
Birth Control and Abortion: H 751; PS 283; STM 206, 225, 245, 255, 303.
     See also: Feminism; Population; Women's Rights.
Birth Rate: H 18, 26, 29, 41, 47; SOC 423. See also: Population.
Black Muslims: H 1030; R 226; SOC 141. See also: Blacks--Religion and
     Religions.
Black Writers: L 140, 204, 241, 259, 269, 319, 329, 350, 394, 441, 443,
     449-450, 462-463, 481, 487-488, 510-511, 516-517, 524, 541, 543,
     552, 563, 582, 593, 598, 601, 616, 619, 645. See also: Blacks--
     Literature; Writers.
Blacks: A-F 118, 166-199, 326, 440; H 16, 28-29, 152, 265-266, 509, 932,
     1012-1094, 1563, 1572, 1603, 1975; PC 12, 848, 856, 862, 916;
     PS 260, 522, 548, 566; PSY 1, 7, 18, 26, 39, 50, 54-55, 103,
     105-106, 116, 133, 143, 173, 178, 182; R 86, 88, 225, 261, 264,
     266, 268; SOC 48-49, 52, 87-88, 99, 102, 106, 111, 117, 164, 169,
     174, 177, 186, 191, 194-196, 198, 208-209, 211, 214, 229, 234,
     238, 241, 243-244, 246, 319, 385, 387, 528; STM 237, 328.
  Art: A-A 35, 51-52, 55, 109, 315, 428; A-F 408; L 462.
  Education: H 351, 1086; PSY 50, 182; SOC 90. See also: Education.
  Film: PC 444-445.
  Folklore and Legends: A-F 188, 370, 390, 394, 403, 421, 423-424, 445,
     450, 462, 465.
  Language: A-F 167, 175, 359, 361.
  Literature: L 204, 449, 462-463, 481, 487-488, 510-511, 516-517, 524,
     541, 543, 552, 560, 582, 595, 598, 601, 616, 619, 622, 645; PC 353,
     848, 856, 862, 916; PSY 143. See also: Black Writers; Literature.
  Music: L 462, 470, 498; M 6, 11, 18, 21, 25-26, 29, 31-32, 35-36, 142,
     147-149, 151, 158, 163-164, 166, 174, 176-177, 184, 189, 195,
     197, 200, 202, 214, 218-224, 226-228, 232, 236, 238-244, 252-254,
     274, 300-301, 329, 351, 378, 417; PSY 143. See also: Jazz; Motown;
     Spirituals and Gospel Music.
  Politics: H 1048, 1064, 1088; PS 203; SOC 99, 114, 122, 125, 141,
     153-154, 176, 180.
  Religion and Religions: A-F 198; R 80, 156, 222-227, 229-239; SOC 96,
     144. See also: African Religion and Religions; Black Muslims.
  Sports: PC 939, 952, 955, 981, 989, 991, 997.
  Women: H 757, 794; SOC 366, 386.

Blacks in Art and Literature: A-A 103; A-F 425; L 466, 470, 477, 525, 542, 593; PC 111, 124.
Blacks in Media: PC 426, 445, 495, 515, 528, 538, 553, 556, 559, 589, 783.
Blue Collar Workers: A-F 110, 125, 131, 155; H 1531, 1539, 1574, 1642; PC 12; SOC 305, 459, 478-479, 481-482, 498, 535, 581. See also: Labor; Middle Class.
Bluegrass Music: M 133, 182, 203. See also: Country and Western Music.
Blues (Music): M 203, 206-213, 217-220, 225-226, 229-236, 239, 242-243, 253-254, 302, 356, 398, 445. See also: Jazz; Rhythm and Blues.
Books and Book Collecting: L 10. See also: Censorship, Pornography, Etc.; Publishing.
Borders: A-F 269; SOC 469.
Botany: STM 107.
Boxing: PC 963, 989.
Bridges: H 1390, 1970; STM 240, 332. See also: Civil Engineering.
Broadcasting: see Mass Media.
Broadway Musicals: see Shows and Musicals.
Buddhism: A-F 134; H 549; R 206-208, 218.
Building Construction and Construction Industry: A-A 411, 496; SOC 581; STM 71. See also: Architecture; Houses (Architecture).
Building Materials: A-A 441; STM 71. See also: Wood and Wood Industries.
Bums: see Homeless, Gypsies, Etc.
Bureaucracy and Public Administration: H 353, 467, 1640, 1892; PS 214, 313, 329, 336, 343-344, 346, 358, 363, 376, 395, 403, 665, 768.
Burlesque: PC 334, 372, 395, 406.
Business: A-F 174, 300, 344; H 396, 540, 544, 546, 625, 1311, 1414, 1646-1819, 1829, 1835-1836, 1839; PC 864; PS 303, 310, 325, 348, 482; SOC 93, 116, 164, 533, 553, 557, 572, 576-577, 589, 615, 623, 631, 663; STM 62, 299. See also: Banks and Banking; Consumerism; Small Business.

Calvinism: R 62, 64, 81-82, 143.
  Literature: L 80.
Canada: A-F 28, 81, 107; H 95; PSY 158; R 8, 19. See also: Borders; Foreign Relations--Canada.
Canals: see Waterways.
Cancer: see Disease and Disease Control.
Capitalism: H 1311, 1649, 1705, 1725, 1831, 1879, 1881, 1885, 1906, 1914-1915, 1922; L 30, 53, 608; PS 28, 32, 39, 45, 270, 322, 325, 354, 359, 369, 509-510, 548, 553; R 108; SOC 557, 560, 589, 603; STM 47, 269.
Carpetbaggers: see Reconstruction.
Cars: see Automobiles and Automobile Industry.
Cartoons, Comics, Etc.: PC 305-322, 443, 525, 565, 595, 600, 869. See also: Wit and Humor.
Catholic Church: A-F 293; H 862, 890, 903, 1002, 1526, 1536, 1629; L 239, 281, 617; PS 483; R 28, 30, 71, 89, 118, 158, 160-161, 164, 168, 170-171, 174-175, 179-180, 184, 265, 279; STM 245. See also: Anti-Catholicism; Ethnic Groups; Irish-Americans.
Cattle Industry: H 1305, 1410, 1435, 1465, 1470, 1750, 1806, 1816, 1869. See also: Cowboys.
Celebrities: see Actors and Acting.
Cemeteries: see Death and Burial.
Censorship, Pornography, Etc.: L 240; PC 438, 440, 459, 571, 597.
Central Intelligence Agency: see CIA.
Ceramics: A-A 357, 361, 370, 378, 387, 393, 396, 413, 420, 430; A-F 381. See also: Decorative Arts.
Charismatic Revivals, Movements: R 269-270, 273, 279-280.
Chicanos: see Hispanic-Americans.

Child Abuse: PSY 5; SOC 281; STM 75. See also: Sex Crimes.
Childbirth: H 837; SOC 379. See also: Midwives.
Children: A-F 65, 76, 172, 299, 313, 322, 342; H 99, 112, 169; PC 18,
    119, 435, 778, 790, 792-793, 797, 801, 809, 828, 833-834; PS 531;
    PSY 7, 18, 25, 42, 50, 59, 63, 67, 69, 75, 81-82, 91, 158, 163;
    SOC 106, 160, 217-218, 259, 262, 281, 325, 327, 361; STM 75, 334.
    See also: Adolescence; Divorce; Family; Psychology; Working Women;
    Youth.
Children's Literature: PC 108-137.
China: PS 637, 668, 678, 683, 726-727, 796; STM 51.
Chinese-Americans: A-F 159, 164; H 844, 863, 955, 970; M 185; SOC 130,
    146, 164, 170, 177, 187, 200. See also: Asian-Americans.
Cholera: see Disease and Disease Control.
Christian Science: R 203.
Christianity: L 647; R 8, 14, 18-19, 21, 43, 52, 100, 102, 128, 137,
    235, 297. See also: Protestantism; Names of Individual Sects.
Church and State: H 123; PS 262, 291, 483; R 36, 43, 46, 62, 250, 253,
    300-311. See also: Civil Religion; Religious Freedom.
Church of the Latter-Day Saints: see Mormons.
CIA: PS 328, 680.
Cigarettes and Smoking: SOC 666.
Cinemas: see Theaters (Architecture).
Circus: PC 330, 342, 350, 367, 369, 383, 396-397, 402.
Cities, Urbanism, Etc.: A-A 439, 443, 502, 508, 608, 619; A-F 32, 61,
    69, 154, 178-179, 302-303, 327; H 65-66, 87, 102, 162, 188, 505,
    932, 1003, 1005-1006, 1024, 1039, 1066, 1073, 1274-1403, 1447,
    1502; L 340, 376, 494, 514, 528, 663, 673; PC 96, 661, 997, 1017;
    PS 335; PSY 14; R 90, 99, 182, 184, 222; SOC 21-76, 124, 172-173,
    175, 225, 428, 480, 527; STM 35, 72-74, 99, 102-103, 220. See
    also: Slums; Urban Architecture; Urban Renewal; Urban Transporta-
    tion.
City Planning: A-A 543, 551, 625; A-F 25, 61; H 1308, 1312, 1324-1325,
    1337, 1367, 1372-1374, 1381, 1402, 1537; STM 42, 73, 131.
Civil Engineering: STM 59, 240, 395. See also: Bridges; Engineering;
    Panama Canal.
Civil Religion: R 2-3, 6, 24, 96, 98, 105, 291-299. See also: Church
    and State; Political Ideology.
Civil Rights: A-F 229, 238; H 24, 333, 398, 1022, 1079; M 148; PS 228,
    264; R 230; SOC 180. See also: Blacks; Desegregation and Inte-
    gration; Equality; Gay Rights; Voting; Women's Rights.
Civil Service: see Bureaucracy and Public Administration.
Civil War: H 8, 25, 43, 268, 272-273, 276, 286, 290-291, 293, 300-302,
    305, 310, 318, 320, 323, 343-344, 355-356, 361, 368, 370-371,
    373, 388, 390, 407-408, 592, 784, 951, 1016, 1431, 1823, 1916;
    R 91-98, 288. See also: Abolition and Abolitionism; Blacks;
    Confederate States of America; Slavery; South.
  Film: PC 614.
  Literature: L 18, 88, 151, 157, 200, 309. See also: South--Literature.
  Music: M 35, 68, 95, 149, 158.
  Veterans: H 284.
Class (Social): A-F 74, 157, 177, 296, 326; H 6, 42, 143, 347, 517, 827,
    878, 1338, 1363, 1859, 1916, 1940; L 329, 603; PS 342; PSY 43,
    112, 154; R 45; SOC 2, 7, 12, 14, 49, 83, 119, 126, 135, 203,
    210, 226, 445-509. See also: Ethnic Groups; Labor; Middle Class;
    Rich; WASPS.
Classical Literature in the U.S.: L 60, 550.
Clergy: see Ministers and Ministry, Religious.
Clothes and Clothing: PC 1025, 1027, 1029, 1045-1046; SOC 11. See also:
    Fashion Industries; Pop Culture; Textile Industry; Textiles.
Coal Industry and Mining: A-F 433-435; PS 394. See also: Mining.

Cold War: H 5, 483, 496; PC 593; PS 357, 586, 602, 621, 644-646, 648, 654, 656, 675, 690, 707-708, 722, 729, 746, 794, 807, 812, 816; STM 337.

Colleges and Universities: A-A 586, 594; A-F 80, 319; H 148, 180, 214, 580, 582, 668, 670, 678, 686, 744, 1302; PC 919, 924, 937, 990, 992; SOC 107, 211, 243, 248, 252, 295, 301-302, 308, 320, 328, 521, 537, 541. See also: Education.

Colonial Life and History: A-A 145, 170-178, 241-247, 277-279, 364, 391, 535-560; A-F 33, 57, 92, 201, 220; H 12, 31, 48-188, 728, 773, 779, 795, 829, 921, 1376, 1436, 1651, 1664, 1729, 1799, 1840-1841, 1862, 1876, 1880, 1901, 1904; L 60, 65-66, 69-70, 74, 77, 82, 85-87, 121, 528; M 70, 104; PC 1033-1034, 1045; R 25-67, 255-257, 284-286, 291, 305, 307-308; STM 26, 75, 263, 282, 356, 376.

Comedy (Theater and Media): L 139, 142, 335, 357, 410, 448; PC 437, 453, 514, 532, 830. See also: Burlesque; Shows and Musicals; Theater; Wit and Humor.

Comics: see Cartoons, Comics, Etc.

Communes: SOC 37, 74-75.

Communism and Literature: L 306, 471, 529, 626.

Communism in the U.S.: H 420, 440, 447-449, 456, 467, 477, 480, 483, 493, 508-509, 1000, 1585, 1590; L 203; M 148; PC 555; PS 540.

Competitiveness: PC 71, 73; PSY 13. See also: Psychology.

Computers and Computer Industry: PC 263; PS 520; PSY 145; STM 137, 158, 357.

Confederate States of America: H 286, 291, 335, 363, 393, 407, 816. See also: Civil War; South.

Confederation: H 213, 215, 236.

Congregationalism: H 142, 153; R 50, 62, 67, 74, 81, 157.

Congress of the United States: H 234, 379, 382; PC 851; PS 106-181, 385, 435, 437-440, 449, 569, 609, 641, 751, 761, 802, 808. See also: House of Representatives; Laws and Legislation; Senate.

Conservation and Environment: H 84, 469, 1308, 1356; L 167, 653; PS 297, 302, 327, 330, 334-335, 337-338, 351, 364, 394, 524; SOC 22, 34, 500, 507; STM 61, 368, 374. See also: Forestry; Pollution (Environment).

Conservatism: H 482, 581, 653, 1426; L 521, 583; PC 573; R 105, 120, 122-123; STM 264. See also: Liberalism (Politics); Political Ideologies; Radicalism; Reactionism.

Constitution: H 5, 221, 1828, 1963, 1965, 1971-1972; PS 126, 235, 245, 247, 254, 268, 271, 277, 279-280, 290, 782; R 303. See also: Bill of Rights; Supreme Court.

Consumerism: PC 20.

Copyright Law: H 1944. See also: Mass Media; Patents.

Country and Western Music: M 138, 141, 153, 156, 159, 170-172, 183, 192, 198-199, 207, 235, 429. See also: Bluegrass Music; Folk Music; South--Music.

Courts: H 1689, 1943, 1955, 1981; PS 1, 228-295; R 302; SOC 628, 656. See also: Judicial System; Supreme Court.

Cowboys: H 1430; M 196, 429; PC 275-276, 284. See also: Cattle Industry; Rodeos; West in Media.

Crafts: see Decorative Arts.

Crime and Criminals: A-F 120, 160, 364, 388; H 112, 163, 756, 885, 907, 947, 971, 1062, 1292, 1332, 1344, 1351, 1363, 1380, 1958; L 579; PC 36, 504-506, 539, 581, 599; PS 225, 258, 328, 496; PSY 53, 147; SOC 431, 495, 606-668; STM 81. See also: Criminal Justice; Drug Addiction and Traffic; Judicial System; Juvenile Delinquents and Gangs; Organized Crime; Police; Prisons; Sex Crimes.

Criminal Justice: H 112, 163; SOC 495, 621, 628, 632; STM 323.

Cuban-Americans: A-F 277. See also: Hispanic-Americans.

Cults (Religions, etc.): H 453; R 15, 186, 191, 193-194, 199, 200, 209-210, 217.

Customs and Manners: PC 5-6, 23, 42.

Dance Music: M 111, 167, 344, 369; PC 368.
Darwinism and Evolution: H 561; R 100, 102, 110, 133; STM 15, 83, 90,
          107, 152, 177, 206, 230, 233, 256, 272, 327.
Death and Burial: A-A 241, 243-244, 246-247; A-F 144, 382, 428; H 38,
          103, 174, 1344; PC 1036; PSY 61, 125-126; SOC 398, 402, 432, 440;
          STM 121.
Declaration of Independence: H 253.
Decorative Arts: A-A 137, 355-432; A-F 405-406, 408; PC 1016, 1026, 1040;
          STM 298, 376. See also: Ceramics; Folk Art; Furniture; Glass;
          Industrial Design; Metalwork; Textiles.
Defense: PS 300, 340, 354, 568, 578-579, 592, 598, 605, 608, 630, 633,
          642, 645-646, 653, 658, 664, 679, 713, 771, 788, 800-801, 803,
          816; STM 19, 95, 112, 120, 197, 210. See also: Arms and Armament;
          Arms Control and Arms Race; Department of Defense; Disarmament;
          Military.
Democracy: H 7, 595, 602, 660, 688, 1914; PS 15, 42-43, 47, 78, 97, 103,
          193, 195, 213, 216, 254, 308, 419, 472, 490, 498, 513, 539, 563,
          724; R 63.
Democratic Party: H 19, 36, 259, 308, 354, 357, 514; PS 3, 224, 426,
          463, 786. See also: Political Parties.
Demography: see Population.
Department of Defense: PS 300, 692, 703. See also: Arms and Armament;
          Arms Control and Arms Race; Defense; Military.
Depression (1890s): H 1868, 1875.
Depression (1920s): A-A 219; H 422, 428, 499, 521, 534, 809, 1524-1525,
          1860, 1884, 1900, 1921, 1927; PS 241, 260, 295, 639; STM 267.
  Film: PC 424, 575.
  Literature: L 274, 292, 306, 341, 353.
Desegregation and Integration: A-F 307; H 1094; PS 241, 260, 295; R 235,
          265-266; SOC 97, 107-108, 152, 206, 244, 246. See also: Blacks;
          Civil Rights.
Detective Literature: PC 138-168, 439. See also: Novel.
Determinism and Free Will: L 556.
Deviants and Deviance: PC 36, 708; PSY 53, 71; R 29, 50; SOC 570. See
          also: Mental Disorders, the Insane; Psychology; Social Work;
          Sociology.
Dialects: A-F 348, 368; L 555. See also: American English; Language.
Diplomacy and Diplomats: PS 615, 669, 694-695, 752, 806.
Disarmament: PS 596, 603, 732, 811, 813. See also: Arms and Armament;
          Arms Control and Arms Race.
Discrimination: H 876-877, 1070; PSY 153; SOC 40, 80-81, 83, 91, 102,
          116, 125-126, 166, 174, 195, 197-198, 202, 204, 370, 562. See
          also: Civil Rights; Desegregation and Integration; Race; Racism;
          Women's Rights.
Disease and Disease Control: A-F 258, 325; H 183, 734; PC 1; PS 367;
          SOC 516; STM 32-33, 100, 116, 133, 220, 307, 314, 319, 328, 341,
          377. See also: Hospitals and Asylums; Medicine; Smallpox;
          Venereal Diseases; Yellow Fever.
Dissidence (Political): H 285; SOC 125, 145.
Divorce: A-F 82; H 513, 786; SOC 249, 266-267, 280, 323. See also:
          Children; Family; Marriage.
Doctors (MD): SOC 368, 382; STM 37, 151, 153, 194, 271, 324, 336. See
          also: Medicine; Nurses and Nursing; Surgery; Women Doctors (MD).
Documentaries (Film and Television): PC 410, 417-419, 491, 517, 579-580,
          609, 724, 763. See also: Newscasting.
Dominican Republic and Dominicans: A-F 272.
Draft: SOC 638, 662. See also: Military; Student Protest.
Drama: L 20, 23, 34, 218, 220, 222, 269, 272, 283, 292, 306, 335, 366,
          404, 407, 412, 449, 450, 465-466, 495, 552, 639. See also: Film;
          Literature; Theater.
Dramatists: L 222, 245, 259, 264, 269, 284, 345, 412, 495, 595.

Dred Scott Case: H 1948.
Drug Addiction and Traffic: A-F 145, 160, 305; PSY 121-122, 139; SOC 607, 630, 664; STM 81, 258. See also: Crime and Criminals; Organized Crime; Social Services.
Drugs: see Pharmacy.
Dutch-Americans: H 881, 956; PC 1020; R 64.

Ecology: see Conservation and Environment
Economics: A-F 332; PS 2, 75; SOC 15, 23, 31, 490; STM 132, 204, 317, 329, 362.
  History: H 4-6, 18, 33, 45, 1036, 1694, 1820-1940.
    17th-18th Centuries: H 72, 77, 85, 113, 137, 159, 225, 241, 245, 602, 1677, 1708, 1763, 1766, 1822, 1832-1833, 1870.
    19th Century: H 602, 1467, 1686, 1688, 1709, 1870; STM 92.
    20th Century: H 531, 1820-1821.
Economy: H 31, 1825-1826, 1928; PS 309, 353-354, 356, 359; STM 316.
Education: A-F 80, 213, 303, 312-315, 317-318, 323, 329-331, 336-337, 345-346; H 23, 53, 140, 351, 551, 569, 573-574, 578, 618, 652, 688, 775, 1296, 1346, 1371, 1639; PS 335, 402-403, 507; PSY 6, 50, 67, 112, 117, 146, 182; SOC 81, 97, 107-108, 194, 196, 206, 209, 211, 243, 246, 248-327, 487, 510, 521, 524, 541; STM 22, 34, 37, 57, 147, 194, 202, 274, 276, 286, 299, 336. See also: Blacks--Education; Colleges and Universities; Hispanic-Americans--Education; Literacy.
Educational and Learned Societies: STM 162.
Egalitarianism: see Equality.
Election Campaigns: H 90; PC 647, 675, 685, 711, 768, 781, 802, 851, 853; PS 406-474. See also: Politics; Presidency and Presidents; Mass Media.
Electric and Gas Lighting: STM 1, 44. See also: Energy Sources and Supplies.
Electric Power Supply and Industry: H 1676, 1766, 1802; STM 1, 242-244, 291. See also: Energy Sources and Supplies.
Electricity: STM 1, 31, 74, 76, 156.
Emancipation: H 1032, 1055, 1189, 1933; PS 5, 10; R 228, 398. See also: Blacks; Freedom; Slavery; South.
Employment: see Unemployment and Employment.
Energy Sources and Supplies: H 1784, 1934; PS 323, 330, 386, 524, 668, 706, 789; SOC 68, 453, 530. See also: Coal Industry and Mining; Electric Power Supply and Industry; Oil Industry and Exploration.
Engineering: STM 5, 18, 29, 59-60, 155, 249, 260, 269, 332, 343, 351, 387. See also: Civil Engineering.
England: R 25, 69, 73, 110, 282. See also: Foreign Relations--Great Britain; Scottish-Americans; War of 1812; War of Independence; WASPS.
Enlightenment: H 202, 637; R 136, 305.
Epidemics: see Disease and Disease Control.
Episcopal Church: R 63. See also: Anglican Church.
Equal Rights Amendment: H 707; PS 240. See also: Women's Rights.
Equality: H 24, 667, 718; PSY 187; SOC 12, 166, 223, 449, 472, 483, 497, 505, 543; STM 229, 237. See also: Civil Rights; Gay Rights; Race; Women's Rights.
Eskimos: H 1256; SOC 557. See also: Indians (American).
Ethnic Groups: A-F 26, 29-30, 67, 70-71, 73, 85, 95, 103, 111, 119, 158, 317; H 12, 22, 28, 35, 39, 517, 841-1011; L 140; M 154; PC 75, 546; PSY 7, 18, 54-55, 69, 104; R 184; SOC 8, 57, 77-247. See also: Catholic Church; Class (Social); Hispanic-Americans; Immigration; Jews; WASPS; and names of specific national groups, e.g., Irish-Americans.
Eugenics: STM 154.

Evangelicalism: H 737; R 12, 54, 68-69, 72-73, 77-78, 85-88, 93, 105,
        107, 119, 121-122, 224, 232, 248, 271, 274-277, 281, 290. See
        also: Fundamentalism (Religion); Revivals and Revivalism
        (Religion).
Evolution: see Darwinism and Evolution.
Expansionism (American): see Manifest Destiny.
Expatriots: A-F 126.
Exploration of America: see North America--Discovery and Exploration.
Exports, Imports: see Foreign Trade.

Fairytales: PC 109, 132. See also: Children's Literature; Folklore
        and Legends.
Family: A-F 64, 152-153, 199; H 39, 41, 88, 831, 1011, 1042, 1049, 1143,
        1382, 1399; L 476; PS 23, 554; PSY 2, 5, 7, 10, 23, 36-37, 41-42,
        50, 58, 68, 75, 86, 89, 91, 100-101, 119, 136, 151; R 201, 247;
        SOC 2, 14, 21, 53, 87, 120, 158, 160, 208, 248-327, 340. See
        also: Children; Divorce; Marriage; Middle Class; Working Women.
Fantasy (Literature): see Grotesque and Fantasy (Literature).
Farms and Farming: A-F 79, 97, 105, 123, 136, 148; H 13, 37, 167, 449,
        473, 524, 946, 1420-1421, 1442, 1446, 1500-1501, 1543; SOC 540,
        564, 587; STM 239, 391-392. See also: Agriculture; Migrant
        Workers; Ruralism and Rural Societies.
  Buildings: A-A 435, 471; PC 1020.
Fashion Industries: PC 1029; SOC 11. See also: Clothes and Clothing;
        Pop Culture; Textile Industry.
FBI: PC 52; PS 328, 360, 400.
Federal Reserve System: H 1830, 1857, 1937. See also: Banks and Banking.
Federalism: H 189, 221, 228, 234, 236, 250, 252, 255, 260, 269, 297,
        334, 623, 1949; PS 182-227.
Feminism: A-A 71, 85; A-F 84; H 12, 24, 707-708, 732, 739, 747, 761,
        777-778, 796-797, 803, 810, 813, 821, 823, 827, 840; L 465, 479,
        488, 502, 578, 609; PC 205, 260, 508, 513; PS 21, 50; PSY 32,
        57, 135, 187; R 240; SOC 329, 332-336, 340, 349-352, 358, 378,
        384, 388, 394; STM 322. See also: Birth Control and Abortion;
        Children; Gay Rights; Women's Rights; Working Women.
Fiction: L 2, 119, 124, 126, 131, 140, 146, 235, 239-240, 272, 277-278,
        280, 293, 303-304, 309, 321, 331, 360, 366, 380, 390-391, 397-398,
        404, 409, 411, 433, 450, 466, 478-479, 483, 527, 531, 544, 558,
        571-572, 575, 595, 604. See also: Detective Literature; Histori-
        cal Fiction; Literature; Novel.
Film: A-F 132; L 260, 347; M 388-389, 425; PC 281, 398, 407-644, 707,
        1022; SOC 378. See also: Actors and Acting; Censorship, Pornogra-
        phy, Etc.; Documentaries (Film and Television); Drama; Mass Media;
        Newscasting; Pop Culture.
Film and Government: PC 438, 440-441, 447, 521, 555, 598.
Film Directors: PC 570, 592.
Finnish-Americans: A-F 432.
Fires and Fire Fighting: A-A 534; STM 297.
Fisherman, Fishing, Fishing Industry: A-F 128; SOC 565.
Folk Art: A-A 291-320; A-F 372, 378, 407-408, 410, 451; PC 1026; SOC 27.
        See also: Art; Decorative Arts.
Folk Medicine: A-F 67, 221, 275, 311, 417, 419; H 735; STM 381, 386,
        398. See also: Medicine; Pharmacy; Surgery.
Folk Music: A-F 422, 466; M3, 131-132, 134-135, 137, 139-140, 143, 146,
        150, 166, 173-174, 179, 186-187, 190-191, 194, 197-198, 200, 212,
        429. See also: Ballads; Bluegrass Music; Country and Western
        Music; Music; Pop Music.
Folklore and Legends: A-F 369-469; L 1, 470, 623, 639; M 161-162; PC 35.
        See also: Blacks--Folklore and Legends; Customs and Manners;
        Death and Burial; Fairytales; Indians (American)--Folklore and
        Legends.

Food and Food Supply: H 13, 22, 35; PS 677; SOC 338; STM 8-9, 389. See
    also: Cafes and Diners; Restaurants; Soft Drinks.
Football: PC 924, 973-974, 982.
Foreign Aid: PS 589, 745.
Foreign Policy: H 207, 271, 315, 337, 345, 419, 457, 546, 1620; PC 852,
    877, 896-897; PS 385, 568-817. See also: Diplomacy and Diplomats.
Foreign Relations: H 12, 271, 315, 345, 451. See also: Berlin Crisis;
    Cold War; Imperialism (American).
  Africa: PS 690, 704, 723, 802.
  Asia: PS 731, 763, 796, 798, 809.
  Canada: PS 790.
  Central America: PS 619, 680, 709-710.
  China: PS 637, 681, 683, 726-727.
  Cuba: PS 572, 618, 699, 762.
  Far East: PS 660, 669, 792, 817.
  Germany: PS 649, 728.
  Great Britain: H 364-365, 392.
  Israel: PS 661, 670, 772, 774, 776.
  Japan: PS 681.
  Korea: PS 611.
  Latin America: PS 651.
  Mexico: A-F 269.
  Near East: PS 707, 714, 734, 756, 758, 760, 769, 773, 797.
  South Africa: PS 588, 671.
  Soviet Union: PS 628, 696-698, 812; STM 118.
  Spain: H 466.
  Third World: PS 634, 667, 745, 767.
  Vietnam: PS 691.
Foreign Trade: H 532, 1699, 1767, 1813-1814; PS 303.
Forestry: H 1962; PS 339, 476; STM 297. See also: Conservation and
    Environment.
France: R 308.
Free Enterprise: H 1850. See also: Regulation and Deregulation of Indus-
    try.
Free Speech: H 227; PC 883. See also: Censorship, Pornography, Etc.
Freedom: H 556, 1019-1020, 1022, 1029, 1032, 1034, 1042, 1044, 1055,
    1074, 1076, 1961; PS 4, 6, 18, 28, 54, 228, 255, 293; R 286.
    See also: Emancipation.
Freemasonry: SOC 241.
Frontier, Frontiersmen: A-A 54, 72, 112, 281; A-F 220, 410; H 128, 559,
    648, 765, 995, 1345, 1372, 1391, 1405, 1417, 1419, 1498,
    1510-1512, 1519; L 100, 113, 130, 159, 187, 190, 340, 448, 460,
    559, 636; PC 277; R 74-75, 79, 106, 298; STM 276. See also:
    Fur Trade; Manifest Destiny; North America--Discovery and Explora-
    tion; West.
Fundamentalism (Religion): R 7, 101-102, 109, 276, 282. See also: Evan-
    gelicalism; Revivals and Revivalism (Religion).
Fur Trade: H 1516, 1726, 1770.
Furniture: A-A 355, 359, 362-365, 368, 372-373, 379-380, 382-384, 394-395,
    400-401, 403, 407, 410-411, 419, 422-423, 426, 431, 455; A-F 459;
    PC 1032. See also; Decorative Arts; Folk Art; Interiors.

Gambling: PC 373; SOC 548, 640, 659.
Games, Riddles and Jokes: A-F 2, 46, 101, 439; L 1; PC 100, 290, 354,
    950. See also: Wit and Humor.
Gay Rights: H 24; PSY 30; SOC 343. See also: Civil Rights; Equality;
    Feminism; Homosexuality; Homosexuals.
General Accounting Office: PS 341, 361.
Geology: STM 141, 230, 234, 248, 330.

German-Americans: A-A 131, 308, 310, 318-319, 385, 587, 590; A-F 433;
     H 665, 846, 871, 875, 890, 897, 914, 946, 957, 982, 1399; M 55,
     65, 90, 125, 134, 188, 201; PC 1044; R 168, 172. See also: Immi-
     gration.
Germany: STM 34.
Gilded Age: H 313, 349-350, 387, 395-396, 405.
Girl Groups (Music): M 417. See also: Bands; Motown; Pop Music; Rock
     and Roll.
Glass: A-A 405-406, 412, 415-416, 432; H 1675. See also: Decorative
     Arts; Folk Art.
Gothic Novel: PC 185, 187, 189-198.
Gothic Revival Architecture: see Revival Architecture.
Government Buildings: see Public Buildings.
Graphic Arts: A-A 147, 269-290, 413-414, 455; L 86; M 367. See also:
     Advertising; Cartoons, Comics, Etc.; Illustration.
Greek-Americans: A-F 147, 413-414, 455; L 550; SOC 185, 190.
Grotesque and Fantasy (Literature): PC 169-182.
Guns: SOC 667; STM 11, 109, 318. See also: Arms and Armament.
Gypsies: see Homeless, Gypsies, Etc.

Handicapped: SOC 622, 626, 636, 642.
Happenings, Performance Art, Etc.: A-A 77, 259; PC 43-44, 46.
Hare Krishna: A-F 91. See also: Oriental Religions and Cults.
Hawaii: A-F 83, 95, 109; M 165; SOC 130.
Health Care: A-F 262, 325; H 1378; PS 206, 298, 319-320, 390; PSY 160,
     176; SOC 338, 380, 420, 439, 454, 534, 569, 599; STM 47, 186,
     193, 253, 302, 308, 320, 371. See also: Insurance and Insurance
     Companies; Medicine; Public Health; Social Services.
Heredity and Genetics: PSY 107, 127, 183; STM 229, 338.
Heroes: A-F 386; L 300, 343, 444; PC 9-10, 18, 33, 35-36, 287, 549, 564.
Hippies: see Beatniks and Hippies.
Hispanic-Americans: A-F 115, 257-294; H 926, 940, 978, 996; PSY 12, 17-18,
     54-55, 69, 105, 133; SOC 95, 145, 147, 203, 213, 643; STM 64.
     See also: Ethnic Groups; Immigration; Migrant Workers; and names
     of individual groups, i.e., Mexican-Americans.
  Art: A-A 303, 320.
  Film: PC 450.
  Folklore and Legends: A-F 259, 273.
  Language: A-F 265.
  Literature: A-F 265; L 467, 510.
  Music: M 174, 186, 426.
Hispanic-Americans in Literature: PC 281.
Hispanic-Americans in Media: PC 639, 670.
Historical Fiction: L 100; PC 296. See also: Fiction; Literature; Novel.
History: H 1-2, 27, 32, 55, 596, 666, 1425, 1482; PC 562, 577, 612; PSY
     11, 33, 88.
  1760-1811: H 189-256, 269, 590. See also: Colonial Life and History;
     War of Independence.
  19th Century: H 257-413, 1493; PC 69; R 91.
  20th Century: H 414-548, 1395; PC 799.
Holidays: PC 49, 971.
Homeless, Gypsies, Etc.: A-F 98, 141, 146; SOC 178, 627.
Homosexuality: A-F 163; H 24, 740; PSY 23, 30, 84, 134; SOC 331, 361,
     365, 392, 646. See also: Gay Rights; Psychology; Sexuality.
Homosexuality in Literature: L 573, 628.
Homosexuality in Media: PC 587.
Homosexuals: A-F 127, 163; SOC 331, 361, 365, 377, 391-392. See also:
     Gay Rights.

Hospitals and Asylums: A-F 86, 96, 99, 137, 144; H 376, 1378; SOC 433,
    552, 569, 590, 605; STM 99, 143, 145, 237, 330, 379. See also:
    Disease and Disease Control; Medicine; Mental Disorders, the Insane;
    Nurses and Nursing; Social Services.
House of Representatives: PS 114, 123, 151, 174. See also: Congress
    of the United States; Senate.
Houses (Architecture): A-A 440, 444, 449, 452, 483-484, 497, 522, 527,
    529, 535-537, 541-542, 544-545, 547-548, 550, 555-556, 559, 562,
    571, 579, 584, 592, 622, 633; PC 1010. See also: Vernacular
    Architecture.
Housing: H 1335, 1350, 1400; PS 208, 388; SOC 39-40, 48, 66.
Human Rights: PSY 145; R 44.
Humanism: L 307, 409, 582, 664; PSY 171.
Humor: see Wit and Humor.
Hutterites: A-F 81, 107-108.
Hymns: see Religious Music.

Idealism: H 44; L 30.
Illustration: A-A 106, 132, 272; PC 108, 129. See also: Advertising;
    Graphic Arts.
Immigration: A-A 89; A-F 158, 279; H 588-589, 729, 791, 848, 852, 855-858,
    868-871, 874-877, 879, 884, 888-891, 893, 896-897, 899, 906-908,
    914, 916-917, 920, 924, 931, 933-936, 941-942, 945, 949-950, 952,
    969-970, 972, 975, 977, 979, 981, 983-985, 987, 989-991, 1001,
    1006-1008, 1011, 1394, 1403, 1556, 1581, 1615, 1644; L 125, 329,
    594, 635; PC 890; PSY 28; SOC 98, 110, 143, 157, 177, 203-204,
    228; STM 35, 154. See also: Ethnic Groups; Labor; Migrant Workers;
    and names of specific groups of immigrants, e.g., Irish-Americans.
Imperialism (American): H 44-46, 262-345; R 106. See also: Foreign
    Relations; Manifest Destiny.
Imports, Exports: see Foreign Trade.
Indian Wars: H 129, 1121-1123, 1127, 1131-1132, 1135-1136, 1158, 1163,
    1172, 1175, 1186, 1189, 1191, 1205, 1215, 1219, 1232-1233,
    1235-1236, 1244, 1259-1260, 1264, 1267; L 93.
Indians (American): A-A 485, 509; A-F 4-5, 13, 49, 60, 200-256; H 31,
    53, 84, 122, 152, 1095-1273, 1511; M 9, 145, 160, 167, 175, 178,
    181, 193; PSY 18, 25, 55, 69, 116, 133, 179; R 249-257; SOC 151,
    177, 225, 567; STM 297, 381. See also Eskimos.
  Art: A-A 1-17.
  Folklore and Legends: A-F 212, 219; H 1125, 1144, 1146, 1150, 1152,
      1156, 1161, 1178, 1181-1182, 1186, 1220; PSY 25.
  Government Policy: A-F 207, 213, 220, 242; H 1097-1100, 1106-1108,
      1112-1113, 1118, 1124, 1126, 1128, 1131, 1134, 1137-1138, 1140,
      1142, 1147, 1149, 1154, 1159, 1162, 1165-1166, 1173-1174, 1184-1185,
      1189-1190, 1192, 1194-1195, 1197-1201, 1204, 1206-1210, 1214-1215,
      1222-1224, 1226, 1231, 1237, 1240, 1245, 1249, 1251, 1253-1255,
      1258, 1262, 1265-1266, 1269; SOC 567.
  Language: A-F 13, 203, 208, 240; H 1155, 1271.
  Literature: H 1160, 1171; L 93, 374, 492, 504-505, 510, 536, 602.
  Religion and Religions: A-F 200, 218, 222, 225, 247; H 122, 1150, 1152,
      1154, 1176, 1178-1179, 1192, 1202, 1211-1212, 1221, 1225-1226,
      1245, 1261, 1270; R 28, 30, 249-257.
Indians (American) in Art: A-A 103.
Indians (American) in Media: PC 420, 471, 561.
Individualism: H 550; L 333; R 298; SOC 6.
Industrial Design: A-A 377; H 1656, 1710, 1751; PC 1016, 1030, 1038,
    1040; STM 213, 246.
Industrial Revolution: H 1393, 1549, 1558, 1719.

Industrialization: A-A 50, 257, 344; A-F 308; H 6, 258, 385, 470, 597,
    852, 856, 1299, 1403, 1445, 1529, 1580, 1671, 1731, 1827, 1834,
    1863, 1930; PS 514; SOC 4, 67; STM 96, 181, 184, 201, 269, 299.
    See also: Automation and Mechanization.
Industries: A-F 155; H 442, 1650, 1665, 1667, 1671, 1700, 1713, 1715,
    1757, 1829; PS 355; SOC 550; STM 4, 16, 44, 46, 87, 98, 105, 110,
    114, 123, 134, 139, 189, 232, 242-243, 267-269, 300, 329, 364,
    376, 393-394, 400. See also: Manufacturers and Manufacturing;
    Regulation and Deregulation of Industry; Textile Industry.
Industrial Research: STM 31, 38.
Insane: see Mental Disorders, the Insane.
Insurance and Insurance Companies: H 1662, 1701, 1727, 1811; PS 319-320;
    SOC 516, 534, 604; STM 175, 271, 273, 287.
Intellectuals and Intellectualism: H 141, 465, 549-697; L 50-51, 69,
    405, 535; STM 124, 178. See also Professional Class.
Intelligence Tests: see Testing (Intelligence).
Interest Groups: see Political Lobbying.
Interiors: A-A 402, 404, 417, 421. See also: Furniture; Textiles.
Inventors and Inventions: H 1877, 1893; PC 1015, 1040; STM 1, 3, 38,
    49, 54, 76, 126, 135, 169, 181, 190, 196, 223, 231-232, 239,
    291-292, 294. See also: Patents.
IQ: see Testing (Intelligence).
Irish-Americans: H 846, 859-861, 864-865, 884, 890, 897, 903, 915-916,
    923, 931, 944, 953, 962, 974, 976, 992, 999, 1007, 1292, 1332,
    1351, 1365; L 239; M 131; SOC 112, 115, 128. See also Immigration.
Ironwork and Ironworking: A-F 461; H 286, 1683, 1765; STM 159, 263.
    See also: Metalwork.
Isolationism: H 437; PS 686.
Israel: H 997, 1004; PS 661, 670, 756, 772, 774, 781; SOC 235. See also:
    Zionism.
Italian-Americans: A-F 467; H 845-846, 858, 873, 882, 910-911, 943, 950,
    959, 971-973, 983, 999, 1003, 1011; PSY 47; SOC 101, 123-124,
    128, 168, 190, 193, 240. See also: Immigration.

Jails: see Prisons.
Japanese-Americans: A-F 113, 320, 334, 339-340; H 537, 870, 877, 942;
    R 207; SOC 93, 156, 161, 164, 177, 182, 197, 655. See also:
    Asian-Americans.
Jazz: M 11, 21, 28, 214, 245-365, 429. See also: Blacks--Music; Blue-
    grass Music; Blues (Music); Ragtime.
Jews: A-F 102, 124, 135, 443, 454; H 235, 605, 705, 841, 846, 848, 850,
    853-854, 857, 867, 880, 883, 885-886, 894-895, 898, 900-902, 904,
    908-909, 913, 916-919, 921-922, 925, 928, 930, 935-936, 939, 947,
    950-951, 960-961, 980, 986, 988, 990, 993-995, 997, 999-1000,
    1002, 1004-1005; L 224; M 405, 436; PC 986; PS 501, 781; R 118,
    159, 162-163, 165-167, 169, 172-173, 176, 178, 181-183, 185; SOC 96,
    103-104, 109, 118, 127-128, 131, 139, 142, 144, 148-149, 159,
    175, 177, 199, 201, 205, 215, 219-222, 224, 235-236, 238. See
    also: Ethnic Groups; Zionism.
  Literature: H 866; L 214, 224, 244, 270, 322, 348, 522, 576, 631.
Jews in Literature: L 505, 523.
Jews in Media: PC 472.
Jive: see Slang.
Jokes: see Games, Riddles and Jokes.
Journalism: see Newspapers and Journalism.
Judicial System: H 292, 1981; PS 1, 228-295; R 301; SOC 628, 656. See
    also: Courts; Crime and Criminals; Criminal Justice; Supreme
    Court.
Juvenile Delinquents and Gangs: A-F 62, 183; H 1330; PC 543; SOC 230,
    625, 639, 644, 650, 660, 665. See also: Crime and Criminals.

Korean-Americans: SOC 155. See also: Asian-Americans.
Korean War: H 25, 43; PS 611.
Ku Klux Klan: H 885, 1336; R 259.

Labor: H 113, 149, 170, 863, 895, 981, 1045, 1437, 1521-1645, 1852, 1890,
        1912; M 152; PS 153, 231, 348, 481, 508, 517; PSY 23, 177; SOC 49,
        227, 234, 271, 277, 290, 318, 381, 410, 494, 510-605; STM 4, 109,
        148, 250, 261, 266-268, 280, 398. See also: Blue Collar Workers;
        Class (Social); Immigration; Labor Unions; Migrant Workers; Unem-
        ployment and Employment; Unemployment Compensation; Working Women.
    Women: H 729-731, 733, 743, 766-768, 798-799, 828, 1586, 1612, 1642;
        SOC 234, 362, 383, 535, 587, 590; STM 82. See also: Working
        Women.
Labor Unions: A-F 155; H 733, 743, 792, 799, 1521-1523, 1526-1527, 1530,
        1533, 1535-1536, 1538, 1540-1543, 1545, 1547, 1550, 1552, 1557,
        1559-1567, 1569-1571, 1573, 1583, 1585-1588, 1590-1595, 1599-1600,
        1603, 1606-1607, 1609, 1612, 1616-1618, 1622-1623, 1629, 1633-1634,
        1636-1641, 1643; PC 583; SOC 537, 542, 578, 590.
Land Law: H 11, 34, 1898, 1951, 1957, 1977.
Language: A-F 7, 265, 349, 352; H 8; L 41, 145, 216, 279, 314, 325, 555,
        572, 604; PC 36, 403, 942; PSY 67, 135, 138, 157. See also:
        American English; Bilingualism; Dialects; Linguistics; Slang.
Latin America: L 39; M 173, 426; PS 651.
Latter-Day Saints: see Mormons.
Laws and Legislation: H 57, 98, 227, 1941-1982; PS 186, 259, 273; R 309;
        SOC 211, 231, 475, 549, 567. See also: Congress of the United
        States; Police.
League of Nations: H 533.
Legends: see Folklore and Legends.
Leisure: H 1307, 1315; PC 12, 17, 19, 34, 39, 996; SOC 3, 10, 513.
Lesbianism: see Homosexuality.
Liberalism (Politics): H 387, 475-476, 495-496, 672, 1052, 1873; L 449;
        PS 1, 8, 34, 42, 44, 53, 59, 103, 488; R 116. See also: Conserva-
        tism; Political Ideologies; Reactionism.
Libraries: L 10; SOC 544.
Lighting: see Electric and Gas Lighting.
Linguistics: A-F 309, 347-368; PC 237; PSY 135, 138, 155. See also:
        American English; Bilingualism; Blacks--Language; Dialects;
        Hispanic-Americans--Language; Indians (American)--Language; Language;
        Slang.
Literacy: A-F 11; H 133. See also: Education.
Literature: See also: Blacks--Literature; Detective Literature; Chil-
        dren's Literature; Drama; Fiction; Historical Fiction; Modernism
        (Literature); Naturalism (Literature); Novel; Popular Literature;
        Post-Modernism (Literature); Realism (Literature); Romanticism
        (Literature); Symbolism (Literature); Science Fiction; Short Story.
    European Influences: L 39, 48, 71, 89, 99, 103, 112, 154, 165, 176, 230,
        233, 237-238, 271, 296, 315, 337, 356, 364, 372, 486, 527, 632.
    History:
        17th-18th Centuries: L 39-87; PC 133.
        19th Century: L 5, 13, 16, 18, 75, 88-202; PC 99, 188, 196, 223.
        20th Century: L 5, 203-436; PC 210-211, 213, 219, 232, 236, 269.
Literature and Politics: L 229, 236, 253-254, 381, 473, 476, 584.
Lithuanian-Americans: H 924.
Lobbyists: see Political Lobbying.
Loneliness: see Alienation and Loneliness.

Machines and Machinery: H 1804; PC 220-221; STM 4, 134-135, 148, 184,
        261, 318, 344, 348. See also: Automation and Mechanization.

Mafia: see Organized Crime.
Magazines and Periodicals: L 58, 76, 133, 149, 170, 313, 319; PC 78,
       86-87, 93, 106, 118, 195, 207, 212, 848. See also: Newspapers
       and Journalism; Publishing.
Malaria: see Yellow Fever.
Management Sciences: STM 4-5, 62, 149, 198, 250.
Manifest Destiny: A-A 72; H 30, 46, 331, 400, 611; PC 1; R 255. See
       also: Frontier, Frontiersmen; Imperialism (American).
Manufacturers and Manufacturing: H 1558, 1611, 1668, 1682, 1773, 1893;
       SOC 523; STM 364, 383. See also: Industries.
Maritime Trade: see Ports, Harbors, Maritime Trade.
Marriage: A-F 284; H 115, 786, 851, 1941; PSY 23, 54, 92, 156, 177; R 201;
       SOC 2, 256, 266, 274, 287, 298-299, 313, 323, 333, 345, 418.
       See also: Children; Divorce; Family.
Mass Media: A-F 24; M 238, 391; PC 9, 14-15, 20, 28-29, 32, 37, 45-46,
       48, 50, 53, 55, 62, 64, 632, 645-710, 810; R 128; SOC 515. See
       also: Censorship, Pornography, Etc.; Copyright Law; Film; News-
       papers and Journalism; Pop Culture; Radio; Television.
Material Culture: PC 1010-1046.
Mathematics: STM 24, 68, 155.
Medicare and Medicaid: PS 352; STM 287. See also: Aged; Medicine--
       Government Policy; Public Health--Government Policy; Social Services.
Medicine: A-A 61; A-F 311; SOC 252, 261, 273, 380, 382; STM 37, 57-58,
       97, 160-161, 186, 247, 309, 313, 336, 339, 371, 380, 385. See
       also: Disease and Disease Control; Doctors (MD); Folk Medicine;
       Health Care; Hospitals and Asylums; Nurses and Nursing; Pharmacy;
       Public Health; Surgery; Women Doctors (MD); Yellow Fever.
  Government Policy: STM 57-58.
  History: PSY 15; STM 14, 20, 26, 35, 40, 43, 47, 75, 86, 97-102, 113,
       115-117, 122, 125, 151, 202, 221, 227, 257, 270, 275-276, 282-283,
       303, 308, 324, 333, 339-342, 353, 358, 379-381.
    18th Century: STM 33.
    19th Century: PSY 35, 78; STM 42.
    20th Century: PSY 35, 78, 139.
Men (Psychology and Sociology): PC 544, 615; PSY 42, 56, 119, 124, 165,
       175; SOC 253, 259, 311, 330, 356-357, 376, 385, 408.
Mental Disorders, the Insane: A-F 20, 133, 137, 189; PSY 15-16, 45, 51,
       53, 70-71, 98, 169-170; SOC 468, 488-489, 617, 645; STM 131, 144.
       See also: Deviants and Deviance; Hospitals and Asylums; Mental
       Health; Psychology; Social Services.
Mental Health: A-F 20, 42, 143, 270, 338; PSY 10, 15, 17, 51, 55, 84,
       89, 98, 100, 105, 109, 121-122, 133, 142, 145, 148, 153, 156,
       160, 162-163, 167, 169, 171, 173, 176, 178; SOC 468; STM 85-86,
       143-144, 312. See also: Mental Disorders, the Insane; Psychology;
       Social Services.
Mesmerism and Hypnotism: PSY 74; R 202.
Metalwork: A-A 363, 367, 375, 390-392, 397-399, 408, 427; STM 263. See
       also: Decorative Arts; Folk Art; Iron Work and Ironworking.
Metaphysics: L 362.
Methodism: R 94, 96-97, 106, 234, 272.
Mexican-American War: H 352, 355, 383, 937; SOC 92, 136, 143, 173, 184,
       207, 214, 227.
Mexican-Americans: A-A 110; A-F 257, 261-262, 269, 275, 278, 280, 282-284,
       287, 291-292, 294; H 38, 963-966, 981, 987; M 131, 161, 179, 186;
       PC 281; SOC 92, 136, 143, 173, 184, 207, 214, 227.
Mexico: A-F 313; L 617.
Middle Class: A-F 168; H 317, 560, 806, 1002, 1382; L 305; SOC 241, 305,
       448, 486, 492, 508; STM 280. See also: Blue Collar Workers;
       Class (Social); Family.
Middle East: H 15.

Midwest: A-A 425; A-F 94, 151, 161; H 258, 326, 511, 842, 899, 938, 973, 980, 1274, 1291, 1306, 1352-1353, 1362, 1382; PC 1044; PS 199, 308; SOC 34, 111, 222, 247, 303, 582. See also: Plains States.
  Architecture: A-A 564, 566, 595, 598, 621.
  Blacks: A-F 192; H 1080; SOC 33, 132.
  History:
    19th Century: H 1420-1421, 1442, 1452, 1476, 1894.
    20th Century: H 1407, 1501.
  Literature: H 1424; L 137, 184, 199, 265, 334, 490.
Midwives: H 735; STM 68, 227, 236. See also: Childbirth; Children; Nurses and Nursing.
Migrant Workers: A-F 176; H 912, 1601-1602; M 161; SOC 506. See also: Farms and Farming; Hispanic-Americans; Immigration; Labor.
Military: A-A 503; A-F 187; H 20, 40, 43, 181, 344, 408, 415, 471, 872, 1451; L 583; PC 289, 297, 437; PS 300, 305, 353, 356, 405, 590, 614, 658, 736, 815; PSY 40, 101, 136; SOC 554, 568, 613, 638, 655, 662; STM 212, 261, 300. See also: Air Force; Arms and Armament; Arms Control and Arms Race; Army; Defense; Department of Defense; Draft; Navy.
Millennium (Religion): R 197, 282-290. See also: Revivals and Revivalism (Religion).
Mills: see Textile Industry.
Minimal Art: A-A 21.
Mining: A-F 433; H 984, 1058, 1488, 1528, 1542, 1547, 1557, 1579, 1594, 1597, 1628, 1654, 1683, 1724, 1805; M 155; PS 302; STM 351. See also: Coal Industry and Mining.
Ministers and Ministry, Religious: PC 382, 385-386, 390, 399, 405; R 32, 44-45, 53, 58, 62-65, 67, 72, 81, 84, 109, 128, 138, 151, 161, 219, 273, 277, 304. See also: Missionaries.
Minstrels and Minstrelsy: M 187, 418; PC 382, 385-386, 390, 399, 405. See also: Shows and Musicals.
Missionaries: H 632; R 28, 30, 240, 250-252.
Modernism (Literature): L 325-326, 337, 365, 377, 382, 397, 409, 431, 469.
Modernism (Theology): R 102, 104.
Money and Coinage: H 1832.
Money Supply: H 1830, 1857-1858, 1878, 1885, 1887, 1904, 1927; PS 737.
Monopolies: H 1659; PC 805; SOC 523.
Moral Philosophy: H 593-594; L 7, 51, 225-226, 282, 333; PS 542; PSY 31; R 138-139, 145.
Moral Theology: R 138.
Morals and Moral Conduct: A-A 62; H 800, 1288, 1681; L 531; PC 886; PSY 80, 155; R 82, 220; SOC 342, 624.
Mormons: A-A 561, 569; A-F 409, 438; H 38, 307, 1408; R 188, 204, 216, 219, 242; SOC 250.
Motion Pictures: see Film.
Motown: M 417. See also: Blacks--Music; Girl Groups (Music); Pop Music.
Movie Houses: see Theaters (Architecture).
Multinational Corporations: STM 335.
Museums: A-A 510; STM 335.
Music: M 2-5, 7, 10, 12, 15-17, 19, 22, 24, 37-38, 42, 52, 57-58, 75, 86, 89, 94, 102-103, 106, 113, 115, 119-120, 129; PC 27, 339, 357. See also: Blacks--Music; Bluegrass Music; Blues (Music); Country and Western Music; Folk Music; Jazz; Pop Music; Shows and Musicals; Symphonic Music and Symphonies.
Music Education: M 124, 164.
Music Publishing: M 59, 80, 83, 99, 128, 379, 410. See also: Publishing; Records and Recording Industry.
Musicals: see Shows and Musicals.

Musicians and Composers: M 27-28, 39, 41, 46-51, 56, 61, 64, 69, 72,
76, 80, 82-85, 87, 91, 99-100, 105, 107, 110-111, 121-122, 130,
188, 191, 209, 236, 244, 249, 257, 278, 347, 385-389, 399; PC 324.
See also: Songs and Singers.
Muslims, Black: see Black Muslims.
Mysticism: R 192, 199. See also: Spiritualism and Parapsychology.

National Parks: see Public Lands and National Parks.
Nationalism: H 28, 32, 257, 281-282, 445, 550, 651, 657; L 6, 191, 268,
389, 396, 442, 480, 557; R 262, 295, 305. See also Patriotism.
Nativism: H 267; R 258, 262, 267.
Naturalism (Literature): L 89, 146-147, 231, 255, 404, 417, 509, 556,
660, 664; PC 363.
Nature: H 612, 642, 644, 654, 695; STM 335.
Nature in Art and Literature: A-A 160, 195-196, 286; L 77, 464, 508,
587.
Navigation Laws: H 204.
Navy: H 20; STM 167. See also: Military.
Negroes: see Blacks.
Neo-Classical and Colonial Style Architecture: A-A 498-500, 570.
New Deal: A-A 39, 90, 98-100, 231; A-F 123, 310; H 421, 438-439, 454,
460, 474, 486, 494, 498, 500, 506, 520, 524, 526-527, 586, 832,
1153, 1173, 1210, 1217, 1251, 1279, 1316, 1384, 1872, 1900, 1964;
L 353; PS 310; STM 264.
New England: see Northeast.
"New Thought": R 190.
Newscasting: PC 465-466, 648, 650, 656, 658-659, 662, 664, 671, 685-686,
694-695, 699, 711, 717, 742, 747, 750, 754, 758, 768, 777, 781,
802-804, 818, 820, 822, 835. See also: Documentaries (Film and
Television).
Newspapers and Journalism: A-F 388; H 195, 811; L 48, 303, 341, 413,
423-424, 426-427, 487, 599; PC 293-295, 302-303, 648, 664, 685-686,
694-695, 699, 836-916. See also: Magazines and Periodicals;
Mass Media; Publishing.
North: H 1416; R 10, 95-96, 222, 288.
North America--Discovery and Exploration: H 48-52, 86, 89, 147, 157,
164. See also: Frontier, Frontiersmen.
Northeast: A-F 105, 156, 178; H 48-51, 854, 868, 872, 897, 986, 999,
1003, 1011, 1067, 1078, 1342, 1346, 1472, 1870, 1974; L 85; PC 1012;
PSY 78; R 26-27, 32, 36, 40, 47, 50-51; SOC 43, 108, 158, 206,
239; STM 32, 159, 310, 367. See also: Puritans.
    History: H 1447, 1456.
        17th-18th Centuries: H 62, 64, 76-78, 91, 92, 94, 97, 99, 108, 114,
        116-118, 120, 134, 150, 162, 176-177, 179, 645-646, 931, 1041,
        1436, 1822, 1973.
        19th-20th Centuries: H 1071, 1286, 1343, 1973.
    Literature: L 40, 52, 61-62, 67-70, 104-106, 122, 132, 134, 142, 182,
        440, 596, 633.
    Music: M 62, 73-74, 93, 96-98, 104, 115, 117, 126.
    Religion and Religions: R 33, 34, 37-40, 42, 44, 47-48, 50-51, 53,
        58, 61, 65, 67, 81, 139-140, 143, 150, 157, 257, 284-286, 291,
        305, 307.
    Women: H 721, 830.
Northwest: H 1497.
    Architecture: A-A 491, 521.
    Art: A-A 68, 138.
    History
        17th-18th Centuries: H 79.
        19th-20th Centuries: H 1002, 1428, 1467, 1705.
Norwegian-Americans: A-F 355.

Novel: L 3-4, 33, 36, 72, 94, 101, 128-129, 136, 141, 149, 157-158, 172,
    189, 195, 209, 212, 229, 232, 234, 251, 275-276, 281-282, 285-288,
    299-300, 302, 311, 321, 328, 331, 340, 343, 346-347, 358, 360,
    362, 367, 374, 377, 383, 394, 401, 410, 415, 425, 440, 460, 484,
    491, 494, 503, 514, 517, 540-541, 551, 567, 576, 583-586, 588,
    597, 605, 610, 624, 628, 660, 669, 671, 673; PC 70, 81, 88, 90,
    92, 97, 101, 278, 280, 566-567. See also: Detective Literature;
    Fiction; Historical Fiction; Literature.
Nuclear Energy: PS 386; STM 129.
Nuclear Weapons: PC 1; PS 578, 581, 585, 591, 593, 620, 635, 659, 685,
    687-688, 696, 719, 750, 778, 788, 814; STM 136, 146, 165-167,
    197, 339, 346-347, 365, 397. See also: Arms and Armament; Arms
    Control and Arms Race; Disarmament; Radioactivity.
Nurses and Nursing: H 735, 776; SOC 552, 590, 593; STM 236, 247, 310.
    See also Doctors (MD); Hospitals and Asylums; Medicine; Midwives;
    Women Doctors (MD).

Occultism: PC 169-182; R 186. See also: Satanism and Devil Worship;
    Witches.
Oil Industry and Exploration: A-F 377; H 532, 1696-1697, 1712, 1716,
    1720-1721, 1738-1739, 1755, 1774, 1815; PS 318; STM 114, 191,
    393-394. See also: Conservation and Environment; Energy Sources
    and Supplies; Regulation and Deregulation of Industry.
Old Age: A-F 89; H 17; PSY 93, 186, 189; SOC 400, 402, 416-417, 420,
    432, 434, 443; STM 2. See also: Aged; Social Security.
Olympics: PC 969.
Opera and Operettas: M 20, 69, 77-79, 101, 110-112, 114; PC 328. See
    also: Shows and Musicals; Songs and Singers.
Organized Crime: A-F 112, 182; H 971, 1292, 1332, 1351; SOC 606, 614,
    648-649. See also: Crime and Criminals; Drug Addiction and
    Traffic; Prostitution.
Oriental Religions and Cults: A-F 91; R 206, 214. See also: Buddhism;
    Hare Krishna.

PACs: see Political Lobbying.
Painting: A-A 146-234, 269, 275, 282, 284, 294, 296-297, 301-302, 304,
    312, 314. See also: Art.
Panama Canal: STM 241. See also: Civil Engineering.
Parks, Amusement: see Amusement Parks, Fairs, Etc.
Parks, National and Urban: see Public Lands and National Parks.
Parties (Political): see Political Parties.
Patents: H 1944; STM 10, 18, 44. See also: Copyright Law; Inventors
    and Inventions.
Patriotism: H 445; L 78; M 158. See also: Nationalism.
Patronage: A-A 95.
Peace Movements: H 443.
Pearl Harbor: PS 638, 753, 810. See also: World War II.
Pediatrics: see Childbirth.
Pennsylvania Dutch: see German-Americans.
Pentecostal Movement: see Charismatic Revivals, Movements.
Performance Art: see Happenings, Performance Art, Etc.
Performing Arts: PC 323-406.
Periodicals: see Magazines and Periodicals.
Pesticides: STM 61, 104, 389. See also: Agriculture; Pollution (Environ-
    ment).
Petroleum: see Oil Industry and Exploration.
Pharmacy: STM 115, 350, 370, 398-399. See also: Folk Medicine; Medicine.
Philanthropy: H 9, 14-15, 1245, 1353, 1759, 1877, 1893; M 66; PS 583,
    793; SOC 558; STM 251.